Suarez On Individuation

Metaphysical Disputation V:
Individual Unity and Its Principle

Suarez On Individuation

Metaphysical Disputation V:
Individual Unity and Its Principle

*Translated from the Latin
with Introduction, Notes,
Glossary and Bibliography*

by

JORGE J. E. GRACIA

Professor of Philosophy
State University of New York at Buffalo

MARQUETTE UNIVERSITY PRESS
MILWAUKEE, WISCONSIN
1982

Library of Congress Catalogue Card Number: 80-84769
© Copyright, 1982, The Marquette University Press
Milwaukee, Wisconsin
Printed in the United States of America
ISBN 0-87462-223-9

CONTENTS

Preface

There is more interest today in the problem of individuation than at any other time in the history of Western philosophy, except perhaps for the period that saw the rise and culmination of scholasticism. Most major philosophers of this century, both in the so-called Analytic tradition and in Continental philosophy, have written extensively about the nature of individuality, its causal explanation and its relation to various other metaphysical and epistemological notions. Moreover, the contemporary preoccupation with this old problem has produced a renewed interest in scholastic doctrines relating to it. The names of Ockham, Scotus and Thomas are frequently found and their theories often mentioned, particularly in recent discussions. Nevertheless, in spite of all this interest, a comprehensive study of the way this problem surfaced and developed in the Middle Ages has not yet appeared. Indeed, even the most rudimentary discussion of the various aspects of the issue is unavailable, leading often to unfortunate misconceptions both about the nature of the problem as faced by scholastics and about the views of individual authors.

The present translation and study of Suárez's Disputation V: On Individual Unity and Its Principle (1597) hopefully will help to close this gap in scholarship. Suárez's text provides a careful, knowledgeable analysis of the problem of individuation, and its critical exposition of the main scholastic views on this issue is simply masterful. In addition, the text presents with great clarity Suárez's own view, which, as is well known, played a leading role in the transition between scholastic and modern philosophy, especially through Descartes and Leibniz.

The Disputation is not easy reading. Like most scholastic texts of this period, the discussion is painstakingly organized, but the issues and arguments are so intricate and the number of technical terms so large, that the philosopher unfamiliar with the period is likely to find the text difficult to understand even in translation. There is, of course, little that the translator can or should do to improve style. I have tried, however, to facilitate the understanding of the text by adding notes where they seemed indispensable, and by providing a Glossary of technical terms. The Glossary clarifies not only Suárez's use of the technical terms, but also the common understanding of them among major scholastics, and when possible identifies their source in Aristotle or his Latin Commentators. In addition, an Introduction summarizes the main points of Suárez's view and places it within a historical framework. Since there are several good introductions to Suárez's life and philosophy,* I have restricted the introductory remarks to the analysis of this Disputation. For other aspects of his metaphysical theory, the reader may consult the Select Bibliography at the back.

In preparing the translation I have made use primarily of Carolo Berton's edition of Suárez's Disputation V: *De unitate individuali ejusque principio*, in *Opera omnia*, vol. XXV (Paris: Vivès, 1861), pp. 145b-201a. Although this is not a critical edition, there are no serious disputes regarding the authenticity or integrity of the text of this Disputation. Nevertheless, I have also looked at Rábade's edition in Biblioteca Hispánica de Filosofía, Madrid, 1960, vol. I, pp. 563-693, for which he consulted a number of older editions and in which he resolved some minor editorial problems present in the Vivès edition. Any additions to Berton's edition based on Rábade are placed within pointed brackets «». Additions based on my understanding of the text, such as unstated conclusions, identification of the referent of relative pronouns, demonstratives, etc. have been placed within square brackets []; important disagreements in the texts of the two editions have been recorded in footnotes. All terms have been translated into English except for *ex natura rei*, a technical phrase not easily rendered by any one word or circumlocution. In cases where terms are used in a multiplicity of meanings depending on context, I have chosen one translation as the principal one, adding the Latin in

---

* See J. H. Fichter, *Man of Spain: Francis Suárez* (New York: MacMillan, 1940) and the brief notes in J. F. Ross, *Francis Suárez. On Formal and Universal Unity* (Milwaukee: Marquette Univ. Press, 1964) and Cyril Vollert, *Francis Suárez. On the Various Kinds of Distinctions* (Milwaukee: Marquette Univ. Press, 1947, rep. 1976). A more scholarly biography is J. de Scorraille, *François Suárez de la Compagnie de Jésus*, 2 vols. (Paris: Lethiellieux, 1912-13). For the various editions of Suárez's works see C. Sommervogel, *Bibliothèque de la Compagnie de Jésus*, 9 vols. (Paris: A. Picard, 1890-1900).

parentheses whenever any other is used. The references made by Suárez in this Disputation have been identified in footnotes whenever possible and the translated titles of the pertinent works have been placed within square brackets in the text.

Finally, I would like to thank Paul Vincent Spade and Thomas Perry for their invaluable help. Spade's masterful reading of the Latin text and the translation purged it of a substantial number of errors which had escaped me. And Perry's detailed suggestions for the improvement of the style and content of the Introduction have greatly enhanced its value. I am deeply indebted to both of them. I am also grateful to John Corcoran for reading the translation of Sects. I and II and offering his sound and sensible advice; to David Winiewiecz, for planting the idea in my mind to undertake this project after hearing me lecture on the subtleties of Disputation V; to Kenneth Barber and Joseph Owens for the useful questions they raised concerning my understanding of Suárez; to Russell Hatton for having contributed substantially to the preparation of the Select Bibliography; and to Marie Fleischauer, without whose expert typing, persevering patience and good humor the preparation of the manuscript would have been both difficult and unpleasant. Also, I would like to express my appreciation to the editor of *The New Scholasticism* for allowing me to use a portion of my article, "What the Individual Adds to the Common Nature according to Suárez" (vol. 53, 1979) in part III of the Introduction.

Jorge J. E. Gracia
1978

"If being is, it must be one."

Melissus (Diels-Kranz, 30B9).

Introduction

When thinking about an individual concrete thing such as a man or a tree, one may consider those features that the thing has or seems to have in common with other things, or alternatively, those features that are peculiar or unique to the thing under consideration. If the common features are part of what distinguishes the thing from a larger group of things and at the same time makes it part of a smaller group of things, the members of which can be distinguished only in terms of individual features, then one is thinking of what was commonly known in the Middle Ages as the thing's "nature." If, on the other hand, one considers those features that set a thing apart from all other things, including those falling together with it into a group, then one is considering the thing's individuality. In either case the content of the thought seems to be different. Take Peter, for instance. A consideration of his nature focuses on his humanity; that is, the feature or group of features such as rationality, capacity to laugh, etc., that make him human and in respect of which he is both indistinguishable from other human beings and distinguishable from non-human beings such as dogs, trees and rocks. A consideration of Peter's individuality, on the other hand, will focus only on that feature or group of features which separate Peter from Paul and any other individual being, whether human or not. In the first case we think of the ways in which Peter is the same as other human beings, in the second of the ways in which Peter is unique. The cluster of philosophical problems concerned with the nature of a thing is usually designated as "the problem of universals," those concerned with individuality are gathered under the term "the problem of individuation." Suárez's attention in Disputation V is directed toward the latter.

Contrary to a widespread misconception, the complexity of the problem of individuation was not ignored by scholastics. Most were aware that there is more than one issue related to individuality, and a few of them isolated and discussed the four most important ones. These are, in logical order: the nature of individuality, the extension of individuality, the ontological status of individuality in the individual and its relation to the nature, and, finally, the cause or causes that bring about individuality. When references to the medieval or scholastic problem of individuation are found in contemporary literature, it is usually the last that is meant. And not without reason, because up to the fourteenth century one seldom finds a careful and clear distinction between these four different issues, and much more effort is put into the solution of the last than any of the others. Yet, it is also evident that as the age progresses they become more and more defined until we find late scholastics like Suárez carefully separating them in their discussions. Some never became quite independent in treatment, however. The first one, the nature of individuality, was usually discussed in the context of the second, the extension of individuality. And even the second does not become the subject of separate investigation until late in the Middle Ages. Only the last two issues, the ontological status of individuality and its cause or causes, were generally discussed in isolation from the others. Suárez's treatise is consistent with this practice. He deals with the nature of individuality in the context of its extension (Sect. I), giving separate analyses of the ontological status of individuality (Sect. II) and its cause in various entities (Sects. III-VII). The last two Sections of the Disputation take up a problem related to the individuality of accidents: whether numerically different accidents can be present in the same subject simultaneously and successively.

I. The Nature of Individuality

Individuality is the distinguishing feature or features of an individual. To ask about the nature of individuality[1] is therefore to ask about the nature of those features and thus about what it is to be an individual as opposed to something else. The term scholastics generally used to refer to individuality was 'individual unity' (*unitas individualis*) although often one finds '*individuatio*' (usually translated as 'individuation') used as one would use 'individuality' in English.[2] The term 'individual' (*individuum*) was also used, for individuality was thought to be what constitutes an individual as an individual. They used the term 'individual unity' because they thought, following Aristotle (*Metaphysics* V, Ch. 6, 1015b15 ff), that to be an individual was to be one, and consequently that individuality was a kind of unity.

Often individual unity was also called 'numerical' (*numerica*) and opposed to "specific" (*specifica*) unity. The latter is the unity a species has despite the plurality of its individual members. All members of a species are one in the sense that they are the same kind of thing or belong to the same type. For example, Peter and Paul are one specifically in that each of them is a man in the same sense in which the other is. Numerical unity, on the contrary, is the separate unity of each individual within the species. It is called numerical because to be an individual is to be one, i.e. to be *a number*, in contrast to being specifically one, which is to be *a kind* of thing such as a *man* or a *dog*. Strictly speaking, however, one may distinguish *conceptually* between numerical and individual unity even though the adjectives 'individual' and 'numerical' can be, and in fact are, interchanged since they refer to the same thing in *reality*, namely, to the unity proper to individuals. Thus the unity of the individual is called numerical, as already stated, because the individual is one in number; but it is also called individual because the individual is not divisible into units that are specifically the same as itself. For instance, a man is not divisible into men but only into parts of a man, or a pile of thirty stones into piles of thirty stones but into smaller piles or just into stones.[3] Individuality, then, is opposed to universality, since to be a universal consists precisely in being divisible into units that are specifically of the same kind as itself. Thus the universal "man" is divisible into men, for each man fully participates in, i.e. is "a part of," man. That men and man are specifically of the same kind is evident from the fact that their definitions are the same. For the definition of an individual is none other than the definition of the species. Or more exactly, the individual *qua* individual has no definition. But the definition of a divisible whole and the definition of its parts are different; the definition of a man and his head are not the same.

For this reason, indivisibility was also called incommunicability, just as divisibility was referred to as communicability. Although there were several senses in which the term 'communicable' was used by the scholastics, the most central and pertinent to the present issue was the one in which the universal, for example, tree, is communicable to its instances, trees. To be communicable, therefore, means to be able to be made common or become common to many. This relation is the converse of the relation of participability. That which is capable of participation is simply what is able to take part in or be a part of something else which by that very fact of participation is made or becomes common to those things that participate in it. An individual, therefore, was said to be incommunicable because, unlike the universal, it could not be made common to many or, what is the same, it could not become participated in by many.

Indivisibility into things of the same specific kind as the original is, for Suárez, the fundamental feature of individuality (Sect. I, §§ 2, 3 and 7). It constitutes its essence, and therefore, we might say, is expressed or contained in the definition of individuality.[4] In addition to indivisibility there are other features that always accompany the individual, such as, for example, the individual's separation or distinction from other individuals, whether members of its species or not. But this feature was regarded by many scholastics, and explicitly by Suárez, as a consequence or result of individuality rather than a constituent of it (Sects. II, § 28 and III, § 12). "Distinction" or "separation" from all other individuals is not part of the essence of individuality, but, one might conclude from the way Suárez refers to it, more like a property of it, similar to the way in which the capacity to laugh is a property of man but not part of his essence. Properties, according to the scholastics, always accompany the being whose properties they are, but they are not part of its essence. Logically, some claimed, they are deducible from the definition but do not constitute it.

This distinction, which Suárez carefully makes in Sect. I, between indivisibility and separability or distinction, clearly shows a conception of individuality as something intrinsic to the individual apart from any relations it may have to other individuals. From this perspective it is altogether possible to have but one individual in the universe and nevertheless inquire, for example, into the ontological status of the individuality of that individual, and into its cause or principle. On the other hand, if one were to hold that individuality has to do essentially with separability and distinction, it would be impossible to have a universe with only one individual in it. Moreover, since individuality would have to do with others on that assumption, one would expect its cause also to include others. But this would be a very unsatisfactory situation, since the cause of the individual's individuality would have to be found in something other than the individual. It would be like saying that X has property M because of Y, which does not itself have property M.[5]

Suárez distinguishes carefully, moreover, between indivisibility and distinction on the one hand and the distinction proper to those individuals which are many within a species on the other. The latter feature is called "numerical distinction within the species" or more often just "plurality." According to Suárez this type of numerical distinction is not proper to all individuals and therefore should not be confused with the indivisibility essential to individuality or even with the numerical distinction which results from it. Plurality within a species is a feature of only some individuals. God, for example, is not one among many within a species, and the same seems to be the case with other purely immaterial substances such as angels (Sect. I,

n. 8). All beings which are numerically distinct within a species, however, are also indivisible and distinct from all other beings.

Many scholastics often failed to make the distinction Suárez makes, a fact which had very serious consequences for their understanding and solution of the other problems surrounding individuality. An important historical source of this failure was Boethius' *On the Trinity* I, one of the places where he introduced the problem of numerical difference to the Middle Ages. In that text he states that "*numerical difference* is caused by the variety of accidents" and later remarks that "it is because men are *plural* by their accidents that they are *plural in number.*"[6] The important expressions here are "numerical difference" and "plural in number;" they indicate that Boethius' concern in this text was restricted to finding the cause of numerical distinction and/or plurality. And of course he understands numerical distinction and plurality to refer not to indivisibility, but to separation from others and multiplication within the species. His problem may be phrased, then, in two questions as follows: (1) What makes an individual different from other individuals? and (2) What makes possible the multiplication of individuals within the species? The answer that suggests itself most easily in both cases is the one he gave — the accidents. For, what else seems to make Paul different from Peter but the fact that he is tall and dark while Peter is short and fair? Unfortunately, although Boethius himself may not have done so, the terminology he used and the way he raised the problem in *On the Trinity* seem to have prevented many scholastics from realizing that in addition to the questions of diversity and plurality, i.e. of numerical distinction or separation and of multiplicity within the species, there was another more basic question which involved indivisibility. It is a mark of those who fail to make that distinction that they set up the problem of individuation in terminology resembling that of Boethius in *On the Trinity*. It is also a mark of their solutions that they identify the cause of individuality as wholly or at least partly accidental, a most unfortunate development as Suárez makes clear throughout Disputation V.

Perhaps the most important case of this is Thomas Aquinas' discussion of individuation in his *Commentary on Boethius' "De Trinitate,"* q.4, where he frames the problem in the context of Boethius' text and terminology. He asks:[7]

1. Whether otherness is the cause of *plurality*.
2. Whether variety of accidents produces *diversity according to number*.
3. Whether two bodies can be, or can be thought of as being, simultaneously in the same place.

4. Whether *difference* of location exerts some influence as to *difference according to number.*

In none of these questions does Thomas ask about indivisibility. His primary concern is with diversity and plurality—what makes the individual distinct from other individuals and a discrete unit within the species. The result is that he identifies the principle of individuation as accidental, at least in part: matter plus quantity, the latter being understood as indeterminate dimensions.[8]

In contrast, and as we have already mentioned, Suárez distinguishes carefully between the notions of distinction and plurality within the species on the one hand and indivisibility on the other, opting for an investigation of the latter as the most basic notion.[9]

II. The Extension of Individuality

Next to the nature of individuality, the most fundamental of the problems surrounding this notion concerns its extension. For even if it is accepted that individuality is a viable concept, we still have to ask whether there are any entities that have it, and if so, which ones. The most widespread view on this issue in contemporary circles is generally regarded as a form of realism. It holds that individuality extends only to what scholastics called "substances," e.g., a man or a tree, and not to the properties and accidental characteristics of such substances. A man, Paul, is individual, but his height, weight, hair color, etc. are not, since some other man, John, may have the same height, weight, and hair color as he. Other contemporary writers hold that individuality extends not only to substances but to their properties and accidental characteristics as well. Not only is a man an individual,—his height is too; for it is his and only his. One may speak, then, of "this height" as well as of "this man." This view is generally regarded as a form of nominalism, although such notorious realists as Plato and Duns Scotus would adhere to it.

On the other hand, one may hold that even within substances there are some that possess individuality and others that do not, for individuality is a characteristic of only certain kinds of beings. Some theists held versions of this view. Created beings are individual, but God is not. And others rejected even the individuality of purely spiritual substances such as angels.

Suárez's Section I, except for §§ 2 and 3, which investigate the nature of individuality, is fundamentally concerned with the extension of individuality. In it he adopts the standard medieval formula, derived from Aristotle: Everything insofar as it exists is individual (§ 5). This formula was used by everyone in the Middle Ages except for a few early realists such as John Eriugena, who believed that only substances were individual — their properties, natures, and accidents were universal.[10] After the period of translations in the twelfth century, every scholastic adhered to this formula. Their understanding of it varied, however. Some, although accepting the individuality of both substances and accidents, did not extend individuality to the metaphysical principles of substances. In Duns Scotus, for example, the nature has a unity and being of its own and therefore cannot be said to be, *qua* nature, one individually. It derives its individuality from the unity of the individual substance, that is, it is an individual only insofar as it is a metaphysical constituent of an individual substance. Man, for instance, as a nature, has a unity and being as such different from the unity and being it has in Paul or Peter. Then, not everything is individual for Scotus, although, strictly speaking, everything that exists exists as an individual either because it is an individual or because it has been individuated. Consequently, Scotus could be said to adhere to the general formula, because in his view the nature cannot be said to exist except in an individual and as individuated. Only substances and their accidents exist; therefore, although the nature has some ontological status considered in itself, and without regard for the individual of which it is part, he could maintain that only individuals exist.[11]

Ockham, on the other hand, dispensed with the ontological status of the nature in itself, reducing the unity and being of the nature to the unity and being of the individual substance. And he went even farther than that, holding that the nature is in fact indentical with the individual, except insofar as it is considered a concept in someone's mind. Man, considered as it exists in reality independent of the mind, is nothing but the actually existing individual men and, considered as it exists in the mind, it is nothing but a concept.[12]

Parallel to this was another point of disagreement, for some scholastics accepted the individuality of all components of an individual substance, but denied that all substances, regardless of their kind, are individual. Some restricted individuality to the realm of material being, excluding all purely spiritual beings (angels and God) from it, while others excluded only God. The tradition that denied individuality of God was well entrenched in the Middle Ages, originating in part in texts of Boethius, where he says that God is not "a this" or "a that" and that he has no number.[13] Some texts from Thomas seem to have been the source of the other thesis, at least among the Latins, that purely spiritual creatures (angels) do not have individual unity.[14]

Suárez's views on both issues are quite clearly stated in Sect. I of this Dispu·tion and elsewhere. His understanding of the extension of individuality is maximal. He rejects all restrictions upon it. For

him, every entity in the universe including substances, their properties and accidents as well as their metaphysical components and
principles, such as matter and form, are individual (Sect. I, §§ 4 and
5). There is indeed only one kind of *actual* unity in the universe, individual unity. And since unity is convertible, i.e. coextensive with being, everything that is an actual being must necessarily have individual unity. As Suárez puts it (§ 5), "to be an entity [i.e. one being]
and to be divisible [i.e. capable of becoming many beings of the
same specific kind as the original being] implies a contradiction."
Individual unity, then, extends to all *actual* being. It does not extend,
however, beyond actual being to include universals and forms. The
latter have unity, but their unity is conceptual. Scotus' view that in
an individual there are, as it were, two unities, the unity of the
individual and the unity of the nature, is completely rejected by
Suárez. For him the unity of the nature in the individual is the same
in reality as the unity of the individual; their distinction is the result
of mental consideration alone (Sect. II, § 10). And the unity of the
nature apart from the individual unity is only conceptual.[15]

With respect to the second issue, whether individuality extends to
every kind of substance, Suárez sets out on his own again, rejecting any
limitation upon individuality. In his universe, all beings including God
and angels are individual. This doctrine contrasts with Thomas' since it
seems that for the latter the unity proper to each level of being is different and concordant with it. God, whose essence is to exist, and who is
therefore unique, has no individual unity so to speak. His unity could
only be one proportional to his being; it might be called, using a term
coined by some contemporary Thomists, "existential." Angels, who are
composed only of form and their act of existence (*esse*) — each of them being a complete essence or species in itself — do not have the same kind of
unity as material beings. Their unity is proportional to their essence,
and thus, according to some of Thomas' critics, it can be called "essential." Finally, material beings, composed of form, matter, and their act
of existence (*esse*) have, properly speaking, numerical unity, caused by
their quantified matter (*materia signata*). It is this that makes possible the
existence of many separate individuals within the species.[16]

For Suárez, on the contrary, individuality extends to all being including God. Indeed, God's individual unity is the model for all
others, since his indivisibility is essential. If God could be divided into beings specifically the same as himself he would not be one but
several gods, at least in potency, a doctrine abhorrent both to faith
and reason, in Suárez's view. Similarly, Suárez holds that angels are
indivisible in this sense since they are not communicable to many
supposits, that is, they are not universals which can be instantiated.
Finally, material beings are also individual.

It would be inaccurate, however, to say that Thomas and the other scholastics who seem to have restricted the extension of individuality in some sense would consequently hold that the substances which did not have individuality were divisible into units of their same specific kind, i.e. that they were universal. For it would be inconceivable that any scholastic should entertain the possibility of a divisible God or even of a divisible angel. What Thomas seems to have rejected, along with many others, was that God and angels are numerically distinct, understanding by this that they are numerically discrete beings within a species. For they seem to have understood individuality primarily as a distinctive characteristic of material beings (Sect. II, § 26). And with this Suárez would agree to this extent: If individuality is primarily distinction understood as separation and plurality within the species, then it is quite probable that angels are not individual. But he would disagree with their conception of individuality; he would argue that their view was limited because it fails to distinguish between indivisibility on the one hand and separation and plurality within the species on the other.

The latter distinction is nevertheless not reflected in Suárez's use of the terms 'individual unity' and 'numerical distinction.' Following common practice, he uses both terms to refer to individual unity, a fact which appears to obscure the distinction. This should not be taken as an oversight, however. The fact is that for Suárez all beings are indivisible, and insofar as they are they must also be distinct from other beings (Sect. III, § 12). That follows logically as we saw earlier. What Suárez rejects is that (1) individual or numerical unity, (2) numerical distinction from others, and (3) plurality within a species are conceptually equivalent. The first two have in fact the same root, since the unity by which an individual is indivisible is also the unity by which it is distinct from all other individuals (Sect. III, § 6). But they are not equivalent notions by any means. And the first two and the third do not even have the same root (Sect. III, § 5). Indeed, the distinction present in all beings and the plurality peculiar to material beings are, for Suárez, rather outward signs of the inward unity that he called individual or numerical unity (indivisibility), and not real constituent features of things.

III. The Ontological Status of Individuality

Once individuality is defined and its scope established, it remains to determine its ontological status in the individual, and its relation to the nature. Philosophers have generally framed this problem in terms of two issues: (1) whether there is some distinction in reality which corresponds to the distinction in thought between individuality and the nature, and (2) what the basis of the distinction is.

In the Middle Ages these two issues were usually considered together under the question, "whether in all natures the individual as such adds something to the common nature." The question meant to ask (a) whether it is the case for all natural beings that an individual, considered as individual, is distinguished by some feature or features from the common nature, (b) the nature of this distinction, that is, whether it is real, conceptual or otherwise, and (c) the ontological status of the distinguishing feature or features. To take an example, the question was (a) whether Peter, considered as Peter, has something that man does not have and, therefore, whether he is different from man, (b) the nature of the distinction between [i] what Peter has that makes him different and [ii] man, and (c) the status of the features which distinguish Peter from man.

Basically there are three positions that philosophers have adopted in this matter. The first not only rejects the distinction in reality, but goes so far as to disregard the conceptual distinction. For obvious reasons there have been few philosophers who have held this view. Indeed, given the pressing witness of experience, it is difficult to reject at the outset the fact that there is at least some sort of conceptual distinction between an individual's individuality and the individual's nature. Nevertheless, although experience seems to warrant this distinction, it should be noted that philosophers have difficulty clarifying it. The main problem appears to be that intellectual consideration takes place always in terms of universal concepts and thus seems to preclude a proper determination and understanding of the individual *qua* individual. Most likely, it was this sort of problem that led Roscelin, in the Middle Ages, to adopt this view.[17]

The second position has been more popular. It accepts the conceptual distinction between common nature and individual, but argues that there is no distinction in reality that corresponds to the conceptual distinction. There are two main versions of this view and they are quite opposed to each other. The first, which is the position usually attributed to Plato, argues that what is real is the nature, that is, the common features of things, and that consequently there cannot be a real distinction between the nature and the individual since there are no two real entities which may be distinguished in reality from each other.[18] The obvious problem facing this view is the explanation of how the conceptual distinction arises, given the lack of distinction in reality. Many attempts have been made to answer this difficulty, most of them in terms of the so called "bundle theory of individuation," but little progress has been made in definitely settling the objections raised against this view.[19]

The second version argues that what is real is the individual, and consequently that the nature is a conceptual phenomenon only. As such there cannot be a real distinction between the nature and the individual. This view was vigorously defended in the Middle Ages by William of Ockham. What he and other supporters of this position failed to explain adequately is the cause or causes of conceptual community, i.e. the causes that give rise to the notions of natures in the mind. In addition, as Scotus made quite plain, this sort of view puts into question the objectivity of scientific concepts, undermining the bases of all science.

The third, more eclectic position is the one that has found more adherents in the philosophical community. Like the second, it does not question experience; it accepts the conceptual distinction between the nature and the individual, but it goes further by positing as well some sort of real distinction between them. What distinguishes them, however, is differently interpreted by different philosophers. Scotus thought of it as formal, while Thomas and others interpreted it in various other ways.

Suárez's view on this matter is discussed in Sect. II of Disputation V. His position borrows elements from Thomas, Scotus and Ockham, but in general it is closer to that of the first and third than it is to the second. With Thomas and Scotus he holds that what the individual adds to the common nature is something real, but at the same time he maintains with Ockham that what is added is only conceptually distinct from the common nature (§§ 8 and 16). In spite of these similarities, however, Suárez's view departs substantially in detail from these standard views of the times. For it was usually accepted by scholastics that if something real is "added" to something else, that means (1) there is a real addition, (2) that to which the real thing is added is also real, and (3) the terms of the addition are really distinct. Those who, like Scotus, accepted that the individual adds something real (or formal) to the common nature, also accepted that a real addition takes place, that both the individual and the common nature are real, and that they are really distinct. On the other hand, those who, like Ockham and Plato, rejected the reality of one of the terms of this pair (of the individual for Plato; of the common nature for Ockham), and therefore their real distinction, were forced to conclude that the individual adds nothing real to the common nature.

For Scotus, what an individual adds to the common nature, i.e. the feature which distinguishes an individual from the common nature, is, like the common nature itself, a formality, — what he or his followers called thisness (*haecceitas*) — , and formally distinct from the common nature.[20] It is formally rather than really distinct from the common nature because neither the nature nor the thisness are realities "as thing and thing." The unity and being of the nature is not the kind of unity and being proper to individual things, i.e.

substances or their accidents; it is "a less than numerical unity" and its being is proper to itself.[21] Thus, according to Scotus, the nature and the thisness cannot be distinguished as two things are, but neither are they to be distinguished only as two concepts. Their distinction follows from their ontological character as formalities with a being and unity of their own, and thus it is less than real but more than conceptual. It is formal.

Thomas, like Scotus, accepts the view that what the individual adds to the common nature is something real, i.e. the feature that individuates the nature. For him this is designated matter, that is, matter under the accident of quantity.[22] What the individual adds to the common nature is therefore not only something real, but also something really distinct from the nature, since quantified matter is a reality distinct from the reality which is the nature. The essence of man and the essence of Socrates, therefore, differ as the undetermined and the determined, that is, as (i) a nature undetermined by individual characteristics (designated matter), and (ii) the nature considered together with those very characteristics.[23] This does not mean, for Thomas, that the nature is to be found separate from individuals, or that it is not part of the individual, but it does mean that the distinction between nature and individuality (the determining features) is a real one, based on the way things are and not on the way the mind considers them. For in an individual the quantified matter that distinguishes it from other individuals is as real as, and as really distinct from, the nature as matter is from form or accidents are from a substance.[24]

For Ockham, on the other hand, the individual is real but the nature is not. Unlike Scotus, Ockham accords to the nature no unity and being proper to itself. The only unity and being there is in reality are individual unity and being, and those are proper only to individuals, not natures.[25] Moreover, what causes the individuality of the individual is not a formality added to it, as it is for Scotus, or matter designated by quantity, as it is for Thomas. Indeed, nothing causes the individuality of the individual; for the individual is such by virtue of itself.[26] It is for this reason that Ockham denies not only that what the individual adds to the common nature is real, but also that the nature and the individual are really distinct. For him the distinction is conceptual and nothing else. The nature is just another way of considering an individual and, therefore, nothing more than a concept in the mind. Even as a concept it is individual, although its signification is multiple owing to the generality of its content.[27]

Suárez differs from all these three thinkers in that he does not assume that the reality of what is added implies (1) a real addition, (2) the reality of that to which it is added, and (3) a real distinction between those terms. For him, the addition of something real implies only that what is added is real, leaving open the question as to the reality of both the addition itself and that to which the addition is made, and also leaving open the nature of the distinction between the terms of the addition. That is, that X adds something real to Y does not imply that there is a real addition of X to Y, that both X and Y are real and, therefore, that they are really distinguished; it implies only that X is real, leaving undetermined the question as to the reality of the addition and of Y, and as to the nature of X's distinction from Y. This by itself does not mean, as Suárez wishes to hold, (1) that the term to which the addition is made, the common nature in this case, must necessarily be conceptual, or (2) that the distinction between it and what is added, the individual unity, is also conceptual, or finally, (3) that the addition itself is conceptual. It only makes it possible. That it is so in fact involves an ontological commitment concerning the status of natures and a sophisticated theory of distinctions which Suárez adopts.

Influenced by Ockham, Suárez accepts the view that the common nature is nothing apart from the individual, and only conceptually distinct from it.[28] In this his position differs from that of Scotus, for whom the nature has being and unity of its own, and from that of Thomas, for whom the nature is something real though never unindividuated except when it exists as a concept in the mind.

Influenced by Scotus, Suárez develops a subtle theory of distinctions: the real, the conceptual, and the modal or *ex natura rei*.[29] It is the conceptual distinction that concerns the individual and the nature. It holds between two ways in which we think about the same thing. Suárez puts it as follows:

> This sort of distinction does not formally and actually intervene between the things designated as distinct, as they exist in themselves, but only as they exist in our concepts, from which they receive their name.[30]

This is the distinction that holds between two attributes in God, or between the terms of the relation of identity when one says that Peter is the same as himself. For God's attributes are not really distinct from each other since his nature is simple, nor is Peter something distinct from himself, although in order to identify him with himself it is necessary for the mind to duplicate him.

It should be emphasized, then, that the distinction is not between conceptual entities. Suárez is clear in pointing out that the terms of the conceptual distinction are different aspects of the same thing, and that these different aspects arise either through mental repetition and comparison or through some inadequacy in conception. In either case the concepts are grounded on a real thing and as such are not misleading as long as the distinction is understood to be conceptual rather than real.

Now let us go back to Suárez's doctrine of what the individual adds to the common nature and see how these points affect it. The doctrine is explained in four parts. First, Suárez states that the individual adds something real (*reale*) to the common nature by reason of which (1) the individual is indivisible and (2) distinct from others. This reality added by the individual to the common nature is, as the title of the Disputation reveals, a kind of unity, what Suárez calls in Section I, "individual unity." Naturally, since unity and being are convertible, and to be real is to be, the unity which the individual adds to the common nature must be considered something real. Secondly, Suárez points out that what is added, this reality or individual unity, is not distinct *ex natura rei* from the nature (§ 9). Indeed, if that were the case, there would be a composition in the individual of at least thing and mode or at most thing and thing. But this cannot be the case, for the common nature, say "man," is not a thing; that is, according to Suárez, it is not something real apart from the individual. What is real (and here we see the Ockhamist emphasis) is the individual man, not the nature "man." Therefore, it is not possible for the nature to be either really or modally distinguished from its individuality, that is from its individual unity, even though the individual unity is real. For in order to be so distinguished the common nature and the individual unity would have to fall into a relation of thing to thing or thing to mode.

But if the distinction between the common nature and the individual is not real, then it must be conceptual. And, indeed, this is what Suárez concludes:

> I say thirdly that the individual adds to the common nature something conceptually distinct from it, belonging to the same category and metaphysically composing the individual as an individual difference which contracts the species and constitutes the individual (§ 16).

What Suárez emphasizes again, however, is that what is added is not conceptual. This means simply that individuality or, as he puts it, individual unity is not something conceptual. On the contrary, it is real, the most real constituent of anything; for indeed, as he notes in Section I, individuality extends to all reality. Certainly there is no reason why a conceptual distinction should hold only between mental entities or concepts. In fact, as explained earlier, Suárez holds that conceptual distinctions do not hold between mental entities at all. They are grounded in reality, although only in one thing which is considered by the mind in two ways. Therefore, that the common nature and the individual are only conceptually distinct does not require that individual unity be a mental being or concept. On the other hand, that individual unity is real does not require that the distinction between it and the common nature be real, for in fact it is real things that are the basis of conceptual distinctions. It is the individual that is conceptually distinguished from its nature, while in reality the nature and the individual are one and the same, just as Peter is distinguished from himself when we make a judgment concerning his identity, although in reality he is himself. Suárez puts the point thus:

> ...for just as the separation of the common nature from the individual difference is only conceptual, so, conversely, the addition of the individual difference to the common nature is to be understood only conceptually; for there is not that proper addition in reality, but in each individual there is one entity really having by itself both natures (§ 16).

In short, there is no real *addition,* that is, a real giving, since there is no real distinction between the individual and the nature. Yet, what is added, i.e. what the individual is over and above the common nature, is something real.

IV. The Cause of Individuality

Having established the ontological status of individuality, it remains (1) to identify its cause or causes, and (2) to determine whether the cause or causes are uniform for all entities.

Scholastics generally spoke of the "principle" of individuation rather than the "cause" of individuation, since they made a distinction between these two notions. The term '*principium,*' which also meant "beginning," "source," "element," among other things, was used more widely than the term 'cause.' Causes were classified as principles, but not all principles were causes. 'Cause' was used by scholastics to refer specifically to physical causes, that is, one of the four types of causes identified by Aristotle as the sources of change (form, matter, the agent, and the end). But principles need not be physical. Logical principles, for example, such as the principle of non-contradiction, the rules of inference, and in many cases, just the premises of particular demonstrations, were called principles because they were considered the starting points of knowledge. Finally, scholastics spoke of metaphysical principles. Like logical principles, these are not separable from the things of which they are principles, but unlike them and like physical principles they are really distinct from that of which they are principles. As such they are neither physical things nor mental concepts, but they are nevertheless real constituents of things.

The most generally accepted of these were form and matter, essence and existence, and substance and accident. For those scholastics who did not identify the cause of individuation with a physical cause such as form, matter or the agent (as for example, Scotus did not) it was very important to maintain the distinction between principle and cause. There was a principle of individuation, but not a cause of it. However, for Suárez, Thomas and others, who identified the cause of individuation with one or several of Aristotle's causes, such distinction was not very significant. In spite of his use of the term 'principle' in this context, Suárez acknowledges in Disp. XII, Sect. I, § 5, that if a principle is understood to have some positive influence, then it is not very different from a cause. In the last analysis, whether the cause of individuation was regarded as a logical principle, a metaphysical principle, or a physical cause depended on the particular theory in question. For Ockham, who thought the individual was individual *per se,* which for him meant essentially, and therefore that individuality was nothing separate from the nature except in thought, the principle of individuation was a logical abstraction since there was nothing to be individuated in the first place.[31] On the other hand, for Scotus, who held that the nature in itself was not individual and therefore required some real or formal addition to be made individual, the principle of individuation was metaphysical. That it was so, meant, for Suárez, that it was a concept and therefore no different in fact from Ockham's logical principle. Indeed, Suárez did not think that either Ockham or Scotus had addressed the question concerning the cause of individuality. This is evident from the fact that he does not discuss their positions in the parts of the Disputation where he deals with the various views on the cause of individuality. Their views are discussed only in Sect. II, where the problem addressed is the ontological status of individuality, i.e. "what the individual adds to the common nature." On the other hand, in Suárez's own doctrine, where the principle of individuation is identified with the individual itself (i.e. its entity, as we shall see presently), the principle of individuation was physical.

Scholastics differed widely as to their understanding of what constitutes the principle of individuation. A few, like Ockham, rejected the idea of any such principle except as a conceptual abstraction, as already stated. But most endeavored to identify it. There were as many theories as logical possibilities. Since within the Aristotelian framework and that of his commentators, the individual is made up of a determinate number of principles (form, matter, accidents, and, for some, existence), scholastics pointed to these, singly or in combination, as the causes of individuality. And sometimes, dissatisfied with them, they sought the solution in the external causes of the individual, such as the efficient cause or agent. Within accidents are included quantity, quality, relations and other appropriate notions.

In addition to the identification of the principle or cause of individuation, scholastics who accepted the Aristotelian distinction between substance and accidents sought to determine whether the source of individuation was the same or different in these. Is what makes Peter the individual he is the same thing that makes the black color of his hair the particular black color it is, namely "this black color"? Scholastics generally separated these two questions, but they differed as to the answer. Some, like Thomas, argued that the principle in each case was different: Peter is the individual he is because of his quantified matter, but the black color of his hair is the particular black color it is because it is his. In short, the principle of individuation of accidents is the substance in which they adhere, that of the substance something else. Others, including Suárez, held that although the principles of individuation for substances and for accidents were different they were nevertheless of the same *kind*. Whatever sort of thing individuates Peter, individuates also the black color of his hair.

A. Individuation of Substances

Concerning the first problem, Suárez discusses only three fundamental views in this Disputation: individuation by designated matter, individuation by substantial form, and individuation by existence. External causes such as the agent are considered too extrinsic to cause individuation (see also V, § 1) and are therefore rejected in passing, in Sect. III, § 2. The efficient and the final causes, he points out, cause individuation only indirectly, by furnishing the intrinsic principle which causes it immediately.

The first view discussed at length is individuation by designated matter (Sect. III). This was not only a popular view at the time among Thomists, but it also was the source of much debate and misunderstanding. Suárez discusses three different interpretations of it. The first is the view of what we might call orthodox Thomists (§ 9). It holds that designated matter is to be understood as matter with quantity or matter affected by quantity. Matter, a substantial principle, is the source of incommunicability, while quantity, an accidental principle, is the source of distinction. Suárez finds many faults with this view. Most of them spring from the fact that quantity is an accident and as such must be posterior to substance. It is inconsistent, then, to maintain that quantity is the cause of an intrinsic feature of substance, namely, individuality. This objection militates also against all other views of accidental individuation — bundle views, relational views (space-time, place, position, etc.), and so on, for which reason Suárez dismisses them (see also Sect. VI, § 2).

A second interpretation purports to understand designated matter as "not intrinsically including quantity itself, but rather as the term of the relation of matter to it" (§ 18). This interpretation comes out of the discussion of indeterminate quantity found in Thomas' *Commentary on Boethius' "De Trinitate"*. There he stated:

> Dimensions can be considered in two ways. In one way according to their termination, and I say that they are determined according to limited measure and figure; and so, as complete beings, dimensions are classed in the genus of quantity, and thus they cannot be the principle of individuation....In another way, dimensions may be considered without this certain determination, merely in the nature of dimension, although they never could exist without some kind of determination...and according to this aspect dimensions are classified in the genus of quantity as imperfect. And by these indeterminate dimensions matter is made to be this signate matter and thus gives individuality...[32]

Thomists, concerned about the problems created by the accidental nature of quantity, found in this passage support for the view that the quantity to be considered part of the principle of individuation was not accidental quantity, such as "three feet wide;" rather, it was the potency contained in matter for this quantity—the capacity of matter to be three feet wide. In a sense, this view seems more concordant with Aristotle's casual statements about the issue, since it tends to put back into prime matter the causality of individuality. But it is difficult to see how such an interpretation can be reconciled with many other texts from Thomas in which he explicitly identifies the principle of individuation of this man, for example, with his flesh and bones.[33] Indeed, many followers of Thomas, including Cajetan, would have nothing to do with this view, as Suárez points out.

Suárez's rejection of this position is based primarily on the unintelligibility and uselessness of the distinction between the potency for quantity in matter and the actuality of quantity present in matter on which this view rested. This is because the potency and act of a kind (in this case, quantity) fall within the same category in the Aristotelian framework. As such, then, the distinction does not add anything to the first interpretation.

Finally, a third group of Thomists hold that designated matter is not the principle of individual unity but only the occasion of our awareness of it; in other words, of its discernibility (§ 28). And the problem here, which Suárez sees, is that even if designated matter were a good principle of individual discernibility, such answer would leave unresolved the original ontological problem concerning the cause of individuality.

The second solution, discussed by Suárez and suggested by some texts of Averroes and Durandus of St. Pourçain, is that the principle of individuation is the substantial form (Sect. IV). In a man, for example, it is his humanity that is responsible for his individuality. The support of this view is derived from the general Aristotelian doctrine which regarded the form as the vehicle for all actuality and existence in the individual. It is only fitting, then, some concluded, that form should also be the cause of an individual's most basic unity, its individuality. Suárez, however, finds it difficult to explain, among other things, how substantial form, so different a principle from matter and accidental forms, could individuate these other components of the individual. This leads him to reject this view insofar as it holds that form alone is the full and adequate cause of the individuation of things. According to him, form is only the principal one (see also Sect. IV, § 16).[34] Matter, as we shall see, plays also an important causal role in this.

In Section V, Suárez discusses the last of the views concerning the cause of individuation which he rejects. And here again, as with the second, he finds partial agreement with the view, provided the terms in which it is expressed are understood correctly. The view in question holds that the principle of individuation is existence.

This alternative had become viable after Thomas introduced the doctrine of the real distinction between essence and existence. In a phoenix, for example, what the phoenix is and the act whereby he exists are really distinct, for there is nothing in the definition of a phoenix which implies its existence. The latter answers the question "whether it is" (*an est*) rather than the question "what is it?" (*quid est*).[35] Although not all implications of this view are easy to see, and some of the common ones thought to derive from it are clearly contrary to the import and intention of Thomas' original doctrine, one at least could be thought to follow easily. For, could it not be argued that the real distinction of existence from essence introduced another element in the constitution of an individual, and that, since existence is so individual and "incommunicable," existence is after all the cause of individuality? It is clear evidence of the depth of scholastic speculation that no one is known to have explicitly and unambiguously adhered to this view, at least in this simplistic way. Suárez obviously found it difficult to reconcile this position with the notion of an individual possible being (Sect. V, § 3); conceptually, there is no difference between an existing Paul and a non-existing, possible Paul.

If existence, however, is not viewed as the act of existence properly speaking, but as entity, then Suárez finds little difference between this view and his own, except for the unfortunate misuse of terminology. To his view we turn presently.

The first two of the three theories discussed by Suárez address the question of individuality in the context of material substances. This is indicated in the titles of the sections in which they are discussed: "Whether designated matter is the principle of individuation in *material substances*" and "Whether the substantial form is the principle of individuation of *material substances*." Spiritual substances are excluded. This is a result of the identification of individual unity with the numerical distinction of the individual from other individuals within the species characteristic of material entities. This identification, mentioned above, was made by many of Suárez's predecessors.

The third view, however, and Suárez's own, assumes individuality to be a feature of all beings, not only of material substances. This is no doubt the consequence of his careful distinction between the notion of individuality as indivisibility, on the one hand, and of numerical distinction and plurality within the species on the other. In Sections V and VI, then, Suárez is able to discuss all created substances. He excludes God, the only uncreated substance, because (as he points out in Sect. III, § 1) "the divine substance…is individual by itself and essentially; whence, there is no more reason to look for a principle of individuation in it than for a principle of its essence or existence." In short, God is individual in the sense Ockham said all substances were: *per se.* To ask what makes him individual is superfluous, since God has no common nature or essence to which individuality may be said to be added. The case of other spiritual substances is different, however. For although they are not numerically multiplied within the species in the way material beings are (it is most probable, according to Suárez, that each of them is, as Thomas held, one of a species), yet they have an essence and common nature to which individuality must be added: An individual angel is *really* more than its angelic nature, even if there is only one angel of such a kind.

But God, angels, and material composites are not the only substantial entities in Suárez's world. It also contains matter, substantial forms, and substantial modes. In all of them the principle of individuation is the same — the entity. If the entities in question are not composites, as is the case of form, matter or a mode, then their entities are the principle of individuation. And if they are composites, as material substances are, then the principle of individuation is the individual matter and the individual form united to each other. Of these, as we said earlier, the form is primary, but not sufficient by itself (§ 15). Individuality in material beings requires both matter and form. The causes of the individuation of individuals are the intrinsic principles that constitute it. In simple beings, the beings themselves as they exist; in spiritual beings, the form as it exists; in composite beings, the principles that compose them. In all cases the principles are physical—, form, or matter, or form and matter—, and therefore the cause of individuation is a physical cause.

This is what Suárez means by saying that the principle of individuation of a thing is a thing's entity. For a thing's entity is nothing but "the essence as it exists" (Sect. V, § 2).[36] In simple beings it is simple, but in composite ones it is the physical composite as it exists (Sect. IV, § 17). And since what exists is individual, we must conclude that it is the individual that is the cause of its own individuation. Indeed, Suárez points out clearly that it is not "form" and "matter" that individuate this composite of which they are parts, but "this form" and "this matter." And what makes this form and this matter individual? Their entities, i.e. the form and matter themselves as they exist in reality.

But then, one may ask, is Suárez's view any different from Ockham's? After all, Ockham had said that individuals were individual by themselves. The differences between the two views are not easily discernible, but nonetheless they are there. In the first place, Ockham speaks of the individuality of individual composite substances apart from the individuality of their components. But Suárez analyzes the individuality of composite substances in terms of the individuality of their components. Second, for Ockham the individual was individual *per se* and this meant for him not only that the individual was individual *by itself* but also *essentially,* because there were, for all intents and purposes, no essences aside from the individual essence. Consequently, there is in fact no individuation. To speak of individuation presupposes that there is such a thing as a non-individual that may become so through something else. And this for Ockham is absurd. But Suárez does not have individuality attach to individuals essentially (Sect. VI, § 1). Individuality is *per se* in simple entities, *per aliud* (their components) in composite ones, but in neither case is it something essential. For what is essential to an individual is what is common to him and other members of his species and genus. Consequently, for Suárez it is possible to speak of individuation since he still holds on to the notion of essence, even if this, considered as such, is only a conceptual abstraction (Sect. VI, n.3).

In spite of these differences, however, it is clear that Suárez's view is closer to that of Ockham than to the views of Thomas and Scotus.

B. INDIVIDUATION OF ACCIDENTS

The inquiry into the cause of the individuation of accidents is briefly undertaken and settled by Suárez in Sect. VII. Contrary to a widespread view, supported among others by Thomas,[37] that accidents are individuated by their subject, Suárez, following the general principle stated in Sect. VI, holds that they are individuated by their entity. Paul's black color of hair, for example, is the particular black color of hair it is because of its own entity, not because it is Paul's color of hair.

Suárez's rejection of the individuation of accidents by the subject is based on the nature of the subject-accident relation. As he puts it (§ 3), "the subject cannot be said to be the intrinsic principle of the individuation of accidents, as intrinsically and essentially composing the accident...since the accident is certainly not intrinsically composed of the subject." The relation between subject and accident is, within the context of Aristotelian metaphysics, an extrinsic one, that is, extrinsic to the subject — which may or may not have the accident in question — and to the accident — which may or may not be attached to a particular subject. It would not do, then, to explain their individuality, which is something intrinsic to them and tied to their very nature and entity, by reference to something extrinsic. Peter's black color of hair is not this black color because of Peter. It is this black color because it is "a this" by itself. That it is Peter's is an accidental matter. It could have belonged to someone else.

V. The Presence of Accidents Differing only Numerically in the Same Subject

In the last two sections of the Disputation, Suárez takes up a problem of widespread concern among scholastics, related to the individuation of accidents: the manner, if any, in which accidents differing only in their individuality, and therefore belonging to the same species, can be present in the same subject. In an example, how can two only numerically different whites be in Paul? The two logical possibilities are explored in Sections VIII and IX respectively. In the first the case is put in terms of simultaneity; in the second, of succession.

With respect to the first, Suárez considers five different opinions which oppose in some measure the view that all accidents differing only numerically can be present simultaneously in the same subject. The views most opposed to the simultaneous presence of numerically different accidents derive their opposition from their doctrine concerning the cause of individuation. If, for example, accidental individuation is caused by the subject, as Thomas holds, then it would certainly be impossible for two accidents differing only in their individuality to be present at the same time in the same subject. For their difference would spring from the subject, and this being the same, the two accidents would have to be the same. If the black color of Paul's hair is the individual black color it is because it belongs to Paul, it could not happen that Paul would have two black colors of hair that were exactly alike in kind but still distinct.

Since Suárez points to a different cause of accidental individuation, however, indentifying it with the accident's entity, it becomes possible, irrespective of other considerations, for two numerically different accidents to be present in the same subject at the same time even though they are not different in any other way. If that were an impossibility, Suárez points out (§ 20), it must be derivable from some other factor than individuation. Accordingly, and with a great deal of caution, he proposes (1) that the proposition, "No plurality of accidents of the same species can be in the same subject [at the same time]" is not to be accepted without exception, and (2) that the occurrence of a plurality of accidents of the same species in the same subject at the same time does not occur naturally.

The answer to the second problem, whether accidents differing only in number can be successively present in the same subject, follows easily from this one. For if, according to Suárez, it is possible that they do so even simultaneously, it would be even more possible for them to do so successively. Indeed, he holds that it is not only possible this time, but also true in fact in the natural order.

VI. Conclusion

In conclusion I would like to stress four important points. The first is the completely philosophical character of Suárez's analysis. Although some theological considerations and examples creep in once in a while, the discussion is guided wholly by philosophical principles. The arguments given are philosophical, and the criteria by which various views and arguments are judged are also philosophical. Often Suárez will explicitly make the point that an argument is not philosophical enough, meaning that it is based on theological assumptions, or that a particular problem that had surfaced in the discussion is theological and therefore outside the scope of his discussion (Sect. II, §§ 30 and 37). It is clear, then, that at this time, and for Suárez at least, philosophy and in particular metaphysics had a place of its own among the sciences, independent of theology. In this sense Suárez is no less modern than Descartes or Leibniz who, as it is well known, read the *Metaphysical Disputations* avidly.

The second point is that Suárez's analysis of individuality is ontological in character. He is not primarily concerned with the discernibility of the individual and its cause, although he is aware both of the problems related to the knowledge of the individual and the epistemological problems related to the way we distinguish between two individuals (Sect. III, § 28 and VII, § 4). The roots of discernibility are always referred to by Suárez, as they are in the scholastic tradition dating back to Thomas, as "signs" or "indications" of individuality rather than its causes or principles.[38] The latter are prior to the former both logically and ontologically, even though the former are prior in human experience. This is why Suárez, like most other philosophers who put ontology before epistemology, cannot adhere to what in contemporary philosophy goes by the name of "the principle of identity of indiscernibles," since such a principle implies a reversal of what Suárez would regard as the proper order between these two sciences. His primary concern is with individuality as it is, independent of human consideration.

Thirdly, I would stress Suárez's contribution to the controversy surrounding the problem of individuation. Besides the subtlety and originality of many of the arguments he proposes, four factors stand out: (1) His identification of the nature of individuality as indivisibility, and of distinction as a result of individuality rather than a constituent of it. (2) His explicit discussion of the extension of individuality, a problem seldom treated separately by his predecessors, whose views on the subject were in many cases no more than implicit uncritical assumptions rather than explicitly discussed philosophical commitments. (3) His original interpretation of Scotus' doctrine of *haecceitas* as an answer to the problem of the ontological status of individuality rather than to the problem concerned with the cause of individuality. (4) The merits of his own view on the causal analysis of individuality, which avoids some of the most obvious pitfalls of other views and presents a unified and economic solution to this most vexing philosophical problem. The numerous other merits of Suárez's analysis will become evident, no doubt, to the careful reader.

The fourth most important point I would stress in closing is the centrality of this problem within Suárez's metaphysics. This is evident from the place that the discussion of individuation has within the whole framework of the *Metaphysical Disputations*. As a kind of unity, individuality is discussed just after the general notion of transcendental unity in Disputation IV. This indicates that he considered it the most important kind of the first of the three basic attributes of being (unity, truth, goodness). Universal and formal unities are discussed only after individual unity, in Disputation VI. For it is individual unity that makes all other unity possible. As such, then, Disputation V reveals the core of Suarecian metaphysics.

NOTES

[1] The term 'nature of individuality' is, strictly speaking, inappropriate. For medievals, except for Scotus, his followers, and a few early medieval figures, did not regard individuality as having a nature. Indeed, for most thinkers individuality was not at all a formal feature of things. The term 'nature,' then, in this context is to be interpreted non-technically to refer to the sort of thing individuality is rather than as referring to "a nature."

² Strictly speaking, 'individuality' and 'individuation' are not equivalent. Individuality is the feature or features which constitute an individual as individual; individuation is the process whereby the individual becomes the individual it is. However, scholastics often used the same Latin term '*individuatio,*' usually translated as individuation, to refer to both. Suárez follows custom on this.

³ The case of collections, such as a pile of stones, present some difficulties. One way of dealing with them is to argue that it is in the essence of a collection to have a determinate number. Therefore, collections of different numbers are essentially different. As such, then, there would be an essential difference, for example, between a pile of thirty stones and one of three, or between one of thirty and one of twenty-nine for that matter. This is the reason why a pile of thirty stones is an individual and different from "man," for example. For the pile would not be divisible into other piles of thirty, while man is divisible into units which are essentially the same as itself. Suárez seems to be quite aware of this problem and of this sort of solution, but he adopts a different one. In Sect. I, § 3, he points out that the individual unity which collections have is not truly an individual unity since it is accidental—it is not essential to a pile to have thirty and only thirty stones. Individual unity is an entitative (for him this means essential) feature of things and as such it is a feature only of those things that have essences, i.e. of instances of natural kinds. The case of homogeneous substances such as water, wood, and the like is raised in the same passage.

⁴ Definition here is not to be taken strictly, since only natural kinds are definable. The definition of "individual" is nominal. The same is the case with the use of the term 'essence' in this context.

⁵ Perhaps in a different framework, which does not rely on the priority of actuality over potentiality, it would make sense to say that it is possible for X to have property M because of Y when Y does not itself have it. But within Suarecian metaphysics it would be absurd to say so.

⁶ Loeb, p. 6; my underlining.

⁷ The point is not that Thomas did not make the distinction at all. There is evidence elsewhere that he may have done so; in *Summa theologiae* III, 77, 2, (ed. De Rubeis *et al.,* vol. V, Turin: Marietti, 1932, p. 140a-b) for example, he reduces individuality to incommunicability. But there are also many places such as the *Commentary on Boethius' "On the Trinity"* where one would expect the distinction and it is not present (*Expositio super librum Boethii de Trinitate,* ed. B. Decker. Leiden: Brill, 1959). In addition, there are some texts where he clearly defines indivisibility as distinction (*Summa theologiae* I, 29, 4. *Ed. cit.,* vol. I, p. 209a). And in at least one important one (*Summa theologiae* I, 13, 9. *Ed. cit.,* vol. I, p. 90a-b), he actually seems to reverse the order between indivisibility and distinction, making the latter appear primary and the former secondary. Moreover, even if one were to grant that Thomas was aware of the differences between indivisibility and distinction, his explicitly stated answer to the problem concerning the principle of individuation (in material substances designated matter—which distinguishes numerically within the species—, in immaterial ones themselves, i.e. the existing essence—which distinguishes them from everything else) suggests that he had in mind primarily the problem of distinction rather than that of indivisibility. See also the recent discussion by D. Winiewicz, "A Note on *alteritas* and Numerical Diversity in St. Thomas Aquinas," *Dialogue* 16 (1977), 693-707.

⁸ *Expositio...,* q.4, a.2, p. 143. Thomas consistently states that "designated matter is the principle of individuation" of material beings, although designated matter is understood as matter under determined dimensions in some works (*De ente et essentia,* Ch. 2, ed. M. D. Roland-Gosselin. Paris: J. Vrin, 1948, p. 11.2), and as matter under undetermined dimensions in others (*On II Sentences,* d.3, q.1, a.4, in *Opera omnia,* vol. VIII, Paris, Vivès, 1850, p. 46a-b; *Expositio...,* text mentioned).

[9] Distinction or separability is viewed by him as a consequence of individuality. Sect. I, § 7 and Sect. III, §§ 5, 17 and 28. Of course, since distinction is a consequence of individuality, the latter is the cause of the former (Sect. III, § 12 and Sect. VI, § 16).

[10] *Periphyseon* IV, Ch. 7; *PL* 765 ff.

[11] *Ordinatio* II, d.3, qq. 5-6, ed. Balic, in *Opera omnia,* vol. VII (Vatican, 1973), p. 477.

[12] *Super quattuor libros sententiarum* VI, d.2, qq.4 and 6, in *Opera plurima,* vol. III (Lyon, 1494-1496; rep. Farnborough: Gregg, 1962) fol. i-iiivb ff and k-iivb. Also *Summa logicae* I, Ch. 16, ed. P. Boehner *et. al.,* in *Opera philosophica,* vol. I (St. Bonaventure: Franciscan Institute, 1974), pp. 54 ff.

[13] *De Trinitate* 2; Loeb, p. 12.

[14] See, for example, *De ente...,* Ch. 5, pp. 10 ff, where Thomas discusses individuation only in the context of material substances. Immaterial substances, except for the human soul, which is naturally joined to matter, are not multiplied within the species; they are only "limited" by their nature and their being. This seems to imply that they are not "individual." However, Thomas states elsewhere (*Summa theologiae* III, 77, 2, vol. V, p. 140a) that "separate immaterial substances are individuated by themselves," a statement which implies that they are indeed individual. Suárez himself believed that Thomas accepted the individuality of immaterial substances (Sect. II, § 6). The question at stake then is not whether he accepted it, but (1) how he interpreted it, (2) what importance he attached to it, and (3) how he was able to account for it.

[15] Because of this, for Suárez, things independent of the mind can be called universals only through a *denominatio extrinseca,* that is, only because they are causally related to the universal in the mind, which is properly called universal.

[16] See n. 14 above.

[17] Roscelin, according to Anselm, held that universals, such as "man" and "dog," were mere particular utterances (*voces*). This would seem to imply that no distinction between the individual and the common nature considered as common is possible, even at the conceptual level. The most there can be is a distinction between individuals, for example, between Socrates and the sound I utter when I say "man." See Picavet, *Roscelin philosophe et théologien d'après la legénde et d'après l'histoire,* Paris, 1911, particularly pp. 130 ff.

[18] The individual is nothing but a mere appearance.

[19] The bundle theory of individuation holds that the individual is nothing other than a bundle of characteristics. For the medievals who held this view (Boethius, *De Trinitate* I; Eriugena — see my article, "Ontological Characterization of the Relation Between Man and Created Nature," *Journal of the History of Philosophy* 16 (1978), 155-166) some of these characteristics were essential and others accidental; for contemporary writers they are usually accidental (see, M. Black, "The Identity of Indiscernibles," in *Problems of Analysis,* Ithaca, N.Y.: Cornell Univ. Press, 1954). In both cases, however, the point is usually made that there is at least one characteristic of a bundle (place for Boethius, identity for Black) that is not shared with other bundles. It is this unique characteristic (or characteristics), then, that makes one individual distinct and, consequently, discernible from other individuals.

[20] *Ordinatio* II, dist. 3, qq. 5-6, reply to the first objection. *Ed. cit.,* pp. 476 and 484-485.

[21] *Ibid.,* q. 1, answer to the question, p. 402 ff.

[22] *De ente...,* Ch. 2, p. 11.1; *Expositio...,* q.4, a.2, answer to the question, last paragraph, p. 143.

[23] *De ente...,* Ch. 2, p 11.9.

²⁴ Whether Thomas in fact held that the individual (the composite of matter and form in the case of man, for example) is really distinct from the nature (the form) is a matter of dispute among scholars. For the present what is pertinent is that the explanation given here is in accordance with Suárez's understanding of Thomas' position. The individual considered as a whole is really distinct from the nature because the nature considered as a whole or as a part does not include the designated matter which belongs to the individual. Indeed, the nature, i.e. the features that make the individual like other individuals of the same species and genus, is something really distinct from individuality, i.e. the features that make the individual unlike other individuals.

²⁵ *Super quattuor...,* I, dist. 2, q.4, answer to the question, vol. III, fols. ira ff.

²⁶ *Ibid.,* q.6, answer to the question, fol. k-iivb.

²⁷ *Ibid.,* fol. k-iiira. Thomas held a similar view about the particularity of concepts; see *De ente...,* p. 28.14.

²⁸ In addition to the texts cited here, see this Section, §§ 15 and 32 and Sect. I throughout.

²⁹ See *distinctio* in Glossary.

³⁰ Disputation VII, Sect. I, § 4. In Vivès, p. 251a: *"Et est illa distinctio rationis, quae formaliter et actualiter non est in rebus quae sic distinctae denominantur, prout in se existunt, sed solum prout substant conceptibus nostris, et ab eis denominationem aliquam accipunt...."*

³¹ *Super quattuor...,* I, dist. 2, q.6, vol. III, fol. k-iivb.

³² Q.4, a.2, answer to the question, p. 143. In Brennan's translation, Herder, 1946, pp. 110-111.

³³ *De ente...,* Ch. 2, p. 11.7; and *Summa theologiae* I, 29, ad 3, and 30, 4, vol. I, pp. 206a and 215b.

³⁴ It is this sort of a statement that may have caused Ross to state that "Suárez... holds that individuation is derived from the *form...*" (Intro. to *Francis Suárez, On Formal and Universal Unity,* Milwaukee: Marquette Univ. Press, 1964, p. 24). If this is to be interpreted as saying that individuation is due to form alone then it is mistaken. If it is to be taken as saying that form is the principal (among others) factor in individuation, then it is correct.

³⁵ *De ente...,* Ch. 4, pp. 12-13 and 18-19.

³⁶ See also Glossary.

³⁷ *Summa theologiae* III, 77, 2, vol. V, p. 140a.

³⁸ Indeed, the causes of discernibility are quite different from the causes of individuality. In the case of accidents, for example, discernibility is due to the subject (Sect. VII, § 4), while, as we have seen, individuality is the result of entity. In Sect. VI, § 17, Suárez points out that the discernibility of material substances is always the result of matter and accidents, for discernibility follows our mode of cognition, which begins with sensation (see also Sect. III, § 33, and VI, §§ 4 and 8). Individuality, on the other hand, as a kind of unity, follows being.

Disputation V
On Individual Unity and Its Principle

We shall inquire about three [things] in this Disputation: First, whether this unity is found in all existing things; next, what it is in them; and, finally, what principle or root it has in each of them. And since the last [of these] cannot be explained in the same way *(ratione)* in all things, we shall inquire separately about [it in] material and spiritual substances and [in] accidents.[1]

Section I[2]

Whether all Things that Exist or can Exist are Singular and Individual[3]

1. The reason for [raising] this question can be:[4] First, that although the divine nature really exists, yet it is not singular and individual, since, according to faith, it is communicable[5] to many. Second, that although each angel is an existing thing, it does not have this numerical and individual unity, but, [speaking] with precision, [it has] essential [unity],[6] such as that understood by us to be in man as such.[7] Therefore, [some things that exist have no numerical and individual unity].[8] Proof of the minor:[9] This individual unity is understood as adding something to the formal or essential [unity], by reason of which the essential nature *(ratio)* can be contracted and, consequently, divided into many individuals. But there is no such addition in an angel, since in it the whole essence is, as it were, separate *(praecisa)* and abstract, for which reason it cannot be numerically multiplied; just as, if man existed as it is conceived in abstraction, it could not be multiplied. Third, in reality man exists in Peter and Paul, and as such it is not something individual and singular. Therefore, not everything existing in the order of things has this unity.

[However], what Aristotle frequently taught against Plato goes contrary to this, namely that everything that exists in reality is individual and singular.[10]

2. It must be granted[11] that individual or singular being is not opposed to common or universal[12] being only relatively, insofar as the individual is [something] placed under the species according to mental comparison or logical consideration. For this [notion of individual being as something placed under the species] does not apply to every individual nature, as it is clear from [the case of] the divine [nature], nor [is it relevant] to what is being considered now. Therefore,[13] [individual or singular being] is opposed [to common or universal being], as it were, privatively, almost in the same way in which unity is opposed to multiplicity. For, that is called "common" or "universal" which is communicated[14] to many [entities] or found in many [entities] according to one single notion. On the other hand, that is called "one in number" or "singular" or "individual" which is one being in such a way that, according to that notion of being through which it is called "one," it is not communicable to many [entities], for example, to [those that are] inferior to or placed under it, or to those that are many under that notion; for these coincide in the same thing. Aristotle refers to them in Bk. III, *Metaphysics*, Ch. 3, text 14, saying: "We call singular what is one in number, universal, however, what is in these."[15]

These [things] are clarified by an example: Humanity as such,[16] in its objective concept, does not express something singular and individual, because that concept is of itself common to many humanities, which are really many, and in them the very notion of humanity is multiplied. Whence it follows, according to reason, that the notion of humanity is superior and common to many as to inferiors, but that, on the other hand, this humanity of Christ, for example, is individual and singular, because the whole notion or objective concept of "this humanity" cannot be common to the many [entities] that are many under the notion [of humanity], that is, to many humanities. However, that [the notion of] "this humanity" be communicable to the divine Word,[17] for example, or even to many supposits,[18] does not go against its singular and individual unity, because [this humanity] is not communicated to them as a superior to inferiors, but as the form to the supposit, or supposits, in which it [i.e. the form] is not multiplied or divided in its proper notion *(ratio)*. Therefore, this singular and individual unity is completed by this negation of communicability or division.

3. This is further confirmed and explained thus: Just as the notion of "one in common" is completed by the negation of division, as it is explained following Aristotle, so the notion of "a particular one"

(talis unius), namely, of "a singular and individual," is also to be completed by negation. [This is] both because there is no more reason for the one [notion to be completed by negation] than for the other, and also because the notions of "more [common]" and "less common" must maintain a proportion. So that, just as the difference by itself and in the same order contracts the genus, so too in general the determination is related to the determinable to which they[19] are subordinated by themselves, as it happens in the present [case]. Moreover, no other negation of division or divisibility that may complete the notion of an individual and singular entity can be thought, except that which has been explained by us, namely, that the entity be such that its whole notion may not be communicable to many similar entities or, what is the same, that it may not be divisible into many entities such as itself. For man as such is not a singular entity for this reason: that it is divisible into many [entities] in [each of] which the whole nature *(ratio)* of man is found. On the contrary, however, this quantity of two feet is individual, because, although divisible, [is] not [divisible] into many [entities], each of which is such as was the divided whole; and so that is a division of the whole into parts, not of the common into particulars.[20]

[But] you will say:[21] This notion of individual is accidentally common to [any] multitude and to being, because a pile of stones, too, is such that it may not be communicable to many [entities] or divisible into many [entities] such as itself, and the same is the case with any number taken in particular. Indeed, no species or genus, man or animal, for example, is divisible into many [entities] which are like the [entities which are] divided.

The answer to this must concede that all those [entities] that participate in that negation are individuals and singulars to that extent, as this pile of stones is singular and individual in that respect *(ratione)*. And similarly this set of two or set of three is a certain individual of a particular species of number, and this genus or this species is one individual under the notion of genus or species. However, these, [i.e. genus and species, participate in that unity] only conceptually, and those, [i.e. pile of stones and sets of two and three, participate] merely by accident in the notion of being[22] or number, that is, of multitude. Wherefore, in order to apply the aforementioned negation or indivision essentially *(per se)* to the being and unity of which we have spoken, it must be taken as essentially *(per se)* joined to entity; for the notion of unity, as we said above, does not consist in indivision alone, but in undivided entity. Therefore, the notion of essentially *(per se)* individual and singular unity consists in that of the entity [considered as] essentially *(per se)* one by its nature and, as stated above, undivided or incommunicable.[23]

[But] you will say:[24] At least this water will not be singular, because it is divisible into many [entities] in [each of] which the whole nature *(ratio)* of water is found.

The answer [to this] is that what is divided [i.e. this water] is not divisible into many [entities] which are [also] "this water," but [rather] which are [just] water; and hence, "this water" is singular, while "water" [is] common.

Solution to the Question[25]

4. Therefore, having explained thus the notion of individual or singular being, it must be said that all things that are actual beings *(entia actualia)* or that exist or can exist immediately, are singular and individual. I say "immediately" in order to exclude the common natures *(rationes)* of beings, which, as such, cannot immediately exist or have actual entity, except in singular and individual entities. If these [individual entities] are removed, it is impossible for anything real to remain, as Aristotle said concerning first substances in *Categories,* Ch. on substance.[26] The stated assertion is evident,[27] as Aristotle proves against Plato in Bk. I, *Metaphysics,* Ch. 6 and Bk. VII, texts 26 and 27, and often elsewhere.[28] Nevertheless, many believe that Aristotle misinterpreted Plato's doctrine of ideas, because he either put them [i.e. the ideas] in the divine mind[29] or separate from individuals, not indeed in reality, but only [separate] by a formal notion. But this does not interest us very much,[30] and besides, we shall discuss it in the Disputation that follows.[31]

Now we prove the assertion that whatever exists has a fixed and determinate entity.[32] But every such entity has necessarily[33] an added negation; therefore, also singularity and individual unity.[34] The minor is evident, because every entity, for the very reason that it is a determinate entity, cannot be divided from itself; therefore it can neither be divided into many [entities] such as itself. Otherwise the whole entity would be in each of them, and consequently, [insofar] as it is in one, it would be divided from itself insofar as it is in another, [something] which involves a clear contradiction. Therefore, every entity, for the very reason that it is one entity in the order of things, is necessarily one in the aforementioned way, and hence singular and individual.

5. This argument concludes that not even by absolute power can a real entity, as existing in reality, not be understood to be singular and individual, because to be an entity and to be divisible into many entities such as itself implies a contradiction. Otherwise, there would be both one and many entitatively, that is, according to the same real entity, [something] which involves a contradiction. This argument shows as well that universals cannot exist separate from singu-

lars, because if the universal man existed outside Peter and Paul, etc., either [1] it would also be in Peter and Paul or [2] it would remain entirely separate from them. If the latter [2] were said, [then] man as such would already be a certain singular thing distinct *(condivisa)* from Peter and Paul [and], therefore, falsely called universal. Moreover, it would follow that neither Peter nor Paul are men, because in order for an essential predicate to apply *(conveniat)* to something, it is necessary that [the predicate] not be separate from it [i.e. that to which it applies]. For, how could [the essential predicate] truly be said of it [i.e. that to which it applies], if [the essential predicate] were not in it [i.e. that to which it applies]? Or how can [an essential predicate] be understood to constitute essentially that in which it is not? If, however, [1] it is in Peter and Paul, it is neither [a] entirely the same really and entitatively in both, and so Peter and Paul will not be two men, but one; or [b] it is distinct in reality and entity in each of them. And so, if [b], that separate and universal man would either [i] be a third [one] distinct from Peter and Paul,[35] and so it would be false to say that it is in them and universal, because it would not be [anything] except something singular distinct from them. Or, indeed, [ii] if it were the same in one and the other, it would be necessary for it to be distinct from itself as well as one and many in reality according to the same essence insofar as it exists in reality. [But] these [things] are clearly contradictory. For this reason, therefore, it is necessary that every thing, insofar as it exists in reality, be singular and individual.

Answer to the Objections[36]

6. To the first: There are theologians who say that the divine essence is neither singular nor universal.[37] But this is false, for those two [notions, "singular" and "universal"], are immediately contradictory;[38] hence, it is impossible that there be a being to which neither of them applies. Moreover, the divine nature is one in itself in such a way that it cannot be multiplied or divided into several [natures] similar [to itself]. It is, therefore, one individual and singular nature; for which reason God is one in number in such a manner that [the divine nature] cannot be multiplied in any way. Therefore, the divine nature has individual and singular unity, and this is not inconsistent with the communicability of that nature to the three persons, because it is not communicated to them as universal to particular or superior to inferior, but as form or nature to the supposits. In these [supposits] it is not [found] divided from them or from itself, for it is wholly [present] in each and in all [of them] simultaneously [and it is] completely indistinct from them; but [more] on this elsewhere.[39]

7. To the second: Some Thomists — as pointed out when discussing Part III of St. Thomas, *[Summa theologiae]*, q.4, a.4[40] — feel that spiritual natures exist in abstraction as in specific essence and perfection alone, without a proper individual contraction. But we speak more suitably in the Section that follows, n.21,[41] concerning this view and the sense it can have in order that it may not [appear to] say something entirely absurd and unintelligible. In terms of what is relevant at the moment, it cannot be denied that every angelic nature, insofar as it exists in the order of things, is singular and individual. For if the divine nature itself, which is supremely immaterial, is singular and individual, much more will any angelic nature be [so]; for it is incommunicable not only to many natures, but also to many supposits, at least from its nature. Then, the reason for the conclusion holds equally about any spiritual nature or entity, because it is impossible for such an entity not to be accompanied by the negation of communicability, that is, of the division of such an entity into several entities similar to itself, because it cannot be divided from itself and be one and many. Finally, whether a spiritual substance and nature can or cannot be numerically multiplied within the same species has nothing to do with this. For, if it can, it is necessary for any individual of that species to have individual and singular unity; nor could the very species exist except in some individual, as has been said concerning other universals. If, however, that multiplication of individuals is incompatible with such a nature, for this very reason such a nature, existing in reality, is more singular and individual, because it is more incommunicable, namely, as it were essentially, in the manner of the divine nature. Therefore, the addition of the aforementioned negation is sufficient for the notion of individual unity which concerns us at the moment. Whether a positive addition to the specific nature may be required for this negation as well will be discussed in the Section that follows.[42]

8. The answer to the third is that man as it exists in the order of things is singular, because it is no other than Peter and Paul. Whether man is distinct *ex natura rei* from them in them will be discussed both in the Section as well as in the Disputation that follow.[43]

Notes

¹ The first problem is discussed in Sect. I, the second in Sect. II, and the third in the rest of the Disputation. Sections III to IX can be subdivided into a first part comprising Sects. III to VI, which discuss the principle of substantial individuation, and Sects. VII to IX, which are concerned with accidental individuation. In particular, Sect. VII deals with the principle of individuation in accidents; Sects. VIII and IX raise a separate issue, the question of the simultaneous or successive presence

of the numerically same accident in a subject. Consequently, this Disputation raises at least five different problems: the extension of individuality, its nature, the ontological status of individuality in an individual and its relation to the nature, the principle of individuation in substances and accidents, and the question of the simultaneous or successive presence of the numerically same accidents in a subject. These issues were not always distinguished by earlier scholastics. The first issue, for example, was one that did not often receive separate attention. Most medievals, except for very few, such as John Eriugena, regarded the doctrine of universal individuality (everything that exists is individual) as almost self-evident; one hardly finds any arguments in favor of it. Even realists such as Duns Scotus repeat the doctrine and apply it not only to substances, such as a man or a dog, but also to their principles (ex. form) and accidental characteristics (ex. white). Indeed, this seems to be one of the features of the medieval controversy concerning individuality that separates it from contemporary discussions, since in the latter one of the predominant views is that the characteristics of individuals are not themselves individual. The reasons for the scholastic commitment to universal individuality are not very clear except perhaps for one: the general statements to that effect found in Aristotle's *Categories*. It must be remembered that this work had an enormous influence in the first part of the Middle Ages, until about 1150, when the new translations of ancient and Arabic works began to enter the Latin West through Spain and to a lesser extent through Sicily. For further details see the Introduction above.

² This Section, like most of the others, follows roughly the organization of a medieval *quaestio*. After the initial identification of the problem to be investigated in a brief, one line question, Suárez presents three arguments in the first paragraph of § 1, which answer the question negatively (the *Contra* part of the *quaestio*). The second brief paragraph of § 1 contains the positive answer (the *Pro* part of the *quaestio*), based on the authority of Aristotle. The brevity of the *Pro* and its purely authoritative nature are explained not only in terms of established scholastic tradition, but also because Suárez offers a detailed discussion and defense of this view in what remains of the *quaestio*. It would have been superfluous to add arguments at this point and repeat them again later. Moreover, owing to the rare treatment of this problem as a separate issue by scholastics, and therefore to the lack of a well established tradition of arguments in favor of the view, most arguments given by Suárez are the result of his own thinking rather than the product of borrowing. For this reason, again, it seems only natural that the arguments be presented as his own, in the *quaestio*'s determination or solution. This brings us to another important point concerning the structure of this Section. Contrary to the explicit division present in the various editions of this text, which identify the *Solutio* as beginning in § 4, the *Solutio* seems to begin in § 2, immediately after the statement of the *Pro*. There are several factors that support this structural interpretation. In the first place, to put the *Solutio* immediately after the *Pro* would be in keeping with scholastic tradition and particularly with the clear and symmetrical structure of the articles of Thomas' *Summa theologiae*, a work for which Suárez had great admiration. Secondly, the linguistic formulas used at the beginning of § 2 ("It must be assumed") and § 4 ("Therefore,...it must be added...") suggest indeed that § 2 is the beginning of the answer and that § 4 is only an addition or further conclusion and elaboration drawn from what has already been established in §§ 2 and 3. And third, it is clear from evidence gathered from other Sections and Disputations that the divisions and subtitles found in the text of this edition are often quite plainly mistaken, and therefore must have been the work of someone other than Suárez — perhaps the editor — who did not follow very well the thread of the argument. Now, the reason the editor, or whoever introduced the subtitles of this Section, confused the place where the *Solutio* begins may be that the *Solutio* is long and complicated, having at least three discernible parts. The first, comprising §§ 2 and 3, clarifies and defends Suárez's understanding of individuality, pointing out its essential features. In § 3 Suárez also anticipates two subtle

objections against the view he adopts, and offers answers to them. The second part of the *Solutio* comprises the first paragraph of § 4. It explicitly states the conclusion of the Section, offers some further authoritative support for it, and explains the addition of the word 'immediately' to the answer. The third part of the *Solutio* comprises the second paragraph of § 4, and § 5. This part proves that "whatever exists has a fixed and determinate entity." The rest of the text answers the three objections raised in the *Contra,* at the beginning of the Section. The answers are contained in §§ 6, 7, and 8 respectively.

³ *Individuum* (used in the text in the feminine plural, *individuae,* because it refers back to *res*), individual, not divided, indivisible, inseparable. For the technical meaning of this term see the Glossary and the Introduction. Although the terms 'singular' and 'individual' are used interchangeably because they refer to the same thing in reality, their meaning is different. This may be the reason why Suárez uses both here instead of only one.

⁴ This is the part of the Section which argues against universal individuality; it is the *Contra* of the *quaestio.* Suárez presents three arguments in it which cover the whole span of reality — God (uncreated spiritual being), angel (created spiritual being), and man (created material — spiritual being). His aim as far as it can be gathered from the text is to present as a strong a case as possible for the opposition in order to settle the problem once and for all. There is no need to add an argument from purely material being, because, within the Aristotelian framework adopted by Suárez, the more material a thing is the less universal or common to many it can be, since it is more restricted by spatio-temporal dimensions. Moreover, in the objections to Suárez's own determination of the *quaestio* in § 3 Suárez will discuss the cases of material things which present particular difficulties, such as homogeneous substances (water) and collections (pile of stones). This procedure of presenting the strongest possible case for the opposition is standard among late scholastics, who priced intellectual honesty very highly. It is particularly important in the case of Suárez because part of his argumentative method is dialectical, that is, by, first, the elimination of all possible alternatives to his own and, second, the answering of all serious objections.

⁵ This is a case of communicability by identity without any division of essence and existence. This is the way the divine essence is communicated, i.e. is common to the three persons of the Trinity. See answer to objection in § 6 and Glossary, under *communicabilis.*

⁶ The unity of the essence considered as separate from individual differences. See Glossary, *unitas essentialis* and *praecisio.*

⁷ This objection is based on the view that angels, unlike beings composed of matter and form, lacked matter and therefore a principle whereby they could be numerically multiplied within one species. As a result, many scholastics, beginning with Thomas Aquinas, concluded that each angel constitutes a single species and that its unity is therefore "essential" rather than "individual." In spite of their spiritual and, as it were, formal nature, however, Thomas thought they were not pure act, but a mixture of potency and act, owing to their composition of essence and existence. See the treatise *On Spiritual Creatures,* a.1, q.1. As it is clear from the answer to this objection (see § 7, below), Suárez rejects the view that because angels are spiritual they lack individual unity and have only essential unity. Moreover, he rejects the view, proposed by followers of Thomas, which thought impossible for God, even by absolute power, numerically to multiply angels within one species (see *On Angels* I, Ch. 15, § 3). However, he does accept as "without a doubt quite probable" the view that angels differ essentially and specifically in Disp. XXXV, Sect. III, § 43. The reason why he can find it only "quite probable" and not "necessary" is simply that, as Suárez will explain in Sect. VI of the present Disputation, § 18, the principle of individuation in spiritual substances is not matter. Hence, he does not have to conclude

necessarily that because angels are not material they must differ essentially. In fact, according to him, they differ in essence and also as individuals. The reason for saying that they might differ essentially is other than their non-materiality. In Suárez's own words "it is more believable and concordant with the perfection of the universe that there be in that level [of being, i.e. the angelic], several species of intelligences essentially diverse" (Disp. XXXV, Sect. III, § 43). Obviously, in spite of Suárez's recalcitrant Aristotelianism, the influence of Plato and "the great chain of being" was not altogether foreign to his thought. On the other hand, the fact that he viewed angels as having individual unity shows that he understood quite well the distinction between individual and essence and that he sided with those who thought of being as primarily individual. In this respect Suárez's metaphysics has a clear advantage over Thomas', since, for the latter, angels would have to be, as it were, existing essences —he blurs the distinction between individual and essence. The only way Thomas could have individualized these angelic essences would have been by making their existence *(esse)* their principle of individuation, since their composition includes only essence and existence. But Thomas never assigned to existence *(esse)* the role of individuator. If he had, he would have ended up with two principles of individuation in material beings (designated matter and *esse*) and would have been hard pressed, moreover, to explain the individuality of possible beings. Consequently, it seems that Thomas' Platonism is much stronger and that his understanding of individuality is less clear than Suárez's in this respect. In fact, the similarities of his view with that of the Platonists are quite evident, since the latter believed that the forms, also identified with "ideal numbers," differed by themselves—not by matter or as individuals—as it were essentially. See Giovanni Reale, *Teofrasto e la sua aporetica metafisica,* Brescia, 1964, Ch. 4, n. 41. Not even Aristotle liberates himself completely of this Platonic view. D. Badareu argued as early as 1936 (*L'individuel chez Aristote,* Paris) that Aristotle does not preserve the individual and does not explain it, since the form is the source of all being for him (p. 146). Perhaps the matter is not so serious as Badareu makes it, but it is true nonetheless that Aristotle's notion of individuality is not completely satisfactory. This becomes particularly evident in the case of spiritual substances. See *Metaphysics* XII, Ch. 8, 1074a31-38. See also W. Jaeger, *Aristoteles Grundlenhung einer Geschichte sener Entwicklung,* Berlin, 1923, p. 481; in Robinson's trans. pp. 352-353.

⁸ Often Suárez does not state the conclusion of arguments. This was a usual practice among scholastics at the time and in the Middle Ages in general. Given the scarcity and expense of writing material (parchment in the Middle Ages and later paper) it was thought economical to leave out what could be easily supplied by the context. Because this creates some difficulty for the modern reader, and particularly for those unfamiliar with the rules of the Aristotelian syllogism used in this period, I have supplied the missing conclusions within square brackets. In this particular case the argument may be interpreted as something like this: 'No angel *is a thing that* is numerically and individually one' (major premise), 'Some angel is an existent entity' (minor premise), 'Some existent entity is not a thing that is numerically and individually one' (conclusion).

⁹ The reference is to the minor premise of a standard syllogism. The term 'premise' or its equivalents (See *propositio* in the Glossary) were often omitted after 'minor' and 'major' for economy's sake. The major premise is so called because it contains the major term, i.e. the predicate term of the conclusion, of the syllogism. The minor premise contained the minor term, i.e. the subject term of the conclusion, of the syllogism. A syllogism, according to Aristotle in *Prior Analytics* I, Ch. 1, 24b18-22, is "discourse in which, certain things being stated, something other than what is stated follows of necessity from their being so." In short, a syllogism is a valid argument, that is a deductive argument in which the conclusion cannot be false if the premises are true.

¹⁰ This brief sentence constitutes the whole *Pro* part of the *quaestio*.

[11] Here begins the first part of the *Solutio*. It covers §§ 2 to 3. The first paragraph of § 2 explains the notion of individual by contrasting it with the notion of the common or universal, and the second paragraph clarifies the point with an example. The first paragraph of § 3 gives some further support to this view while the second and fourth paragraphs present objections to it, the answers to which are contained in the third and fifth paragraphs respectively.

[12] *Universale,* belonging to all, universal; from *universus,* all together, whole. Here it is used by Suárez as a synonym of 'common.' For *universale,* see Glossary.

[13] The reader would rather expect "but also that" instead of "therefore" *(ergo).* Although the grammatical construction "not only...therefore" is not frequently found in English, its sense is clear: If *A* is not only *x,* it is therefore *y* because....If a man is not only animal, therefore he is rational because....

[14] The passive indicative used here *(communicatur)* indicates that, according to Suárez, what is common must be actually communicated to many things. If it is not actually communicated it is not common but communicable. On the other hand, what is numerically one must not only be actually communicated to many, but also not capable of being communicated.

[15] *Metaphysics* III, Ch. 4, 999b33. *In Aristotelis opera cum Averrois commentariis* VIII, Venetiis apud Junctas, 1562-1574; Frankfurt, 1962, fol. 52vb. All future references to Aristotle will be to this edition, which was a standard text at the time and may have been used by Suárez. The term 'text' or 'common text' *(textus communis)* refers to the divisions introduced by Averroes in Aristotle's text.

[16] *Humanitas ut sic.* The term *humanitas* can mean not only mankind and the quality of being humane or philanthropic, but also human nature, what it is to be human. The latter is by far the most common use in philosophical discourse. When coupled with *ut sic,* as such, it means human nature considered only as human nature, that is, considered as including only what is contained in its definition. Scholastics also spoke of "someone's humanity" as the individual form of that human being. Thomas Aquinas explains the distinction between the terms 'man' and 'humanity' in *On Being and Essence,* Ch. 2, § 13, thus: "The term 'man' expresses the essence of man as a whole because it does not prescind from the designation of matter, but contains it implicitly and indistinctly, as we said the genus contains the difference. That is why the term 'man' can be predicated of individuals. The term 'humanity,' on the other hand, signifies the essence of man as a part, because its meaning includes only what belongs to man as man, prescinding from all designation of matter. Consequently, it cannot be predicated of individual men." For quotations to *On Being and Essence* I am using Maurer's trans., with occasional modifications, throughout (PIMS, 1968).

[17] Christ, the second person of the Trinity. The term 'communicable' here refers to the fact that Christ or the Word has or may have his own humanity. For his humanity "to be communicable" is simply for his humanity "to be possessed" by him. This is, of course, an odd use of the term *communicabilis.* In the more common use of the term, humanity is said "to be communicable" if it is or can become common to *many* things, as animality is or, if it were not, could become common to many animals.

[18] The divine persons; see Glossary, under *suppositum.*

[19] The reason for the unexpected plural is that *determinatio,* although in singular, is taken collectively as referring to the various determinations of what is determinable.

[20] A particular quantity of two feet, for example, the length of a particular skirt, is not divisible into many quantities of two feet, for it is a whole and as such it cannot be divided into parts equal to itself. This is contrasted to the division of the common into particulars, for the common is divisible into parts which are of the same specific kind as itself—man is divisible into men, each of which is fully man. The difference

between man and men or man and a man is not in kind—they are both human in the same sense—but in their ontological status—man is the species, a man is an individual member of the species.

²¹ This marks the beginning of the first objection; it takes up a full paragraph. The answer to it is contained in the paragraph which follows it.

²² The expression "participation in being" or "participation in the notion of being," as used by Suárez here, conveys the point, concordant with his formalistic metaphysics, that being may be treated in some sense like a form. This would be quite contrary to the spirit of Thomistic thought, for example, where being is not formal. When Thomas uses expressions such as these, they are always to be understood as referring to efficient causality rather than formal causality. Being for him is not a form which may be shared, but an act. See J. Owens, *An Elementary Christian Metaphysics,* (Milwaukee: Bruce, 1963) p. 107. Although Suárez accepts a formalistic interpretation of "participated being," he also adopts the Thomistic interpretation of the term as implying efficient causality. In this sense, for him, "participated being," i.e. created being, is opposed to "essential being," i.e. God. He draws the distinction in Disp. XXVIII, Sect. I, § 13: "Being is divided into being by essence and being by participation...." That being is called "being by essence which by itself and in virtue of its essence essentially has being, neither participated nor received from another. On the contrary, that being is called being through participation which has no being except as participated and communicated by another....Only God is a being by essence, the rest are beings by participation, because only in God his being is his essence...."

²³ The notion of individuality, therefore, consists for Suárez in entity, indivision and distinction from others. Properly speaking, however, individuality involves indivision alone. Distinction from others, as he points out throughout the text, is a result of indivision, while entity is a prerequisite of it. Entity should not be confused with actual existence, since, as Suárez argues elsewhere, an actually existing individual and a possible one are the same conceptually. The entity, then, which is a prerequisite of individuality is not actual existence, but the being which as a transcendental is convertible, i.e. coextensive, with unity and therefore possessed by both actual and possible individuals.

²⁴ This is the second objection.

²⁵ The solution to the question begins in § 2. This subtitle is a later addition.

²⁶ Ch. 5, 2b5; Junctas, vol. I, fol. 26vb: *"Non ergo existentibus primis substantiis, impossibile est aliquid aliorum esse."*

²⁷ *Per se evidens* or *per se nota,* evident in itself or self-evident. Here, as in most places in this treatise these expressions are used in a weak sense, meaning simply "evident" or "clear." See Glossary.

²⁸ *Metaphysics* I, Ch. 6, 987a30 ff. and II, Ch. 6, 1031a30 ff.; Junctas, vol. VIII, text 5, fol. 7rb ff. and fol. 175vb and 176va-b.

²⁹ The author who interpreted Plato as positing the ideas in the divine mind was not Aristotle, but Augustine. He borrowed the doctrine from the neo-Platonists and modified it according to his theological needs. See Augustine, *Concerning Eighty-Three Questions,* q.9. Scholastics, however, consistently blamed others for this historical mistake.

³⁰ Although Suárez's Disputations contain much history of philosophy, giving rise to the statement, that he is "the first historian of Scholasticism" (C. Vollert, *Francis Suárez: On the Various Kinds of Distinctions,* Milwaukee: Marquette Univ. Press, 1947, p. 8), Suárez's remark here, taken together with many others scattered throughout the text, show that he had little interest in the history of philosophy as such. The philosophical opinions he discusses are taken as views to be studied and criticized for their philosophical merits, rather than their historical importance. Indeed, seldom does Suárez issue historical judgments about philosophy, and when he does they

are, as the one made here, incidental to the discussion. He does, moreover, follow on occasion the medieval tradition of "interpreting" authorities in order to show how their opinions support his view. However, even then, his attitude is critical, for he often and openly disagrees not only with philosophical authorities like Aristotle, but also with theological authorities like Thomas Aquinas, Alexander of Hales, and others.

[31] Disp. VI, *On Formal and Universal Unity,* Sect. III, trans. James F. Ross (Milwaukee, Wisc.: Marquette Univ. Press, 1964).

[32] This paragraph begins the third part of the Solution. It adds to the first two the proof for the determinate and fixed nature of every thing that exists. The first, it should be remembered, dealt with the notion of individual as indivisible into many entities of its kind ("the same as itself") and as separate from others; and the second argued for its application to all actual beings.

[33] The necessity involved is of nature (see Glossary, under *necessarius*): It is in the nature of an existing thing to have "an added negation" and hence "singularity and individual unity."

[34] The syllogism may be interpreted as follows: 'Every singular and individual entity is a fixed and determinate entity' (major premise), 'every existing entity is a singular and individual entity' (minor premise), and 'every existing entity is a fixed and determinate entity' (conclusion). Strictly speaking, there is a middle step in the argument which connects "added negation" to "singularity and individual unity." I have omitted this step because, given Suárez's discussion of individuality in §§ 2 and 3, the connection between these two notions seems sufficiently clear.

[35] This is a clear use of the so called "third man argument," of Platonic origin. See Plato's *Parmenides,* 132, and *Republic,* 597.

[36] Suárez and other scholastics of this period followed very strict rules in their replies to objections. Ross has explained these briefly as: "(a) Do not deny the major premise; only a fool uses a false major premise and politeness demands that such an argument be ignored; nor should one reject an argument as formally invalid, for the same reason. (b) If the minor premise is false, then deny it, show it is false and proceed to deny the conclusion. (c) If the minor premise needs to be *distinguished* (that is, if two or more senses can be assigned it), make the distinction, and make a corresponding distinction in the conclusion. (d) If the major premise needs to be distinguished, do so; then 'counter-distinguish' the minor (that is, show that it trades on the double-meaning of the major) and proceed to deny that the conclusion follows." Translator's Introduction, in Francis Suárez, *On Formal...,* p. 4. It should be added, however, that Suárez did not always adhere in practice to these rules.

[37] See Durandus and others, *On I,* dist. 35. Lat. editor's note.

[38] Predicates that are both exclusive and exhaustive. Literally, predicates that "include an immediate contradiction," i.e. imply an immediate contradiction *(includunt contradictionem immediatam).*

[39] Sect. II.

[40] The reference is to Suárez's *Tertia pars Summa theologiae...cum commentariis...,* in *Opera omnia,* vol. XVII, Paris: Vivès, 1860, pp. 501-502.

[41] Sect. II, § 21.

[42] Sect. II.

[43] Sect. II and Disp. VI.

Section II

WHETHER IN ALL NATURES THE INDIVIDUAL AND SINGULAR THING AS
SUCH ADDS[1] SOMETHING TO THE COMMON OR SPECIFIC NATURE

1. We have shown that there is in things an individual and singular unity; now we begin to explain what it is, which cannot be better done than by explaining what it adds to the common nature, that is, to what is conceived abstractly and universally by us.[2]

Exposition of Several Views

2. The first view affirms generally that at least in created things the individual adds to the common nature a real mode, distinct *ex natura rei* from the nature, and that, together with it, it makes up the individual.[3] This seems to be the opinion of Scotus, *On II [of the Sentences]*, dist. 3, q.1, and in *Quodlibet*, q.2, and *Metaphysics* VII, q.16;[4] and there also Antoninus Andrea, *[Metaphysical Questions]*, q.17.[5] This view seems to be defended by Fonseca [as well], *[Commentary on the Metaphysics]*, Bk. V, q.3, sect. 2, q.5, throughout.[6] And John Baptist Monlerius defends it very forcefully in the special work on universals, *[Detailed Disputation on Universals]*, Ch. 6.[7]

The basis of this view can be perhaps what, according to Aristotle, caused Plato to posit ideas of universals separate *(abstractas)* from singulars, namely: That sciences and demonstrations are about universals and not about singulars; again, that there are essential and proper definitions of universals and not of singulars; again, that properties, which are essentially *(per se)* in things, come to them by means of universal natures, so that it is true to say that Peter has the ability to laugh because man has the ability to laugh, just as, on the contrary, contingent predicates come to common natures by reason of individuals, for man runs because Peter runs. Therefore, all these [considerations] indicate a distinction *ex natura rei* between the individual and the common nature. But there cannot be such a distinction except insofar as the individual adds something to the common nature, since [the individual] includes the whole [nature]. Therefore, [the individual] cannot be distinguished from it [i.e. the common nature] except as adding something to it.

3. Second, I argue that man, for example, is not essentially an individual something *(quid)*. Therefore, when it is made an individual, something outside the essence of man is added to it; therefore, it is necessary for that [something] to be distinct *ex natura rei* from man as such. The antecedent is evident, because if man were essentially this individual, it could not be multiplied into many; nor indeed could it be conceived without some individuality *(individuatione)* and singularity, — because a thing cannot be conceived without that which belongs to its essence; man, however, can be conceived distinctly, and indeed can be defined essentially, without any individuality *(individuatione)*; — just as God, [who], because he is essentially this singular individual, can neither be multiplied nor truly and properly be conceived unless he be conceived under this individual and singular notion. The first consequence seems to be evident, because to be an individual is [to be] something in the order of things, and it is not essential to the common nature. Indeed, neither [is it essential] to the individual itself, as is commonly said, because all individuals [of the same species] have the same essence. Therefore, it is necessary [for the individual] to add something to the common essence. And hence the second consequence is easily proven, because what belongs to the essence and what is outside the essence seem to be distinguished *ex natura rei* — indeed, those [things] are maximally distinguished which do not belong to the same essence. But what the individual adds to the species is outside its essence, as has been shown. Therefore, [what the individual adds to the species must be distinct *ex natura rei* from it.][8]

4. Third, Peter as Peter and [Peter] as man are not formally constituted by the same [thing], both because that by which a man is constituted [to be a man] is common to Peter himself and to other men, but that by which [a man] is constituted to be Peter *(in esse Petri)* is proper to him; and also because otherwise man could not be better conceived under a common concept than Peter. Here can be added all the arguments with which it is usually proven that universals are distinguished *ex natura rei* from [their] inferiors. We dealt with some of these above in the discussion concerning the concept of being, [and] we shall deal with the others in the Disputation that follows.[9]

5. The second view is at the contrary extreme [from the first one]: The individual adds absolutely nothing positive and real to the com-

mon nature, whether really or conceptually distinct from it; rather, every thing or nature is essentially *(per se)*, primarily and imme- diately individual. The nominalists adhere to this view in *On I [of the Sentences]*, dist. 2, where Ockham, qq. 4 and 6,[10] and Gabriel, qq.6, 7 and 8, [do so].[11] This view may also be attributed to Henry, *Quod- libet* V, q.8, where he holds that the individual adds only a negation to the species.[12] We discuss this view in detail in the following sec- tion, under opinion 3.[13].

The bases of this view are [the following: First], that nothing can be understood to be real unless it be singular, as it was proven in the preceding Section.[14] Therefore, it is inconsistent for a thing to be made singular by the addition of something real to the common na- ture. Second, that no thing can be made one by the real addition of something positive, as it was shown above, [and] therefore neither [can it be made] singular and individual. The consequence is clear, both because singularity is a kind of unity, and also because there is no true and real unity beyond singular and individual unity. Third, that what is added is either essential or accidental. If essential, it fol- lows [1] that the species can be divided by essential differences, [something which goes] against Porphyry, *[Isagoge]*, Ch. on species.[15] Whence, it follows further [2] that individuals differ essentially, and that the species does not express the whole essence or quiddity of individuals, [something] which goes against Porphyry and all dialec- ticians. Finally, against Aristotle, *Metaphysics* VII, text 53,[16] it fol- lows [3] that individuals can and should be defined by a proper and adequate essential definition. If, on the other hand, what is added is accidental, it follows [1] that the individual is a being by accident. It follows also [2] that the accident does not come to the individual sub- ject, but constitutes it, which is impossible, because if one of the two is individuated by the other, it is more appropriate for the accident to receive individuation from the subject rather than vice versa.

6. The third view uses the distinction between spiritual and material things: In immaterial things the singular adds nothing to the com- mon nature, while in material [things, it adds] something. This dis- tinction seems to be based on Aristotle, *Metaphysics* VII, Ch. 11, text 4,[17] where he says that in immaterial things that which [the thing] is *(quod quid est)* is not distinguished from that of which it is *(eo cuius est)*, while in material [things] it is distinguished.[18] Here, by "that which [the thing] is" *(quod quid est)* he understands the essence or essential definition, which can refer *(comparari)* both to [what is] defined itself and to the individuals in which [what is] defined and the definition exist. Aristotle referred to them in the first way in *Metaphysics* VII, Ch. 6, texts 20 and 21,[19] and he taught in general that in essential *(per se)* beings that which [the being] is *(quod quid est)* is the same as

that of which it is *(eo cuius est)*, which is to say, the definition with [what is] defined, because they express the same essence and differ only in the confused or distinct manner in which they are conceived. This is common both to simple and to composite substances and to accidents, if they are defined insofar as they are one essentially *(per se)*. For accidental beings either [1] cannot be defined by a definition or [2], if they can be defined in some way by the unity due to the accidental form, such definition is in some way distinct from the subject to which it is attributed.

In the latter way, however, which is the pertinent one at present, Aristotle refers to them in the other place cited. And in this way he says that in immaterial things that which [the thing] is *(quod quid est)*, which is to say, the specific essence which is expressed by the definition, is the same as that of which it is *(eo cuius est)*, which is to say, as the individual or singular thing, although he says the case is different for things composed of matter and form. He feels, therefore, that an immaterial thing is individual in itself, without any addition, while it is not so with a material [thing]; rather, [a material thing] is made this individual by an addition. This is the way St. Thomas and others explain this text.

In *On the Soul* III, text 9,[20] Aristotle says that in some things the thing, that is, the individual, is different from the specific quiddity of the thing. He says this with these words: "Magnitude is one [thing], to be of a magnitude[21] another." But he adds that this distinction is not found in all things. This is understood by all the commentators to have been said on account of immaterial things, in [the case of] which individuals are nothing but the very subsistent specific natures. Averroes, Philoponus, and St. Thomas [give this interpretation] everywhere. St. Thomas himself seems to teach this view in *[Summa theologiae]* I, q.3, a.3, and in *On Being and Essence,* Ch. 5,[22] in which places and in *[Summa theologiae]* III, q.4, a.4 Cajetan thinks the same.[23] This view seems to have been accepted also in the School of St. Thomas, as will become clearer from what we shall say in Section IV.[24] For the basis of this view is to be found in [the things] that will be discussed there, namely, that since immaterial substances neither have matter nor display a relation to it, nothing can be thought to be added to their essence in them, and hence they are individual in themselves. In composite things, however, designated matter is added, from which it can be gathered that the individual adds something to the species.[25]

The Cause of the Difficulty is Exposed

7. First, it is accepted by all authors that the individual adds to the common nature a negation, which formally completes or constitutes

the unity of the individual. This is evident from the notion of unity explained above, added to what we noted in the preceding Section[26] concerning the meaning *(rationem),* that is, the what *(quid),* of the name 'individual.' Even more, if we speak formally of the individual, insofar as it is one in a particular way, it adds a negation in its formal concept, not only to the common nature abstractly and universally conceived, but also to the whole singular entity conceived with precision under a positive notion. For this whole entity is not conceived as one singularly and individually until it is conceived as incapable of being divided into many [entities] of the same kind *(rationis)* [as itself]. Therefore, the present difficulty does not concern this negation, whether it may formally pertain to the notion of this unity or not. For concerning this there are also [various] opinions, about which we have already said in the preceding Disputation,[27] which one we think is closer to the truth. The difficulty concerns rather the foundation of the negation. For, since it does not seem that [the negation] can be founded in the common nature alone, — since it [i.e. the common nature] is indifferent of itself and does not include *(postulat)* such a lack of division into many similar [entities], but rather it is divided into them —, therefore, we ask what there is in the singular and individual by reason of which such negation comes to it.

Solution to the Question

8. I say, first, that the individual adds something real to the common nature, by reason of which it is a particular individual and there comes to it the negation of divisibility into many [individuals] similar [to itself].[28] In this conclusion we agree with Scotus. It is also taken from St. Thomas, *[Summa theologiae]* I, q.40, a.2, who says that wherever there is something common to many, there must also be something distinctive.[29] And in *Contra gentiles* I, Ch. 42, arg. 7, he says that the distinctive [feature] must be something added to the common intention.[30] Thomists do not disagree with this conclusion, as it is clear from Cajetan, [commentary to] Bk. I, *Posterior Analytics,* Ch. 4, and in [his commentary to Thomas'] *On Being and Essence,* Ch. 4;[31] Soncinas, *[Questions on] Metaphysics* VII, q.31;[32] Capreolus, *[Defences of Theology]* II, dist. 3, q.1;[33] Hervaeus, *Quodlibet* III, q.9;[34] Soto, in *Logic,* q.2 concerning universals.[35]

The proof [of this assertion] comes from what we just said. For the common nature does not include *(postulat)* of itself such a negation, and yet such negation pertains essentially *(per se)* and intrinsically to the nature as it exists in reality and has been made "a this." Therefore, something has been added to it by reason of which it [i.e. the negation] has been joined to it [i.e. the nature], because every negation pertaining intrinsically and necessarily to some thing is founded in something positive that cannot be conceptual, but real, since indeed that unity and negation pertains to the very thing truly and from itself.

This argument can be stated in another way as well, because the specific nature, in itself and insofar as it is the proximate object of the common concept of man, lion, etc., has nothing incompatible with communicability, and thus it is said to be negatively indifferent, as we shall see below. Owing to this individuation, however, its indifference is removed and it is made incapable of such division insofar as it has been made singular. Therefore, it is necessary to understand that something positive has been added to it by reason of which this [division] becomes incompatible with it.

Finally, Peter and Paul agree in common nature and differ from each other in proper notions; therefore, they add them [i.e. the proper notions] to the common nature. But they [i.e. the proper notions] are positive, for they are not constituted by negations in the notion of a particular substance. Therefore, [the individual adds something positive to the common nature]. The same conclusion is also reached by the arguments given in support of Scotus' opinion.

9. I say secondly[36] that the individual as such does not add anything distinct *ex natura rei* from the specific nature. So that in an individual, Peter for example, humanity as such and this humanity, or rather that which is added to humanity in order that it be made "a this" — which is usually called thisness *(haecceitas)* or individual difference — may be distinguished *ex natura rei* and, consequently, may constitute a true composition in the thing itself. All those who oppose Scotus' opinion must agree with this assertion, as do Cajetan, [commentaries on Thomas'] *"On Being and Essence,"* q.5, and [on *Summa theologiae*] I, q.5, a.6;[37] Soncinas, [*Questions on*] *Metaphysics* VII, q.3[2];[38] Niphus, Bk. IV, [*Explanations on the*] *"Metaphysics,"* disp. 5;[39] and others. They do not make sufficiently clear, however, whether they oppose Scotus' whole doctrine, including the addition of an individual difference to the specific [nature], or only the distinction *ex natura rei*. And for this reason their arguments, which seem to be used for both, are not very effective.

Those who deny that the nature is universal in reality, as do most authoritative[40] philosophers and theologians and the whole School of St. Thomas, as we shall see in the following Disputation,[41] must agree necessarily with the previously stated assertion. That is, one [i.e. the fact that they must agree] follows from the other [i.e. the fact that they deny the nature to be universal in reality],[42] because if in individuals, that which the individual adds to the common nature is distinct *ex natura rei* from it, therefore conversely too, the nature in reality prescinds from such an addition or individual difference. And so, in reality the nature and the thisness are two, if not as two things, at least as a thing and a mode. Therefore, each of them has its own *(per se)* unity, because it is unintelligible that some [two things] be two unless they are one and one, for number presupposes unities. Therefore, the nature, [insofar] as it prescinds from the individual difference, has unity in reality [and], therefore, either individual or universal unity. The first cannot be said according to the aforementioned view, otherwise the nature would be individual before [receiving] the individual difference, and so, such a difference would be superfluously added. Therefore, according to this view, it is necessary to say that the nature, insofar as it really prescinds and is distinguished *ex natura rei* from the individual difference, has universal unity. [But] this is impossible, as can be gathered from what has been said in the preceding Section[43] and from what we shall show in more detail below.

10. In accordance with Scotus' doctrine, the answer to this can be that the nature, [considered] as separate *(praecisam)* in reality from individuality *(individuatione)* has neither individual nor universal unity, but rather [formal] unity. This is as it were a middle [ground] between the aforementioned unities, being no other than the unity of essence expressed by the definition.

Against this is, first, that although in such a nature this formal unity could be distinguished conceptually from the individual unity, nevertheless it is inconceivable that in reality it be separate *(praecisa)* in its own entity and distinct *ex natura rei* from the individual unity, and that as such it may lack also universal unity. This is proven because that [i.e. the nature] as such is either common or incommunicable, for these two [predicates] are immediately opposed[44]; if incommunicable, it is individual; if common, it is universal. Again, either [1] the nature which in Peter is distinct from the thisness of Peter is really distinct by itself from the nature which is in John, — just as it is also distinguished *ex natura rei* from his thisness — , or [2] it [i.e. the nature] as such is not distinct. If the second is said, the nature will be common. If, however, the first is said, it is necessary that those natures as such be individual and singular, because they do not differ except as distinct in number and reality within the same species.

11. After this, I argue secondly by showing directly that there cannot be in things such a distinction that is a true and actual distinction *ex natura rei,* preceding every operation of the intellect. For every such distinction must be either [1] between real entities or [2] between a real entity and its mode. And indeed, if the former [1], it will be a real distinction, which will presuppose necessarily that each [of these] entiti[es] be singular and individual in itself, [something] which is

evident and as such denied by no one, because a distinction between entities presupposes that each entity is constituted in itself and, consequently, [that it is] one and singular. If, however, the distinction is between an entity and its mode [2] as it is said here, in order for it to be a true distinction *ex natura rei,* it is necessary for such an entity, separate from the mode *(praeciso modo),* to be understood in reality as having a true real entity; otherwise the distinction *ex natura rei* between the mode and the entity is unintelligible. For, either [a] the mode intrinsically and formally constitutes the entity or [b] not. If it constitutes it [a], then it is not distinct *ex natura rei* from it, since it is intrinsically and essentially included in it, so that nothing could be conceived in the entity that may not include the mode. On the other hand, if the mode is not understood thus to constitute the entity intrinsically and formally [b], it is necessary to understand [the mode] as presupposing it as [already] constituted in its entity and as really coming to and modifying it, since [the mode] is posited in reality as distinct from it. But it is impossible to understand this type of distinction between the individual difference and the common nature. Therefore, [there cannot be in things such a distinction that is a true and actual distinction *ex natura rei,* preceding every operation of the intellect]. The proof of the minor is that, if [considered as] separate from the mode *(praeciso illo modo),* the nature is understood to have its own entity, [and] then the entity by itself, and [insofar] as it is prior to the mode, must necessarily be singular and individual. Therefore, it does not require a superadded individuality *(individuatione),* nor can it be distinguished *ex natura rei* from it. [This is] just as if the line could not be understood to be constituted in the nature *(ratione)* of line without straightness, [in which case] straightness could not be conceived as a mode distinct *ex natura rei* from the line and coming to it. Now, however, if it is conceived as a mode distinct *ex natura rei,* then it is because the line can be conceived as existing in reality and constituted in the nature *(ratione)* of line without such a mode.

12. The proof of the first consequence is that every entity existing in reality must be necessarily singular and individual in itself: First, because as such it is understood to be outside its causes and to have real actuality and existence. Therefore, as such it is understood to be singular, because nothing can terminate the action of causes or be capable of existence except what is singular.

Second, because such an entity, conceived thus as prior to a mode distinct from itself, is incommunicable to many inferiors, that is, [to those entities] that belong to the same species *(rationis)* [as itself], because it cannot be divided from itself or be made many. Therefore, it is as such already individual.

Third, because the mode of thisness that constitutes Peter is singular and proper to him, and it is said to constitute and compose Peter by modifying the nature. Therefore, if the modification is due to a true distinction and composition in reality, it is necessary that to the mode, which is as it were a certain particular act, there correspond also a particular entity similar to *(per modum)* an actualizable potency. Therefore, the entity presupposed by such an act must be individual and particular.

This is explained, fourthly, because in Peter and Paul, for example, there is a double composition of common nature and individual difference. Therefore, not only is the individual difference of one really distinct from the individual difference of the other in both, but also the entity of the nature which is in one from the entity of the nature which is in the other. Therefore, the two natures are intrinsically and entitatively distinguished as two singular things, even prescinding conceptually from individual differences, because a real distinction between actual entities is not intelligible except insofar as they are individual and singular.

13. [But] you will say that they are indeed distinguished by individual differences, just as two matters are said to be distinguished by forms or quantities. But we shall discuss this example later. For in general I think that it cannot be [the case] that a thing be really distinguished from another by [still] another [thing] distinct from itself, but [only] by its very entity, by which it is constituted into the being it is *(in tali esse),* because, preserving the proper order, a thing is distinguished by what constitutes it. But in the present [case] this is evident, because in Peter and Paul there are two individual differences really distinct from each other, and each of them actualizes a real nature, from which it is distinguished *ex natura rei* and [together] with which it composes its individual as completely and really distinct from the other, not only with respect to the difference, but also with respect to the whole entity of the nature. Therefore, it is necessary that, even having conceptually prescinded from the differences themselves, what remain in reality in Peter and Paul be really distinct and, thus, singular. Otherwise it would be necessary to say that a thing completely the same in reality is contracted by the individual differences [which are] in Peter and Paul. Nor is it enough to say that it is not the really same nature that is contracted, but [only] the formally same [nature]. For this formal identity, insofar as it can exist in reality, is only a certain similarity which presupposes the real distinction, and, consequently, the individuality *(individuationem)* of those [things] which are said to be similar. But insofar as it is conceived as a unity, it is not a real unity, but a conceptual [unity] derived only by denomination from the mental concept, as we shall say later.

14. Fifth, this can be explained, because the individual differences themselves of Peter and Paul are really distinguished from each other as two incomplete things, although singular and individual in the way they are; and nevertheless, they have similarity and conformity *(convenientiam)* to each other, because they are truly more similar to each other than to the individual difference of a horse or a lion. And in them it is not necessary to distinguish *ex natura rei* something in which they may be similar and [something] in which they may be distinguished, otherwise the process would go to infinity, which in [the case of] things or modes distinct *ex natura rei* is inappropriate, as was said above in a similar [case]. Therefore, the same could be said about the individuals themselves, Peter and Paul, because, although they may be distinguished from and similar to each other, it is not necessary to distinguish *ex natura rei* in them that in which they are similar from that in which they are distinguished. Therefore, there is no [reason] why the individual difference should be distinguished *ex natura rei* either from the common nature, as from a basic component *(extremo componente)* of the individual, or from the whole individual, as from the entire composite. Nor does it matter if someone answers that those individual differences are more simple and are that whereby individuals are constituted and [whereby] they are distinguished and thus that they can be better distinguished by themselves. For, although perhaps with regard to the mental distinction or concept this may add something relevant, as I shall say immediately, nevertheless, if this distinction were in things, the argument would apply, because those differences must be considered as two real modes existing in reality and distinct *ex natura rei* from any other entity; because, since they have, as it were, numerically distinct formal effects, namely, to constitute this or that individual, so they are likewise numerically distinct. And although they may be accidental *(quo)* with respect to the individuals, nevertheless, insofar as they are something *(aliquid)* in themselves and real beings, however incomplete, they are also something *(quod)* at least incompletely, as we noted above in a similar [case] when discussing the concept of being, [and] as Cajetan also noted in [his commentary to Thomas' *Summa theologiae*] I, q.11, a.1, in *ad* 1.[45] [Together] with this distinction and simplicity, however, they have between them a real conformity *(convenientiam)* in the common nature *(ratione)* of such modes, as the same Cajetan says, [in the commentary to Thomas'] *On Being and Essence*, q.5.[46] Therefore, either the common nature *(ratio)* must also be distinguished from the particular ones *(propriis)* in these, or certainly this sort of argument is fallacious in [the case of] any individual. Some answer that between these individual differences there is no real conformity *(convenientiam)* from which a common concept could

be abstracted. But this is difficult to believe, as it will be generally shown in the following Disputation.[47]

15. The sixth reason is taken from this, because the whole distinction, which is supposed to be *ex natura rei,* between the nature and the individual, is taken from the manner of conceiving and of speaking concerning the conformity *(convenientia)* and distinction which are found among individuals themselves. This sign, however, is in no way an indication of a distinction *ex natura rei,* and elsewhere one finds many [things] which indicate more forcefully that there is no such distinction in reality. Therefore, [there cannot be in things such a distinction that is a true and actual distinction *ex natura rei,* preceding every operation of the intellect].[48] The major is established from the arguments given in favor of Scotus. The first part of the minor is evident, not only from the example given concerning individuating differences themselves, but also from what has been discussed above concerning the concept of being, — the same arguments can generally be given about both — and also because otherwise it would be necessary to distinguish *ex natura rei* all common from particular concepts, something I shall show to be false below. Finally, this part will be further established by the solution to the objections. The other part of the minor, however, has been sufficiently proven by the arguments given. It is also confirmed by the sign of inseparability. For those [things] which, although conceived by us in different ways, are so related in reality that one is not and could not be separated from the other even by absolute power, are without reason *(causa)* supposed to be distinct *ex natura rei,* as I shall explain more extensively in the Disputation dealing with distinctions.[49] But in Peter the nature *(ratio)* of man and Peter's own individuality *(individuatio)* are so related that they could not be separated in any way, nor such a mode from the nature, nor the nature as it is in Peter from such a mode. Therefore, [there is no distinction *ex natura rei* between the nature and the individual]. Nor does it help any to say that the nature *(rationem)* of man is separable from Peter because it can be in Paul, because this is not to consider the nature *(rationem)* of man as it really exists, but only as conceived in the mind. And thus, it is not sufficient for the distinction *ex natura rei* which must exist between those [things] which exist in reality, if it is a distinction between positive things or between a thing and a real positive mode. Hence, the distinction which is understood between the common nature *(rationem)* abstractly understood and the individual is only conceptual, because the nature as such is nowhere except objectively in the mind. If anyone called that distinction "formal" because the mind conceives a different definition of man as such and of Peter, he makes a verbal distinction,[50] because, with respect to reality, the distinction is not

really found in such a way that those [two things] are understood as distinct *ex natura rei* in Peter and Paul, or as making up a composition in reality, as has been shown.

16. I say thirdly[51] that the individual adds to the common nature something conceptually distinct from it, belonging to the same category and metaphysically composing the individual as an individual difference which contracts the species and constitutes the individual. The first part of this assertion follows from the two preceding [ones]; for in the first it was asserted that the individual adds something to the common nature, and in the second it was denied that it [i.e. what is added] was distinct *ex natura rei*. Therefore, it is necessary for it to be distinguished at least conceptually, because if it were not distinguished in any way, it would not be added [to it] in any way. Nor, indeed, does it follow from this that what is added is something conceptual. For, just as it is one thing to be distinguished conceptually and another to be only [a being] of reason — for it can happen that real things be distinguished only conceptually —, so also that which is added can be real, as it truly is, although distinguished only conceptually. [But] you will say: The addition is only conceptual. I answer: As far as the added thing is concerned I deny it, but as far as the mode of addition, contraction,[52] or composition, I accept it. For just as the separation of the common nature from the individual difference is only conceptual, so, conversely too, the addition of the individual difference to the common nature is to be understood only conceptually. For there is not that proper addition in reality, but in each individual there is one entity really having by itself both natures *(rationem)*.

17. The second part of the conclusion also follows clearly from what has been said. It is taken from St. Thomas in *[Summa theologiae]* I, q.29, a.1, where he says that substance is individuated by itself,[53] and in q.10, *On the Power,* a.3, [where] he denies that substance could be constituted accidentally.[54] Therefore, this added [thing] is not outside the genus of the thing itself, but in substances it is substance, at least incomplete, because in reality there is nothing but individual substance.

Finally, the third part is easily evident, because this added [thing] is not a physical part of substance, since it is predicated of the individual as expressing its whole essence, [something] which is not expressed by a physical part and, thus, is not predicated of the whole. Nor is it something like a whole when directly placed in the category of substance. Therefore, it is something incomplete, like a difference. Again, it contracts the common nature and divides it into individuals and it metaphysically constitutes the very individual as essentially *(per se)* one in its genus.

18. But against this conclusion one can object by a previously given argument. For, if the individual adds something, at least conceptually distinct, a progression to infinity of conceptually distinct objective concepts follows, [something] which we already judged inappropriate in a similar [case] above. The consequence *(sequela)* is clear, because the individual is said to add something conceptually distinct to the species, because it agrees with another individual in the specific notion and differs in the individual. But the individual difference itself agrees also with another similar difference in a common notion, and it differs numerically from it. Therefore, it also adds conceptually to the common notion of such a difference something conceptually distinct; and again the same argument would be given about that which is added, and so to infinity.

The answer to this can be, first, that in these, our concepts, it is not entirely inappropriate to admit a progression of this kind, because the intellect divides [those things] which are completely indivisible in reality, and thus one should not marvel if the intellect could proceed to infinity in these divisions or concepts. Second, someone could philosophize about the concept of species and individual as we reasoned above concerning the concept of being and its inferiors. For we said that inferiors add something conceptually distinct to being, so that, however, the inferior concept, immediately conceived under the concept of being, may not be properly reducible to two concepts, but that it may be only a simple concept better expressed and determined than the concept of being. So, therefore, in the present [case] it can be said that the concept of individual is not properly constituted in and reducible to the concept of another mode or individual difference. Rather it is only a better expressed concept of the specific nature itself as it exists in reality in such an entity, in which neither such an entity nor anything of that entity can be conceived without the specific nature *(rationem);* nor can the specific nature *(ratio)* itself be distinctly conceived as it exists in reality, unless as contracted in such or such an entity. This argument easily avoids the progression to infinity, as it is evident from what has been said in the similar [case] of being.

19. But this way of answering might seem inconsistent with the philosophers' common way of thinking and speaking, who explain this contraction of the species into individuals by way of metaphysical composition. It is not without reason that this seems to be commonly affirmed, because the genus and difference are not distinguished in the thing in which they are joined together, as we shall show below, and nonetheless, owing to several similarities *(convenientias)* and dissimilarities *(disconvenientias)* which are found among many things, the intellect forms the diverse concepts of genus and difference, neither of which is

included in the other. Wherefore, the same point can also be made concerning the species and individuals; for there is almost the same proportion between them and the same difference with respect to the concept of being. For that [i.e. the concept of being] is transcendent, and thus it cannot properly be contracted by way of composition, nor [can] something be conceptually added to it in which it [i.e. the concept of being] may not be included. But, on the other hand, the concept of species — as well as the concept of genus — is from itself limited and not transcendent, and, thus, it is not necessary for it to be included in every one of its determinative concepts. Therefore, it could be contracted by way of composition, and, consequently, the individual could also be reduced to the concept of species and individual difference. For that [i.e. the individual difference] is not man, or Peter, for example, but the difference contracting man and constituting Peter.

[But] you will say also that there is a difference between genus and species, because the generic notion, not only as made abstract and universal in the mind, but also as existing in reality, can be separated *(praescindi)* by the mind and distinguished conceptually from the specific difference, as we shall see below. The specific notion, however, cannot be distinguished even conceptually from the individual difference, except as made abstract and universal in the mind, because it cannot be conceived as existing in reality except as it includes individuality *(individuationem)*. And because every composition, even conceptual, must be understood in reality as it exists in act, hence it is easier to understand such a composition between the generic and specific notion than between the specific and individual [one]. But, in spite of this, the metaphysical composition of the individual must not be denied, because it is enough for it that the specific notion could be [considered] with precision *(praescindi)* by the mind as not included in this individual difference.

20. Thus, having admitted this kind of composition and reduction of the individual, it is answered, thirdly, that it is not necessary to proceed to infinity. For the same mind which conceives the individual as composed of the objective concept of the species and the individual difference, conceives the individual difference as completely simple and irreducible, because it does not conceive it under the concept of the species, but only of the difference, to the notion of which it belongs to be simple and not composed of a common notion and another contracting difference. This can be seen also in the specific or subalternate differences themselves. For the sensible or the rational are not formally composed of other differences, but because of this very reason, that they are notions of difference, they differ by themselves from the others. Therefore, individual differences must also

be conceived in this way; in them, to this extent, one can admit that way of determining being to themselves by a simple determination of the concept without composition. And the notion of individual difference, insofar as it can be conceived as a real and common notion, will also, as it were, transcend each individual difference, because nothing could be conceived in them in which such a notion may not be included. And thus the common notion will be determined to each difference, not by a new composition, but by the simple determination of a better expressed and determined concept, and so any further reduction and progression ceases.

21. I say fourthly[55] that the individual adds something conceptually distinct to the species not only in material things and accidents, but also in created and finite immaterial substances. We exclude the divine nature from this conclusion, because, since it is essentially so determined numerically to this nature, that it is completely incompatible for it to be multiplied, the common notion of deity—if true—cannot even be conceptually abstracted from such a deity; because for this very reason, [namely], that it is so abstracted, true deity is not conceived, because it belongs to the true concept of deity to be numerically "a this" and not another, because its infinity requires it. It can be concluded from this, consequently, that "this individual deity" does not add anything even conceptually to the concept of true deity. Hence, Cajetan is justly censured for having said, in [his commentary to Thomas' *Summa theologiae*] I, q.3, a.3 and other places,[56] that 'God' can be taken in one way as signifying [what is] concrete, [and], as it were, specific in the divine nature. For such a truly common concept is incompatible with true divinity, the essence of which is to be this singular nature, and thus no more can the true God be conceived by a common concept abstracted from "this God" than [can] Peter.

22. From this exception, however, which is unique and applies specifically to God because of his infinity, is confirmed the stated conclusion and the contrary rule in all creatures, even if they are immaterial. The proof of this is that in any individual and finite immaterial substance, for example, the Archangel Gabriel, the mind conceives both this individual, insofar as it conceives numerically this entity, and its essential and specific notion, which does not include essentially this numerical entity nor the positive inconsistency that it could be communicated to another individual. Therefore, the mind conceives there something common and something which is conceptually added to it, so that it may be determined to this individual. Therefore, with respect to this [feature], strictly (*praecise*) [speaking], there is no difference between immaterial substances and other things.

It might be said perhaps, that any essence or angelic species is essentially and intrinsically determined to this individual, and, consequently, that this individual adds nothing really positive, or even conceptually distinct, to the species itself, but [that it adds] only the negation of communicability to many [entities] similar [to itself, something] which pertains to such a species immediately from its own nature *(ratione),* without any addition.

23. This seems, indeed, to have been the sense of the authors cited in the third view. Those who deny that angels differing only in number could be created within the same species, even by absolute power, think likewise. For this cannot be denied of the divine power by any other reason than that it is judged to be against the intrinsic and essential notion of such a nature. Moreover, this view is founded in St. Thomas, in [*Summa theologiae*] I, q.50, a.4, and the *Questions on Spiritual Creatures,* a.8, and *Contra gentiles* II, Ch. 95, *On Being and Essence,* Ch. 5,[57] where Cajetan has it, q.9;[58] and Capreolus, *On II* [*of the Sentences*], dist. 3, q.1, concl. 5;[59] and Abulensis, *Paradoxes* IV, Ch. 34.[60] And Aristotle seems to favor it considerably, *Metaphysics* XII, text 40;[61] and Avicenna, *Metaphysics* V, Ch. 5.[62]

24. But this view assumes, in the first place, that designated matter is an adequate principle of such an individuation, by means of which the individual adds something positive to the notion of the species which can be called positive individuality *(individuatio).* But this assumption in the aforementioned sense is false. The major is clearly evident from the aforementioned authors. The reason for it is clear, because they do not deny this type of individuality *(individuationem)* in the aforementioned substances for any other reason than that they lack matter. Therefore, they assume matter in itself, or as designated by quantity, to be an adequate root of such an individuality *(individuationis)* so that from the principle, "If affirmation is cause of affirmation, negation is cause of negation," they infer lack of the aforementioned addition or individuality *(individuationis)* from lack of matter. The minor proposition, however, will be proven extensively in the following Section,[63] even for material substances. But even if we granted that an individual difference of this kind were taken from matter in material substances, it could not be effectively inferred that matter is the adequate principle of such a difference in the whole extension of created being; for diverse substances have diverse principles appropriate to their natures. Nor can a conclusive argument for things of a superior nature *(rationis)* be taken from the mode of composition or individuation found in inferior[64] things; otherwise, somebody, using the same argument, could deny that angels have a metaphysical composition of genus and difference, because in material [entities] the genus is taken from matter and the difference from form,

as many with propriety wish it to be understood.[65] Again, anybody could as easily say, that the individual does not add anything positive, not even conceptually distinct, to the species in heavenly bodies, either because they have no matter, as Averroes thought, or indeed because they have matter of another kind[66] *(rationis)*. For, if it is true that matter is the only root of individual difference in these inferior things, we can only attribute it to this inferior matter; for concerning the superior we cannot infer by any conclusive argument whether this also applies to it, since it is of a different kind *(rationis)*. They will say perhaps that that matter lies under a quantity of the same kind *(rationis)*, and that this is enough for it to be the principle of the same type of individuation. But this is not conclusive, for, as I shall show below, quantity, being an accident, cannot enter in any way in the principle of individuation of substances. Therefore, substances of a superior order can agree in metaphysical composition with substances of an inferior order, and have its principle in a more perfect and simple way. And so, an effective argument cannot be made from the negation of matter.

25. Next, I return to the unfinished argument. From the fact that the divine nature essentially includes its positive individuality *(individuationem)* and incommunicability with respect to inferiors comes precisely [the fact] that such a multiplication is incompatible with its infinity. But every created immaterial substance is finite. Therefore, there is no [reason] why it should be incompatible [for created immaterial substances] to have another, completely similar essence, although really distinct in entity.

The answer [to this] can be that, although spiritual substance is absolutely *(simpliciter)* finite within the genus of being,[67] it is, however, infinite in its species and has all possible perfection in its species, because, being abstract and separate from matter, it does not have any way to be limited, and thus cannot be multiplied within the species. But this sort of infinity is not only asserted without sufficient basis, but what it is can hardly be explained except by begging the question.

26. I ask, therefore, whether this infinity is intensive or extensive. The first cannot be asserted, because the whole intensive perfection of a particular angel is contained within the determined degree and limit of the particular species [to which it belongs], in which [species] there is no formal intensive infinity,[68] unless perhaps [the species] is called infinite in a certain respect, because it can contain under itself syncategorematically[69] infinite species of an inferior order. This, however, does not indicate infinity, but a certain perfection of superior nature *(rationis)*, according to which [perfection the species] can be common to the species of material things, as it is clear in [the case

of] the human species, under which the species of brutes can be multiplied to infinity. This type of perfection or infinity, therefore, has nothing to do with the question which concerns us, nor can it be the reason why a species is individual by itself and cannot be multiplied in individuals. Indeed, even if we were to admit such an intensive infinity, true and formal, in some intrinsically limited degree, it does not follow that such a perfection could not be found in many similar individuals, because the latter has no necessary connection with the former; just as, even if an infinitely intense grace were present in the soul of Christ, the Lord, for example, it does not follow from this that other numerically distinct kinds of grace, whether finite or infinite, could not be present [in it]. This argument makes clear that a proper and formal intensive infinity cannot be present in substances anymore than in accidents.

27. On the other hand, if we speak of extensive infinity, first, a question is begged, because this extension is no other than the multiplication of individuals in that species. Next, what is said involves a contradiction; for the individual is, formally and in itself, only one: How, then, can it contain in itself an extensive infinity, which consists in the sole multiplication of individuals? You will say that it contains it virtually, not formally.[70] But this does not explain in what this virtual infinity or containment consists or on what it is founded, since it does not consist in the intensive infinity of such a nature, nor could it be founded on it, as it has been proven. Therefore, no reason is given why to be communicated to many individuals similar in essential perfection is incompatible with the perfection of such a nature. Substances of this kind, therefore, although separate *(abstractae)* from matter, are absolutely *(simpliciter)* finite. For, it is also not necessary that they be limited by matter properly speaking — irrespective of what the case may be with material forms — , but [they could be limited] [1] by a difference of their own either by [the difference] itself or by [its] entity, or [2] because they have received a particular being, or finally [3] because they exist in a particular supposit through its nature. Therefore, no reason can be derived from infinity that shows how immaterial natures of this kind are essentially individual and incommunicable.

28. It can be said, on the other hand, that a conclusive argument is derived from immateriality alone, because things that lack matter cannot be multiplied materially, as is quite obvious. Therefore, [they can be multiplied] only formally and essentially or specifically; therefore, [they can] not be multiplied individually or according to numerical multiplication, because this is [the same as] material multiplication.

But even this argument, if the words 'materially' and 'formally' are properly taken in the first antecedent, is not enough and begs the

question. For it assumes the very conclusion of the argument, namely, that numerical distinction is taken from matter or that it is the
same to differ in number as to differ materially. For, although there
is some truth to this in [the case of] material things, something we
shall examine later, nevertheless, from this no conclusive argument
can be derived for [the case of] immaterial [substances]. The individual distinction, therefore, is clearly more broad than the material
difference as taken in the stated way. For to differ numerically is to
be distinguished only in proper entity, with conformity *(convenientia)*
and similarity in the whole essential nature *(ratione)*, [something]
which can be common to spiritual and corporeal things. Whence, if
'material' and 'formal' are taken more broadly, insofar as 'formal' expresses the precise essential nature *(rationem)* and 'material' [ex-
presses] everything that contracts and determines it [i.e. the nature]
to such an entity, then two angels of the same species, although they
may be distinguished as two whole forms, can be said not to be distinguished formally but materially or entitatively, in the same way in
which two rational souls are distinguished from each other.[71]

29. This view can be confirmed, first, by this example, for the rational soul, considered physically, is also a simple and spiritual entity, and yet, is not individual from essential nature *(ratione)*, but
[rather] adds something conceptual [to the individual]. But they say
that the rational soul has a transcendental relation to the body, and
is individuated by it. But this, in the first place, is doubtful, for perhaps it is as true that this soul thus expresses such a relation to the
body because it is such [a relation] itself as the contrary. And next,
whatever be [the case] about this, it is of no import here; for proportionally the same argument can be taken. For the rational soul,
which has its specific nature *(rationem)* with a transcendental relation
to the body, is not individuated precisely in virtue of that [relation],
but from a conceptual addition, whereby the relation is determined
to such a body, or rather, to such a relation to the body. Therefore,
in the same proportion, the angelic substance, which has an absolute, essential nature *(rationem)* without [any] transcendental relation, will not be individual in virtue of that [relation], but from
something proportioned and conceptually added to it.

A similar argument can be derived from spiritual accidents, in
which the individual adds something to the species, not only with
respect to diverse subjects, but also with respect to itself. For, thus
can these accidents be distinguished and multiplied numerically with
respect to the same subject, at least successively, as it is clear from
the diverse acts of the same nature *(rationis)* in the same angelic intellect. If, therefore, there is found in those acts the same spiritual specific nature *(ratio)* contractible into diverse individuals not from

diverse subjects, but from diverse individual differences with respect to the same subject, why cannot the same substantial and spiritual specific nature *(ratio)* be similarly contracted by individual diffe-rences proportioned to itself? Certainly, no sufficient reason can be given [for this].

Similar arguments can be derived from other simple entities that can be distinguished numerically by themselves, such as two matters or two quantities, as we shall see more extensively in the following Section.[72]

30. Finally, divine power is limited without reason, so that it could not create many angels similar in essence and species, or, if it had wished to annihilate the evil angels, it could not have created other similar ones, which is certainly something incredible in itself. And thus, nearly all remaining theologians teach that it can be done by God, in *On II* [*of the Sentences*], dist. 3: Scotus, [*Ordinatio*], q.7;[73] Durandus, q.3;[74] Gabriel, q.1, and others;[75] and Marsilius, *On II* [*of the Sentences*], q.3, a.3.[76] Alexander of Hales, [*Summa theologica*] II p., q.20, last member, a.2, and [*Commentary on the*] *Metaphysics* VII, text 41.[77] Also, Ferrara (from Thomas, *Contra gentiles* II, 93)[78] says that this type of numerical distinction among spiritual substances is not incompatible with absolute power, although he denies that it exists in the natural order of things. St. Thomas favors it in *Opuscle* 16, [*On the Unity of the Intellect against Averroists*], last chapter, where he teaches extensively that an immaterial substance is one in number, singular and individual, because it is not from itself naturally participated by many.[79] He adds, however, that it is proper to the clumsy mind to gather from this that it cannot be multiplied by God. But whatever be [the case] with this manner of speaking, — whether this is said to be possible by absolute, or natural, that is, ordinary power, which is perhaps only a verbal matter—, nevertheless, by whatever reason that may be possible, it is concluded with sufficient force that imma-terial substance is not individual in virtue of its specific and essential nature *(ratione)*. For, if this were the case, it would be contradictory for such a substance to be multiplied individually, as the numerical multiplication of the same individual implies. Hence, it is also per-fectly obvious that those who say that in angelic natures there is an objective concept truly specific and, as they say, logically universal, and that, however, that nature is from itself so incommunicable that for it to be in many individuals distinct only in number implies a contradiction, do not know the proper [meaning of the] word, for this is an open contradiction. For, if that nature cannot be in any way in many individuals, it is because it is incommunicable in this way from itself and from [its] proper essential concept. Therefore, if it is such, it is incompatible with it to be abstracted from this indivi-

dual and to be rendered communicable or indifferent, because this very abstraction is against its nature and essence, as it is obviously clear in [the case of] the divine nature. Therefore, it is more suitable and more true to say that just as in immaterial substances there are true and proper species, likewise there is the individual, which adds something conceptual to the species, and consequently, that there can be several similar individuals [within the same species]. However, whether there are in fact [any], and what in this [matter] is more consistent with the Scriptures and the Fathers, [is something that] pertains to theological disputations.

Answer to the Bases of the other Opinions[80]

31. The answer to the basis of the first view is that all those [things] considered in the first argument indicate only that the specific nature expresses an objective concept separate *(praecisum)* conceptually from individuals, and, on the other hand, that the individual adds something conceptually distinct to the specific nature. For human science is about things conceived universally, with which definitions and demonstrations are immediately concerned. And it is sufficient for this that they can be conceptually abstracted, although they might not be found separate in reality. This is evident from what has been said concerning the concept of being, the subject of science and demonstrations, although it is evident that in reality [being] is not found separate *(praecisum)* from the proper notions of beings, but only abstracted conceptually.[81] Whence this distinction is sufficient also for the causal expressions *(locutiones),*[82] 'because man is capable of laughter,' 'Peter is capable of laughter,' because in them there is not found a real and physical cause which may be interposed between Peter and the capacity to laugh, but [rather] the adequate reason and origin of that property is explained.

32. The answer to the second is that in such arguments, — as I noted above, when discussing the concept of being —, an equivocation is easily committed when arguing from our manner of conceiving and from the [ordinary] use of words with which we signify things as conceived by us to the very things as they are in themselves, deriving a real distinction from a conceptual distinction; for this is a fallacious argument. Therefore, the answer is that man, signified and conceived as such, does not express or include in its essential notion any individual difference, as the argument rightly proves. This is clear, because [man] is conceptually separate *(praescinditur)* from all those [individual differences] and it can be conceptually contracted and determined by several differences of this kind. Whence it can be rightly concluded that something outside the essence of man so con-

ceived must be added in order for it to be made singular. I deny,
however, that a real distinction between the common nature of man
and its individual difference follows from this, because human nature is not found in reality as common and abstract, in the way it is
conceived by the intellect.

Now, when it is said that what belongs to the essence and what is
outside the essence are distinguished *ex natura rei* and not only conceptually, the answer is that there are two ways of understanding
that something is outside the essence: In one way, according to reality, that is, considering things themselves as they are in reality; in
another way, according to the notion that separates *(praescindentem)*
one from another, although [the one] might not be separate *(praecisum)* in reality [from the other]. In the first way it is true — particularly in finite things — that all that is outside the essence in reality
must be distinguished *ex natura rei* from it, because it cannot be said
to be outside the essence in another way *(ratione)*. But I deny that the
individual difference as existing in reality, for example, of Peter and
Paul, is outside the essence of man in this way. For man does not
exist in reality except in Peter, Paul, etc..., and in each its proper
difference belongs to the essence of man as existing in it. [But] you
will say that it follows from this that man differs essentially in Peter
and Paul or that Peter and Paul do not have the same essence. The
answer to this is that they do not have the same essence really, but
[rather] that they have it conceptually, which in reality is nothing
other than having a similar [one]. And because "to differ essentially,"
thus put, does not signify only the real distinction of essences, but
also denies essential similarity and conformity *(convenientiam)* and
thus conceptual unity of essence, therefore, it is not granted without
qualification that those [things] which differ only in number differ
essentially. If, however, those words are taken only in the first sense,
it would be true that Peter and Paul differ essentially; according to
this meaning we deny that the Father, the Son, and the Holy Spirit
differ essentially in God, because they do not have either essential
difference or distinction of essences. However, [if those words are
taken] in the latter way, namely, with conceptual precision, all that
without which such a conceived notion can be preserved is said to be
outside the essence of the objective concept. In this way it is not
necessary that what is said to be outside the essence be distinct *ex
natura rei* from the other; but it is enough that it be conceptually distinguished, because the word 'outside' itself does not signify absolutely to be outside the thing, but to be outside the concept, that is,
to be outside the thing [insofar] as [the thing is] conceived.[83]
33. Hence, the answer to the confirmation uses an almost identical
distinction. For in reality man is not constituted as man with preci-

sion, nor as separate in itself, but is constituted as Peter, Paul, Francis; hence, in each of them, man is constituted by the same [thing] that Peter. Nor is there in reality something truly one, constitutive of man, that is common in reality, but [rather] there are many [things] constitutive of each man in which the common nature *(ratio)* is said to be fundamentally, owing to the conformity *(convenientiam)* and similarity which they have among themselves, as we shall discuss in more detail in the following Disputation.[84] On the other hand, according to reason, just as the common man is abstracted, so also it is understood to have an adequate and common constituent. From this, however, it can only be concluded that it [i.e. the common constituent] is conceptually distinct from the singular differences which specifically constitute individuals.

The answer to the third is that, from what was said concerning the concept of being, it is evident that those arguments do not prove a distinction *ex natura rei.* We shall show the same concerning universal and inferior natures in the following Disputation.[85]

34. The answer to the first argument of the second opinion is that [the argument] rightly proves that a thing is not made singular by the addition of a reality or mode distinct *ex natura rei* from the nature which is said to have been made singular, because every such distinction presupposes entity and consequently singularity in each term.[86] But the argument does not prove that it [i.e. a thing] could not be made singular by the addition of something conceptually distinct, because this distinction does not presuppose actual entity, and consequently, neither [does it presuppose] singularity in each term, because, since this distinction is conceptual, it can be easily understood [to hold] between a thing universally conceived and its mode.

35. According to this doctrine, some [objections] raised by Cajetan in [his commentary to Thomas'] *On Being and Essence,* Ch. 2, q.4,[87] against Scotus' doctrine, are easily solved to the degree they can be used against the first and third conclusions reached by us. For example: A singular act presupposes a singular potency, *Physics* II, Ch. 3, text 36;[88] but what the individual is said to add to the species is an act of singular nature; therefore, it presupposes a singular nature, because it is related to it as a potency. For the answer [to this] is that the major is true [in the case] of a real act and potency distinct *ex natura rei,* of which Aristotle speaks in the cited place, but not [in the case] of a conceptually distinct act and potency for the explained reason. Likewise, a specific act does not presuppose a specific potency, but rather a generic [one].

Another of his arguments is that what is compatible *(convenit)* with one individual and incompatible with another presupposes their distinction. But the individual difference is of this sort. Therefore, [the individual difference] does not cause the distinction, but presupposes [it].

But this argument is formally weaker [than the previous one]. For it is easy to deny the major, as it is clear in the [following argument of] similar form: What is compatible *(convenit)* with one species and incompatible with another presupposes their distinction. For it would have to be added: "or it causes it." Therefore, the same would have to be added in the present [case]. However, if the argument were not made for individuals themselves, but for the nature which is contracted by this individual difference, it can be effective against [the view which posits] a distinction *ex natura rei* between the individual difference and the nature, although not against our view. For in distinct individuals there are also really distinct natures. Whence, if individuating differences are distinct *ex natura rei* from them, it is necessary that the difference, compatible *(convenit)* with one and incompatible with the other, presuppose their distinction rather than cause it, because it presupposes, as has been said, a singular potency proportioned to itself, and consequently, distinct from another not proportioned to it; and so, it will not already be the individual difference as we have also argued above. However, having discarded the distinction *ex natura rei,* the argument does not apply [in the case] of the nature to be contracted, because this is not [a case of] two natures, so that the difference could be compatible *(convenire)* with one and be incompatible with the other, but it is [a case of] conceptually one [nature]. If, however, we are speaking about the nature not as contractible but as contracted, then the very thing which is constituted and distinguished from another by the same difference is already individual.

36. The answer to the second is that [the argument] applies only to the last formal notion of one, that is, of the individual unity consisting in negation, concerning which we grant it does not add anything to the individual entity except negation. We, on the other hand, discuss the basis of this negation and what the singular entity adds to the common nature, by reason of which it is capable of such a negation.

37. To the third, some say that what the individual adds to the species is accidental. But that this is false is convincingly shown not only by the arguments given there and the others that[89] will be given in the following Section,[90] but also from what has been said. For if this that is added is only conceptually distinct from the substance or essence of the thing and joined to it by itself, as it were determining by itself the common nature to the particular, how can it be accidental? Therefore, others simply call this "essential" to the individual, not to the species, which is indeed so, if we consider the thing itself,

for what wholly [and] intrinsically constitutes and composes this individual is its proper difference together with the common nature; this individual cannot only not be, but it cannot even be conceived, without such a difference. Nevertheless, conceptually and according to the manner of speaking of dialecticians and metaphysicians followed in our way of thinking, this individual difference is not called "essential," but "entitatively intrinsic" and as it were "material," in order to distinguish it from the specific difference, which is most formal. For [the specific difference] is taken from the degree to which individuals formally agree or are similar. Consequently, it seems this is to be explained thus, that individuals of the same species have, [together] with an integral and perfect similarity in nature, a real distinction in which they differ from individuals of the same genus but different in species, which [individuals] do not have among themselves so much or so perfect a similarity. Therefore, it follows from this that our mind conceives that in which those individuals agree among themselves as something *(quid)* one and as that which is formal in them and which confers science by itself. For the distinction in entity alone is considered to be as it were accidental, and thus it is called "material." For the same reason there is no scientific definition except of the common and specific concept. In this sense the last species is called "the whole essence of individuals," namely, taken and conceived formally and with precision and insofar as its knowledge serves for human science. [For human science] does not descend to particulars in accordance with their proper and individual notions, because it can neither perceive them as they are in themselves nor do so with the accidents proper to the individuals, because they [i.e. the accidents] either agree contingently and accidentally or, if perhaps they are something completely peculiar *(propria)* to the individual, they are as concealed as individual differences themselves. Finally, because it would be exceedingly laborious and almost interminable to descend to every particular. Nonetheless, however, there is no doubt that individuals, even if they differed in number alone, have distinct essences in reality, which, if conceived and explained as they are in themselves, will be made clear by diverse concepts and definitions. And they will have also distinct properties at least in reality or according to some mode of their own, under which notion they fall under angelic or divine science.[91]

38. Answer to the bases of the third opinion. To [the text of] Aristotle in *Metaphysics* VII, it can be answered, first, with Alexander of Hales in the same place, that when Aristotle says that "in [things] separate from matter that which [the thing] is *(quod quid est)* is not distinguished from that of which it is *(eo cuius est)*," he does not take matter with every property as prime matter or as the proper subject

of some form, but as any supposit which may be in some way distinct in reality from its nature.[92] [This is] similar to the way in which no created substance can be said to abstract from matter, because in all [created substances] the nature is in a supposit distinct from it in some way. This doctrine is true, but I do not believe Aristotle spoke in that sense in that place. Alexander of Aphrodisias expounds the text in a different way.[93] He thinks, and this is indeed very probable, that Aristotle, in both places cited above, speaks of the same substances, and that he compares in the same way that which [the thing] is *(quod quid est)* with that of which it is *(eo cuius est)*. This can be confirmed by the words of the Philosopher himself, for he says in text 41: "It has been said above that the quiddity and each [singular thing] are the same in some [things], as [it is the case] in first substances."[94] Alexander reads it thus himself. And, although in the text in that place, the phrase, "it has been said," is not usually repeated, nevertheless, what had preceded it a little before includes also this clause, as is clear enough from the context. Therefore, by "first substance" Alexander does not understand immaterial substances, as St. Thomas [does], because in the latter place Aristotle refers to those [things] which he had mentioned in the former [place], and there he had said nothing in particular concerning immaterial substance. Nor does he give any particular reason in the other [place] why he may regard this as the difference between material and immaterial substances. Nor is there any indication why we might believe he uses the term 'with that of which it is' *(cum eo cuius est)* equivocally, taking it in the former place for the definition and here for the supposit, so that, when compared, both places [may say something] different. Finally, Aristotle had never used the name 'first substances' to signify especially immaterial substances. For although in Bk. IV, Ch. 3, text 7,[95] it may seem that he uses those words in that sense, nevertheless, there the Commentator[96] understands by "first substance" God, and whatever be [the case] concerning that text, no argument is derived from it in support of the one we are discussing. And so, according to this interpretation, Aristotle's meaning *(sententia)* is the same in both places. By "first substances," therefore, Alexander understands any substantial supposits, from which that which [the thing] is *(quod quid est)*, that is, the common nature, is not separated. Indeed, what Aristotle says below: "I call 'first substance' that which is not said [to be] in some thing *(eo quod)*, as one [thing] is in another, as in a subject or matter," Alexander interprets of substance, which is not signified as one [thing] in another [thing], but as one [thing] consisting in itself,[97] [and] in this it differs from an accidental composite, such as a white, for example, or a snub, which signify something existing in a subject as in matter. For of this sort of composite of such a subject as matter and an accident existing in it, Aristotle adds that in it, since it is one accidentally, that which [the thing] is *(quod quid est)* is distinguished from the subject in which it is *(quo est)*. Consequently, according to this interpretation, nothing can be gathered from the aforementioned text against our view.

In addition to this probable interpretation, however, that text has perhaps another, more probable [one]. But, because it pertains to the question concerning the distinction between the nature and the supposit in immaterial things, it will be discussed more easily below, in the Disputation on the distinction between the nature and the supposit in created things.[98]

39. Answer to the other text from *On the Soul* III: If the common interpretation is to be maintained, nothing can be answered except that Aristotle held the view in question, [something] which Scotus finally concedes in *On II [of the Sentences]*, dist. 3, q.7, *ad* 1,[99] where he says that Aristotle thought angels were essentially *(per se)* necessary beings, and thus, that he could not think possible as a result that there could be many angels in one species. For, if it were possible, it would be so in fact, because in essentially *(per se)* necessary eternal [beings], to be and to be possible are the same. Similarly, if it were possible that there could be many, it would also be possible that they be multiplied to infinity and, finally, that they be actually infinite. But, the basis of this argument, namely, that Aristotle thought angels to be essentially *(per se)* necessary beings is doubtful. Perhaps Aristotle, when he posits this difference between material and immaterial individuals, does not speak precisely and metaphysically concerning the individual [insofar] as it expresses singular substance alone, but [rather] he speaks physically concerning the individual [insofar] as it is found in reality, modified by its accidents. He seems to speak in this way in the mentioned place of *On the Soul* III; for he says that the material individual is such that the sense is concerned with it, [something] which is not true about the individual taken with rigorous and metaphysical precision, but only [when taken] in an *a posteriori* and physical sense. And so, the difference between the material and spiritual individual can be easily ascertained.

40. The answer to the argument for the aforementioned view — whatever be [the case] concerning the opinion that in material things the principle of individuation is designated matter, something we shall discuss immediately — , is that, even if this is not the principle of individuation in immaterial things, yet there must be something similar [to it], because those substances are also individual, not in virtue of the specific nature *(rationis)*, but [in virtue] of the singular [one]. Whence, when the spiritual substance is said to be individual in itself, if 'in itself' is understood as "in virtue of its specific nature"

(rationis), one begs the question and assumes what is false, as it was proven. If, however, 'in itself' is understood as "by its own entity," this is certainly true, but nothing prevents the specific nature *(ratio)* and the individual difference from being conceptually distinguished in the very entity, and the same entity from being the principle and basis of both in different ways. For in this respect almost the same argument can be made concerning material substances. For, whether designated matter or something else is said to be their principle of individuation, nevertheless, it cannot be anything that may not be the very entity essential to the thing either as a whole or in part. Hence, it is necessary to distinguish in it the specific nature *(rationem),* on account of which it is said to be the essence or part of the essence, and another nature *(rationem),* not really, but conceptually *(ratione)* distinct, on account of which it is said to be the principle of individuation.

NOTES

¹ To add is used here in a technical sense not usual in English. In English one speaks of X as adding Z to Y (X adds Z to Y) if X is the person who makes Z and Y come together. Alternatively Z is added to Y when Y and Z are joined. Seldom does one say that the union or product, i.e. Y-Z adds Z to Y or Y to Z. However, this is exactly the sense of addition used here: 5 adds 3 to 2 or, to put it in the language of the text, the individual (individuality + common nature) adds individuality to the common nature. For further details see the Glossary and Introduction.

² This Section, together with Sections I and VI, is one of the most important ones of this Disputation. Its main purpose is to clarify exactly the ontological status of what an individual is over and above the common nature. There are four parts to it: The first (§§ 2-6) presents three different views together with arguments and texts in their support. The first view, clearly intended as Scotus', affirms that the individual adds a real mode to the common nature, at least in the case of created beings. After textual support is given (first paragraph of § 2) Suárez proceeds to offer three arguments in its favor (second paragraph of § 2, § 3 and § 4 respectively). The second view holds, against the first one, that the individual adds nothing real and positive to the common nature (first paragraph of § 5). This is intended as Ockham's view. It is supported by four arguments (second paragraph of § 5). The third view holds that in the case of material things there is a real addition, but not so in the case of spiritual beings (§ 6). This is presented as a standard interpretation of Aristotle also held by Thomas and Cajetan. The argumentation here is based wholly on an analysis of Aristotle's view and thus may be considered authoritative in tone. The reason for this special concern for authority is simply that even at Suárez's time Aristotle was, for scholastics, the metaphysician *par excellence.* To disagree with him required sound and clear bases. It turns out, of course, that Suárez finds them and that he disagrees with both Aristotle and his interpreters. The second part of the Section is a brief but very important statement (§ 7) offered as a clarification of the issue at stake: The problem is not whether the individual adds a negation (of communicability and divisibility) to the common nature – with that everyone agreed, according to Suárez – but rather what the basis of such negation is in the individual. This is followed in the third part by the Solution. The latter is given in four state-

ments: First, the individual adds something real to the common nature (§ 8); second, the individual as such does not add anything *ex natura rei* distinct from the specific nature (§§ 9-15); third, the individual adds something conceptually distinct to the common nature (§ 16-20); and fourth, this addition takes place not only in material things and accidents, but also in created and finite immaterial substances (§§ 21-30). The Section ends with answers to the three views proposed at the beginning (§§ 31-40).

[3] The terminology seems confusing at this point because the Latin term '*individuum*' was used often by scholastics to refer both to a concrete individual, such as Peter Dominoes, and what distinguishes an individual as individual, Peter Dominoes' individuality. Such usage is clearly inappropriate and confusing in cases where the concrete individual is seen as the result of the real union of what distinguishes him as individual (the individuality) and what distinguishes him as a member of the species (the common nature) — the case under consideration presently. For Suárez, however, it is not so, for, as he makes perfectly clear in Sect. VI, what distinguishes an individual as individual, the individuality, and the common nature, are in reality the same. So, it is quite acceptable to speak of the individual and the individual's individuality as one and the same and, therefore, to use the same term to refer to both. It should also be added that the term '*individuatio,*' individuation, was also used by scholastics to mean "individuality." When translated thus I have put the Latin in parentheses.

[4] *Ordinatio,* in *Opera omnia,* vol. VII, ed. C. Balic (Vatican, 1973), pp. 402-404. *Quaestiones quodlibetales,* in *Opera omnia,* ed. Wadding, vol. XXV (Paris: Vivès, 1895), perhaps p. 63b. *Quaestiones subtilissimae super libros metaphysicorum Aristotelis,* in *Opera omnia,* ed. L. Wadding, vol. VII (Paris: Vivès, 1891), pp. 443 a-b.

[5] *Quaestiones in metaphysicam Aristotelis,* q.18 instead (Venice, ca. 1473-77), fol. 67 va ff.

[6] Chapter 6. *In libros metaphysicorum Aristotelis....*(Cologne: Zetzner, 1615; rep. Hildesheim: Olms, 1964), vol. II, cols. 366-368 and 380-394. Key passages appear on cols. 381 and 382.

[7] *De universis copiosa disputatio,* in *In analytica priora seu de ratiocinatione* (Frankfurt, 1593), pp. 446-462.

[8] Strictly, the second consequence is "it is necessary for that something to be distinct *ex natura rei* from man as such." The consequence I have given in the text, however, seems to fit better the more general formulation of the argument.

[9] This third argument in favor of Scotus' view marks the end of the *Pro* part of the "state of the question" section of the discussion. Next, Suárez takes up the *Contra,* for which he chose the view he adscribes to Ockham and Gabriel Biel. Four basic arguments are offered in its support. The Disputation that follows is Disp. VI, "On Formal and Universal Unity."

[10] *Super quattuor...,* I, q.4, sect. C-D and q.6, sect. E-Q, in *ed. cit.,* vol. III.

[11] *Epitome et collectorium ex Occamo circa quattuor sententiarum libros* (Tübingen, 1501; rep. Frankfurt/Main: Minerva, 1965), fols. Ff-iiirb ff.

[12] *Quodlibeta,* ed. I. Badio Ascensio, vol. I, (Paris, 1518; rep. Louvain; Bibliothèque S. J., 1961), fol. CLXVIr.

[13] Sect. III, §§ 38 ff.

[14] Sect. I.

[15] *Introductio in Aristotelis categorias a Boethio translata,* ed. A. Busse, in *Commentaria in Aristotelem graeca,* vol. IV (Berlin: Reimer, 1887), p. 30.

[16] Ch. 15, 1039b20; Junctas, vol. VIII, fol. 201vb.

[17] 1037a34-1037b6; Junctas, Ch. 13, text 41, fol. 193ra.

¹⁸ The term *quod quid est* can be read in two ways, as "that which is," i.e. the individual thing, and as "that which it (anything) is," i.e. the essence of a thing. In this particular case the sentence that follows clearly points out that the second reading is the appropriate one. The subject of the '*est*' is the essence. This sort of terminology begins with Boethius who uses terms such as '*quod est,*' '*quo est*' and '*id quod est*' in *Quomodo substantiae* (in the Loeb ed., p. 40).

¹⁹ 1031a15 ff; Junctas, vol. VIII, Ch. 5, fol. 168vb-169ra-b and 170va-b.

²⁰ Ch. 4, 429b10; Junctas, Suppl. II, fol. 155v.

²¹ That is, to be of such and such a size or number.

²² *Summa...,* vol. I, p. 19b. *De ente...,* pp. 39 ff.

²³ *Pars prima summae theologiae cum commentariis Thomae de Vio Caietani,* in Leonine ed., vol. IV, p. 41b, coms. VII and VIII. *In de ente et essentia d. Thomae Aquinatis commentaria,* q.9, ed. M. H. Laurent (Turin: Marietti, 1934), § 84, p. 134. *Tertia pars summa theologiae cum commentariis Thomae de Vio Caietani,* in Leonine ed., vol. II, p. 83b.

²⁴ Of this Disp., where Suárez discusses form as principle of individuation and rejects it.

²⁵ This is the logical end of the *Status quaestionis*. But apparently Suárez is not satisfied with the clarity with which the views he presents discuss the issue. For this reason, and significantly contrary to traditional form, Suárez adds a paragraph of clarification about the nature of the problem at stake before undertaking its solution. The paragraph is short but extremely important, for it clearly indicates that Suárez is looking for the cause of individuality, i.e. the cause of the incapacity of an individual thing to be divided into many things of its own species.

²⁶ Sect. I.

²⁷ Disp. IV, "On Transcendental Unity in General." For these opinions see *unitas individualis* in the Glossary.

²⁸ This is the first conclusion Suárez reaches. It is first substantiated with authorities and then with three arguments.

²⁹ *Ed. cit.,* vol. I, p. 270a.

³⁰ *Summa contra gentiles,* in Leonine ed., vol. XIII (Rome: R. Garoni, 1918), p. 68b.

³¹ *Aristotelis posteriorum analyticorum cum Thomae a Vio...annotationibus,* in *Praedicabilia...praedicamenta et libros posteriorum...commentaria* (Venice, 1599). Specht does not find anything under ch. 4 and suggests ch. 7 instead, p. 110a. *In de ente...,* q.7, pp. 63 ff.

³² *Conclusio tertia. Quaestiones metaphysicales acutissimae,* ed. Jacubus Rossettus Vincentius (Venice, 1588; rep. Frankfurt, 1967), p. 164a-b.

³³ Q.1 is very long. Passages that may support Suárez's interpretation are found in a.1. *Defensiones theologiae divi Thomae Aquinatis,* ed. Paban and Pèques (Tours: Cattier, 1899-1908; rep. Frankfurt: Minerva, 1967), vol. III, p. 201b.

³⁴ *Ad tertium.* In *Quolibeta,* ed. M. A. Zimara (Venice, 1513; rep. Ridgewood, N.J.: Gregg, 1966), fols. 81vb ff.

³⁵ *Commentarii in librum praedicabilium Porphyrii,* in *In Porphyrii isagogen, Aristotelis categorias, librosque de demonstratione, absolutissima commentaria* (Venice: D. Guerra and I. Baptista, 1587; rep. Frankfurt: Minerva, 1967), pp. 35 ff.

³⁶ This is the second part of Suárez's answer. It is very long (§§ 9-15). He proceeds to explain the initial statement briefly and then to cite those who agree with it, among whom he counts Thomists. Then he gives a counter argument by Scotus and a first (§ 10) and second (§§ 11-15) reasons why it fails. Most of the space dedicated to

the discussion of the second reason is taken up by a substantiation of the claim (already proven in Sect. I) that every entity existing in reality is necessarily singular and individual. Six arguments are offered in its support (1-3 are given in § 12; 4 extends from § 12 to 13; 5 is given in § 14; and 6 is given in § 15).

37 *In de ente...*, Ch. 2, § 35, pp. 50 ff. *Pars prima...*, vol. IV, p. 65a-b, but the text says nothing about individuation.

38 *Ed. cit.*, pp. 165a-166b.

39 *Dilucidarium metaphysicarum disputationum in Aristotelis decem et quatuor libros metaphysicorum* (Venice: Hieronymus Scotus, 1559; rep. Frankfurt/Main: Minerva, 1967), pp. 118a-121b. The solution is found in p. 121b.

40 The term used here is *gravior*, from *gravis*, weighty. At other times Suárez refers to these weighty opinions as the views of *auctores*. The latter term meant often just 'author' or 'writer,' as it does in contemporary English. Sometimes, however, *auctor* was the author of an authoritative opinion or text *(auctoritas)*, which served as the basis for argument. This did not mean that "authorities" could not be contradicted or interpreted — they were often so. What it meant was that these views had to be given serious consideration, since they had been tested by the passage of time and had survived criticism. In the Middle Ages authorities were hierarchically ordered, beginning with the *Scriptures*, which were in turn followed by the writings of the Fathers of the Church, the Doctors of the Church, the Masters of the Schools, and finally the philosophers. The philosophers were non-Christian writers such as Aristotle, Avicenna and Averroes. Bonaventure lists these authorities in order in the *Commentary on Genesis (Collationes in Hexaemeron)*, Vision III, Disp. VII. The way these authorities were used for argumentation varied. According to Suárez in *On Predestination* II, Chs. 13 and 14, there were two main modes of argumentation: 1) Direct or positive — this consisted in the use of a text which clearly stated a view concerning the issue at hand; and 2) indirect or negative — this involved extracting from a text, through interpretation, a view relevant to the issue under discussion.

41 Disp. VI, "On Formal and Universal Unity."

42 Or perhaps "That is, one [i.e. the fact that the individual as such does not add anything distinct *ex natura rei* from the specific nature] follows from the other [i.e. the fact that the nature is not universal in reality]...."

43 Sect. I.

44 *Communis* (common) and *communicabile* (communicable) are not synonyms. That which is communicable, for example, a nature, may not be common if it is not instantiated, i.e. actually communicated to several. Communicability, therefore, is the capacity of being communicated (being made common) to several; community (or commonality) is the actual characteristic of being common to many. The point that Suárez makes here is that what is common cannot be incommunicable since it is already communicated, and what is incommunicable cannot be common because it cannot be communicated. Therefore, either a thing is common or not; if it is, then it must be communicable; if it is not, then it can be either communicable or incommunicable. For this reason to be common and to be incommunicable are contradictory predicates.

45 *Pars prima...*, vol. IV, 109a-b, com. VI.

46 See n. 37 above.

47 Disp. VI, "On Formal and Universal Unity."

48 This argument can be roughly interpreted like this: "The distinction between the nature and the individual is a distinction taken from the way of conceiving..." (major premise), "No distinction *ex natura rei* is a distinction taken from the way of conceiving..." (minor premise), therefore, "No distinction *ex natura rei* is a distinction between the nature and the individual" (conclusion). The minor in fact has two parts: The first asserts the exclusion of the two classes 'distinction *ex natura rei*' and

'distinction taken from the way of conceiving...;' the second, the exclusion of the classes 'existing thing' and 'distinction between nature and individual.' The major premise is to be interpreted as a universal affirmative proposition, an A type.

⁴⁹ Disp. VII.

⁵⁰ *Quaestio de voce,* a matter of language rather than a *quaestio de re* or matter of fact.

⁵¹ This is the third part of the Solution to the question in Sect. II. It goes up to § 21. Suárez explains its three parts in the rest of § 16 and in § 17. In § 18 he raises an objection which is answered with three reasons. In § 19 a further difficulty is taken up and dismissed.

⁵² Berton reads *'contradictionis.'*

⁵³ *Ed. cit.,* vol. I, p. 204a.

⁵⁴ *Quaestiones disputatae. De potentia,* in *Opera omnia,* vol. XIII (Paris: Vivès, 1875), p. 303a.

⁵⁵ This begins the fourth and final part of the answer. It covers §§ 21-30. The length of this part is justified by the importance of the view rejected, namely, Thomas' view that in immaterial substances the individual does not add something conceptually distinct to the species. For him an immaterial substance, such as an angel, is composed of nothing more than its essence and existence. Since existence cannot be conceptualized, the individual angel is, from the point of view of conception, simply an essence.

⁵⁶ *Pars prima...,* vol. IV, p. 40a.

⁵⁷ *Summa theologiae, ed. cit.,* vol. I, p. 342b. *Quaestiones disputatae: De spiritualibus creaturis,* in *Opera omnia,* vol. XII, (Paris: Vivès, 1875), p. 38b. *Summa contra gentiles,* in Leonine ed., vol. XIII, p. 568b. *De ente..., ed. cit.,* pp. 39 ff.

⁵⁸ See n. 23; in that text, pp. 126 ff.

⁵⁹ Art. 1. *Ed. cit.,* vol. III, p. 206a.

⁶⁰ Not found. The *Paradoxa quinque* are found in *Opera,* vol. XII (Cologne, 1613), but I have not seen the work.

⁶¹ Ch. 7; 1073a4; Junctas, vol. III, fol. 323vb.

⁶² *De prima philosophia,* in *Opera omnia* (Venice, 1508; rep. Louvain, 1961), fol. 90ra.

⁶³ Sect. III.

⁶⁴ The text reads *exterioribus;* it should read *inferioribus.* This is either an editorial or a typographical mistake. The sense is clear from the arguments that follow.

⁶⁵ The point is discussed at length in Thomas' *On Being and Essence,* Ch. 2.

⁶⁶ Medievals discussed extensively the composition of heavenly bodies. Averroes, for example, believed that they were not composed of matter and form. The reason: they were incorruptible. But Thomas opposed this view, pointing out that incorruptibility was not a sufficient reason to conclude to their immateriality as long as their matter was interpreted differently than sublunary matter. Suárez did not find either of these two views irrefutable, but thought the Thomistic more probable (Disp. XIII, Sect. 10, §§ 7-8).

⁶⁷ Strictly speaking, being is not a genus. Suárez was well aware of Aristotle's view on this matter. His use of the term 'genus' here, then, should not be taken as technical. The term may very well be translated as "class" or "universe of discourse," etc.

⁶⁸ That is, the angel, as a creature and, therefore, by nature, is formally limited by its species and as such cannot possess any perfection to the highest degree (intensive infinity).

⁶⁹ In this context the term 'syncategorematically' means "potentially." Species or perfections are said to be syncategorematically infinite because they are "potentially"

infinite. Here Suárez is speaking of the extensive infinite instantiation of a particular perfection. See Glossary.

⁷⁰ "Virtually" is opposed to "formally" in this text, not to "actually" as it is often the case. See Glossary.

⁷¹ Rationality is the specific difference of man; it is in his nature to know through reason. Angels, on the other hand, do not reason; they do not "compose and divide;" their mode of knowing is intuition. Some scholastics rejected, further, the notion that angels discoursed (Thomas), while others accepted this view (Scotus). Suárez finds a middle way based on what is meant by 'discourse.' See *On the Nature of Angels* II, Chs. 32 and 33.

⁷² Sect. III, where Suárez discusses Thomas' view that designated matter is the principle of individuation of composite substances.

⁷³ *Ed. Vaticana,* vol. VII, p. 500.

⁷⁴ *Petri Lombardi sententias theologicas commentariorum libri IIII,* (Venice: Guerra, 1571; rep. Ridgewood, N.J.: Gregg, 1964), vol. I, fol. 138ra.

⁷⁵ Art. 2. *Epitome...,* fols. CC-iiivb ff.

⁷⁶ Art. 1 instead. *Quaestiones super quattuor libros sententiarum,* (Strasburg, 1501; rep. Frankfurt/Main: Minerva, 1966), fol. CCXIIva-b.

⁷⁷ *Summa theologica,* vol. II (Quaracchi: S. Bonaventurae, 1928), p. 156a-b. Also art. 3, p. 157a-b. *In duodecim Aristotelis metaphysicae libros dilucidissima expositio* (Venice, 1572), fol. 227ra.

⁷⁸ *Thomae Aquinatis summa contra gentiles cum commentariis Francisci de Sylvestris Ferrariensis,* com. VI, 3, in Leonine ed., vol. XIII (Rome: R. Garroni, 1918), p. 565a.

⁷⁹ *De unitate intellectus contra averroistas,* Ch. 5, in *Opuscula philosophica,* ed. R. M. Spiazzi (Turin-Rome: Marietti, 1954), §§ 249ff., pp. 85ff.

⁸⁰ There were three of these opinions. The response to the first is given in §§ 31-33, to the second in §§ 34-37, and to the third in §§ 38-40.

⁸¹ Note the very important point that for Suárez science has to do with "the concept of being," not "being." This indicates a drastic departure on his part from the views of earlier scholastics, such as Thomas. See Glossary, under *Metaphysica.*

⁸² Following the text, I have translated *locutiones* in the plural. This is contrary to contemporary usage in which 'Because man is capable of laughter, Peter is capable of laughter' would be considered one expression rather than two. Clearly, Suárez considered it to be composed of two expressions, 'Because man is capable of laughter' and 'Peter is capable of laughter.' Both are causal not because they both are causes, but because one expresses the cause of the other, which expresses the effect.

⁸³ To see the relation of the last sentence to the rest of the paragraph one must keep in mind that the term *res* in Latin means both "reality" and "thing." It is translated as reality earlier, but here it must be translated as thing.

⁸⁴ Disp. VI, "On Formal and Universal Unity."

⁸⁵ *Ibidem.*

⁸⁶ The terms of a distinction were called extremes *(extremi)* because they represented complete opposites. The word *extremum* means, in fact, end, outermost limit.

⁸⁷ Q. 5 instead. *Ed. cit.,* § 36, pp. 51 ff.

⁸⁸ 195b12-20; Junctas, vol. IV, fol. 62vb.

⁸⁹ Berton reads '*quae*' instead of '*quod.*' The reference is clearly to the arguments.

⁹⁰ Sect. III.

[91] By science here is meant knowledge. See Glossary.

[92] *Ed. cit.,* fol. 183rb.

[93] *In Aristotelis metaphysica commentaria,* ed. M. Hayduck, in *Commentaria in Aristotelem graeca,* vol. I (Berlin: Reimer, 1891), pp. 483-484 and 516-517.

[94] Bk. VII, Ch. 11, 1137a30; Junctas, vol. III, fol. 193ra.

[95] 1005b1; Junctas, vol. III, fol. 72rb.

[96] The "Commentator" was Averroes. He was known by that title because his commentaries on Aristotle's works became a constant source of interpretative information for the later Middle Ages. It should be noted, however, that Averroes was not considered "the Commentator" for all of Aristotle's works. Eustratius of Nicaea, for example, was "the Commentator" for the *Nicomachean Ethics.*

[97] The most common formula is *"per se subsistens,"* subsisting by itself. The formula used here is *"per se consistens,"* which makes sense only if one keeps in mind that Suárez is emphasizing the composite character of accidents, which are "things in other things."

[98] Disp. XXXIV, "On the Primary Substance or Supposit and Its Distinction from the Nature."

[99] *Ed. Vaticana,* vol. VII, p. 505.

SECTION III

1. We omit the divine substance, since, as we said, it is individual by itself and essentially; whence, there is no more reason to look for a principle of individuation in it than [for a principle] of its essence or existence.

The Sense of the Question

2. Now, in order to understand the sense of the question, it should be taken from what has been said in the preceding Section[2] that in this sort of created substances one can consider a metaphysical composition, conceptually composed of the specific nature and the individual difference. For just as what the species adds to the genus is, according to metaphysical consideration, the divisive difference, that is, [the difference] contractive of the genus and constitutive of the species, so likewise, what the individual adds to the species is rightly called the contractive difference of the species and the constitutive and distinctive [difference] of individuals, which are truly and properly said to differ in number. Indeed, for this reason the species is said to be predicated of many numerically different [things]. Again, we show that what the individual adds to the species, although only conceptually distinct, nevertheless, is real and positive, founding the negation or indivision proper to the individual, because it is by itself incommunicable and distinct from others, that is, incommunicable to other individuals. Hence, [when] added to the species, it constitutes [together] with it an individual, one by itself, under the species. Therefore, it lacks nothing in order to have a true nature *(rationem)* of difference. For this reason some think this is to be identified as the

principle of individuation, and that no other is to be searched for, as it can be seen in Scotus, *On II* [*of the Sentences*], dist. 2, q.6,[3] and Fonseca, Bk. V, [*Commentary on the*] *Metaphysics,* Ch. 6, sect. 1.[4] But this sense of the question is not under dispute, nor is there truly a diversity of opinion on that [question] among those who dispute concerning the principle of individuation.[5] Therefore, the sense of the question concerns what basis or principle the individual difference has in reality. For these metaphysical predicates are usually taken from real constitutive principles of reality, in the same manner in which the genus is usually said to be taken from matter and difference from form.[6] And substantial predications *(denominationes)* are taken from matter sometimes, as when man is said to be material, sometimes from form, as when [man] is said to be rational, [and] sometimes from the whole composite nature, as when [man] is said to be man. Therefore, in accordance with this, we inquire presently what the principle of this individual difference is.

From this statement, it is clear we are not looking here for extrinsic causes or principles of individuation, or rather, of individuals, such as are the final and efficient causes. For these do not cause individuation except [insofar] as they cause the individual entity, that is, by furnishing the intrinsic principle of individuation. Therefore, it is the latter that we look for. And although the general question [of individuation] concerns all created substances, nevertheless, because material [substances] are better known to us, we shall discuss them first, and then it will be more easily determined what we can conclude concerning spiritual [substances]. Moreover, since there are several opinions concerning this matter which require detailed consideration, we shall discuss them one by one.

3. There is a famous view which affirms designated matter to be the principle of individuation.[7] This is the view of St. Thomas, [*Summa theologiae*] I, q.3, a.3, *ad* 3, and q.50, a.4, III, q.77, a.2, and *On IV* [*of the Sentences*], dist. 12, q.1, a.1, *quaestiuncula* 2, and *Opuscle* 29, [*On the Principle of Individuation*],[8] and *On Being and Essence,* Ch. 2, where Cajetan discusses and defends it in detail;[9] and Capreolus, *On II* [*of the Sentences*], dist. 3;[10] Soncinas, [*Questions on*] *Metaphysics* VII, q.33 and 34;[11] Ferrara, [*Commentary on*] *Contra gentiles* I, Ch. 21,[12] and others to be cited below. It is believed as well that this is Aristotle's view; for in several places he holds that numerical distinction and identity is to be attributed to prime matter. Whence, in Bk. V, *Metaphysics,* Ch. 6, text 42, he says that "[those things] are one in number of which matter is one."[13] And, in Bk. VII, Ch. 8, text 28, he says that "the form in these fleshes and bones is Socrates and Callias."[14] And in Ch. 10, text 25, he says: "The singular is already Socrates, owing to the last matter."[15] And concerning this principle he con-

cludes in Bk. XII, *Metaphysics,* Ch. 8, text 49: "The first mover cannot be but one in number, because it lacks matter," holding as necessary that those [things] that agree in species and differ in number
have matter and differ by matter.[16] Similarly, in *On the Heavens* I,
Ch. 9, he proves that there cannot be another world, because this
world comprises all the matter of natural things.[17]

From these texts it appears, therefore, that this was Aristotle's
view, according to which, consequently, it must be said, — as the
aforementioned authors say—, that in immaterial substances there
is no positive principle of individuation or proper individual difference, but only the nature incommunicable of itself.

4. If we follow reason, I find almost no basis [given] for this view
that does not recall the authority of Aristotle, namely, that matter is
the principle of multiplication and distinction of individuals within
the same species, as Aristotle states in the cited places. But what is
the principle of numerical distinction is the principle of individuation; therefore, [matter is the principle of individuation]. Second,
because what is incommunicable to inferiors similar [to itself] is individual. But matter is the primary foundation of that incommunicability; for form, since it is act, is communicable of itself, while
matter, since it is primary potency, is incommunicable of itself, and
form then is limited and determined when it is contracted to this
matter. Third, because the individual is the primary subject in
metaphysical coordination; for all [things] superior [to it] are predicated of it, but it [i.e. the individual] is not [predicated] of others.
Therefore, the first principle and foundation of the individual as
such must be that which is the primary subject among physical principles, and matter is such; therefore, [matter must be the principle of
individuation].

The Arguments for the Stated View are Examined

5. But before we proceed further, [note that] these arguments, apart
from authority, do not have great weight. The first can be easily
answered by denying the major; for what is a principle of distinction
is more a principle of multiplication [than of individuation].[18] Moreover, the principle of distinction is not matter, but rather form, for,
as the common saying goes, "act is what distinguishes." Whence, St.
Thomas, in *Contra gentiles* II, Ch. 40, explicitly proves that matter is
not the primary cause of the distinction of things.[19] And although he
is primarily concerned with essential distinction [there], nevertheless, the arguments he gives seem to apply also to numerical distinction, [and] in particular what he says in the second argument, that
"form does not follow the disposition of matter as first cause, but
rather, and conversely, matter is so disposed in order that a particular

form may follow." Again, what he says in the same place, that "those [things] related to matter as to a first cause are outside the agent's intention and are produced by chance." If, therefore, matter were the primary cause of the individual, the individual as such would be produced by chance and outside the agent's intention. Again, what he says in the same place in the fourth argument, that "one matter requires something distinct from itself in order to be distinguished from another matter;" therefore, it is not the primary cause of distinction, as it was taken in the argument given.

For this reason, having been convinced by these and other arguments, many of the authors who follow the aforementioned opinion acknowledge that, since there are two [things] which belong to the notion of individual, namely, to be incommunicable to inferiors and to be distinct from other individuals, matter is the principle of individuation with respect to the first, and quantity is [so] with respect to the second, for [quantity] is what distinguishes the matters themselves. We shall examine later the truth and consequence with which this is said.[20] For now we shall consider only the force of the stated arguments.

The first argument, however, concerned only individuation with respect to the distinction of one [thing] from another, about which the already aforementioned authors acknowledge that it does not originate from matter. Notice, moreover, that the arguments given are not convincing with respect to every distinction. For, as I shall state below, matter has its own way of distinguishing one [thing] from another, insofar as it has some entitative act. They do prove, however, that there is no [reason] why the primary reason of all numerical distinction should be attributed to it [i.e. matter] rather than to some form.

6. The second argument deals with the primary root of incommunicability, in which the notion of individual consists first [of all], as was stated above; for distinction from another is rather a consequence [of it], as was stated above concerning unity in general. Hence, if the argument were effective, it would be sufficient to prove that matter is the principle of individuation. But, if one considers this [argument] carefully, there is an obvious equivocation committed in the reasoning. For, when matter is said to be the principle of the incommunicability of the individual because it is the primary subject, incommunicable of itself in the highest degree, either the word 'incommunicable' is taken equivocally or something false is assumed in the proof. For matter can be understood to be incommunicable in many ways: First, as incommunicable to something, such as a physical subject which it may inform or in which it may inhere.[21] And this sense is most true, and it is rightly proven from the fact that

matter is the primary subject. This, however, has nothing to do with the topic under discussion, both because to be incommunicable to another as to a subject does not belong to the notion of individual as such, — since accidents are individuals and yet they may be communicated in this way, and so too are substantial forms — , and also because that incommunicability is not sufficient for the notion of individual. For matter is incommunicable in this way in virtue of its species and, nevertheless, it is not an individual in virtue of the species, but common to many numerically different matters. Therefore, that incommunicability is not the primary root of individuation, even in matter itself; therefore, much less could matter be the primary principle of individuation of substance by reason of this incommunicability.

Matter can be said to be incommunicable in another way as well, either in the manner of a cause, in the manner of a part, in the manner of a nature to a supposit, or in the manner of a superior to inferiors. But all these ways are false. For matter is communicated to form in the way in which it is its cause and sustains it. Again, matter is communicated to the composite as part to whole and also as cause to effect, which it does not cause otherwise than by intrinsically communicating its entity to it. Again, matter as part of a nature is communicated only to [its] proper supposit, if we speak naturally. Supernaturally [speaking], however, [matter is communicated] also to another [supposit], as one may see in the [case of the] humanity of Christ. But none of these ways [of understanding the incommunicability of matter] is pertinent to the present case, as is intuitively *(per se)* obvious.

Moreover, the last way — in which alone the terms used in the aforementioned argument would be taken univocally — is clearly false, as the argument given above convincingly shows, because matter as such, by virtue of its species is communicable to many inferiors, which can stand under [it] in the order of predication but cannot be subjects of inherence. And if you say that matter as such is common, while the designated matter about which the statement is made is incommunicable, [then] against this there is [the fact] that designated matter, whatever it may be, does not have incommunicability from the notion of primary subject on which the argument given was based. If, therefore, designated matter is incommunicable, it will be so on account of another cause, which could be common to forms or to other things, as we shall see in what follows. Wherefore, the notion of primary subject does not pertain to the incommunicability belonging to the notion of an individual; for angelic forms and God himself are incommunicable in that way, even though they are completely acts and not potencies. Hence, when form is said in that same place to be communicable of itself, this is also irrelevant. For form as form is communicable to matter as to a subject, not as to an inferior; it is also communicable to distinct forms according to its own specific notion, and thus it is not individual according to that notion. Nevertheless, this form is as incommunicable as this matter. Therefore, in this respect there is no better reason for one [to be principle of individuation] than for the other.

7. Now, it is evident from these [considerations] that the third conjecture is not effective, because the notion of the subject of inherence and [that] of the subject of predication are very different *(diversa)*. For, although it may be possible to think of a certain proportion between these two subjects, since the superior is compared to the inferior [which is] its subject as the form that gives [it] being, nevertheless, they simply do not have the same notion, nor is one founded on the other. Whence, in simple substances, there is subjection or subordination of inferiors to superiors without subject of inherence or of information.

It should be added that what is the subject of predication is not of itself more imperfect than its superior predicate, as matter, which is the primary subject, is inferior to form. And thus it is not necessary that what is a primary subject in the order of generation and imperfection be the first principle and foundation of the individual, which is the primary subject in the order of predication, containing in itself all the perfection of the superiors and adding something proper whereby it, as it were, completes and perfects that [perfection].[22]

Many Objections are Raised against the Stated View

8. But we must see whether this view, although not demonstrable *(convinci non possit)* by reason, may [still] be suitably defended and maintained, for this will be [reason] enough for us, at least because of the authority of Aristotle and St. Thomas, to defend it.[23] The first source *(ratio)* of difficulty concerning it [i.e. this view] can be that matter is common of itself not only insofar as it, according to specific notion, is common to many individuals of matter,[24] but also that the numerically same matter can be under many forms, whether specifically distinct or only numerically diverse, at least successively. In that way, therefore, can matter be principle of individuation? For the principle of individuation must be particular *(proprium)* in the highest degree and in no way common to many individuals, whether simultaneously or successively. Because of this difficulty, the view adds that not matter in just any way, but [rather matter] designated by quantity is the principle of individuation. But what is signified by the term ['designated matter'] is so obscure that the defenders of this

view differ among themselves greatly in the way they try to explain it. It is necessary, therefore, to refer and examine their various interpretations in order to assess more clearly the suitability of this view.

The First Way of Explaining Designated Matter is Rejected

9. The first interpretation is that matter designated by quantity is nothing other than matter with quantity or matter affected by quantity. For they hold that the principle of individuation is, as it were, composed of these two, so that matter may give incommunicability and quantity distinction, as we said above. Thus states Capreolus in *On II [of the Sentences]*, dist. 3, q.1, a.1, concl. 5, and in a.3, in the answer to the arguments against it[25]; again, Ferrara, *[Commentary on] Contra gentiles* I, Ch. 21,[26] and Soncinas, *[Questions...]*,[27] Bk. VII, q.34. St. Thomas favors it in *On Truth*, q.2, a.6, *ad* 1, where he explains that natural designated matter is matter "with the determination of these or those dimensions."[28] And in *On Evil*, q.16, a.1, *ad* 18, he says that "matter subject to dimensions is the principle of numerical distinction in those [things] in which many individuals of one species are found."[29] And commenting on Boethius' *On the Trinity*, q.4, a.2, he says that "quantity distinguishes material things."[30] This seems to be based on Aristotle, in *Metaphysics* III, Ch. 3, text 11, where he holds that specific distinction is the result of form, while numerical [distinction is the result] of quantity.[31] And in Bk. X, Ch. 3, text 4, he posits only two types of division, namely, according to form and according to quantity.[32] And in *Metaphysics* V, Ch. 13, he attributes to quantity to be principle of division, whence he says that "a quantum is what can be divided into those [things] each of which is born to be this something."[33] And in *Physics* III, Ch. 7, text 78, he says that "number is born from the division of a continuous quantum."[34] In fact, the reason can be that in order for matter to be the principle of individuation, it is necessary that something distinguish this matter from that [one]. But this [something] is not matter itself, since the distinction must be made by an act. Nor is it form, for rather this form is distinct from that [one] because it is made and received in a distinct matter. [Therefore, it must be quantity.]

10. But this view is false and can be attacked with serious arguments. We can proceed in two ways: First, assuming the other view held by the aforementioned authors, that quantity is not in prime matter but in the whole composite, and that it is destroyed when the substance is corrupted, and that it is newly acquired for the generation of substance. From which it is concluded that, absolutely *(simpliciter)* speaking, numerically this substantial form is first introduced in this matter and [then] quantity follows. Whence the argument is

completed, because this form, when it is first understood to be received in this matter, is also understood to be received in a matter distinct from the others. Therefore, it is not made formally and intrinsically distinct by quantity. Again, this substantial individual results from matter and form conceived with precision and as preceding quantity. Therefore, that [i.e. the substantial individual] as such is one, not with conceptual unity, but with real, singular and transcendental unity.[35] Therefore, just as it is undivided in itself in virtue of its substantial entity, so also it is substantially and entitatively distinct from all others. Therefore, it does not have distinction through quantity. Nor is it relevant if you say that quantity is prior in matter in the order of material cause, both because that cannot be said to follow properly from that view, as will be discussed below, and also because at least it cannot be understood according to a true inherence of quantity in matter, because, according to that principle, quantity may never inhere in matter in real duration, but [only] in the composite. Therefore, [quantity] cannot agree with it [i.e. matter] in some sign of priority, because what does not agree in reality and in real duration can neither agree in prior nor posterior. Moreover, quantity does not divide a thing or [render it] distinct from others, except by inhering in and informing [it]. Therefore, quantity does not have in any way *(signo)* this effect primarily in matter, but [only] in the whole composite. Therefore, [quantity] presupposes it [i.e. matter] as already individual, and, consequently, as distinct by another prior division. Finally, also because for the argument's force it is enough that matter, as it precedes quantity, be distinct of itself in some kind of causal role *(causa)* that is absolutely *(simpliciter)* prior. Finally, the argument can be concluded thus: Form is received in matter without quantity; therefore, this form [is received] in this matter, because generation takes place in the singular; therefore, this individual results from these [i.e. this form and this matter] before the advent of quantity. Indeed, that [i.e. quantity] comes to the already constituted individual, which God could preserve as distinct from all others without quantity. Therefore, quantity does not intrinsically and formally enter into the principle of individuation, whether of the whole composite substance or of each of its parts, namely, form and matter.

11. Second, we can proceed to the other view, that quantity is in prime matter and remains the same in what is generated and corrupted. And then an argument no less effective is taken from another place, because not only this matter in itself, but also [matter] as affected by this quantity, can be under diverse forms and, consequently, in numerically distinct individuals. Therefore, [matter designated by quantity] can no more be the principle of individuation

than matter alone [can]. It will be said, perhaps, that matter with indeterminate dimensions can be under diverse forms, and as such is not the principle of individuation, but, on the other hand, matter with these determinate dimensions is proper to this individual and that as such is the principle of individuation. But I ask what these determinate dimensions add to quantity. For dimensions can be called indeterminate only because they do not express a fixed limit of length or width etc., and so a determinate quantity will only add fixed dimensional limits. But this is not enough for the present [purpose], because the same matter, existing in this way under the same fixed and determinate quantity, can be under distinct forms, as it is clear from [the case of] the same branch, first green, later dry, and in similar [cases].

In another manner, that quantity can be called indeterminate which is not affected by fixed dispositions, such as a particular rarity or density or by other qualities by which matter is determined to this form rather than to another. In this sense it can be admitted that matter, affected by quantity or dimensions so determined, that is, [matter] so immediately *(proxime)* disposed, is so proper to this individual that it could not be in another.

The mentioned authors, however, cannot be speaking in this sense, nor is this part of their true view. The first is clear, because they say that quantity distinguishes one individual from another by its proper notion and formal effect. Therefore, this [i.e. that quantity distinguishes...] does not agree with that [i.e. that matter, affected by fixed dispositions...] by reason of the other qualities or dispositions. Otherwise, not matter designated by quantity, but [rather] matter insofar as it is designated by qualities must be said to be the principle of individuation. The second is clear, because otherwise it would follow that the accidents by which matter is disposed to form are intrinsically included in the principle of individuation of substance. But the consequent is false.[36] Therefore, [this cannot be their true view]. What follows is clear, because designated matter, according to this view, intrinsically and formally includes these accidents as inhering in itself and determining it to a particular form. Now, the minor is proven, first, because the substantial individual is one by itself [and] directly placed under the species in the category of substance; therefore, it does not intrinsically include accidents, although it may, nevertheless, intrinsically include the principle of individuation. Second, because it was shown above that the individual difference in reality is not distinct *ex natura rei* from the substantial nature, and that, therefore, it is the individual substance itself. Therefore, its intrinsic principle cannot be an accident, but the substance.

12. These arguments can be effective also against the other view, that quantity is not in prime matter, but [rather] in the whole composite, because quantity is an accident. Therefore, in whatever subject it may be, it cannot intrinsically enter into the constitution of the substantial individual. Therefore, it cannot cause its distinction.

Hence, leaving these views aside, we can argue thirdly that, although a thing's being one in itself is by nature prior to its being distinct from others, nevertheless, the latter follows intrinsically from the former without any positive addition being made to the thing itself that is one, but only by negation, by which, having posited the other term, it is true to say that this is not that. Accordingly, the same positive [thing] that is the foundation of unity with respect to the first negation or indivision in itself, is subsequently the foundation of the later negation of distinction from another. In this sense it is usually said with great truth that a thing is distinguished from others by that by which it is constituted in itself, because it is distinguished by that whereby it is.

Almost in the same sense St. Thomas says, [*Summa theologiae*] I, q.76, a.2, *ad* 2, that "each thing has unity in the same way in which it has being."[37] This is clear in [the case of] specific unity, for the same difference which constitutes the species one in itself, renders it distinct from other species. Hence, what is a principle of such a difference is also a principle not only of unity, but also of specific distinction. Therefore, likewise in [the case of] individual unity, what is a principle of the individual with respect to its constitution and its incommunicability or indivisibility in itself is also a principle of its distinction from others; and, conversely, what is a principle of distinction must also be a principle of constitution. If, therefore, matter by itself and separated from quantity constitutes the individual as incommunicable and one in itself, it also distinguishes it from others, or [alternatively], if distinction is impossible, so is the incommunicability of individuality *(individuationis)*. This is confirmed: For that is called "incommunicable" in this way, which is so one in itself that it could not be divided into many [entities] similar [to itself]. Moreover, what is such is distinguished from others precisely in virtue of this — provided others exist. And conversely, the same argument can be made concerning quantity, because if that [i.e. quantity] is what distinguishes substantial individuals, it [i.e. quantity] must constitute them as well. And, conversely, if it cannot constitute [them], — which is more true, because, being an accident, it is outside the whole realm of substance, presupposing rather the individual subject — neither can it distinguish them.

13. Some answer that this argument rightly proves that quantity does not cause the first distinction among substantial individuals,

but it does not prove that it does not cause any distinction, such as the numerical and quantitative, which is enough for quantity to be able to pertain intrinsically in this respect to the principle of individuation.

But this answer falls into an equivocation, for if quantity does not cause the first distinction, but [rather causes] another, I ask, which is the one it presupposes [and] which is the one it causes? Surely the former cannot be any other but the entitative distinction, whereby this matter is not that [one] or this substance is not that [one], both because [1] no other prior distinction can be thought, and also because [2] this [distinction] is the most intrinsic to each entity. For, just as nothing more intrinsic to any being can be conceived than its entity, so no distinction or separation from another being is prior to that which is stated by this negation: "This being is not that [one]." Hence, it is unintelligible that one entity be distinguished from another entitatively and primarily by something other than itself.

14. Whence it follows also — [something] which is a new and sufficient argument against this whole view — that to distinguish entitatively one matter from another, or a part of matter from [another] part of matter, is not a formal effect of quantity, because just as quantity presupposes matter as subject, so does it presuppose its individual entity, which by itself is entitatively distinct from another similar entity. Therefore, distinct quantities presuppose distinct subjects in which they are received and distinct parts of quantity [presuppose] as well entitatively distinct parts of a subject. For here Cajetan's argument is relevant, that a singular act presupposes a singular potency, which is especially true in [the case of] a really distinct act and a potency. This is particularly so because, since quantity is a thing distinct from the matter in which it is, it cannot make it really distinct from itself. Therefore, [quantity] presupposes in it [i.e. matter] an entity which can be distinguished by itself from its quantity. Therefore, by the same [entity, matter] will be distinguished from all other [things] which are not itself. Therefore, this [distinction] is not a formal effect of quantity.

Finally, the same can be confirmed *a posteriori*. For, if God, abstracting from quantity, preserved the substance of Peter's body, for example, the partial entities of matter which are in the hands, the feet, the head, etc., would always remain entitatively distinct, whether they remained united or not. The reason for this is that although one entity could be united or separated from another, nevertheless, it would be openly incompatible for one to become the other or for both to be united into one indivisible [entity] which preserved its entity, because they would be both distinct and not distinct.

15. Therefore, the distinction that quantity presupposes in substance is an entitative and substantial distinction, and it is one that pertains by itself to the individual unity we are discussing. For through this [distinction] the individual is understood to be distinct from all others, whether under the same species if it is compared with [individuals] similar [to itself], or also under the genus or under any common predicate if it is compared with all other [individuals]. Therefore, if quantity confers any distinction, it will be accidental to the notion of individual and coming to it from outside; therefore, it is not for this reason that quantity will pertain to the principle of individuation presently under discussion. This is explained by [the nature of] the thing itself [i.e. quantity], for since quantity gives quantitative unity to substance, it can only give [to it] either a quantitative or a place distinction. The former of these consists only in this, that one substance is under diverse limits of quantity from another, and so that it is not continuous with the continuity proper to quantity. And the latter consists in this, that one substance is outside the place or location of the other. Hence, [the fact] that quantity distinguishes in the way it constitutes is also preserved. For, first, it makes substance extended in itself, quantitatively united and determined and to have this corporeal mass, but, as a result, it makes it to occupy local space; and similarly, it first distinguishes [it] quantitatively and then locally. This whole distinction, however, is outside the notion of individual substance, and [it is] accidental to it, as is [the case] with quantity itself.

16. Surely this is evident in [the case of] the place distinction, because [the place distinction] is exceedingly extrinsic and mutable, and however much the quantified thing may change place, it remains numerically the same. Indeed, by the power of God, the numerically same corporeal substance can be preserved without place, whether without quantity or with it, in the manner in which the body of Christ is [preserved] in the Eucharist. Similarly, the same quantified thing can be constituted in two places by the power of God, as I showed extensively when discussing the mystery of the Eucharist,[38] and two distinct bodies can be located in the same place, — this is often done by God, as it has been demonstrated in the matter of the resurrection.[39] Therefore, the place distinction has nothing to do with numerical unity and distinction. The same can be affirmed, moreover, concerning the quantitative distinction as concerning the very quantity and unity arising from it, which we showed above to be accidental to the intrinsic and entitative unity of material substance. Hence, although it [i.e. the quantitative distinction] naturally follows in the manner of a property, nevertheless, in the order of nature, it [i.e. the quantitative distinction] presupposes

it [i.e. the unity of material substance], and it is rather caused by it than causes it. Finally, material substance could be preserved by absolute power as numerically the same without its quantity, and consequently, [it could] retain the whole individual unity with substantial incommunicability and distinction without quantitative unity or distinction.

17. Wherefore even Soncinas and Ferrara finally acknowledge that material substance does not have transcendental unity from quantity, although [they insist] that it is numerically one through quantity. But it is astonishing that they should depart so easily from the true sense of the question and use terms equivocally. For, as we have often warned and everybody assumes and they themselves — I believe — know, when we discuss numerical unity here, we do not take number as a species of quantity, but as it can be found in any entity, as St. Thomas points out in *Opuscle* 16, [*On the Unity of the Intellect against Averroists*],[40] the last chapter, where he says thus, that "even immaterial substance is numerically one." Likewise Aristotle also distinguished numerical, specific, generic and analogical unity in *Metaphysics* V.[41] Therefore, this numerical unity is transcendental in each thing, just as the specific or formal unity is transcendental in its own manner with respect to the common nature. Therefore, if material substance has transcendental individual unity, and [this is] not through quantity, quantity does not intrinsically pertain to the principle of individuation of substance. [To this] it must be added that in the same way in which substance is categorically one in number through quantity, [it is] not only distinguished, but also constituted and made in itself undivided and quantitatively incommunicable by the same quantity. For quantity could not make something one in its genus unless it also made [it] undivided, since the notion of one consists in this [indivisibility]. Therefore, if they speak consistently and univocally concerning the incommunicability and distinction of the same genus, they badly distribute these functions, assigning one to matter and another to quantity. If, however, they speak at one point of substantial incommunicability, [and] afterwards of quantitative distinction, they do not preserve the true sense of the question and equivocate in the use of words.

The Second Way of Interpreting Designated Matter is Rejected

18. The second interpretation is that matter, designated by quantity, does not intrinsically include quantity itself, but [rather it includes it] as the term of the relation of matter to it. For matter is capable of quantity by its nature, but as such it cannot be the full principle of individuation, because it is indifferent to any quantity,

just as to any form. Moreover, by the agent's action prior to generation, it is determined to have a capacity for this quantity, and not for another, and as such it is said to be the principle of individuation. Moreover, in this place we understand by quantity not only mathematical quantity, if I may call it so, but physical [quantity], that is, [quantity] affected by physical qualities and dispositions. Cajetan explained this point thus in [his commentary to Thomas'] *On Being and Essence,* Ch. 2, q.5.[42] He is followed by Iavellus, [*Questions on the*] *Metaphysics* V, q.15,[43] and before them, Egidius, *Quodlibet* I, q.5, a.1.[44].

This view, however, displeased Cajetan himself, [in his commentary to the *Summa theologiae*] I, q.29, a.1,[45] because of the argument to which I shall refer below, and thus he found another manner of speaking, if indeed it is different. For he says that matter is the principle of individuation not [insofar] as it is in potency to this quantity, but [insofar] as it virtually pre-contains this quantity or is the root and foundation of this quantity. Nevertheless, I do not understand sufficiently what is signified by these words "distinct *a priori,*" because matter—particularly in the view of Cajetan and other Thomists—does not pre-contain quantity as an efficient cause, but [rather quantity] is caused by an extrinsic agent or results from form. Therefore, [matter] can only pre-contain it [i.e. quantity] as a material cause. But this is nothing other than to have it in receptive potency, or what is the same, to have a potency for it. [For] just as matter, [insofar] as it pre-contains form, can be nothing other than matter as it is in potency toward form, or rather, as it is [in] receptive potency toward form, because it does not pre-contain [it] otherwise than as material cause, so likewise with the present [case], for the same reason. Therefore, all those words, matter as "foundation," as "root," as "cause," amount to the same, because matter is not the foundation of quantity, except in a material and in a passive [way]; nor is it the root except as the primary subject, nor the cause, except the material [one], which consists in the nature *(ratione)* of receptive potency from which form is educed. Therefore, under all those words there can lie nothing other than the potency of matter itself. Wherefore, the argument of Cajetan himself and those which we shall give go equally against this view, which for this reason need not be given separate consideration.

19. To these must be added another [view] as well, which holds that designated matter is nothing other than matter immediately *(ultimo)* disposed to this form, because it is not disposed except by quantity affected by particular qualities. This view, however, can be stated in two ways: First, understanding that quantity and other dispositions inhere and remain in matter and absolutely *(simpliciter)* precede in

the order of nature the introduction of form. And thus, matter, disposed and designated to form, can be rightly understood. However, to posit designated matter as principle of individuation in this way is to fall back into Capreolus' earlier view, because this designated matter intrinsically includes quantity and accidents, which, as we showed, cannot be included in the principle of individuation. If it is said that these dispositions, although inherent in matter, nevertheless, are not intrinsically and formally included in the individual, but are, as it were, required conditions, against this is [the fact] that from this follows that the principle of individuation is intrinsically and formally only something common to many individuals, namely, matter itself as such. But this is impossible, as we argued above. Hence, this would not be to point out what in itself and in reality is the principle of individuation, but, at most, what can be a sign of individuation for us, or an occasion of the production of a particular individual with respect to an agent. We shall speak about these matters later.

This view can be taught in another way, presupposing that quantity and other dispositions are not in matter, but in the composite, and that, as they produce the last disposition, they follow form. In this sense it is the same [thing] for matter to be disposed as to have an order or determined potency to this quantity with these dispositions; and thus this manner of speaking coincides in this with the second interpretation given.

20. Therefore, I think this whole interpretation is false. In the first place, it is assumed in it that matter does not have quantity and other dispositions inhering in itself, which, although defensible *(probabile)*, nevertheless is not perhaps as defensible *(probabile)* as the contrary [view]. Next, assuming this view, — Cajetan argues in [his commentary to *Summa theologiae*] I[46] —, the potency of matter for the reception of quantity falls in the genus of quantity, since potency and act are in the same genus, as Aristotle says in *Metaphysics* X.[47] Therefore, the potency toward quantity cannot intrinsically belong to the principle of individuation of substance, otherwise the substantial individual would not be one by itself, for it would be made up of things belonging to different categories. This argument, however, taken by itself is not effective. For, as Iavellus correctly answers,[48] potency belongs to the genus of its primary act, toward which it is primarily ordered by itself, and from which it takes the species in its own way. Matter, however, is not in potency to quantity in such a way that it may be primarily ordered to it by itself, but [it is so in potency] to substantial form, and thus it is not necessary that [its potency] belong to the category of quantity. Moreover, what Fonseca adds in Cajetan's favor in [*Commentary on*] *Metaphysics* V, Ch. 6,

q.4,[49] that although the potency of matter may not belong to quantity absolutely *(simpliciter),* even though it belongs to that category as receptive of quantity, this — I say — is not a serious difficulty. For the reduplication of matter as receptive of quantity does not add a real potency to matter itself, but explains that potency only according to our manner of conceiving and speaking by relation to a secondary term, that is, quantity, and thus, it is not necessary that for that reason it should belong to the category of quantity. Therefore, Iavellus' answer is good with respect to the force of the argument based in the maxim, "act and potency are in the same genus," as we shall point out more extensively later, when discussing the material cause of accidents.

21. However, an effective argument against this very opinion is taken from the same answer. For if the potency of matter is related to substantial form prior to [being related to] quantity, then it also determines its potency to this substantial form prior to [determining its potency to] this quantity. Therefore, [matter] is not designated or determined to this form by a potency to this quantity. The first consequence is clear, both because [1] potency is determined to act in a way proportionate to it [i.e. act]. If, therefore, potency itself is substantial and is not related to accidental act except by means of a substantial [act], it is not determined except by the same relation and proportion. And also because [2], according to the view of these authors, matter does not receive this quantity in reality, except by means of this form, and because it receives this form, therefore it receives this quantity. Therefore, similarly, its capacity [i.e. of matter] for this quantity is not determined in potency, except insofar as it is determined to this form.

The same argument applies to Cajetan's other manner of speaking about matter as "pre-containing quantity," because matter does not pre-contain quantity except insofar as it pre-contains the form which is followed by quantity. Therefore, neither does it pre-contain this quantity with dispositions, except insofar as it pre-contains this form, after which this quantity and these dispositions follow. Therefore, [matter] cannot be designated to this form by the fact that it pre-contains this quantity.

Finally, the same form of argumentation can be used against the other manner of speaking about matter as "disposed with an immediate *(ultima)* disposition," because matter is not determined to such an immediate *(ultima)* disposition except by means of form. For we assume that [the immediate disposition] is not received in it [i.e. matter], but in the composite. Therefore, matter cannot be designated either by the relation to such a disposition, or by the very disposition as actually received, since in either case the determination of this matter to this form absolutely *(simpliciter)* precedes both the relation and the actual reception. This argument is effective, on the one hand, for the last *(ultima)* disposition which is present in the instant of generation and follows form. If, on the other hand, someone contends that matter is designated by immediately preceding dispositions, another argument must be found.

22. Hence, I argue in a second principal [way] against this whole interpretation,[50] because matter is of itself indifferent to this quantity and these dispositions, and to others. But in the instant of generation, according to this view, naturally prior to the reception of substantial form, [matter] is left bare of all accidents and without any entity added to it. Therefore, it remains equally indifferent as it exists of itself. Therefore, its potency is not determined to this quantity, since it is unintelligible that potency, indifferent of itself, be determined without any addition or change made in it. Therefore, [matter] is not designated by such an indeterminate potency. The major is self-evident from the nature of matter. The minor is also self-evident in the principles of the view we oppose, because nothing else substantial can be preconceived to be added to matter before substantial form. For, what would that be, or by what would it be made, or on what basis, or what would its purpose be? Not even something accidental [can be understood to be added] because no accident precedes substantial form in matter and, according to every view, no accident precedes quantity itself in matter.

Some say that a certain real mode, distinct *ex natura rei* from matter, is added to matter in the instant prior to the introduction of the substantial form with its quantity and other dispositions, and that matter is designated by this mode. Some call this mode substantial, others accidental. But all of these speak gratuitously, nor can they explain or give a reason for what they say, which is [something] foreign to the true nature *(ratione)* of philosophizing. For I ask, first, what this mode is for. They say: So that matter may be determined to this form. [But], on the contrary, it [i.e. matter] is indifferent to this mode, and to an infinite [number] of others. Therefore, by what is matter determined to receive this mode in that instant rather than any other? For, if you say that it is determined by another mode, we proceed to infinity. But, if you say that it is determined by immediately preceding dispositions, it would be better to say that matter is immediately determined to form, and thus this mode is superfluous. Besides, the arguments by which we shall show at once that matter cannot be determined to form by preceding dispositions prove in the same way that [matter] cannot be determined by them to the reception of such a mode. Finally, if it is said that matter receives this mode by virtue of the agent, without any prior determination, why not may the same be said of form? Therefore, this mode is introduced without reason or basis.

23. Second, I shall inquire when and by what this mode is produced. For either [1] it is produced gradually while matter is being disposed, or [2] it is produced in one instant, whether [a] prior to generation or [b] in the very instant of generation. None of these, however, can be appropriately understood or explained. For, if [1] it is said to be produced successively and gradually with the dispositions, it will be subject to intensification like them; therefore, it will be an accident and as such it will be corrupted at the instant of generation.[51] Again, for this reason, the principle of individuation will be subject to intensification and remission, and matter will also be designated in itself and modified toward form before it receives it [i.e. the form] in time. Consequently, since this mode is immediately incompatible with the other mode of determination, which matter has with respect to the form under which it exists, it follows that matter also loses it gradually. For the same reason it could be inferred that it gradually and successively loses the union with such a form, all of which is absurd and improbable.

The same [things] follow more clearly if [2a] this mode is posited as produced all at once in an instant before the instant of generation. For, then, matter would be all at once under one form and immediately *(ultimo)* designated by another. Besides, no reason can be given why it may be made in one instant rather than another, when speaking about those [things] in which matter is not apt for the reception of form. If, however, [2b] it is said to be produced all at once at the instant of generation, it follows that, naturally prior to the reception of such a mode, matter is left bare, and consequently, no resistance is offered to the agent, which acts in matter as much as it can. Therefore, just as it is said that it produces such a mode immediately, it would be much better to say that it produces its [i.e. matter's] form immediately.

24. Third, I shall inquire what this mode is. For it is not substantial, first, because what it may be is inconceivable, since it is neither a nature nor part of a nature, subsistence or existence. Or, next, it is completely separate *(absolutus)* even according to transcendental relation, and this could not be said to follow, both because matter is said to be determined by it to this form or quantity, and also because matter is said to be designated by it. If, therefore, it [i.e. the mode] is wholly separate *(absolutus),* designated matter will be something wholly separate *(absolutum)* from quantity and from a relation to quantity, [something] which contradicts the stated doctrine.

Almost the same argument is made if the mode is posited with some kind of transcendental relation. For, in order for the mode to be substantial, it is necessary that the primary term of the relation be the substantial form and not quantity, and so also, in no way will a relation to quantity pertain to the principle of individuation. Moreover, if the mode is posited as accidental, what it is or the category under which it falls cannot be explained. Moreover, [the fact] that accidents are not in prime matter is inconsistent with that view. It follows also that the principle of individuation is an accidental being composed of substance and accident, and that the individual adds an accidental mode distinct *ex natura rei* from substance to the species, which is [something] completely false.

25. For these reasons, others answer that the potency of matter is determined to this quantity in that instant by the agent itself, without any thing or intrinsic mode added to it. But this involves an open contradiction. For, if the expression refers to the agent as preconceived in first act before its action, — and in this way it is impossible that the intrinsic potency and capacity of matter be determined by it, since they are wholly distinct things and the one as such does not actually change the other, — hence, if in that instant the agent were anihilated before it acted in matter, and another were applied, it would induce in it a different form, proportioned to itself.

If, however, the expression refers to the agent in second act, that is, to its action, it is necessary to understand that the agent determines matter by its action and that it puts nothing intrinsic in it in order to determine it, because such an action of the agent is in the patient *(passo)* in which it necessarily has some end.

26. The answer to this can be that the agent determines matter by its action, not by the one it has in the instant of generation, but by the one it had immediately before that instant. This answer coincides with the view which holds that the dispositions preceding immediately before leave the potency of matter determined, even though they leave nothing real in it. [But] this cannot be understood by any means about an intrinsic and positive determination on account of the argument given, that the capacity of matter is universal and indifferent of itself. Therefore, [matter] cannot be intrinsically limited unless something be added to it or it be changed in itself somehow. But nothing of this sort happens to it. Moreover, the relation to preceding dispositions is only a sort of conceptual relation or extrinsic determination.

This is confirmed [thus]: For, if preceding dispositions determine matter, [they determine it] either efficiently or formally. For those accidents can have no other kind of causality in matter. For, although by comparison with form they may be said to concur materially, nevertheless, with respect to matter [they do not do so] in any way, because they are not compared to it as potency, but as act.

Therefore, they can determine it only formally or efficiently. But [they can] not [determine it] formally, because the form which does not exist has no real formal effect. Hence, just as matter lost those accidental forms in that instant, it lost all their formal effects. Nor [can they determine it] efficiently both for the same reason, that what does not exist does not have effects, and also because matter receives nothing before form, as has been shown. Therefore, the potency of matter cannot be understood to be in any way intrinsically determined to this quantity, so that it could be the principle of individuation in this way.

This whole argument can be used against Cajetan's latter manner of speaking, because matter of itself does no more pre-contain this quantity than another; nor is it more the root of this [one rather] than of another. I ask, therefore, what determines it, so that in the instant of generation it may pre-contain more this quantity than another or be root of this [one] rather than of another; and the whole argument is reproduced.

This is effective in the same way against the other way of interpreting designated matter, [that is], that matter is disposed by preceding dispositions—for about the [dispositions] that follow enough has already been said in the first argument and in the arguments given against Capreolus' view. For those dispositions leave nothing in matter, since, as it is supposed, they are wholly corrupted. Therefore, they cannot leave it [i.e. matter] intrinsically and positively disposed, as is convincingly shown by the arguments given; for it makes no difference whether you say "disposed" or "determined," since these words stand for the same thing.

27. Moreover, I always say "intrinsically and positively," because negatively, in virtue of preceding dispositions, matter is left without incompatibility to the introduction of this form, which is rather to remain indifferent than determined. On the other hand, extrinsically, [matter] can be said to be here and now, naturally determined to receive this form, because, perhaps with a certain natural consequence this agent here and now, with respect to this subject, is determined to the introduction of this form immediately after this alteration in the natural order. But, in truth, this is rather a determination of the agent than of matter, and thus, this determination cannot cause matter to be the intrinsic principle of individuation, since [this determination] is an extrinsic principle from the part of the agent. And especially so also because, according to this mode of determination, the agent is understood as determined to the introduction of this form before [it is determined to the introduction of] this quantity and other dispositions. For it induces this form by itself, but this quantity and the dispositions as results of this form, according to the view under discussion.

Hence, finally, a general argument can be given, because matter is not disposed or determined primarily by itself, except to this form and on account of this form, and because of it, it receives these accidents. Thus, in itself and in the order of nature, form cannot be "a this" on account of these accidents, or on account of a relation to them, and consequently, neither [can it be "a this"] on account of matter designated by a relation to some accidents. Therefore, designated matter, interpreted this way, cannot be the principle of individuation.

Third Way of Interpreting the Same View Concerning Designated Matter

28. The third interpretation is that we can speak about the principle of individuation in two ways: First in itself, that is, insofar as it is truly the principle constituting the individual such as it is in reality, and [insofar as] it is the root or foundation from which the individual difference is taken. Second, we can speak of the principle of individuation with respect to the production or multiplication of individuals, which is to ask what the principle and root is whereby substantial individuals are multiplied, or why this individual is produced rather than another, that is, why it is produced distinct from the rest. On the other hand, in either case, it may be inquired [1] what the principle of individuation is by itself and in itself, or only [2] what the principle is whereby one individual is distinguished from another with respect to us, or [3] only what the occasion of such distinction is.

First, therefore, speaking about the principle constituting the individual in reality, and from which the individual contractive difference of the species and constitutive of the individual is truly taken, this opinion denies that matter designated by quantity is the principle of individuation, because the arguments given seem to conclude this.

29. Second, this opinion states that matter is the principle and root of the multiplication of individuals in material substances. The proof of this is that [matter] is the origin of generation and corruption whereby the multiplication of individuals is accomplished. Again, because [what is] composed of such matter is corruptible by reason of it, and, from it, it has that it cannot be preserved forever; and thus, the multiplication of individuals is required for the preservation of the species. Therefore, matter is the root of this multiplication.

It can also be added that this root is matter affected by quantity, because matter without quantity would not be capable of physical alteration and change owing to various and contrary dispositions, from which this variety and multiplication of individuals is born.

This function, however, does not belong to matter as designated and determined to a certain form or quantity, but absolutely in itself, because hitherto we have not discussed the root of this individual in particular, but absolutely the root of the multiplication of individuals within the same species. And matter is not the root of this multiplication absolutely insofar as it is determined to one form or quantity, but rather, insofar as it is determinable to many.

[But] you will say: In this way too matter will be said to be root of multiplication of the species in substances subject to generation and corruption. For, indeed, they can be multiplied from the same matter, because it [i.e. matter] has a capacity for all forms, and [it is] in itself indifferent to them and to their various dispositions.

The answer to this is that the case (*rationem*) is not similar. For, although that property of matter may be necessary for the multiplication aforementioned, nevertheless, properly [speaking], it is not the first root of that variety. [And this] both because, [1] since all that matter is of one species and its parts or portions are distinguished in themselves only numerically, that [matter], insofar as it exists of itself, is contained in numerically distinct forms; and also because [2] the specific distinction is [found] by itself in things, and, thus, it in the end comes from form, which by itself provides the species. Thus, this distinction is without doubt found in material and in immaterial, corruptible and incorruptible [things], [something] which is not the case with the numerical distinction, nor does it seem so necessary.

30. Third, this opinion states that matter, designated by quantity, is the principle and root, or at least the occasion, of the production of this individual as distinct from the rest. This is explained because this individual can be compared either to the remaining existing individuals or to other possible [ones] which can be produced from the same matter, even by the same agent. In the first way, the first and sufficient reason why this individual is produced as distinct from the rest is that it is produced from numerically diverse matter, because, since the numerically same form could not be in numerically diverse, whole matters, [therefore], for the very reason that matter is numerically diverse, it is necessary that form at least be numerically diverse. Hence, it is not necessary for this distinction that other dispositions or another designation of matter be added, because [for this] is sufficient the numerical distinction of matter in itself, or [of matter] with its quantity, which, nevertheless, is not sufficient for this matter to be the root of the distinction of this individual from the rest that do not exist or that are made or can be made from the same matter. Hence, some say that Aristotle did not point out the principle of individuation whereby the individual is distinguished from all [those individuals] that do not exist, since these are sufficiently

distinguished by contradiction alone, but that he pointed out only a principle which distinguishes in the aforementioned way one individual from other existing [individuals]. This was taught by Fonseca in [*Commentary on Metaphysics*], Bk. V, Ch. 6, q.4, sect. 4.[52] And he took it from Hervaeus, *Quodlibet* V, q.9,[53] and Cajetan, [in his commentary to Thomas'] *On Being and Essence,* Ch. 2, q.5.[54]

It must be added, moreover, that by matter, considered in the aforementioned way, the individual is not only distinguished from other existing [individuals], but also from all other possible [individuals] whatever, even non-existing [ones], which can be generated from other numerically distinct matters. [This is so] especially in those [individuals] whose forms are educed from matter, because it is very likely that the numerically same form cannot simultaneously, or even successively, be educed from numerically diverse matters. However, in individuals that can be generated from the numerically same matter, there is no place for a distinction between one existing individual and another existing [individual], because many individuals, having the numerically same matter, cannot exist simultaneously, and thus, such a distinction is always between an existing thing and a non-existing [one].

31. Moreover, although this contradictory opposition is argument enough for the distinction of such individuals, nevertheless, one can still investigate the principle and root [1] why they are so distinguished, one as existing [and] the other as not existing, or [2] why numerically this form is introduced in this matter rather than another that could be made. For the cause of this cannot be found in prime matter alone, since [prime matter] is successively the same in each individual, which is also true perhaps of the quantity cotemporal (*coaeva*) with the same matter. Therefore, other dispositions and circumstances of the action must be added, namely, that this action takes place from this subject thus prepared and disposed at this time by this agent. For it is the case that, although prime or remote matter be the same, nevertheless, from it this individual is made distinct from all others that are made or could be made from it, since the production takes place under diverse dispositions and circumstances. This is confirmed and explained [thus]: Fire, for example, has of itself the potential to produce many forms similar to itself in species and distinct in number, and nevertheless, here and now it introduces numerically this form rather than others in this matter. And this determination cannot come [1] from fire itself, since [fire] is a natural agent and of itself equally potential to the introduction of any form; nor can it come [2] from the form itself to be educed, because that does not yet exist and does not have the means to determine the power of the agent; nor does it come [3] from remote mat-

ter, because that is also equally indifferent of itself. Therefore, it comes either from [4] the dispositions, if those remain in matter, or from [5] the natural order of acting here and now, with these circumstances, for no other natural cause can be easily thought. For, what some think, that this is to be referred to [6] the divine will, although true in relation to the effects which come immediately from God himself, nevertheless, does not seem philosophical when attributed to all natural causes. And in theology it creates a special difficulty, owing to the determination of free acts and particularly of the bad [ones], which we shall discuss when treating God's cooperation (*concursu*) with secondary causes. Therefore, in this way, matter designated and affected by these circumstances is the principle or occasion of such an individuation, because neither matter without circumstances, as has been said, nor circumstances without matter, is sufficient. For, if this [i.e. matter designated and affected by these circumstances] is diverse, its effect will also be diverse.

32. [But] you will say: Therefore, the same matter will be the intrinsic principle constitutive of the individual in its being; for just as a thing is related to [its] production, so is it related to [its] being.

This is answered by denying the consequence, both because [1] it is one thing for this thing to be a particular individual but another thing for this individual rather than another [one] to be produced now, and thus, these can come from diverse roots; and also because [2], according to this interpretation, designated matter is not so much the principle of individuation as the occasion for inducing this form rather than another into a subject. This form, however, is not this because it is produced in this subject, at this time and by this agent. For these things are accidental to it [i.e. the form] in itself and it could be made numerically the same by God without these circumstances — and speaking of dispositions, they are the ones that are ordered to a particular form rather than the contrary. Therefore, matter, designated in the stated way can only be the occasion why this form is produced by a natural agent in the natural order, whereby the power of the natural agent was determined to cause such an effect rather than another in a particular subject attached to and affected by particular circumstances.

33. Fourth, this opinion adds that matter, designated by sensible quantity, is called "principle of individuation" in relation to us, because by it we know the distinction of material individuals among themselves. Thus, St. Thomas, in *Opuscle 32, On the Nature of Matter and Indeterminate Dimensions,* Ch. 3, says, "the substantial individual is made from this prime matter and this form, but it is not shown to be here and now without determinate dimensions; and thus," he says, "matter under fixed dimensions is called a cause of individuation,

not because dimensions cause the individual, since an accident does not cause its subject, but because by fixed dimensions the individual is shown to be here and now, as by an inseparable sign proper to the individual."[55] And he points out the same in *Opuscle* 29, *On the Principle of Individuation*.[56] Hence, when in other places St. Thomas says that the individual adds accidents to the specific nature, as in [*Quodlibet*] I, q.3, and *Quodlibet* II, a.4 and *On Truth*, q.2, a.6, *ad* 1, and in other places cited above, it seems that this is to be interpreted in terms of our knowledge.[57] For that [i.e. the accident] is the sign whereby we distinguish *a posteriori* one individual from another, not, however, that whereby the individual is distinguished in itself. St. Thomas himself, in other places and opuscles cited, seems to have explained and even to have proven [this] with an excellent argument, namely, "that accidents do not cause their subject," especially when St. Thomas himself, in [*Summa theologiae*] I, q.29, a.1, and *On the Power*, q.9, a.1, *ad* 8, says that substance is individuated by itself and by its proper principles, while accidents are individuated by substance.[58] Therefore, since in other places he posits accidents, or the relation to accidents, among those [things] that individuate substance, it is necessary to explain [this] either in terms of our knowledge or in terms of the occasion that they offer for the production of a particular individual substance, as it has been stated. Moreover, this is attributed to matter by reason of quantity rather than by reason of quality, because even the numerical distinction of qualities themselves is known to us primarily through quantity. For, if two images are very similar to each other, we do not distinguish them except by numbering them in quantitatively diverse subjects. And in the same sense it seems it must be understood that quantities themselves are numerically distinguished by place. For, that is true with respect to us, since we sensibly distinguish and number them because we perceive them in diverse places. Nevertheless, this is not true in itself, since, rather, quantities occupy diverse places because they are distinct in themselves. Therefore, [this is so] only because quantity is by its nature such that it constitutes a part outside a part in a body outside a body with respect to place, and [because] we lack a more suitable principle to distinguish material individuals with respect to us.

Solution to the Question

34. This whole opinion is indeed probable in itself and it was acceptable to me once. I am afraid, however, that it does not express satisfactorily the thought of Aristotle and St. Thomas, not only because [1] otherwise they would have given us a very deficient and exceedingly equivocal principle of individuation, if having omitted what is

truly and in itself the constitutive principle of the individual, they
had given us only either the *a posteriori* signs or the occasions of distinguishing or producing individuals; but especially because [2] they
seem to have concluded from this principle that [things] separate
from matter are not many individuals since they do not have this
kind of principle of individuation. Moreover, many and learned
men find hard to believe what was expressed by that view concerning the determination of agents to particular effects and forms from
matter with the circumstances of the action, because if the issue is
considered carefully, all [circumstances] are reduced to the circumstance of time, which seems too extrinsic in order for this determination to come from it. But I shall discuss in more detail this last point
in the following Section.[59]

Concerning the other [matter] relating to the thought of Aristotle
and St. Thomas, insofar as St. Thomas is concerned, it is evident
that the interpretation is based on other of his writings and words,
which cannot be reconciled in any other way. Insofar as Aristotle is
concerned, he does not seem to have ever explicitly and metaphysically investigated and explained this principle,[60] but [rather] to have
taught only from sensible [things, and] in a physical way, that one
material individual is distinguished from another. However, what
the mentioned authors concluded from this, [namely], that in immaterial substances there is no multiplication of individuals within the
same species, this can have at most a probable force, namely, that
we do not have the reasons and principles to distinguish numerically
distinct spiritual substances that we have for material [ones]. Indeed, many extend this also to incorruptible material substances, in
which too we do not have as many principles in order to know or to
posit a numerical distinction as we have in corruptible substances, to
which apply especially everything said. Finally, when Aristotle says,
in *On the Heavens* I,[61] that there can be no other world than this one
because all matter is in this one, it seems certain that he had in mind
either [1] that God created the world from matter but that he could
not have created matter itself, or [2] that God acted from a necessity
of nature and, thus, that he could not have created more matter than
he created, or, indeed, [3] that God was so determined in his way of
acting that he could not have fashioned any integral and material
substance in time from nothing, as we shall see in the course of this
work. And so, from that statement, it can only be gathered for the
moment that, according to Aristotle's thought, material substances
are not multiplied except through matter. Whatever these authors
may think, however, it is clear that this view, so stated, does not give
us the proper and internal principle of individual difference even in
material things. For the arguments given against other interpreta-

tions of this view plainly conclude that designated matter cannot be a principle of this sort.

NOTES

[1] In Sects. III to VI, Suárez takes up a different issue from those discussed in Sect. I (whether everything that exists is individual) and Sect. II (what the individual adds to the common nature); he seeks to identify the principle of individuation. In Sect. III in particular he discusses and rejects one of the most widespread views on the subject, Thomas' doctrine that it is matter designated by quantity that individuates. Like most other sections of this Disputation, the present one is structured after the fashion of a medieval question, although it is significantly different from the traditional structure in some respects. In the first place, Suárez adds an explanatory part (§ 2) in which he repeats much of what he had stated in Sect. II, § 7, clarifying the nature of the problem at hand and distinguishing it from the problem discussed in Sect. II. This provides a justification (1) for the separate consideration of each of these problems and (2) for the exclusion from consideration of the views of Scotus and Ockham in the problem discussed in Sections III-VI. In §§ 3 and 4 (the *Pro* of the question) he presents what was generally regarded as the view of Thomas and Aristotle and the textual and rational bases behind it. In § 4 in particular, he gives three arguments used generally in support of this view. They are rejected in §§ 5-7, the *Contra*. These arguments, however, do not prove, according to Suárez, that the view cannot be maintained; they only prove that the view is not demonstrable by reason (§ 8). For that further analysis of the notion of "designated matter" is necessary. In §§ 9-33 he provides such an analysis. The discussion is divided into three parts, according to the three traditional ways of interpretating this notion. The first is presented in § 9 and rejected with arguments in §§ 10-17. The second is presented in §§ 18 and 19, where two varieties of the second interpretation are given, and rejected in §§ 20-27. The third is presented and rejected in §§ 28-33. Finally, § 34, entitled "Solution to the Question," summarizes the main reasons why the view that holds designated matter as the principle of individuation is untenable. In particular it rejects the ascription of this view to Thomas and Aristotle by rejecting the textual support for it given at the beginning of the Section, in § 3.

[2] Sect. II, § 7.

[3] Dist. 3, instead. *Ed. Vaticana,* vol. VII, pp. 480 ff.

[4] Question 5. *Ed. cit.,* col. 381D.

[5] The point is not that they agree on this matter. It is clear they do not think they do. The point is rather that, in spite of what they think, their views come down to the same thing, according to Suárez.

[6] Scholastics generally adhered to this principle. Thomas explains it in *On Being and Essence,* Ch. 2, § 9 (Maurer's trans.): "A genus is not matter, but it is taken from matter as designating the whole; and a difference is not form, but it is taken from form as designating the whole....The concept 'animal' signifies the nature of a being without the determination of its special form, containing only what is material in it with respect to its ultimate perfection. The concept of the difference 'rational,' on the other hand, contains the determination of the special form."

[7] Here begins the discussion of the matter of this Section properly speaking.

[8] *Summa theologiae,* a.2 instead of a.3, *ed. cit.,* vol. I, pp. 19a, 342b, and vol. V, p. 140a. *In quartum...,* p. 292b. *De principio individuationis,* ed. R. M. Spiazzi in *Opuscula philosophica* (Turin-Rome: Marietti, 1954), § 428, p. 151.

[9] *Q. 5 In de ente...,* § 37, pp. 53 ff.

[10] Q.1, a.1, *secunda conclusio. Ed. cit.,* vol. III, pp. 200b-202b.

[11] *Ed. cit.,* pp. 166b-170a. See also, q.35, pp. 170a-171a.

[12] Com. IV. *Ed. cit.,* vol. XIII, pp. 65b-66a.

[13] 1016b32; Junctas, vol. VIII, com. 12, fol. 114rb.

[14] 1034a5 ff; Junctas, vol. VIII, fol. 177vb.

[15] 1035b30: Junctas, vol. VIII, com. 35, fol. 185va.

[16] 1074a33: Junctas, vol. VIII, fol. 333rb.

[17] 278a26: Junctas, vol. V, com. 95, fol. 63va.

[18] The point made here is quite important, for it shows that Suárez distinguished quite clearly between what contemporary writers call "the problem of diversity" and "the problem of individuation." The problem of diversity or "multiplication," as Suárez calls it here, becomes important when the possibility or actuality of many individuals within a species is taken into consideration. But the problem of individuation, i.e. of what accounts for an individual's individuality, is present even if the possibility of multiplication is disregarded. See Introduction.

[19] *Ed. cit.,* vol. XIII, p. 359.

[20] That is, not only the truth of what is being said, but also whether it follows from what it is claimed it follows.

[21] The point is that matter is not communicable, i.e., cannot inform a subject in the way forms do.

[22] The individual actually perfects the superior, that is, it completes its perfection because it is the individual that is real.

[23] Scholastics regarded many positions as defensible although not demonstrable (conclusive, convincing). These were positions for which there was some evidence (usually evidence from authority) but not sufficient evidence (demonstrative) to decide the matter conclusively. The non-eternity of the world was, according to Thomas, for example, one such view — it could be maintained on the basis of revelation but outside of faith there was no demonstrative evidence in its support. Consequently, although the non-eternity of the world was more probable than the contrary position, and therefore defensible, it could not be said to be demonstrable, and the contrary view could very well be held without fear of contradiction.

[24] This is an odd expression. The point being made seems to be that "matter" is common to many "matters," that is, "individuals of matter," and not to just "material individuals," that is, composites of matter and form. P. Spade called my attention to this point.

[25] *Ed. cit.,* vol. III, pp. 205a-206b, and 226b ff.

[26] See n. 12 above.

[27] *Ed. cit.,* pp. 168a-170a. There is no mention of *"materia signata"* in the text, but Soncinas does speak of matter and quantity as the principle of individuation.

[28] *Quaestiones disputatae. De veritate* in *Opera omnia,* vol. XIV (Paris: Vivès, 1875), p. 364a.

[29] *Quaestiones disputatae. De malo,* in *Opera Omnia,* vol. XIII (Paris: Vivès, 1875), p. 571a.

[30] *Ed. cit.,* p. 143.

[31] 998b20; Junctas, vol. VIII, fol. 49va. The text in the English translation is very different from the Latin.

[32] Ch. 1, 1053a20; Junctas, vol. VIII, fol. 253ra. The English translation is very different from the Latin.

[33] 1020a7; Junctas, vol. VIII, com. 18, fol. 124vb.

[34] 208b1 ff; Junctas, vol. IV, com. 68, fol. 117rb-va. Both the Latin of Junctas and the English translation differ substantially from Suárez text.

35 For Suárez these are equivalent in reality if not conceptually. Transcendental unity is singular unity conceived as common to all actual beings and therefore to all categories; singular unity is transcendental unity conceived as the unity of the individual; real unity is transcendental and singular unity conceived as having some ontological status.

36 Namely, that the accidents are intrinsically included in the principle of individuation of substance.

37 *Ed. cit.*, vol. I, p. 488b.

38 Vol. III, Part III, Disp. LII, Sect. III. Ed's note.

39 Vol. II, Part III, Disp. XLVIII, Sect. V. Ed's note.

40 See Sect. III, n. 79.

41 Ch. 6, 1016b32; Junctas, vol. VIII, com. 12, fol. 114va.

42 See n.9 above.

43 *In duodecim libros metaphysices* (Lyon: Junctas, 1568), p. 755b.

44 *Quodlibeta*, ed. P. D. de Coninck (Louvain: H. Nempaei, 1646; rep. Frankfurt/Main: Minerva, 1966), pp. 24a-25a. The text is from d.4, q.11; there are no articles.

45 *Pars prima...*, vol. IV, p. 329a, com. IX.

46 *Ibidem.*

47 Perhaps Ch. 7; 1057b1 ff.

48 Q.15. *Ed. cit.*, p. 756b.

49 Sect. 3. *Ed. cit.*, col. 376C-F.

50 Berton reads *dispositionem*, which although it makes some sense, since Suárez is rejecting all theories of disposition, does not make as much sense as *expositionem*, interpretation, the reading chosen by other editions.

51 The instant in which the substance is generated. Being an accident it must be corrupted at the instant of generation of substance, since the matter of a substance has no accidents apart from the accidents of the substance, and those are subsequent to the substance.

52 *Ed. cit.*, col. 379D.

53 Rather *Quod.* III, q.9. *Ed. cit.*, fols. 81vb. ff.

54 *Ed. cit.*, § 36, p. 52.

55 *De natura materiae et dimensionibus interminatis*, Ch. 3, ed. R. M. Spiazzi, in *Opuscula philosophica* (Turin/Rome: Marietti, 1954), § 378, p. 134.

56 See n.8 above.

57 *Summa theologiae*, a.3, *ed. cit.*, vol. I, p. 19b. *Quaestiones quodlibetales*, in *Opera omnia*, vol. XV (Paris: Vivès, 1875), p. 382b. *De veritate*, Vivès, vol. XIV, p. 364a.

58 *Summa theologiae*, *ed. cit.*, vol. I, p. 204a. *Quaestiones disputatae. De potentia*, in *Opera omnia*, vol. XIII (Paris: Vivès, 1875), p. 260a.

59 Sect. IV. Not much is said about this matter there.

60 The point is well taken by Suárez. The problem of individuation was never identified and separately discussed by Aristotle or, for that matter, by any of the Ancients. This problem is, therefore, like many other philosophical issues inherited by the modern world, of medieval origin.

61 See n.17 above.

SECTION IV

WHETHER THE SUBSTANTIAL FORM IS THE PRINCIPLE OF
INDIVIDUATION OF MATERIAL SUBSTANCES[1]

1. There is another important view on this matter: The internal principle of individuation is the substantial form. This is usually attributed to Durandus, *On II [of the Sentences]*, dist. 3, q.2,[2] although he does not exactly affirm it, as I shall say later. Averroes, however, seems to have taught it in [his commentary to Aristotle's] *On the Soul* I, Ch. 7, and Bk. II, at the beginning, and in comments 7, 8 and 9, and 60,[3] and in [the commentary to] *Physics* III, comment 60, and Bk. IV, comment 38;[4] Avicenna is also cited, *Book of Nature* VI, Part I, as saying that form "gives numerical unity to the subject."[5] Zimara holds it, Theorem 97,[6] and [so does] Sebastian, Bishop of Osma, *On the Soul* II, Ch. 1.[7] Moreover, Aristotle favors it in the same place, when he says that "form is what constitutes 'this something.' "[8] And the primary basis of this view is to be taken from this text of Aristotle, for the principle of individuation must be what [1] intrinsically constitutes[9] this substance and [2] is most proper to it. Therefore, by reason of the former property [1], it must be something substantial; for accidents, as it has been often said, do not constitute substance or this substance, for this substance, even [insofar] as it is "a this," is a being by itself and substantial. Moreover, by reason of the latter property [2], this principle cannot be matter, but form, because this matter is not most proper to this individual, since it could be under other forms. Therefore, form is the principle of individuation.

2. Whence, I argue, secondly, that the principle of unity and entity is the same. For this reason St. Thomas said in the single question [in the *Commentary on Aristotle's*] *On the Soul,* a.1, *ad* 2, that "every single [thing] has being and individuation from the same [thing]."[10] But every single thing properly has being from form; therefore, [it] too [has] individual unity [from it]. The major is evident, because unity is an attribute that follows entity, and adds to it nothing but negation; therefore, it cannot have another positive and real principle, except what is a principle of the entity itself.

3. But someone will object against this view and argument that, although it may rightly prove that form contributes to unity, nevertheless, [it does] not [prove] that it [i.e. form] alone is the principle of individuation. For matter also is an intrinsic principle constituting the entity of a thing, and thus, it too will be a principle of individuation, if not alone, at least [together] with form.[11]

[To this] it could be answered according to Durandus' view, *On IV* [*of the Sentences*], dist. 44, q.1,[12] that form not only has the power to individuate the composite, but also [to individuate] matter itself, because form gives being not only to the composite, but also to matter. Hence, it follows, — he says —, that it [i.e. matter] is numerically the same because matter is joined to the numerically same form.[13]

But this view of Durandus is false, and is rejected with reason by other theologians, as I showed in [my commentary to Thomas' *Summa theologiae*], vol. II, Part III, Disp. XLIV, Sect. II.[14] For one and numerically the same matter, which was in [what has been] corrupted, remains in [what has been] generated, otherwise the subject in which generation takes place would not be numerically the same. Again, because it is impossible either that the thing which was numerically distinct from another before become that [thing] afterwards, that is, numerically the same with it in an indivisible way, or that a thing which was one numerically become afterwards numerically another distinct in its whole [entity]. Therefore, the matter that is numerically one under the form of food cannot be made numerically another by the fact that it begins to be under the form of soul. And the matters of Peter and Paul, which are numerically distinct, will not be made numerically one even if they should be under the form of Peter and Paul successively. Finally, otherwise, the numerically same matter, once annihilated, would be restored by the mere union of another matter to the same form. And we speak of true unity according to real and physical entity and not only according to appearance or the common way of speaking, in which way a thing that is in continuous flux and changes only gradually is usually called one. For thus, even if the change were made in the form, such unity can be preserved, as it is clear in a river, or in a tree, or in a brute.

4. Therefore, it can be answered in another manner that,[15] indeed, it is true that form and matter are the adequate intrinsic cause of the individual unity of a material substance, as the argument concludes. Nevertheless, if these two are compared to each other, [it is true] that the principal cause of this unity is form, and in this sense it [i.e. form] is especially said to be the principle of individuation. For although matter is also necessary for the notion, that is, the specific unity, since the notion of man or humanity as such cannot be constituted without matter, and the same is true concerning the generic notion of animal, of living being, etc., nonetheless, the specific notion is said to be taken absolutely from form. [This is so] because it [i.e. form] confers the last complement, and presupposes only matter as something potential and indifferent. Therefore, for the same reason, it [i.e. form] will be said [to be] the principle of individuation, because it confers the last substantial complement to the individual, although it presupposes matter as potential of itself and indifferent. For this reason Aristotle said above, and in *Physics* I, Ch. 7, text 69,[16] that "form constitutes 'this something.' " And since, as we said above, a thing is constituted by the same [thing] by which it is distinguished, the same form that constitutes this something distinguishes it from others, since "act is what distinguishes," *Metaphysics* VII, Ch. 13, text 49.[17] Therefore, it is form that completes the notion of an individual.

The common manner of thinking and speaking confirms this, for if to Peter's soul, for example, there should be united a body composed of matter distinct from the body which it first had, although the composite would not be in all its parts the same[18] it was before, nevertheless, strictly *(simpliciter)* speaking, the individual is said to be the same by reason of the same soul. And yet, on the contrary, if a numerically distinct soul were united to a body composed of the same matter it will not be judged to be the same individual strictly *(simpliciter)*, but a distinct [one]. Therefore, this is a sign [of the fact] that individuation is taken primarily from form.

5. But it is still objected against this view and the argument given[19] that, although form as such confers specific being, nevertheless, it does not confer individual and numerical being except [insofar] as it is "a this." Therefore, not form as such, but that through which form itself is "a this" is the principle of individuation. But [form] is "a this" by reason of matter; therefore, matter is rather the first root of individuation. The minor[20] is proven, first, because form is not by itself "a this;" otherwise the same could be said concerning any entity, nor would it be necessary to ask for another principle of individuation. Therefore, [form] is "a this" through matter, for no other root [of individuation] can be thought. Second, [the minor is proven] because

form has all its being in relation to matter, and therefore, its individuation. Therefore, matter is the principle of individuation of form,
and consequently, of the whole composite. Third, (the minor is pro-
ven] because forms are numerically multiplied insofar as they are
received in diverse matters, and thus, separate forms are not numerically multiplied, since they are not received in matter. Therefore,
[forms] are individuated also by the relation to matter. Therefore,
the last determination *(resolutio)* of this individuation takes effect in
matter; for this form is "a this" because it is received in a particular
matter. Therefore, the first root of individuation is matter.

6. These objections are the bases of the opinion discussed in the preceding Section,[21] which rather explain and confirm the view we are
discussing now, for almost all can be twisted and made to refer to the
same [subject] matter.[22] Accordingly, I grant that form is not the
principle of individuation of the composite according to its specific
notion as is evident, but [rather] insofar as it is "a this." But this same
[thing] must be said concerning matter, because matter also has a
specific and common notion according to which it is not sufficient for
the constitution of the individual. Therefore, if [matter] constitutes
[the individual], it does [so] insofar as it is "a this." Therefore, I will
ask in return whence it is "a this." Some answer: Because God wished to create this [matter] rather than another. But this is irrelevant,
for here we do not inquire about the extrinsic, but about the intrinsic
principle of individuation. Otherwise, one could also say that this
soul is "a this" because God wished to infuse this [one] rather than
another, or that this form is "a this" because God determined his cooperation *(concursum)* to it, something quite probable, as we shall say
in the following Section.[23]

Others answer that this matter is "a this" by reason of this quantity. But this is false and does not evade the difficulty. The first,
[namely, that it is false], is clear from what was said above, because,
since this matter is absolutely *(simpliciter)* presupposed by this quantity, [matter] cannot be individuated by it. Again, because the arguments given above completely prove that nothing substantial can be
individuated by an accident added to it. For this matter too is something one by itself, constituted under the specific notion of matter,
which it contracts by itself. Indeed, matter and this matter are not
distinguished *ex natura rei,* as it was shown above [to be the case] concerning any individual with respect to the common notion. Therefore, this matter cannot be intrinsically individuated by quantity,
which is a thing distinct from it, nor [can it be individuated] by the
relation to it, since it is "this quantity" which expresses a relation to
"this matter" rather than the reverse.

The second, [namely, that it does not eliminate the difficulty], is clear concerning quantity, because about it too I may ask whence it is "a this," since it is not such from its specific notion. And, since it is impossible to proceed to infinity or to fall into a vicious and useless circle, one will stop in some thing which is "a this" by itself. Therefore, this must be attributed to substance rather than to accident, since it [i.e. substance] is a prior and more absolute entity. Or, if it is to be admitted that two incomplete beings are individuated by their mutual relationship to each other, according to diverse kinds of causes, it will be said of matter and substantial form with respect to one another rather than with [respect to] any accident, because they are more connected by themselves and [more] related to each other. Therefore, all the arguments given could conclude the same concerning matter as they assert concerning form, for there is between them [i.e. form and matter] a certain equality with respect to this. And, on the one hand, matter surpasses form only in the fact that it is a certain occasion of producing diverse *(varias)* and individual forms, as was stated above, while form surpasses matter.in the fact that it principally constitutes the individual, and that it is more proper to it, and that matter exists because of form rather than the reverse, as it is said in *Physics* II, Ch. 9, text 91.²⁴ Therefore, having weighted all [these things one must conclude that] form is more than anything else the principle of individuation.

Solution to the Question

7. Therefore, this view, as explained by us, is quite defensible, and comes very close to the truth. Strictly *(simpliciter)*, however, it must be said that form alone is not the full and adequate principle of individuation of material things, if we speak of their whole entity, although it may be the principal one, and thus, according to the formal manner of speaking, it is sometimes judged sufficient for the denomination of the same individual. All these [things] will be explained and proven extensively in Section VI.

NOTES

¹ This question is organized in three parts. The first must be considered the *Pro;* it supports the view that form is the principle of individuation. It includes §§ 1 and 2. In § 1 the arguments are based primarily on the authority of Aristotle and his commentators. In § 2 the arguments are supported by reference to Thomas. The *Contra* and the answer to the objections it presents have been put together by Suárez in the same part of the question. There are two objections to the view (first paragraph of § 3 and § 5) which are followed respectively by their answers (second paragraph of § 3 and § 6). The second and third paragraphs of § 3 are respectively a tentative answer to the first objection based on Durandus' opinion and its counter-objection. The last part of the question consists in a short paragraph, § 7, in which Suárez summarizes and clarifies his view with respect to this opinion. It may properly be regarded as the *Solutio.*

² *Ed. cit.,* vol. I, fols. 136 va-137rb.

³ Junctas, Suppl. II, text 90, fol. 46r: *"Omne enim quod est, est unum; et continuum non est per suam materiam, sed per suam formam;"* and Bk. II, Ch. 1, text 2, fol. 49r: *"Secundus autem est forma, per quam individuum fit hoc."* Text 7, fol. 51v; text 8, fol. 52v and 53r; text 9, fol. 53v; text 60, fol. 81r.

⁴ Junctas, vol. IV, text 60, fol. 114; text 38, fol. 138va.

⁵ *De anima, qui sextus naturalium Avicennae dicitur,* Ch. 1, in *Avicennae perhypatetici philosophi ac medicorum facile primi opera,* ed. C. Fabrio (Venice, 1508; rep. Frankfurt: Minerva, 1961), fol. 1vb and elsewhere. There is nothing as clear as Suárez says.

⁶ *Theoremata seu memorabilium propositionum limitationes* (Venice: Junctas, 1563), fol. 193 ra-b.

⁷ Not found. I owe the identification of the author to James Robb.

⁸ *On the Soul* II, Ch. 1, 412a6; Junctas, Suppl. II, fol. 49r: *"...aliud formam et speciem, ex qua demum dicitur hoc aliquid."*

⁹ *Constituo,* see Glossary. In this particular passage Suárez seems to have in mind senses two and three listed in the Glossary: Accidents are said not to constitute substance because they can neither establish nor be intrinsic parts of it. The principle of individuation, on the other hand, constitutes the substance in both senses specified. Suárez discusses the term *'constituo'* in Bk. VII of *The Holy Mystery of the Trinity,* where he deals with the constitution of the divine persons. In Ch. 3, § 9 he states that a *constitutio* can be conceptual if it depends on the way we think about something, or real if it refers to the actual components of a thing.

¹⁰ *Quaestiones disputatae. De anima,* q.1, *ad* 1 instead of *ad* 2, in *Quaestiones de anima,* ed. James H. Robb (Toronto: Pontifical Institute of Mediaeval Studies, 1968), p. 61.

¹¹ Up to this point Suárez has presented the opinion which holds that substantial form is the principle of individuation in material substances. He has also given authoritative and rational substantiation for this view. Now he presents the contrary position, in the *Contra,* that substantial form is no such principle. The view is presented in the form of a brief objection.

¹² *Ed. cit.,* vol. II, fol. 395va.

¹³ Durandus' argument is used to answer the objection against the view that matter is the principle of individuation in material substances. However, Suárez finds the argument unacceptable, because it rests on the view that form individuates matter, while Suárez holds (see Sect. VI) that matter, just as form, is individuated by its own entity. He proceeds, then, to argue against Durandus first by authority, referring to texts he cited elsewhere, and then by reason, on the bases of three distinct arguments. The arguments are contained in the paragraph that follows.

¹⁴ *Ed. cit.,* pp. 746b ff.

¹⁵ At this point Suárez gives his own arguments against the first objection raised against the view that substantial form is the principle of individuation in material substances. He argues first in terms of reason, then on the basis of Aristotle's authority, and finally on the basis of reason again. The last argument is based on the "common way of thinking and speaking." Although Suárez does not put much stock on ordinary language to prove philosophical or theological points, he is willing to use arguments based on usage as confirmation that the points made are reasonable. This is a common practice in the *Disputations.* It clearly undermines the charge often made against scholastics by Renaissance humanists, and particularly against Suárez, that he had no regard for ordinary usage or common sense.

¹⁶ 191a9-12; Junctas, vol. IV, fol. 40va. Text 69 is by no means unambiguous.

¹⁷ Bk. 2, Ch. 13, 1039a9; Junctas, vol. VIII, Ch. 15, fol. 199ra: *"Actus enim dividit."*

¹⁸ Suárez raises the issue of identity or sameness not because he confuses it with the problem of individuation. He discusses the problem of identity in Disp. VII, Sect. III, § 2 (see Glossary, *identitas*). The issue is addressed here because it was raised by Durandus in his attempt to discredit the theory of formal individuation (see § 3 above). Suárez is aware, however, of the fact that individuality is a necessary condition of identity, as this text seems to imply, and thus of the close relation between the two notions.

¹⁹ At this point Suárez proceeds to give the second objection against the view that substantial form is the principle of individuation of material substances. This argument is accepted by those who hold that matter or matter designated by quantity is the principle of individuation of such beings. Although Suárez already discussed this view and its possible interpretations in detail in Sect. III of this Disputation, he refutes the view again in § 6.

²⁰ The minor is: "Form is 'a this' by reason of matter;" the major is: "That whereby form itself is 'a this' is the principle of individuation;" and the conclusion is: "Matter is the first root of individuation." "Form is 'a this' by reason of" and "that whereby form itself is a this" are regarded as equivalent here. Likewise with "principle of individuation" and "first root of individuation."

²¹ Sect. III.

²² At this point Suárez argues against the second objection to the view that substantial form is the principle of individuation of material substances. This is done in two parts: First he argues against the view that posits matter as principle of individuation and then against the view that makes quantity such a principle.

²³ Sect. V: Whether the Existence of the Singular Thing is the Principle of Individuation.

²⁴ 200b1; Junctas, vol. IV, fol. 84vb.

SECTION V

WHETHER THE EXISTENCE OF THE SINGULAR THING IS
THE PRINCIPLE OF INDIVIDUATION[1]

1. There is no lack of those who have affirmed so.[2] Scotus refers to their views in *On II [of the Sentences]*, dist. 3, q.3,[3] and Soncinas in *[Questions on] Metaphysics* VII, q.32,[4] and Henry points it out in *Quodlibet* II, q.8;[5] and the Carthusian attributes it to him and favors it in *On II [of the Sentences]*, dist. 3.[6] Fonseca, however, in *[Commentary on the Metaphysics]*, Bk. V, Ch. 6, q.2, sect. 2,[7] refers to Henry's *Quodlibet* V, q.8,[8] as denying that individuation is due to existence or to anything intrinsic, but only to the agent. But I have seen no one assert this, being improbable as it is by itself, for although the agent is an extrinsic cause of the individual, nevertheless, its effect is distinct from the agent itself. Moreover, [the agent] causes the individual and confers on it an individual nature; therefore, that whereby the nature is [made] individual is something intrinsic to the individual itself [even though it is caused by an extrinsic cause]. And so, Henry, in the same place, acknowledges explicitly that that whereby the individual is "a this" is something other than matter and other than the agent, which he explains as the notion or disposition of the supposit. Hence, he seems to feel that subsistence is the principle of individuation in all created substances, and so, in the first place where he made the distinction, he was speaking either about existence or about subsistence, and thus, it will be necessary to say something about each [of these here].

2. The opinion concerning existence is rejected by everybody as completely false and indefensible.[9] Moreover, one can proceed [to argue] against it in two ways: First, assuming that existence is distinct *ex natura rei* from the essence of the individual; second, according to the opinion which asserts that existence is nothing other than the actual entity of each thing.[10] In the latter way this view coincides in reality with the opinion which asserts that each thing is individuated by itself, and that it needs no other principle of individuation in addition to its entity. Hence, in fact this opinion does not deserve more censure than the one about which we shall speak later.[11] It can be censured only because it uses obscure and ambiguous terms, and because it attributes to existence rather than to essence the reason for individuation, even though this does not apply to existence except insofar as it is the same with essence.

If, however, one takes up the prior view,[12] it will be formally true indeed that each thing within the notion of an existent has some individual feature *(rationem)* from existence itself; just as "this white," with respect to the formal notion of white, is constituted by whiteness, although absolutely *(simpliciter)* "this white" is not constituted by whiteness because it is taken as subject. Hence, also in the [case] proposed, speaking materially — if I may say so — concerning the existing thing, that is, numerically this essence, the assertion that is individuated by the existence whereby it exists, if this [i.e. existence] is a thing distinct from it or a mode diverse *ex natura rei,* is indefensible.

3. First,[13] indeed, because essence remaining within the realm of essence is made individual, and the specific essence is contracted and determined in it. But the specific essence is not contracted by something distinct *ex natura rei* from itself, as was proven above; therefore, it is not contracted into the individual essence by existence. The major is evident, both [1] because man, for example, is common of itself to many individuals, whether they exist or not, and also [2] because Peter and Paul, as abstracting from actual existence, that is, as possibles, intrinsically include their individual natures *(rationes),* by which they are distinguished; and finally, [3] because specific, that is, essential, differences accrue to the species by a necessary connection, according to which propositions in which essential predicates are predicated are said to be perpetually true; [and] so, [likewise], its individual difference accrues to the individual. Hence, it is as necessary for Peter to be this man, as to be man, and it is as necessary for Peter to be placed under man, as [it is] for man [to be] under animal. Therefore, this contraction and subordination is not caused by actual existence, which comes contingently to the fully constituted and individuated essence.

4. Second, the argument from Cajetan given above is appropriate here, that a singular act presupposes a singular potency. This principle we said to be true in [the case of] an act and a potency distinct *ex natura rei,* because then potency is really subordinated to act *(supponitur actui)* in the order of nature, and is something *(quid)* one, distinct from its act, and one not in thought, but in reality itself, and thus it cannot happen that it have unity formally and intrinsically from its act. But essence and existence are compared in this way according to the aforementioned opinion. Therefore, by the same mode whereby essence has by itself the entity of essence distinct from existence and apt to be acted upon by it, so too does it have its unity and individuation. Otherwise it would be necessary to understand existence to be an act of the specific and universal nature, something quite absurd.

5. Third, because in existence itself there can be considered the common notion of human existence, for example, and the notion of "this existence" of Peter and Paul. Therefore, concerning existence itself, it remains to be asked what makes it "a this." For [it is] not "a this" from essence, since, according to this view, it is not assumed as individual, but as common. Nor [is it "a this"] from some accident, as is evident and sufficiently proven above. Wherefore, then? If you say that it [i.e. existence] is made "a this" by itself, why do you not say it with more reason concerning the essence, since [the essence] is both prior in the order of nature and also in perfection, and since it is in a way more absolute? For existence is the act of this essence. Hence, this existence will be "a this" rather because it actualizes this essence; just as in general the existence of a man and of a lion differ also, either because they are the result of or are related to diverse essences, having presupposed the aforementioned distinction. Whence a new proof[14] can be derived, because, just as human existence in general is outside the essence of man in general, so this existence of Peter is outside this individual essence of Peter, and just as in Peter and Paul there are numerically two existences, so [there are] numerically two humanities having distinct individual entities of essence.

Finally, there is an argument *a posteriori,* because, assuming that view, either the same individual entity is preserved without its existence or it changes several existences, as [is the case with] the humanity of Christ, [which] in that opinion lacks an existence of its own and, nevertheless, is individual and has an intrinsic principle of individuation. Similarly, numerically the same entity of prime matter, insofar as it changes forms, is said to change existences and, nevertheless, it always remains numerically the same.

6. Moreover, from these [considerations] it is easy to understand what is to be concluded concerning this opinion, if speaking not

about existence proper, but about subsistence.[15] For, either we speak [1] formally of the supposit, or [2] abstractly of the nature, or [3] concretely and formally of the individual [insofar] as it is contained under a particular species of substance, namely, of this man. In the first way it is true that the supposit is individuated by this subsistence, because it is formally constituted by it. And for this reason there are three supposits in the Trinity, although there is one nature, because there are three subsistences. The person of Christ, however, is numerically one and a numerically one supposit, although it has a double nature, because it has only a numerically one subsistence. Therefore, the supposit as such is individuated by subsistence. Concerning subsistence itself, however, the question remains: "By what is it made 'a this?' " For even the notion of subsistence, for example, of human [subsistence], is common and specific,[16] while in Peter it is numerically this subsistence or [numerically] that [subsistence]. The same will have to be said about this question as about [the question concerning] other substances or substantial modes, which we shall discuss below.

7. In the second way, that is, speaking of the whole substantial nature in the abstract, for example, about humanity, it is false and indefensible that it be individuated by subsistence, as it is clear *a fortiori* from all the arguments given concerning existence. For it is certain that subsistence is something distinct *ex natura rei* from the substantial nature, even taken individually. It is also certain that such a nature can be preserved as individual without the natural subsistence that accompanies it *(sua connaturali subsistentia),* as it was preserved in Christ, the Lord; therefore, it cannot be intrinsically individuated by it. But if somebody says perhaps that [such a nature] is individuated at least by a relation to it, he will say so gratuitously and without basis, because, if one [of these] is to be individuated by the relation to the other, [then] subsistence is "a this" by the relation to this nature rather than the reverse, since the nature is prior and more perfect, while subsistence is only a certain mode and end-term of the nature. Again, in the divine nature we find a unique individual nature with three subsistences; therefore, [the divine nature] is a sign [of the fact] that the individuation of the nature is wholly separate *(absolutam)* from subsistence.

8. Wherefore, Henry seems plainly to have erred in this respect, for he feels that the nature itself is made "a this" and individual by reason of the supposit. He also teaches something else which is completely false and indefensible concerning this, namely, that the supposit adds to the specific nature only a double negation, indivisibility in itself and division from anything else, and that, by this double negation, the nature is made formally individual without any other

positive addition to the specific nature. This contains three errors: The first is that the supposit adds only a negation to the nature, something we shall discuss in the appropriate place later. For, speaking with respect to the individual nature, it is less indefensible, although not true; nevertheless, with respect to the specific nature, it is wholly indefensible. Second, it is false that the individual nature adds only a negation to the specific [nature]. This is evidently clear from what was said in the Second Section, because otherwise the individual substantial nature, as such, would not be a real being, but would only be a specific nature with the negations, [something] which cannot even be conceived by the mind. Again, because that negation required a positive foundation, which the specific nature alone cannot be, as was sufficiently shown above. The third, however, is [still] more [clearly] false: That the individual nature is made by those very negations by which, according to Henry, the supposit is constituted. For it follows from this either that the humanity of Christ is not individual or that it is a supposit; and both [of these consequences] are in error. The consequence is explained [thus]: For, when in that double negation [the individual] is said to be undivided in itself and divided from any other, either [1] this "being divided from any other" signifies that it is not united to another, that is, that it is not in another, and this either [a] does not belong to the notion of individual substantial nature, or [else] [b] the humanity of Christ, the Lord, is not individual. Or [2] "being divided from another," which Henry openly holds, removes only identity, and affirms distinction from any other entity or similar nature, and in this way either [i] that double negation is not sufficient for the notion of supposit, or [else] [ii] the humanity of Christ, the Lord, is a supposit. Therefore, in no way does subsistence, in whatever way its notion be explained, pertain to the individuation of nature.

9. Moreover, even speaking in the third way, concretely and formally concerning an individual of a specific nature, it must be said that it, properly *(per se)* speaking, does not take its individuation from subsistence, but from the nature. For the theologians say so: If three persons took one humanity, there would be numerically one man, just as they are now numerically one God because of the one divine nature; therefore, the man would have numerical unity from the individual nature. And Christ, the Lord, now, insofar as he is "this man," is the numerically same man that he would be if he subsisted in his own *(propria)* nature, even though the person and the subsistence are very diverse from the proper and connatural [nature] of such humanity. Therefore, the individuation of this man must not be taken from the subsistence but from the nature. The reason is, however, that an individual is formally constituted under the species

by reason of the nature and not by reason of the subsistence. Hence, it is the case that, although it may happen that the subsistence be diverse in genus or species, nonetheless, if the nature is of the same species, the individual would be univocally and most properly contained in such species—for this reason Christ is univocally man with other men. And for a similar reason, if the nature is numerically the same, the man is numerically the same, even if the subsistence should be diverse.[17]

Conclusion of the Whole Question[18]

10. Moreover, I said "properly *(per se)* speaking," because here it was insinuated the question of whether the numerically same individual could exist *(esse)* with a double nature owing to the unity of subsistence. Indeed, it is disputed by theologians whether the divine Word would be one man or many if he assumed two humanities. For, from what has been said, it seems to follow that there would be numerically many men owing to the numerically many humanities, because it was said that the individuation of the concrete [thing] is taken from the individual nature. Yet, nonetheless, as I said with St. Thomas in [my commentary to the *Summa theologiae*], Part III of volume I[19], he will be said to be one man in a simple *(simpliciter)* and ordinary manner of speaking, not [speaking] properly *(per se)* and formally, but, as it were, materially, by reason of the supposit, in the same way in which an artist is said to be one who possesses many arts, not only numerically, but also specifically distinct. Moreover, this unity is different *(diversa)* from the preceding [one], which is taken from the unity of nature, nor is it the unity of the individual formally contained in the species, as the argument proves. [This is] just like the unity of the artist who possesses many specifically distinct arts, [which unity] is not the unity of the species contained in the genus, but is a material or supposital unity. This [unity] is judged sufficient for that manner of speaking, because of the real or substantial union of many natures in one supposit, because the substantive name signifies the nature as [something] standing by itself *(per modum per se stantis)*, as it was extensively explained in the mentioned place.

Therefore, from all this, it is clear enough that neither subsistence nor existence correctly constitutes the principle of individuation of the substantial nature or of the individual constituted by it.

Notes

[1] This Section is organized thus: In § 1 Suárez gives what might be considered the *Pro* of the question. He refers to the authorities who support the view that existence is the principle of individuation of singular things, adding some of the reasons

usually provided in its favor. He also points out that the term 'existence' as used by supporters of this view sometimes refers to existence and at other times to subsistence. § 2 opens the *Contra*. In §§ 2-5 Suárez discusses various views of existence as individuator; in §§ 6-10 he discusses the views of subsistence as individuator. The Section, contrary to the editor's belief, does not contain a solution or conclusion except perhaps for the very last sentence of § 10. The part identified as a conclusion is not a conclusion at all, but part of the discussion immediately preceding the paragraph in question, as will become clear later. In § 2 Suárez gives two possible interpretations of the view which holds existence (as opposed to subsistence) to be the principle of individuation (existence considered as a mode of a thing and existence considered as the entity of a thing, rejecting the first, but identifying the second with his own view. Four arguments are given against the first—one in each §§ 3 and 4, and two in § 5. In § 6 Suárez takes up the view that holds subsistence (as opposed to existence) to be the principle of individuation. Three interpretations (subsistence as supposit, nature, and individual) are discussed and rejected: the first in § 6, the second in § 7, and the third in §§ 9 and 10. In § 8 Suárez identifies Henry of Ghent's view with the second of these and offers further objections against it.

² The first paragraph presents the various authorities who refer to the view of existence as principle of individuation. None of them is said to hold the view except for Henry of Ghent, who, according to Suárez, held a modified version of it. This seems to imply that Suárez knew of no one and no text that would support a strict view of existential individuation. Indeed, as far as I know, no one adhered to this position. It may have been discussed by Suárez for any or all of the following reasons: First, because it was a distinct possibility given the doctrine of a real distinction between essence and existence which had been proposed by Thomas; second, because Henry's view, or even the view of Suárez himself as presented in Sect. VI of this Disputation, could have been loosely interpreted as a view of existential individuation; and third, because this view had been taken up separately and discussed by Scotus and others before.

³ *Ed. Vaticana*, vol. VII, p. 418.

⁴ *Ed. cit.*, p. 165b.

⁵ *Ed. cit.*, vol. I, fol. XXXIIv.

⁶ *In sententiarium librum 2 commentarii locupletissimi*, q.2 (Venice: A. Raphael, 1584), vol. I, p. 98a.

⁷ *Ed. cit.*, cols. 362F-363A.

⁸ *Ed. cit.*, vol. I, fols. CLXVv-CLXVIr.

⁹ At this point Suárez gives the arguments which go against, *contra*, the position which holds existence (as opposed to subsistence) to be the principle of individuation. Since there are two ways of interpreting this position—existence as a mode (distinct *ex natura rei*) and existence as entity—, the discussion is divided accordingly. Suárez identified his own position with the view that interprets existence as entity, leaving its discussion for Sect. VI. The view that interprets existence as distinct *ex natura rei* from essence is criticized in the second paragraph of § 2 and in §§ 3-5.

¹⁰ This is Suárez's own view, although, as he points out in the rest of the paragraph, badly expressed. See Sect. VI, *Responsio*.

¹¹ Sect. VI.

¹² The view in which existence is seen as a mode, that is, as distinct *ex natura rei* from the essence of the individual.

¹³ This is the first of four arguments given against the view that existence, considered as a mode, is the principle of individuation of singular things. The others are given in § 4 (second) and § 5 (third and fourth).

¹⁴ Not new in the sense of being independent of the other four and thus added to them.

¹⁵ Beginning with this paragraph and up to the end of the Section except for the last sentence, Suárez discusses the view that interprets existence as subsistence.

¹⁶ This text shows that Suárez viewed subsistence in a formalistic way, otherwise he could not have stated that subsistence "is common and specific." He makes the same point earlier about existence (§ 2) when he compares the relation of existence to an existent to that of whiteness to a white. This view seems to be in great contrast to Thomas' view. For Thomas existence can never be specific; it is always particular and most proper to the individual.

¹⁷ This implies, of course, that it is possible for numerically the same individual to have numerically diverse subsistences at different times. This is possible because, according to Suárez, subsistence is a mode of the substance and, therefore, if there is a change in the constitution of the substance, the subsistence would change. For this reason there is nothing contradictory in saying that a particular man subsists in a particular way while he is in this life and in another way in the future life. This way of speaking is largely a result of Suárez's formalism. Form in the last analysis is the most important principle in the individual, although, as he makes quite clear, form must be interpreted in this context as being always individual. In an existential metaphysics such as Thomas', the matter takes an entirely different turn, as I have argued elsewhere.

¹⁸ This part of the Section is not the conclusion to the whole question as the editorial subtitle suggests. For one thing, 'properly speaking,' to which Suárez refers in the first line, is found in the preceding paragraph (§ 9), and for another, the whole paragraph suggests that Suárez is still dealing with "the third way of speaking," i.e. "concretely and formally of the individual insofar as it is contained under a particular species of substance…" (§ 6). The only part of the Section that can truly be called a conclusion consists of its very last sentence.

¹⁹ *Ed. cit.,* vol. XVII, pp. 489a ff.

SECTION VI

FINALLY,
WHAT THE PRINCIPLE OF INDIVIDUATION
IS IN ALL CREATED SUBSTANCES[1]

1. From what has been said thus far against the views above, — and after as it were, a process of elimination[2] — it seems that every singular substance « is singular in itself, that is, by its entity» [3] [and] needs no other principle of individuation in addition to its entity, or in addition to the intrinsic principles which constitute its entity. For, if such a substance, physically considered, is simple, it is individual from itself and from its simple entity. If, however, it is a composite, — for example, of matter and form united, — [then], just as the principles of its entity are matter, form, and their union, so [likewise] these same [principles], taken in the individual, are the principles of its individuation. Those [i.e. simple substances], however, since they are simple, will be individual in themselves.

Aureolus held this view with Capreolus, *On II* [*of the Sentences*], dist. 3, q.2;[4] and, in fact, Durandus holds the same [view], *On II* [*of the Sentences*], dist. 3, q.2.[5] Fonseca, however, referring to it, [*Commentary on the*] *Metaphysics* V, Ch. 6, q.3, says in sect. 2, that it is the most confused of all, and, reduced to its true sense, leaves the question unsolved.[6] Nevertheless, it seems to me [to be] the clearest of all, and both he and almost everyone else seem to end up in it, because, in fact, the foundation of unity cannot be distinguished from the entity itself. Hence, just as the individual unity as formal cannot add anything positive [and] real to the individual entity, because, with respect to this, its notion and [the notion] of every unity are the same, so [too] the positive foundation of this unity, with respect to the negation it expresses, can add nothing positive, physically speaking,[7] to that entity which is called *(denominatur)* one and individual. Therefore, that entity by itself is the foundation of this negation, and in this sense is said to be itself the principle of individuation, according to that opinion. For this opinion does not deny that the common nature can be conceptually distinguished from the singular entity in these individuals, and that this[8] individual adds something conceptually distinct to the species, [something] which, from a metaphysical perspective, involves the notion of individual difference, as was said in the preceding Section.[9] And Durandus does not deny [this], but rather seems to assume it. But, nevertheless, this opinion adds something which properly pertains to the present question, namely, that in the individual substance the individual difference does not have some special principle or foundation which is distinct in reality from its entity; and, thus, in this sense it says that each entity is by itself the principle of its individuation. Therefore, this view is true if rightly explained. Nevertheless, in order that it may be made more clear, we shall discuss all the substantial realities [i.e. matter, form, modes, the composite, spiritual substances] separately.

The Principle of Individuation of Prime Matter

2. First, therefore, beginning with prime matter, it must be said that it is individual in reality, and that the foundation of such unity is its entity by itself as it is in reality, without any extrinsic addition. This is proven, because the matter which is under this form of wood is numerically diverse from the [matter] which is under the form of water or man; it is, therefore, individual and singular in itself. The foundation, however, of such unity in it is not the substantial form, nor a relation to this or that form, as was proven above against Durandus, since, when any substantial form changes, the matter remains always numerically the same, which [matter], although it may actually be united to this or that form, nevertheless expresses of itself a common and indifferent relation to any form it can receive.

In turn, quantity also cannot be the foundation of this individual unity of matter, as the same argument proves, if it is true that matter loses and acquires various quantities depending on changes in substantial forms. Again, because, according to the same opinion, matter, naturally prior to receiving quantity, is subject to the action of the agent bringing forth the form or quantity; it is not, however, subject [to it] except insofar as [it is] individual and singular, since actions concern singulars. If, however, we hold the same quantity to be cotemporal *(coevam)* with matter, the same argument can be made to fit, at least with respect to God's power. For God can remove this quantity from this matter and give another to it, or [he can] preserve [this matter] entirely without quantity; therefore, the matter would be numerically the same without numerically the same quantity. Therefore, quantity is not the foundation of such unity of matter, otherwise [matter] could in no way preserve its unity without it. Furthermore, there are all the common arguments given above: That substance is not individuated by an accident, nor by a relation to an accident; for matter is substance, although in part. Again, that an individual substance is a being by itself. Again, that an accident presupposes its subject as it is in reality, and consequently [as] singular. Again, that the individual difference is not really distinct from the entity which it constitutes [and], hence, cannot be founded on a distinct entity.

3. *Corollary.* Moreover, these arguments are *a fortiori* applicable to any accidents or dispositions of matter. Wherefore, when it is usually said by some that matter is individuated by the agent, insofar as its indifference to "this form" is individuated and contracted by dispositions, for [this] to be true in some sense *(ratione)*, it must be understood in a correct manner; because in order for the agent to act on matter it must presuppose it [to be] individual, and by its action it cannot remove or change the individuality *(individuationem)* of it [i.e. that matter]. Otherwise, it would destroy it [i.e. the matter] and introduce another in its place; nor could it happen either that what is already individual in reality should receive in itself another individuality *(individuationem)* by the addition of some entity. Matter is said, therefore, [to be] limited by dispositions or to be determined by the agent to this form, not in relation to being, but in relation to the action of the agent itself and to the reception of form. And this [is so] either [a] only accidentally and, as it were, negatively, because the obstacles to this action and to the introduction of this form are removed by the dispositions, and [b] in some way essentially *(per se)* and positively, if such dispositions are naturally necessary for the eduction or union of this form with this matter. For this is disputed among philosophers and is not relevant to the present problem, because this coadaptation by dispositions is, as it were, extrinsic to matter itself, which, even taken in the individual, is of itself capable of any form; and if dispositions are required, it is by reason of form rather than by reason of matter itself. Therefore, this is in no way relevant to its intrinsic individuality *(individuationem)*.

4. *Answer to several objections.* [But] you will say: This matter is not distinguished from another except by quantity, because, since it is pure potency, it cannot be distinguished except by act. Again, matter is essentially related to form according to its species. Therefore,

this individual matter must be individuated by form or by a relation to this form.

The answer to the first is that one matter is distinguished from another with respect to place by quantity, while it is entitatively and really distinguished by its entity, as has been said above, because, just as matter has some entity from itself, whether of existence or of essence, so by reason of it [i.e. that entity] it has some entitative actuality, whereby it can be transcendentally distinguished from another.

The answer to the second is that in the same way in which matter essentially has a transcendental relation to form, so this matter has, for[10] this [reason], a transcendental relation to form, because it has numerically this capacity and potency, and [so too] man is individuated by a relation to form. But this is [what it is] to be physically individuated by itself, because its [i.e. of matter] entity essentially includes this relation. It is not, however, necessary that this individuation be made by the determination of form — which is the sense in which the objection *(argumentum)* should proceed in order to have some force *(difficultatis)*[11] — , because not only matter specifically, but also numerically this matter is related to form in general as to the adequate object of its capacity, even taken in the individual. And, thus, matter is not rightly said [to be] individuated by this form, but [rather] to be individuated by the individuated relation to form. [This is] just the way the power of sight specifically expresses a relation to color in general, and in an individual, likewise, it expresses a relation not to this or that color, but to color in general, and, thus, it may not be properly individuated by this color, although it may be individuated with a particular or by a particular transcendental and entitative relation to color.

The Principle of Individuation of Substantial Form

5. Second, it must be said that substantial form is intrinsically "a this" by its very entity, from which its individual difference is taken in the last degree or reality. This conclusion can be proven by arguments analogous to those by which the preceding one [was proven], and it can easily be confirmed from the above, especially from what was said concerning the first and second opinions. For, in the first place, no accidents can be the intrinsic principles of individuation of substantial form, because even such a form as this is, is a being by itself, although incomplete, and belongs to the category of substance, and is placed under the specific notion of such a form, although reductively. Again, this form is either [1] absolutely *(simpli-*

citer) and in every sense *(ratione)* prior to accidents and [is] their origin, or [2], if it presupposes some [of them] as a material cause, it does not express by itself a relation to them, but, at most, requires them as necessary conditions or dispositions for the preparation of the subject; therefore, in no way can it be individuated by accidents. Next, matter cannot by itself be the intrinsic principle of its entity; and the principle of unity and the principle of entity are the same, as has often been said, because unity adds no thing to entity, except for the negation intrinsically accompanying it. The antecedent is clear, because matter is an intrinsic principle of the composite, since it composes it through its entity. But it does not so compose the entity of form; therefore, it is not an intrinsic principle of it. With respect to those forms which depend on matter for [their] production and being, however, matter is by itself in its genus the cause of form, not as intrinsically composing it, but as sustaining it, which is a certain, as it were, extrinsic kind of causality. And in this way matter can be said [to be] in its genus a cause and principle of individuation of such forms, in accordance with the stated principle, that the cause of entity is the cause of unity, and because matter does not cause form, except for the singular and individual; therefore, causing the entity it causes its individuation. Nevertheless, because the individual difference is intrinsically predicated of the individual thing, it is not taken from any sort of extrinsic causes of the individual thing itself, but from the intrinsic principle, that is, its entity; and thus, in this way, matter cannot be the intrinsic principle of the individuation of forms. This is stated *a posteriori* with respect to divine power. For this substantial form can be preserved without matter, and then, just as it retains its individual difference, so likewise, [does it retain] its intrinsic principle of individuation; therefore, matter is not an intrinsic principle of this sort. Moreover, this is more obvious in the rational soul, in which, just as being is not caused by itself from matter, so likewise neither is unity or individuality *(individuatio)*, as St. Thomas noted, *Contra gentiles* II, Ch. 75,[12] in the solution to the first argument, and Ch. 81, in the beginning.[13] Therefore, matter not only is not the intrinsic principle of individuation of the soul, indeed it is not even an essential *(per se)* cause of it, although it may happen, as it were, that, if a particular body is produced, God would create in it a particular soul.

6. *Small doubt.* But the difficulty lies in whether form is individuated by matter at least as by the term to which it is related. For the difference between matter and form seems to be this, that matter, because it stands under many forms as numerically the same, cannot have an individual determination from the form to which it is related; while form does not have such indifference, but is determined to actualize

this matter, and, thus, can be individuated by this matter as by the term to which it is related, [insofar] as [it is] such a form. Thomists generally think thus, and they interpret St. Thomas in this way in the places cited above and in others, where he says that form is individuated by matter. And in the same way can be explained what he says in the unique question *On the Soul,* a.3, *ad* 13, that the principles of individuation of forms do not concern their essence, but that this is true only in composites.[14]

But, in the first place, the argument given does not apply to the rational soul, which, [while] remaining numerically the same, can actualize diverse matters. For, first, it so actualizes simultaneously the diverse parts of the matter composing the same body that it is wholly in each part; therefore, it cannot be individuated by the coadaptation to the whole body and to each of its parts. But it is more important that it can successively inform wholly diverse matters, as when by continuous nutrition all of the matter in which the form was first introduced is gradually lost, and a new [matter] is acquired, and is informed by the same form. Again, it is accidental to nutrition itself that it be made from these or those foods and, nevertheless, from this it comes about that the soul informs this or that matter afterwards; therefore, this is also contingent and accidental to it. Therefore, [the soul] is not individuated from it [i.e. matter], nor is it of itself coadapted to numerically this matter.

7. Perhaps someone will say that this soul requires of itself to be introduced in a particular matter at least in the beginning, although afterwards it could leave it and inform another, and that for this reason it is individuated by the matter in which it was first introduced.

But, in the first place, this is said gratuitously; for, if the same soul can naturally inform various matters at different times, this is a sign that its informative power or aptitude to inform is not related as an adequate term to numerically this matter. Therefore, on what basis can it be said to require of itself in the beginning one matter more than another, or to be intrinsically related to one more than to another? Otherwise, in the same way matter could be said to have required by its nature that it be created under numerically those forms under which it was created, and to have been individuated by them, although it were preserved under other forms afterwards. Therefore, just as this would be said gratuitously there, so also it is said without basis concerning the soul. For, imagine that numerically that matter which an offspring acquires and informs by its own nutrition were previously under the form of the maternal blood, from which the body of the same offspring had been formed in the beginning. Certainly, just as numerically this form could have been introduced afterwards into that matter predisposed by nutrition, so also, if it had been predisposed by the maternal blood in virtue of the seed in the first formation, similarly the same form could have been naturally introduced into it; for no philosophical reason can be given why it could not. Therefore, this soul, even as "a this," is indifferent to informing many matters, whether in the beginning in the production, or afterwards in the preservation.

8. *Important theological* [*point*].[15] It is not relevant if you should say that these matters are judged one and the same, because the change takes place gradually under the dispositions and organization of the same nature *(rationis)*; because this unity of matter or body is more in external shape and appearance than in the true and physical entity of the body or of the matter. In addition, even if it happened that the whole matter were produced by the complete separation of one body and by the union to another matter, nonetheless, the soul would naturally inform both, just as it is probable that this will happen in the resurrection. Consequently, if it should happen in this life that two souls informed two exactly identical matters, the body [composed] from one matter could be given to the other [soul], which [soul] will not inform it [i.e. the body composed from that matter] less naturally than if it were composed from the first matter [it had]. Therefore, this is a sign that this soul, [insofar] as [it is] apt to inform, is in no way determinately related to this matter, and, consequently, that it is not individuated by this matter [insofar] as it is "a this," [not] even as by the term of its transcendental relation, because it is not the adequate term of it. Therefore, this soul is individuated by itself and in virtue of its entity, and, consequently, because it intrinsically has such an individual aptitude for informing the human body, in the same way as we were saying a little before concerning the relation to matter.

Toletus teaches this about the rational soul in particular, in Bk. III, [*Commentary on*] *"On the Soul,"* q.18, conclus. 2 and 3, confirming it by an argument given by us above[16]: That in pointing out the principle of individuation one must stop at something which is individuated by itself. Therefore, if matter or quantity are said to be individuated by themselves, much more must that be said concerning the rational soul, which is subsistent by itself, and which gives being to the others rather than receiving [it] from them. Therefore, the plurality *(varietas)* of bodies is the best *a posteriori* sign of the distinction of souls, because it is, as it were, the occasion of the production of diverse souls, although it is not their proper and intrinsic principle of individuation.

9. But, on the basis of the argument given just now, it does not seem possible to decide whether the case *(ratio)* might be the same for all other substantial forms which depend for their being on matter, be-

cause these forms inform numerically this matter in such a way that they are completely determined to informing it, and are not able to inform naturally another numerically distinct matter, since they could not also be separated from this [matter] neither all at once nor gradually. This applies also to the souls of perfect animals if they are extended and divisible, as the general and perhaps more probable opinion holds — for if they are assumed to be indivisible, the argument given concerning rational souls applies to them. Therefore, it can be rightly said that the material substantial form is indeed intrinsically "a this" by the coadaptation to numerically this matter, and by the matter itself, as by the term of this relation. But, nonetheless, this cannot be properly said even concerning these material forms, because either the dispositions whereby this matter is prepared by the agent for this form are included in numerically this matter, or this prime matter is understood solely in its naked entity. But in neither way can this be satisfactorily understood or explained. 10. The first is clear,[17] because matter with accidents cannot be the reason for the individuation of form, [not] even as a term of its relation, because, since this relation is transcendental and substantial, it does not include accidents in its primary and essential (per se) term. Again, because, if we suppose the dispositions [present] in [what is] generated not to be the same that preceded [them] in [what was] corrupted, [then] the arguments given above apply: That the form, prior[18] in nature, absolutely and without qualification informs matter stripped of accidents. It informs it, however, [insofar] as [it is] individual and singular; therefore, it is related to it in the same way, according to its individual aptitude and coadaptation. If, however, we suppose the dispositions which were [present] in [what was] corrupted to remain in matter, then, also, form does not inform matter [insofar] as [it is] affected by accidents, even if those [accidents] are presupposed either as necessary conditions or perhaps only because they are left from the preceding alteration. Therefore, this form, [insofar] as [it is] "a this," is not related to accidents, but to matter alone. This is particularly so because, even if numerically these accidents were changed, whether gradually [and] naturally, or at once [and] supernaturally, and other similar ones took their place (dentur), the numerically same form will be preserved in the same matter. Therefore, in no way is this form, [insofar] as [it is] "a this," related to numerically such accidents, so that it may be individuated by them. Moreover, even if we granted that this form requires numerically these accidents, the form itself would not for that reason be such in the individual on account of the accidents, but rather conversely, such accidents would be required [to be such], speaking a priori and without qualification, on account of such a form; although with respect to us, whether with respect to production or generation, such dispositions are the principle or occasion for distinguishing forms.

11. Moreover, the second, namely, that this prime matter taken as such *(pure)* could not be in this way the principle individuating form, is proven, first, because this matter can be common to many forms, whether diverse in species or in number. Therefore, as such [matter] is not a sufficient principle for individuating form, because what is common of itself as such cannot be a principle of individuation. Second, from the side of the form, because even though this form once made in this and from this matter could not be [placed] in another because of [its] dependence on it (This dependence is such that neither could that form be naturally preserved without the genus of material causality, nor likewise would there be any natural way or manner whereby this form could be transferred into another matter in order to be preserved by it.), nonetheless, however, if the entity of such a form is considered in itself, its intrinsic aptitude does not seem determined to informing numerically this matter in such a way that it would be intrinsically unsuitable to informing naturally any other numerically distinct matter. Therefore, [the form] does not receive its intrinsic individuation from numerically this matter, [not] even as the term of its informative relation or aptitude. The proof of the consequence is that this matter is not an adequate term of the relation, since the aptitude of this form in itself could be exercised equally naturally in any other matter if [the form] were placed in it. For the fact that [the form] is placed in this matter alone and not in another by natural causes does not remove its intrinsic aptitude, nor cause this matter to be the adequate term of it; just as perhaps there is, in the universe, some portion of matter which has always been and will always be under the numerically same form, while perhaps there is no natural way to change it, and [yet] the aptitude of the matter was not determined of itself to such a form because of that.

12. Moreover, the antecedent can be defended with many conjectures which are common even to rational souls. The first, that by absolute power this form can be transferred into another matter and inform it; therefore, this is a sign that there is in such a form a natural [and] intrinsic aptitude for informing it, insofar as [the aptitude] is [derived] from it [i.e. the form]. The proof of the consequence is that even if the action or transmigration of this form from matter into matter were supernatural with respect to its manner [of production], nevertheless, the produced term would be natural; for the composite of such a form and matter would subsist naturally. The second: Any other numerically distinct matter is capable, insofar as [the capacity] is from itself [i.e. the matter], of any individual form,

even though [the form] might happen to be in another numerically distinct matter. For someone might think, [though] without basis, that the capacity of this matter is of itself numerically limited to these forms rather than to those, owing to the fact that, perhaps, in the order of nature, natural agents could not cause in it those individual forms which they cause in other matters. Because, since matter is of itself pure potency and indifferent, such determination cannot be attributed to it on the basis of an appropriate reason. Therefore, numerically that matter which in fact is under this form of this horse, insofar as it is [apt] from itself, would be capable of another numerically distinct soul of a horse, which, in fact, informs another matter; therefore and conversely, that soul also is apt, insofar as it is [apt] from itself, of informing this or that matter. The consequence is clear, because natural potency and act mutually correspond to each other; whence potency is not naturally related, except to that act which has a natural aptitude for informing it.

13. Third, because if this equine soul, for example, were apt from itself only to informing numerically this matter, all equine souls which could inform numerically that matter at different times would have among themselves some real agreement. [And] this [agreement] they would not have with the equine souls informing other matters, because all of them would have an aptitude for informing numerically this matter, which other equine souls could not inform. The same argument can be made for all the forms of water, fire, and similar ones, because obviously under the same species of the form of fire, for example, there may be a certain number of individuals related only to numerically this matter, and another number of others related to numerically this matter, and likewise for the others. And so under the specific concept there could be an objective substantial concept common to many individuals of that species and not to others. [But] this seems absurd; for that agreement, since it would be real and substantial, will be also essential to such forms, and, consequently, the last species will be divisible by many essential differences, [something] which involves an open contradiction. But this objection (ratio) is more apparent than effective, because there can be several counter-objections (difficultates) to and ways of evading it which we shall touch upon more easily in following Disputations. Nevertheless, there are other effective arguments which we shall establish and explain further in the following Section.[19]

Therefore, the stated conclusion, that the intrinsic principle from which the individual difference of the substantial form is taken is the entity itself of the form, insofar as [the entity of the form] has from itself a particular aptitude for informing matter, remains sufficiently proven. For all [principles] extrinsic or distinct from the form itself are excluded, because [the form] could not be individuated from them. From this it results that form is not "a this" because it is related to this matter but only insofar as it has a particular aptitude for informing matter.

The Principle whereby Substantial Modes are Individuated

14. I say thirdly: The substantial mode, which is simple and in its own way indivisible, also has its individuation from itself, and not from some principle distinct *ex natura rei* from itself. This is made clear, for instance, in the union of form to matter, or of matter to form, which I assume, from what is said below, to be a substantial mode. Again in the subsistence of a simple [entity], and the same would be [the case] concerning existence, if it were a real mode of essence distinct *ex natura rei* from it. Accordingly, it is certain that the union which my soul has to my body now is numerically one and individual, both because it is something real and existing in reality and distinct *ex natura rei* from the soul, and also because it differs numerically and not specifically from the mode of union of another soul to its body. Therefore, it has its individual difference and, therefore, [it has] some intrinsic principle or foundation of that. Therefore, we say that this principle can be nothing other than the entity of the mode itself, of whatever kind that entity may be.

Moreover, this can be proven, first, with the general reasons given: [1] that thus each thing is one insofar as it is; and [2] that the negation which unity adds is immediately founded in the thing's entity as it is in itself; and, finally, [3] that each simple entity is itself intrinsically such, that is, it is constituted in its being in the [same] manner we understand [it], and consequently, it is also distinguished from others by itself. Second, it is proven by excluding other principles from this individuation. For, if there were any, it would be most of all this soul or this matter in the case of this union — to continue with the example with which we began, and omitting accidents, however, because they have been already sufficiently excluded by the arguments given concerning matter and form. But this mode is not properly individuated by this matter and this form; because, although this mode of union in the individual could not be in another form because of the special real identity which it has with this form, [and although] it could not also be made or preserved in another numerically distinct matter, because it is related to this [matter] not according to an aptitude, but according to a certain actual nature *(rationem)* which is adequately determined to this matter;[20] nonetheless, however, this soul and this matter could be united by another numerically distinct union. For it is not necessary that, if the union of this soul and matter[21] were now dissolved and perished and this matter and this form were united by God again, they should receive the numerically same union which they had before. For, even if we granted that this can happen, [something] which some also doubt, there is no [reason] why it should be necessary; because in other modes, [for example, in modes] of figures, sittings, or similar [things], it is not necessary that the numerically same [union] be reproduced; indeed, it is not natural. Therefore, those unions can be numerically distinguished in the same form with respect to the same matter; therefore, its principle of individuation is not sufficiently taken from this form or this matter. Therefore, it is necessary that such a mode have from itself an intrinsic foundation of its individuation, although, according to it, it may be related to this form and this matter by a transcendental relation, because this is the nature of such a mode.

The Principle of Individuation of the Substantial Composite

15. Fourth, it must be said, that in a composite substance, [insofar] as it is such a composite, the adequate principle of individuation is this matter and this form united to each other. [And] between these the primary principle is the form, which alone is sufficient for this composite, insofar as it is an individual of a particular species, to be judged the same numerically.

This conclusion follows from the preceding and from what was said in Section IV, and is in agreement with the opinion of Durandus and Toletus discussed above.[22] And Scotus and Henry do not really disagree, nor [do] any of the nominalists. Fonseca also does not disagree, in Bk. V, [Commentary on the] Metaphysics, q.5,[23] although he might say that our manner of speaking is improper when we say that this matter and this form are "physical principles of individuation," because neither this form nor this matter nor both together could be added to the specific nature of man in order to constitute [together] with it this man, and also because this matter and this form are individuals, constituted by their specific natures and by their proper principles of individuation. But in these reasons he passes from the physical notion to metaphysical composition. For, when this matter and this form are called "physical principles of individuation of this composite," they are not compared to the common specific nature, but to the physical composite which they compose. And thus, it is not necessary that they be added to the common specific nature, but [only] that they compose it by composing the individual in which it is included. Whence, according to the same physical constitution, such principles are simple; nor do they have other [principles] by which they are physically individuated, but they are individuated by themselves, as has been explained. Therefore, the expression is not improper, but true and proper, because the intrinsic principles of individuation are the same as the intrinsic principles of entity, as has often been said, because individuality *(individuatio)* follows entity [insofar] as it is a certain negation; however, [insofar] as it includes [something] positive, it is the very entity and adds nothing to it. But this matter and this form, united to each other, are the intrinsic principles of the whole entity of the composite substance which we are discussing; therefore, they are also the intrinsic physical principles of individuation. This is confirmed, for matter and form, taken absolutely, are physical principles of the species of the composite substance and of its specification. Therefore, this matter and this form will be physical principles of the individual and of its individuation. In the same way it can be concluded that neither by itself, but both taken together are this adequate principle. Because this composite, in order to be numerically the same, wholly and completely, requires not only this form or this matter, but both together. And when either one of them is changed, [the composite] does not remain absolutely *(simpliciter)* and in every respect numerically the same composite that it was before, because its entity has been changed in some respect. Therefore, matter and form are the adequate principle of the numerical unity of the whole composite [insofar] as it is such. This is confirmed by the argument given: That the principles of unity are the same as the principles of entity; but this matter and this form are the adequate intrinsic principle of this composite entity, and, therefore, of unity and individuation.

16. *Inference. An objection is solved.* It is clear from this also that this numerically same union is required for the perfect unity of such a composite, because in its way it is intrinsically related *(concurrit)* to its constitution. For the entity of the composite intrinsically includes not only the entity of matter and form, but also their union to each other. Therefore, when the union is changed in some way, the entity is changed and, consequently, [so is] the unity of the composite itself; therefore, it is required for [its] perfect unity and individuation. Therefore, for this reason, this union could also be counted among the [things] which complete the perfect principle of individuation of the composite itself. It is not, however, as necessary as matter and form, because these are the absolutely *(simpliciter)* essential principles of such a composite; the union, however, is, as it were, a required condition or causality of matter and form, as stated in [my *Commentary to the Summa theologiae*], vol. II, Part III, Disp. XXXIV, Sect. II.[24]

Also, comparing matter and form to each other, the primary principle is form, not only with respect to the specific nature, considering the form in the species, but even with respect to this individual, considering the individual form; because this form is most proper to this individual, and because it is what completes numerically this whole substance. For, this matter only lays the foundation *(inchoat)* for it [i.e. this substance] and, insofar as [what] it is of itself, it does not lay the foundation for this more than for another. Again, because this form is the primary principle of being, and, consequently, it is also the primary principle distinguishing this substance from others. But the principle of unity and the principle of being and distinction of it [i.e. this substance] from others are the same. Therefore, [this form is the primary principle of unity and individuation].

[But] you will say that form is the principle of specific distinction, because it causes [the thing] to differ formally; therefore, it cannot be a principle of numerical distinction, otherwise, numerical distinction would be formal and essential.

The answer to this is that form, according to its specific and essential notion, causes the specific and essential difference, but the individual form, according to its entity, causes the entitative and numerical distinction. For Peter and Paul differ numerically from each other more because they have numerically distinct souls, than because they have distinct bodies. And, from this, the last part of the conclusion is clear, which is also sufficiently proven from the common manner of speaking which we noted above. For a man is judged the same absolutely *(simpliciter)* not only in appearance but also in truth, who has the numerically same soul, even if the body has changed. The reason is that form is judged absolutely *(simpliciter)* to constitute the species, and similarly this form [is judged to constitute] this individual under a particular species.

17. *Question [and] answer.* But you will ask whether the individual difference is taken, strictly [speaking], from the complete principle, namely, matter and form, or rather from one of them alone. For it seems that authors more frequently feel it to be taken from one alone; for, since this difference is simple, it does not seem that it should be taken from the whole composite, nor from a twofold, partial principle, but only from a simple one. They disagree, however, for some say that the principle is matter, as [do] Cajetan and others; others, however, say that it is form, as [does] Scotus; and Durandus leans toward the same. This latter [view] is more true, if a prior principle *(fundamentum)* is assumed, namely, that the individual difference must be taken from only one of these principles. We speak, however, about the thing itself as it is. For, with respect to us, who derive our knowledge from material things, the distinction among

individuals is often taken from matter or from the accidents which follow matter, such as quantity and other properties. But truly, as it is, just as difference must be taken from a substantial principle and not from an accidental [one], so also among the substantial principles themselves it must be taken from that which is primary and a more proper and the last constituent of the thing itself; such, however, is form, as has been shown. Again, this is true speaking about an individual of a particular nature or species, insofar as it is formally constituted in it.

For this reason we said above that the supposit is numerically one, if it has a numerically one subsistence, even if the nature is not one, because the formal constituent of the supposit is the incommunicable subsistence, from which alone the individual notion of the supposit as such must be taken. But, on the contrary, we said that the individual unity and difference of the singular thing, as constituted under a particular substantial species or essence, must be taken from the substantial nature, which formally constitutes such an individual. In this way, therefore, we say now that the individual difference of this man, taken formally [insofar] as he is an individual of the human species, is taken from this soul. But, if we speak about this composite [insofar] as it is perfectly and in all respects one, it will be more truly said that its individual difference is taken from its entire entity, and, thus, from the adequate physical principle, which includes matter and form, in such a way that it will also be verified that the whole composite is individuated by itself, that is, by its entity; for by that it has identity absolutely (*simpliciter*) in itself and diversity from all others. Nor is it inappropriate that the difference, which is, from a metaphysical perspective, simple, — that is, not composed of genus and difference — , be taken from the entity, that is, the physically composite nature insofar as it is one and is conceived as one individual nature.

That whereby Complete, Spiritual Substances are Individuated [25]

18. Finally, from what has been said, it is obvious enough what must be said concerning immaterial substances, in which individual differences are also found, as we have shown; because, since in them there is nothing but the complete, simple, substantial entity, it is clear that in them there cannot be another principle of individuation in addition to the entity itself of each thing, which is such from itself, and distinguished from others by itself. And, in this, all those who hold these substances to be individual agree, whatever the reason they give for their individuation. Moreover, those who say that they

themselves, [i.e. these substances], agree in a particular spiritual specific nature, much more and *a fortiori* teach that they are individuated by their entities, as is clear from Capreolus, *On II [of the Sentences]*, dist. 3;[26] Cajetan and others, [in *Summa theologiae*] I, q.3, a.3, q.50, a.4;[27] Soncinas, [*Questions on the*] *Metaphysics* XII, q.49;[28] Iavellus, [*Questions...*], q.25;[29] Ferrara, [*Commentary on*] *Contra gentiles* I, Ch. 21.[30] However, those who think that even in immaterial things individuation is caused by the addition of a difference, also teach necessarily that it must be taken from the substantial entity of the angel in itself; because it must not be taken from accidents, nor is there anything else whence it could be taken; all of which have been sufficiently proven from what has been said.

Moreover, the common argument, that if these substances differ by their entities, they would necessarily differ formally and essentially, has already been refuted in a similar [case] concerning other forms. For those entities, however formal, can be wholly similar in essential notion; and then, although they be distinguished by themselves, nonetheless the distinction is numerical, because it is in the entity, not in the formal notion. Moreover, they are said to be distinguished by themselves, not because they are not similar, but because one is not from itself the other; for similarity does not exclude distinction, as will be said below.

NOTES

[1] Strictly speaking, this is the only section of Disp. V that is not structured as a *quaestio*. It is intended as the *Solutio* or answer to the problem posed by the Disputation considered as a whole. In fact, however, the solution given here solves only the problem concerning the identification of the principle of individuation, not all the problems which surround individuation. This solution and this problem were regarded by Suárez as central to the whole issue. Indeed, the identification of causes or principles is the primary function of science within Aristotelian philosophy and so it is only appropriate that the fundamental issue concerning individuation be precisely the identification of its cause. The other problems — which things are individual; what is the nature of individuality; etc. — are only propaedeutic or consequent to the main enterprise. The Section is organized as follows: In the first paragraph of § 1 Suárez gives a general statement of his view which is then supported with authorities and clarified in the second paragraph. The purpose of the reference to authorities here is more to distinguish Suárez's position from others than actual substantiation. After this initial statement, he turns to the individuation of the various kinds of entities which fill the universe. Since the subtitles of this Section are self-explanatory, we may dispense with further discussion of its structure.

[2] The way Suárez establishes his view of individuation is dialectical. Instead of directly giving arguments in support of his position, he argues against all the possible logical alternatives. Finding all of them at fault, he is left with only one possible view — his own. The argumentation is not altogether negative, however. In rejecting all views contrary to his own, he determined certain criteria which the correct view must meet. In this Section he confronts his view with these criteria and finds, not

surprisingly, that it meets all of them. The dialectical procedure in argumentation goes back to Aristotle's text in *Prior Analytics* (24a20), where he distinguishes a demonstrative from a dialectical premise as one which consists in "the assertion of one of two contradictory statements...whereas the dialectical premise depends on the adversary's choice between two contradictories." A dialectical mode of argumentation, then, begins with a list of alternatives which are then reduced according as the argument progresses.

³ The text within pointed brackets is missing in a number of editions, such as Vivès. The reason for its exclusion may be (1) that Suárez never wrote it or (2) that later editors thought it spurious because they did not understand how it fitted with Suárez's view. Since we have no way of establishing the first point with any degree of finality here, there is no point in dwelling on it. There are some obvious bases for the second view, however, for the added text seems at first sight to coincide with Ockham's view, discussed and rejected by Suárez in Sect. II, § 5, above: "it holds that every thing or nature is by itself, primarily and immediately individual." However, the two *formulae* are by no means equivalent. Ockham's view as rendered by Suárez implies that a thing needs no principle of individuation because it is *primarily* and *immediately* individual, while Suárez's own view identifies a thing's entity as its principle of individuation. Therefore, the 'by itself' is to be read differently in each case: in one it should be read as "essentially," in the other literally as "by itself." There is, moreover, another difference. For Ockham, according to Suárez, the individual and the common nature are actually equivalent in being and individuality adds nothing real to the common nature. But for Suárez the individual does add something real to the common nature, distinguished at least conceptually from it (Sect. II, §§ 8 and 16). It is for this reason that Suárez can say that there is a principle of individuation; for Ockham such talk would be nonsense. Consequently, although Suárez's formula appears very much like Ockham's, it is by no means equivalent to it, and so, although it may have misled some editors into leaving out the present passage, there is no reason to support such an action.

⁴ Rather q.1, a.2, § 2. *Ed. cit.* vol. III, pp. 209b and 215b-216a.

⁵ *Ed. cit.,* vol. I, fol. 137ra.

⁶ *Ed. cit.,* col. 368A.

⁷ Suárez, like most scholastics, put great emphasis on the distinction between physics and metaphysics and as a result on the distinction between "speaking physically" or "arguing physically" and "speaking or arguing metaphysically." In general, physics is interpreted as the science of nature, that is, of material things, while metaphysics is concerned with non-material being. The distinction is, of course, found in Aristotle's *Metaphysics* VI, Ch. 1, 1026a5, but the immediate source for medieval writers was Boethius, particularly in *On the Trinity,* Ch. 2, where he writes: "Physics deals with motion and is not abstract or separable; for it is concerned with the forms of bodies together with their constituent matter, which forms cannot be separated in reality from their bodies....Theology [another term for Metaphysics] does not deal with motion and is abstract and separable, for the divine substance is without either matter or motion...." (Loeb. p. 9).

⁸ Several editions (Rábade and others) add the term *modo* at this point. The text, however, makes sense without it. Suárez wants to point out two things this view does not deny. If *modo* is introduced, then some sort of causal relation between the first and second is introduced.

⁹ Sect. V.

¹⁰ Some editions (Rábade, for example), omit a *per* which precedes *hanc* (this), preferring to read *hanc* with *habitudinem* (relation). However, it is clear from the example Suárez gives at the end of the paragraph that he does not mean to say that "matter" has a transcendental relation to "form" and so that "this matter" has also a

transcendental relation to "this form," but rather, that "this matter" has a transcendental relation to "form in general," not just to "this form," precisely because "matter" has a transcendental relation to "form."

¹¹ The point is that if an objection has or presents no difficulty it will not be effective; its difficulty, therefore, constitutes its force.

¹² Berton mistakenly reads "I."

¹³ *Summa contra gentiles,* chs. 95 and 68, in Leonine ed., vol. XIII, pp. 568a and 440a.

¹⁴ *De anima,* q.3, p. 86.

¹⁵ Suárez occasionally brings theological considerations into the discussion. He, like all other scholastics, felt that no philosophical doctrine which contradicted the articles of faith could be true. But this criterion was used only negatively and, in this particular work, sparingly and adventitiously. Suárez refrained from using authority, whether theological or philosophical, as the basis for arguments to prove or substantiate his philosophical doctrines. When he uses it, the purpose is to show how faith and reason may come to the same conclusions although by different paths, or alternatively that philosophy does not contradict faith. The use of theological authorities is always preceded by ample and, in his view, decisive philosophical argumentation. In this sense Suárez may be regarded as a modern philosopher, not greatly different from Descartes and Malebranche, for example.

¹⁶ *Commentaria una cum quaestionibus in tres libros de anima* (Cologne, 1583), fol. 159ra and rb.

¹⁷ Suárez lists various different reasons in §§ 10-13.

¹⁸ *Prius.* Some editions read *potius.*

¹⁹ Sect. VII.

²⁰ Another possible reading: "which is adequately terminated (ended, fulfilled) in this matter."

²¹ The text reads *forma* instead of *materia,* but the sense is clear. Although the text of Suárez is generally clean, it does contain occasional errors. These ought to be attributed to the printer, certainly. It is quite probable that Suárez's autograph may have been heavily abbreviated and that the printer misread the abbreviations or simply substituted one word for another. The standard medieval abbreviations for *forma* and *materia* are fᵃ and mᵃ respectively. In cursive they could appear quite similar.

²² For Durandus see n. 5 above; for Toletus see n. 16 above.

²³ Ch. 6, sect. 1. *Ed. cit.,* cols. 380F-381B.

²⁴ *Ed. cit.,* XIX, p. 751b.

²⁵ This subtitle appears as part of § 18 in the Latin text.

²⁶ Q.1, a.1, *quarta conclusio. Ed. cit.,* vol. III, pp. 203b ff.

²⁷ *Pars prima...,* vol. IV, p. 41b, com. VII and vol. V, p. 10a, com. I, and p. 11a, com. III.

²⁸ *Ed. cit.,* p. 376a-b.

²⁹ Bk. XII, q.24; *ed. cit.,* p. 902b.

³⁰ Com. I. *Ed. cit.,* p. 64b.

SECTION VII

WHETHER THE PRINCIPLE OF INDIVIDUATION OF ACCIDENTS IS
TO BE TAKEN FROM THE SUBJECT[1]

1. Almost the same opinions that were given in the preceding Section[2] can be given in this question. However, because the same doctrine stated concerning substantial forms is to be proportionally applied to accidental [forms], therefore, this matter can be very briefly expedited by adding a few [things] peculiar to accidents.[3]

Therefore, we assume from what has been said in Section II,[4] that individual differences are necessary in accidental forms; [and that these individual differences are those] which the individual forms add to specific natures *(rationibus),* from which they are distinguished at least conceptually; for the doctrine stated there is general and the arguments given apply to all species and individuals. Whence it is [the case] that, speaking about the metaphysical principles constituting and distinguishing things, no question remains concerning the principle of individuation of accidents. For there is in them an individual difference, which is proper to each and contracts the species to the being of a particular individual. Therefore, it remains to be asked only what the physical foundation and principle of this difference is, and [it is] in this sense that we investigate here the principle of individuation of accidents, just as we did with substances. And thus, here we have no disagreement with Scotus, who thought he had put an end to this question with his thisnesses *(haecceitatibus)* — which are nothing other than individual differences. For we also admit those differences, although we inquire further about the physical root of their differences.

2. Therefore, only two opinions can be discussed here. The first is that accidents are individuated by the subject.[5] Thus teaches St. Thomas, in [*Summa theologiae*] I, q.29, a.1 and q.39, a.3, and *Opuscule* 29, [*On the Principle of Individuation*], at the end.[6] But in *Quodlibet* VII, a.19, he restricts this view and says that it is true for accidents other than quantity, which he says is not individuated from the subject, but from place; the remaining accidents, however, [are individuated] from the subject, at least from quantity.[7] Whence, he infers that, although individual quantity could be preserved by God without a subject, [this could] not [happen], however, in [the case of] whiteness or the remaining accidents, which necessarily require the subject, [or] at least quantity itself, in order to be made individuals. For this reason St. Thomas often teaches that there cannot be two separate and only numerically distinct whitenesses, because they would not have [anything] whereby they might be distinguished, [*Summa theologiae*] I, q.50, a.4, and q.75, a.7.[8] And Capreolus teaches and defends the same in *On I* [*of the Sentences*], dist. 54, a.2, concl. 2.[9]

The bases of this view are the same as those given above to prove that substantial form is individuated by designated matter. This is confirmed, first, because an accident has all its being in relation to the subject. Therefore, it should have individuation from the subject, for each thing should be individuated by the same principles by which it has being. Second, because if accidents were not individuated by the subject, many accidents only numerically diverse could be received in the same subject, since, in spite of the subject's identity, they could be distinguished among themselves, [and] hence, no reason could be given to rule this out *(repugnantiae)*. We see, however, that the same subject cannot receive two whitenesses or two heats. Therefore, the whole reason for this is that they are individuated by the subject; and hence, because they are received in the same subject, they are one, and not two, in fact.

3. *The opinion of others.* The second opinion is that each accidental form is physically individuated by itself, [insofar] as it is a particular entity in act or in aptitude, and that it does not have any other intrinsic principle of individuation in addition to its entity.[10] This is taken from the opinion of Durandus discussed above. And all the arguments which we used in [the case of] substantial form prove the same concerning accidental form. In short, it is that each thing is formally and intrinsically one in number — with respect to the foundation of the unity or negation which "one" expresses — , by the same [thing] by which it is or is apt to be a being in act in the order of things; because every such being is singular, as has been shown above. But every thing is intrinsically and formally such a being in

act by its entity; therefore, it is something singular and individual by the same. Therefore, this applies to accidents as well.

This is confirmed, because the subject cannot be the principle individuating accidents; therefore, only the intrinsic entity of the accidents themselves can be such a principle. The antecedent is clear, because, in the first place, the subject cannot be said to be the intrinsic principle of the individuation of an accident, as intrinsically and essentially *(per se)* composing the accident, because we are not now discussing the composite of subject and accident, but the accidental form itself, which is certainly not intrinsically composed of the subject itself; nor is the subject its intrinsic principle of individuation in this way. In turn, the subject, as term of the relation or of the aptitude of such an accident to inform such a subject, cannot be said to be the principle individuating the accident either: First, because with respect to the numerically same subject two accidents distinct only in number can have the aptitude for informing it. Therefore, those aptitudes cannot be numerically distinguished from the subject; therefore, [they are distinguished] by themselves. Second, this is most pressing concerning some accidents, which according to their relation do not stand in the subject, but refer to it or lead to another in some way, as is [the case with] relations, acts, habits and similar [ones]. For if an accident is said to be individuated by the subject because it is naturally related to it, why may not these accidents be said to be rather individuated by the final terms to which they naturally refer, especially since they take their essential or specific natures *(rationes)* from them and according to their common natures *(rationes)?* Third, that numerically this accident has a natural coadaptability and relation to this subject alone is said without basis. For, although perhaps by natural causes it could only be made in it, yet, nonetheless, the very same [accident] is apt of itself to inform any subject capable of such an accident. [This is] just as, on the contrary, it can happen that this subject could naturally have only this whiteness or this quantity, and yet, its capacity is not, because of this, to be understood to be from itself so limited and determined to this accident that it would not be sufficient of itself to receive similar accidents. Finally, the same point can be defended with all the reasons we gave in [the case of] substantial form.

Solution to the Question

4. This controversy is to be dissolved and explained by the distinction introduced above. We said, then, that we can speak of the principle of individuation in two ways: First, with respect to being and to the proper constitution of a thing in itself; second, with respect to

production, insofar as the agent is determined to produce a distinct individual or to cause one rather than another, and, consequently, with respect to our knowledge insofar as sensibly, — if I may put it so — , we can distinguish one from another. Therefore, according to the former consideration, — which is the most *a priori,* and the most proper to this science — , the second view is true, [the one that] teaches that accidents do not have their individuation and numerical distinction from the subject, but from their proper entities, as the reasons given here and in the preceding Section sufficiently prove, and as it will become more clear in the solution to the arguments.[11] However, according to the latter consideration, — which is more physical and *a posteriori* — , accidents can be said to receive individuation from the subject, as it were, from a root, or rather as the occasion of their multiplication and distinction. This, however, is not to be understood concerning the subject taken bare, but [rather] as together with other circumstances or conditions necessary for action, as it will be explained more conveniently in the solution to the arguments.

5. The bases of the first opinion, therefore, insofar as they are the same reasons with which it is usually proven that matter designated by quantity is the principle of individuation, and [insofar as] they can be inconsistent with the first part of the view proposed by us, have been sufficiently discussed and untangled in the preceding Section.[12] Indeed, the first confirmation proves only that an accident has its individuation in relation to the subject and that it naturally depends from it, not, however, that the individuation of the subject is the intrinsic principle of individuation of the accident. In the second confirmation and in the latter bases of the view, however, is presented a common problem which cannot be overlooked here, but which requires its own separate question.

NOTES

[1] Sections VII through IX comprise a self-contained treatise on the individuation of accidents. Section VII in particular raises the question concerning their principle of individuation. The discussion is preceded by two paragraphs (§ 1) in which Suárez explains the similarity between the problems of accidental and substantial individuation. In § 2 are given the first view of accidental individuation (first paragraph) and its argumentative support (second paragraph). In § 3 a second view is given (first paragraph) and supported with arguments (second paragraph). § 4 comprises the solution to the question, and § 5 is an answer to the arguments in favor of the first view, which Suárez rejects.

[2] Sect. VI.

[3] For Suárez, the problem of individuation as it applies to accidents and substances is basically the same. This is so primarily for three reasons: First, accidents, like substances, are always individual except when found in the mind as abstractions

or universals; second, in both cases their nature is conceptually distinct from the individual unity that distinguishes them numerically from other instances of the same species; and third, the foundation of the individual unity of accidents is, like that of substances, their own entities. The latter point separates Suárez drastically from Thomas and, I believe, Aristotle. For the last two, the principle of individuation of substances and accidents was not the same sort of principle, since substances were individuated by matter or matter and quantity, while accidents were individuated by the subject.

⁴ This paragraph, as it is clear from Suárez's reference to Section II, is meant to establish that accidents, just like substances, possess an individual difference which individuates them. As in Section II, Suárez interprets Scotus' view of *haecceitas* as an answer to the problem of whether there is such an individual difference and not as an attempt to point out the principle of individuation. This is, of course, Suárez's own interpretation of Scotus. For his part Scotus explicitly stated that he was giving an answer to the second problem and not to the first. See *Opus oxoniense* II, dist. III, qq.1 ff.

⁵ This is the opinion later rejected by Suárez. He cites only Thomas and Capreolus as supporters of this view. This position, however, was very common among scholastics.

⁶ *Summa theologiae*, vol. I, p. 204a and 258a. For *Opuscule 29*, see Sect. III, n. 8, also § 429.

⁷ There is no article 19. The reference is probably to a.10. *Quaestiones quodlibetales*, in Vivès, vol. XV, p. 509b.

⁸ *Ed. cit.*, vol. I, pp. 342b and 474b-475a.

⁹ Rather, in d.43/44, *quaestio unica*, a.2. *Ed. cit.*, vol. II, pp. 536b-537a.

¹⁰ This is the view adopted by Suárez.

¹¹ Suárez refers twice to the explanation and clarification he will provide in "the solution to the arguments." Yet the solution to the arguments or answer to the objections is hardly that clear or detailed; it comprises only a short paragraph. Perhaps the reference should be understood to point to Sections VIII and IX. These explore whether it is possible for two accidents, diverse only in number, to be present in the same subject at the same time or successively. This issue was raised in § 2 of this Section, in the context of an argument in support of Thomas' view; whence Suárez's way of referring to his discussion of it as a "solution to arguments."

¹² Section VI.

SECTION VIII

WHETHER IT IS INCOMPATIBLE FOR TWO ACCIDENTS, DIVERSE
ONLY IN NUMBER, TO BE SIMULTANEOUSLY [PRESENT]
IN THE SAME SUBJECT OWING TO THEIR
INDIVIDUALITY (*individuationem*)

1. There are two ways in which accidents [present] in the same subject may differ only in number, namely, simultaneously or only successively. Both [ways] are under dispute, but we discuss only the first in the present Section.[1]

The First Opinion is Discussed[2]

2. The first opinion denies that not only accidents of the same species but also of diverse species, provided they be contained in the same proximate genus, can be simultaneously [present] in the same subject. It may be seen in St. Thomas, [*Summa theologiae*] I, q.85, a.1, where he says: "It is impossible for the same subject to be perfected simultaneously by many forms of one genus and of diverse species, just as it is impossible for the same body in the same respect to be simultaneously colored by diverse colors or shaped by diverse shapes."[3] Moreover, in q.8 of *On Truth,* a.14, he states it concerning forms existing in perfect act.[4] Thomists commonly adopt this explanation, and in this way they solve the difficulties concerning the many intelligible or sensible species contained within the same proximate genus — such as the species of man and horse — and existing simultaneously in the same power. [They] also [solve the difficulties] concerning two sciences, for example, or two moral or theological virtues,[5] which, although differing in species and contained under the same proximate genus, could be simultaneously [present] in the same power, even with perfect intensity. For they say that these and similar [things] are simultaneously [present in the same subject] only in incomplete act, because they are simultaneously [present] in it only in first act or in habit, not in second act.

3. But it is truly difficult to hold this opinion without qualification and absolutely in all its generality, first, because no sufficient reason can be given for it. For, as Scotus correctly objected, *On I* [*of the Sentences*], dist. 3, q.6, "Therefore, to the question...,"⁶ in the examples which St. Thomas gave above, those accidents different in species cannot be simultaneously [present in the same subject], because they include some opposition with respect to the subject. For two colors are always opposed, whether as extreme contraries, or as extreme and middle, or as closer to one of the extremes. [And] shapes also include an incompatibility of place or of straightness or obliquity or any other similar thing. It is not necessary, however, that all accidents different in species have this sort of opposition with respect to the subject. And so Durandus does not incorrectly put forth, *On II* [*of the Sentences*], dist. 3, q.8, the argument concerning intelligible species,⁷ — although he misuses it to reject intelligible species. Accordingly, he argues that, although the intellect may not actually understand, there are many perfect and complete species, with respect to the act of informing; for actual operation has nothing to do with the complete being of form. Cajetan answers, [in his commentary to *Summa theologiae*] I, q.85, a.4, that this is true [in the case] of the real being of species, not however, in their intelligible being.⁸

But, leaving aside [the fact] that there is a sort of begging of the question in the matter which he discusses there, namely, whether the intellect could simultaneously have many acts of understanding, because, as he himself points out, to be intelligible is nothing but actually to move a power to actual consideration; leaving this aside, as I say, it is enough for the question with which we are concerned that two accidents may, with respect to their real being, simultaneously have the complete act of informing in the same subject. And the same argument can be given concerning the habits of moral virtues or of sciences, in which there is no place for the distinction between real and intelligible being. And, from this, the argument can be extended also to acts. For it will not be incompatible, either as far as they themselves are concerned, or as far as their receptive power is concerned, for them to be simultaneously [present in the same subject], if the active power that could cause them to be [present] simultaneously is not lacking, because outside of this there is no greater incompatibility among acts than among habits belonging to the same genus, provided they are not opposed for other reasons.

4. Likewise is solved the problem *(ratio)* St. Thomas raises in the mentioned q.8 of *On Truth,* namely, that acts belonging to the same genus are related to the same power, determining it, while the same power cannot be simultaneously determined by many acts.⁹ The answer to this is, then, that this is true in [the case of] acts adequate

to the same power, but not in [the case of] inadequate [acts]. For instance, in the present [case] one species or one habit is not the first adequate act of the intellect, because it does not perfect it with respect to its adequate object; and thus, there could simultaneously be many [acts present] in it, even if they belonged to the same genus, until they wholly and adequately perfect it. And the same must be said concerning any accidental form, as, for example, heat and dryness. These, although perhaps agreeing in proximate genus, can be simultaneously [present] in the same fire, because neither of these qualities fulfills by itself the natural capacity of fire, — neither the passive [capacity] which it has by reason of matter, nor in any way the active [capacity], which it has by reason of form by natural dimanation. Therefore, in order for the proposition of St. Thomas to be true in some sense, it must be understood to refer to forms which completely and adequately actualize the potency of the subject within a particular genus or nature *(ratione),* as it will become more clear from what will be said. For this opinion, which has been discussed thus far, is not founded in the individuation of accidents, and so it did not refer to the present question. Yet it was necessary to present [it] first, both in order to complement the doctrine and also because it throws some light on what we shall say later.

Second Opinion[10]

5. The second opinion is also extreme: No accidents whatever belonging to the same species can be simultaneously [present] in the same subject. This is thought to be Aristotle's [opinion] in *Metaphysics* V, Ch. 10, text 15,[11] where he says that those accidents differ in species that, being [present] in the same substance, have a difference. In that place, lect. 12, St. Thomas gives the general reason for that assertion: That it is impossible for many accidents belonging to the same species to be in the same subject. He teaches the same in [*Summa theologiae*] III, q.35, a.5, where he rejects as well [the presence of] many relations only numerically diverse in the same father with respect to many children, or in the same child with respect to the father and mother.[12] And so, generally, this opinion is defended by Capreolus, *On I* [*of the Sentences*], dist. 7, q.2;[13] Cajetan, [in his commentary to the *Summa theologiae*] III, q.35, a.5;[14] [and] Hervaeus, *Quodlibet* III, q.9, and *On III* [*of the Sentences*], dist. 8, q.1;[15] [also] there Paludanus, q.2;[16] Soncinas, in [*Questions on*] *Metaphysics* VII, q.4, where he gives many arguments.[17] But the principal [argument] is taken from individuation. For the distinction among forms is only either formal, which is the specific [distinction], or material from the subject, which is the numerical [distinction], according to

Aristotle, *Metaphysics* III, Ch. 3 and Bk. V, Ch. 6.[18] Therefore, where none of these takes place, there cannot be a distinction; therefore, where there is specific unity of accident in the same subject, there cannot be numerical plurality. This is confirmed, because otherwise, by the reason whereby two accidents, diverse only in number, are simultaneously [present] in the same subject, they could also be multiplied to infinity, since there is no more reason for one multitude than for another. Whence it will be inferred that there are infinite relations [present] in the same subject, and other similar unsuitable [consequences].

6. But it is also difficult to maintain this view in all its generality without some exception, because there are several examples which we shall present immediately in which plainly it does not seem to work. And thus, although no author teaches the view at the contrary extreme strictly speaking *(simpliciter)*, namely, that any accidents differing only numerically, whatever their species, can be simultaneously [present] in the same subject, — for this is not only openly incompatible with Aristotle and all other philosophers, but also with experience itself, as it was touched on above, and as it will be established from what will be said in more detail later — ; nevertheless, they bring up many exceptions and qualifications to the aforementioned view. Because it is difficult to choose a middle course and to give the reason for it, however, they do not agree among themselves in making this exception.

Third Opinion[19]

7. The third opinion is that of the Thomists, who distinguish accidents in complete and incomplete act. For they deny that there can, in the former way, be simultaneously [present] in one subject accidents differing only numerically, owing to the reasons given and the authority of Aristotle and St. Thomas, which they so interpret. They admit it, however, in the latter way. Thus Cajetan in [his commentary to *Summa theologiae*] I, q.95, a.4,[20] [and] more clearly Capreolus, *On II [of the Sentences]*, dist. 3, q.2, [in the answer] to the arguments against conclusion 9;[21] Iavellus, [*Questions on*] *Metaphysics* V, q. 16.[22] These seem to have taken it from St. Thomas, *On Truth,* q.8, a.14.[23] And they seem to be primarily led by the argument of intentional species, because they cannot deny that many only numerically different [intentional species] could be [present] in the same subject, namely, in the same intellect, or in the same imagination, or in the same part of the same medium.

8. But, in the first place, this distinction is not sufficient. For we shall show below that not only these intentional accidents, but also

many others, in their whole complete being, can be simultaneously [present] in the same subject. Next, the argument given above is given again concerning these intentional accidents, namely: By what reason are they said to be incompletely [present] in the subject? Is it because they do not cause [it] or because they do not fully inform [it]? This latter is false, because they are [present] in it in their whole being; therefore, they inform [it]. Moreover, the first seems irrelevant, because the complete being of an accident does not consist in causing, but in informing. Finally, it will be [the case] that if these accidents cannot be [present] in the same subject owing to individuation, then, whether they are or not in actual operation, the outcome will be the same, because before they operate they have their individuation from the subject. Therefore, either that argument is not suitable, or it proves equally that these accidents cannot be numerically distinguished in the same subject, even while they are not in operation.

Fourth Opinion [24]

9. The fourth opinion is that proper accidents, that is, accidents which emanate intrinsically from the subject, cannot be many in the same subject while differing only numerically; but, [on the other hand], common accidents can be [there] simultaneously. Thus states Jandun, in [*Commentary on the*] *Metaphysics* V, q.36.[25] The reason for the first part is that nature abhors superabundance. Hence, since a proper accident is intrinsic to the nature, and one [accident] is enough for the function and end of the nature, [a proper accident] is not multiplied. The reason for the second part is taken from this: For, since a common accident often comes [to the subject] extrinsically and accidentally, it is not inconsistent that it be multiplied in the same subject, and so it happens that many heatings[26] are simultaneously produced by diverse fires in the same wood.

10. But this view, although true with respect to its first part, nevertheless is not universally true with respect to the second, because neither many whitenesses nor many heats can be simultaneously [present] in the same subject, even if they were common accidents. Nor is it true what is said concerning many heatings. For when two fires heat the same part of the same wood, just as they cause one heat, so likewise [do they cause] one heating, which is partially from each and from both simultaneously as from a whole cause. Furthermore, if that rule were generally true, it would follow that two sciences of the same species and ordered to the same object — [and] similarly with two temperances, diverse only in number — , could be simultaneously [present] in the same [subject], [something] which is not defensible. Finally, a general reason goes against [this view],

because even in external and accidental changes, the extrinsic agent intends to assimilate the patient to itself. Hence, if it finds [it] similar [to itself], it does not act on it again; otherwise, after it had assimilated the one similar to itself, it would act on it again and again, and so the action would proceed to infinity, at least insofar as the multiplication of accidental forms is concerned. And, for the same reason, things completely similar in the same accident would change each other reciprocally, and they would multiply in themselves similar accidents. Indeed, by the same or a better reason, the same [thing] would act on itself, producing by one accident another [accident] similar to it, or, if it had two already, it would cause a third, and so on to infinity. [But] all of this is plainly false and absurd. Whence it is gathered that even in these accidental changes, their principle on the part of the subject is the privation of a similar form; and thus, this kind of change does not extend to the multiplication of accidents of the same species in the same subject.

Fifth Opinion [27]

11. The fifth opinion distinguishes the accidents produced by a proper motion from those produced without motion, and it denies that the former could be simultaneously [present] in the same subject, owing to the given reason, that motion is produced from contrary to contrary. On the other hand, concerning the latter, it affirms that accidents diverse only in number can be simultaneously [present] in the same subject. Fonseca mentions this opinion in [*Commentary on the Metaphysics*], Bk. V, Ch. 10, q.1, sect. 1,[28] and it is usually attributed to Scotus, Gabriel, Durandus, and others, in *On III* [*of the Sentences*], dist. 8. Durandus, however, says nothing about it there, in q.3, but rather, in the solution to 1, he admits, concerning only absolute accidents, that those which are of the same species could be [present] in the same supposit according to different parts; while in [the case of] relative ones, [they can be present in the same supposit] according to different foundations.[29] Gabriel, however, in the same place, a.3, doubt 1, makes no distinction, but simply denies that it be incompatible for two accidents differing only numerically to be [present] in the same subject.[30] And Scotus speaks almost in the same way there, in the sole question.[31] Nevertheless, he points out that the multiplication of qualities of the same nature *(rationis)* in the same subject is not caused by the operation of a natural agent, because a natural agent intends to perfect a preexisting imperfect form, and thus, it does not induce a completely different form, but a certain degree or, as it were, a part which it unites to the preexisting [one] in order to perfect it. By this he refers to the distinction between acci-

dents which are produced by motion and [those which are produced] without it. This is also suggested by Antoninus Andrea in [*Questions on*] *Metaphysics* V, q.8;[32] for he says that relative accidents differing only numerically can be [present] in the same [subject]. He distinguishes [further], however, concerning absolute [accidents], for some are educed from the potency of the subject, and these are not numerically multiplied in the same subject; while others are not [so] educed, and these can be multiplied. And he thinks light to be one of these. For perspectivists *(perspectivi)* contend concerning it that two lights *(lumina)* are produced in the same part of the subject by two sources of light *(luminosis)*, because they cause two shadows, and because, if one source of light is removed, some light is corrupted and some [light] remains in the air.

12. *All accidents inhering in a subject are educed from its potency.*[33] But these [things] are partially false, partially unsatisfactory. And, to begin with the latter,[34] it is false that there are some accidents [present] in the subject which may not be educed[35] from its potency in the same way they are produced in it, because all [accidents] depend on the subject for [their] production and [their] being. And especially concerning light, it is certain that it is educed from the potency of the subject. For it is not created, nor is it produced only in the subject, but from the subject, — air concurring to its production, obviously, as a kind of material cause in fact. It is false, moreover, that lights are numerically multiplied in the same subject; nor is there any experience by which this could be proven. For experience teaches only that, other [things] being equal, two sources of light make more [light] on the same area than one alone. But that is not due to the multiplication of lights, but due to the greater intensity of the same light. From this it comes about that if one agent is removed, the effect appears diminished even in that part affected only by the action of one [of them] and not of another, [and this] not because one light is removed *(corrumpatur)* and the other remains, but because the same [light] is diminished and preserved. From this it comes also that sometimes two shadows may result, because a shadow is nothing other than the lack or diminution of light. And it often happens that when a body is interposed between two distant sources of light, in one place it obstructs the action of one, and in another distant [one it obstructs] the action of the other, while in the intermediate place the action of neither is obstructed; whence it happens that several shadows may appear. Hence, the first distinction concerning accidents which are produced by motion or without it is easily refuted. For, if motion is taken strictly as successive motion which is caused by the contrary, by the example of light it is made clear that the latter part is false. For light is not produced by motion, but by

instantaneous change, nor is it made from a contrary positive term, but from a privative [one], and nevertheless it cannot be multiplied in the same subject.

Again, the distinction seems too accidental. For, what does this numerical distinction or identity of accidents have to do with [the fact] that they may be produced by motion or by change, since the distinction of accidents is not taken from there, but either from themselves or from the subject? For, if the subject is only in potency to one heat that is successively produced, why not say also that it is only in potency to one light, even if it may be simultaneously produced? Or, on the contrary, if it is in potency to many lights, why will it not be in potency to many heats? For, if it is said that in those [accidents] which are produced successively, the agent does not intend to induce a new accident, but to perfect the preexisting [one], the same will be said concerning light and any other similar quality, which, just as it is produced in an instant from the opposite privation, so also can it be intensified in an instant from the privation of so much intensity. Hence, there is a place here also for the argument from Scotus discussed above,[36] because not only successive motion, but every natural action of the agent aims to render the patient similar to itself; and, hence, it does not act upon a [patient] similar to [itself], but requires privation in the patient as a principle of its action. Therefore, when four degrees of light are in the air, and a new source of light is applied, [the new source of light] will not act on the air insofar as it is similar to four degrees, but rather insofar as it is dissimilar in additional degrees. Therefore, the same argument can be made concerning accidents which are produced by change or by motion.

13. For, if "motion" is not taken so strictly in that distinction, but as including change, so that the sense is that those accidents which are produced essentially *(per se)* by a proper action are not multiplied numerically in the subject, although others may be multiplied, the distinction can also be assailed thus: First, because it is established in terms of those [things] which are too extrinsic and accidental for the numerical distinction of accidents. Second, because neither part seems too certain; for sensible species are produced by proper action, and nevertheless, they are numerically multiplied in the same part of the medium. Sound also seems to be produced essentially *(per se)* by proper action, and nevertheless, it is numerically multiplied in the same subject, as experience seems to prove. For we hear the harmony of many voices at the same time and through the same medium, [something] which could not be possible unless the sounds were diverse. On the contrary, however, shape is not produced essentially *(per se)* and primarily by motion, and nevertheless, it can-

not be numerically multiplied in the same subject. And the same is [the case] with all similar absolute accidents, because they cannot be multiplied by the change of something extrinsic, as relative [accidents are]. And hence, just as they are not produced essentially *(per se)*, so neither can they be multiplied essentially *(per se)* in the same subject; nor [can they do so] concomitantly, since the form, which is produced essentially *(per se)* and which they follow, is not numerically multiplied in the same subject.

14. *Relative accidents can be multiplied under the same species in the same subject, but not all of them.* Furthermore, the distinction between absolute and relative [accidents] is not satisfactory in all respects. For, if relative [accidents] are taken strictly as relative in the order of being and in the categories, it is certainly true that these [relative accidents] can be numerically multiplied in the same subject sometimes, as we shall say when dealing with relations. But this is not universally true; for the relation of "creature"[37] cannot be multiplied in the same subject.

But the other part about absolute [accidents] is less universally true, as is clear from the examples given concerning species and concerning sounds, and similar [things]. Fonseca uses another distinction in the place cited above, [i.e. *Commentary on the Metaphysics*] sect. 3, which coincides in most parts with what has been said above.[38] In short, he says that of the accidents naturally acquired by motion, or by change together with motion, there cannot be many of the same species in the subject. And in the fourth [conclusion][39] he explains in terms of these Aristotle's statement,[40] which in this sense he understands as universally true and without exception. He adds below, however, that it is necessary for accidents not subject to intensification and remission, — whether they be acquired by motion, or by change together with motion, or in any other way — , to be many of the same species in the same subject. Hence, it seems that he limits the first view to those accidents which are subject to intensification and remission; and so, the former view is not completely general, as he indicates in the fourth conclusion.

But not even with that limitation does this view seem universally true, because intentional species can be intensified or diminished, and, nonetheless, they are multiplied in the same subject. It is also probable that sound may be subject to remission and intensification, which, however, he says, is multiplied in the same subject.

Concerning what he also adds there, that in terms of God's absolute power there cannot be many numerically distinct accidents [present] in the same subject when they are such that they are united in a more intense numerical one by their nature, it is difficult to believe [it], as I shall make clear immediately in more detail.

Solution to the Question as to the Way in which Many Similar Accidents can be Simultaneously [Present] in the Same Subject[41]

15. In the midst of so many opinions, it is difficult to prescribe some fixed rule in this matter and to point to the true reason for it. Nevertheless, two[42] [things] seem certain to me in this matter: One is that this universal negative proposition, "No plurality of accidents of the same species can be [present] in the same subject," cannot be verified absolutely and without qualification, that is, without some limitation. This is proven to me above all from examples of intentional and relational species, assuming they are something real, distinct *ex natura rei* from absolute [beings]. Moreover, the example given about sound is not so convincing, both because it is not certain that sound is produced essentially *(per se)* [and] primarily by that motion or action, and above all, because it is not sufficiently certain that many sounds heard are [present] in the same part of the subject. For they are always produced at the beginning in distinct places, and there they are properly perceived. Moreover, when they arrive at the sense of hearing *(auditum)* or at the part of the medium near the sense of hearing, perhaps they do not arrive already as real beings, but only as intentional [beings].

Other examples are usually given concerning the continuities and durations of two motions which can be produced simultaneously in the same [subject]. For example, the same wood can be simultaneously heated and dried, in which two motions, although they be diverse in species [themselves], nevertheless their continuities and durations seem to differ only in number. But these examples are not altogether conclusive, both [1] because it is very probable that neither [i] is duration an accident or a mode distinct *ex natura rei* from the existence of the enduring thing, nor [ii] is the intrinsic or entitative continuity in reality continuous, and also [2] because, even if we grant accidents of this sort, they are not [present] in the mobile immediately, but by means of the motion which they cause; and thus, they are not properly [present] in the same subject in the same respect. Nevertheless, the former examples are sufficient, to which it can be added that the same power can have simultaneously many numerically distinct acts, although perhaps not completely similar or perfect to the highest degree, as if the will or appetite simultaneously loved two men by diverse acts; or if the blessed — as many pretend — loved God necessarily and freely simultaneously out of charity.

16. *Concerning the accidents which are to be judged able to coexist in one subject and [the accidents] which are not.* Second, it is certain that it cannot happen naturally in any species of accident that many [accidents]

differing only in number be simultaneously [present] in the same subject. This is certain concerning: [1] all properties which belong intrinsically, [such] as quantity, which belongs intrinsically by reason of matter; [2] the powers or connatural faculties which emanate from form in each thing and are never multiplied in the same part of the subject within the same species, as it is clear enough from induction; again [3], the real and absolute qualities, whether the first, with which matter is disposed, or the second, which result from these, as experience can also prove, — for the counterexample usually given concerning degrees of intensity is not [pertinent] to the matter, for they [i.e. the degrees of intensity] do not properly differ in number ([we shall speak] about these elsewhere); again [4], it is more probable, finally, concerning light and similar [accidents].

Moreover, I have found nothing that would satisfy me on all accounts concerning which general rule should be given, or which reason should be pointed out for the difference. We can explain it, however, in this way: Certain accidents differ only in number in such a way that in addition to the distinction of entities they have certain similarity and agreement in everything else, such as in the function or service to which they are destined and in any relation they express, for example, in the case of two heats, two whitenesses, and similar [ones]. There are others, however, which, although they may agree in specific notion and differ under it only in number, nevertheless do not have so much similarity among themselves, but differ either in function or in relation, [such] as, for example, two visible images *(species)* of Peter differ numerically in the former sense. The two visible images *(species)* of Peter and Paul, however, differ numerically in the latter sense; for they are not so similar to each other as the former two, since they have diverse transcendental relations to the objects and are ordered to diverse functions.

17. Therefore, I say, third, that accidents of the former sort cannot be multiplied numerically in the same subject, although those of the latter sort can be multiplied. Both [claims] can be proven by induction and the given examples. Indeed, completely absolute accidents are never numerically multiplied in the same subject, because they are similar in the first way. Relative accidents, however, whether with a categorical or a transcendental relation, can be multiplied, because they can have some dissimilarity, as it were material, with the specific unity, by reason of which they can be multiplied. Whence it happens that they can never be multiplied in relation to the same [term]. And thus, the relation of "creature" cannot be multiplied, because its term can only be one, and relations cannot be multiplied with respect to the same term.[43] Hence, also, even if we granted that the relations to father and mother are many and only

numerically diverse, nevertheless, the relation to father cannot be multiplied in the same son.

Moreover, the reason for the difference between both [types of] accidents can be determined with sufficient probability from what has been said. First, from the final cause, because when accidents are completely similar, their multiplication in the same subject would be superfluous and idle, [something] which nature abhors. When, however, they are diverse in some way or are ordered to diverse ends, as it is clear in [the case of] intentional species, or [when] they are the result of things ordered to diverse ends and they participate because of it in diverse dispositions *(habitudines)*, as it happens with relations, then numerical multiplication is not superfluous, nor outside the proper end of the nature.

18. Second, from the part of the agent, because, when accidents are completely similar, no agent by itself intends either their plurality or to induce another [accident] in the subject already having one completely similar [to the first], because the agent only intends to render the patient similar to itself, for which only one [accidental] form of this sort is enough. But, on the other hand, when accidents are not similar in the aforementioned way, this reason ceases [to operate] and the subject requires greater assimilation, and thus, the agent also sees to it. For example, although the medium, having received Peter's species, be intentionally similar to it, it is not sufficiently similar to Paul, and thus, the power to induce the species whereby it [i.e. the medium] is rendered similar to himself [i.e. Paul] remains in Paul, and likewise with other [cases].

19. Hence, third, an argument based on the capacity of the subject is given: For just as prime matter, although indifferent to all substantial forms, nevertheless does not have a capacity to have them all simultaneously, or even many, because it may be sufficiently actualized by one form; so also the subject of accidents, although it may be, primarily [and] by itself, capable of some species of accident and, consequently, indifferent to any of the individuals belonging to it [i.e. such a species], nonetheless, is not capable of receiving simultaneously all or many individuals of such a species, insofar as the specific nature *(ratio)* is found in them in the same way, because a capacity of this sort is sufficiently actualized by one form of such a species. This happens when individual forms are completely similar and of the same nature *(rationis)* and disposition *(habitudinis)*. When, however, accidents are dissimilar and they have similar dispositions *(habitudines)*, then one is not sufficient to fulfill the capacity of the subject. Thus, it can happen that they be multiplied in the same subject until they fulfill completely its capacity. For example, while the intellective power, insofar as it is capable of a natural knowledge

(scientiae)[44] of God or man, is sufficiently disposed in the first act by a numerically one knowledge *(scientia)* of metaphysics or of philosophy, and thus, it does not remain capable of another similar knowledge *(scientiae)* any more; nevertheless, the same intellective faculty, [insofar] as it is capable of actual knowledge of men, is not fully actualized by the one act whereby it knows Peter and Paul, nor by one intelligible species. Therefore, it is capable of many, until its faculty is sufficiently fulfilled, because those many do not actualize it altogether in the same way, but in relation to diverse [things].

Whence it is concluded, finally, from the distinctions made above, that the view that distinguishes between absolute and relative [accidents] is closer to the truth: For absolute [accidents] are not multiplied, because they are always completely similar. Relative [accidents], however, whether according to being or word *(dici)*, or [according to] categorical relation or transcendental disposition *(habitudine)*, can be multiplied when they are related to diverse terms or [when] they are ordered to diverse functions, owing to the dissimilarity they have to each other. [And this] because none of them fully actualizes the subject, as has been made clear. The text of Aristotle in *Metaphysics* V is to be interpreted according to this. For it is not necessary that the sign of specific diversity be altogether the same for all accidents, but [only] for those which are perfectly similar in the individual.

Formal Answer to the Question insofar as Individuation is Concerned

20. The formal answer to the present question is gathered from these [considerations]. It is for this reason that all these [things] have been said, namely, that from individuation it cannot be essentially *(per se)* derived that some accidents diverse only in number could not be simultaneously [present] in the same subject. For, although they may be simultaneously [present] in it, they could best be understood to be numerically distinct by reason of their entities, in the manner in which those [accidents] which can be simultaneously [present in the same subject] are distinguished, as has been said, or in the manner in which those [accidents] which are successively [present] in the same subject are distinguished, as will be said immediately. But that some cannot be [present] in it derives from the natural incapacity of the subject and the proportion *(adaequatione)* which is found between its receptive potency and such an act, and, consequently, from the lack of the natural agent which could effect such multiplication.

21. Whence I infer, further, that in terms of absolute power it is not incompatible for many accidents differing only in number, even if

they were completely similar, to be simultaneously placed in the same subject; because there is no incompatibility from their individuality *(individuatione)* and distinction, and God can act in a subject beyond its natural capacity. And if God wished to do so for the demonstration of his power, [the action] would not be totally superfluous.

Some [authors], however, restrict this to those accidents which are neither subject to intensification nor remission. For, concerning those which are subject to intensification *(intensionem)*,[45] they think it impossible, even by absolute power, that many accidents differing only in number could be placed in the same subject without producing a more intense quality, if both of them inhere in the subject, because by this very fact they are necessarily united with each other in a more intense one. For two degrees of heat do not require any other union in order to produce one more intense heat than that they be in the same subject. Whence, if one of them inheres in the subject while the other does not, but in some other way is sustained by the same subject without inhering in it, then it will not be incompatible that they be simultaneously [placed] in or perhaps be sustained by the same subject, because then they do not have between them the unity necessary for the production of a more intense quality. Egidius in *On I [of the Sentences]*, dist. 17, [and] *On II [of the Sentences]*, dist. 1, q.2, first article, is cited as an example of this view;[46] but he says nothing [about it] there.

22. This view, however, seems to assume false principles concerning the intensification of qualities. First, [it assumes] that intensification is produced by the addition or congregation of many degrees of the same quality completely similar among themselves. Second, [it assumes] that those degrees form no union among themselves, either in a common and real positive term, or in another kind of union such as an act or a potency, but that they are only united in the subject and in the same part of the subject, if [the subject] has parts. Third, [it assumes] that those degrees are not related to the subject in any order, but [that they are] all [related] with equal immediacy, so that there is not among them an order of first, second, and third degrees, except perhaps with respect to generation and production. If, however, they are produced simultaneously, all are equally first. From this doctrine it follows easily that God cannot multiply the degrees of heat inhering in the same subject without their producing one more intense [heat]; because such intensification is nothing other than the congregation of many similar degrees [of heat] in the same subject. Moreover, without these principles, I do not see the basis on which that limitation could rest, as I shall show immediately. Indeed, the view, explained thus, does not properly limit God's

power to put any qualities subject to intensification, diverse only in number, in the same subject, but adds that by this very fact, that he puts them, it is necessary that they produce one more intense [quality].

23. The doctrine, however,[47] concerning intensification involves some inconsistencies, which, being irrelevant to the present discussion, cannot be explained in detail, although they will be identified briefly. For those degrees from which the intensified quality is said to be composed, for example, eight degrees of heat, are either indivisible in themselves, or they have a particular degree *(latitudo)* of intensification and remission. The first cannot be said: First, because otherwise intensification could not be a continuous motion; for any of those degrees should be acquired necessarily at once as a whole, otherwise it would not be indivisible. Therefore, the whole intensification should be produced by momentary and indivisible changes, [and] thus not by continuous succession. [And] this goes against sense and experience and against reason, because when the natural agent overcomes the patient, there is no [reason] why it should interrupt the action, otherwise it would not have the power to repeat it afterwards; nor could there be given a philosophical reason why it may cause it now rather than before or after. Second, because otherwise the degrees of heat would in no way produce one heat essentially *(per se)*, but they would unite in the same subject merely by accident, just as whiteness and sweetness [do]. Moreover, this is not enough for them to cause one individual heat, anymore than if God put two intellects in the same soul. Indeed, if that were sufficient for intensification, no reason could be given why, if God put two intellects in the same soul, they would not cause a more intense one. For, if you say that intellects are not qualities capable of coming together to that opinion, in order for qualities to be able to come together and be constituted into a more intense [quality] nothing else is required except that, since they are completely of the same nature *(rationis)*, they be able to be united in the same subject. And the intellects would have this, at least by divine power. Third, many absurdities follow from that view, namely, that a diminished quality could intensify an equally diminished one or even a more intense [one], causing all the degrees it has in itself. Or, if similarity goes against it, it follows that a more intense quality cannot intensify a more diminished [one], because they are completely similar in form. It follows also that no natural reason can be given whereby, when form is diminished, one degree is abandoned rather than another, and other similar [consequences] which would take long to pursue.

Therefore, it is necessary to say that in those degrees of heat intensification, for example, which we divide mentally, there is a degree *(latitudo)* according to which there can be in them a continuous intensification and remission. It is necessary that this degree *(latitudo)* be infinitely divisible, otherwise a continuous alteration could not be produced owing to them, because continuous motion should necessarily be infinitely divisible. Whence, consequently, it is also necessary that these degrees be joined together among themselves by some common term, because otherwise there cannot be conceived in them continuity or true real union, without which the degree *(latitudo)* cannot be understood; because if two degrees are not united to each other in this way, then, neither will the two parts or halfs — if we may put it that way — of one degree be united to each other, since the whole quality is as composed from many degrees as any degree is composed of two or three equal parts. Moreover, these cannot be understood without the said unity anymore than a continuum divided in every one of its parts could be understood.

24. Moreover, from these contrary principles concerning intensification, it plainly follows that God can put in the same subject many qualities subject to intensification different only in number [and that these qualities] do not cause a more intense one, as, for example, two heats of eight degrees, since he can put them as inhering in the subject and as not having any essential *(per se)* union among themselves, but only [as having] an accidental [union] by reason of the subject, which is not enough for intensification.

Nor can a new contradiction be found in this. The doctors think so frequently in *On Sentences I*, dist. 17, where Gregory [discusses it], q.5;[48] Ockham, q.7.[49] [And] Egidius, [does so in] *Quodlibet* IV, q.1,[50] where he adds a conjecture of no small value: Since God can intimately place two quantities different only in number in the same place, preserving their distinction and without any real union between them, whereby they cause a greater quantity, therefore, why could he not put two whitenesses in the same subject, preserving their distinction, and without a union by reason of which they compose a more intense [whiteness]?

NOTES

[1] The second issue is discussed in Sect. IX. Sect. VIII is structured in two parts. The first, covering §§ 2-14, presents five different opinions, their support and weaknesses. The second constitutes Suárez's answer (§§ 15-23).

[2] The first opinion is discussed in §§ 2-4. In § 2 Thomas is identified as the source of this view and the justification for its adoption by Thomists is given. The justification consists primarily in the fact that it solves certain philosophical problems. In §§ 3 and 4 Suárez shows both that the view involves inconsistencies and that it is not needed to solve the problems which it was supposed to solve.

[3] Art. 4 instead. *Ed. cit.,* vol. I, p. 563a.

4 *De veritate,* vol. XIV, pp. 515a-516a.

5 The theological virtues—faith, hope and charity—were so called because they have God as their object and are freely given by him. The moral virtues were generally reduced to the four cardinal virtues—prudence, justice, fortitude and temperance—and distinguished from the intellectual virtues—wisdom, understanding, science, and art. Man is said to be good if he is morally virtuous, wise if he is intellectually virtuous. Suárez discusses these various classifications in *Treatise on Grace* III, Bk. 6, Ch. 8, § 20 and Ch. 9, §§ 1-2.

6 *Ed. Vaticana,* vol. VII, perhaps on p. 476.

7 *Ed. cit.,* vol. 1, fol. 141ra.

8 *Pars prima...,* vol. V, p. 340b, coms. VII and VIII.

9 Art. 14. *De veritate,* vol. XIV, p. 515a-b.

10 The second opinion is supported by authority first and then by what Suárez calls "the principal argument" (§ 5). In § 6 the opinion is rejected on the bases of its incompatibility with the Aristotelian view (adduced in its support in § 5) and experience.

11 1018a2 and 1018b1; Junctas, vol. VIII, fol. 118vb-119ra.

12 *In XII metaphysicorum,* in *Opera omnia,* vol. XXIV (Paris: Vivès, 1875), p. 54a-b. There is little here to support Suárez's argument. In *Summa Theologiae,* vol. IV, p. 612a ff.

13 Art. 2. *Ed. cit.,* vol. I, pp. 284a ff., particularly *ad tertium Aureoli* and *ad argumenta Scoti et Adae* (pp. 288a ff.).

14 *Tertia pars summae theologiae cum commentariis Thomae de Vio Caietani,* in Leonine ed., vol. XI, pp. 357 ff.

15 *Quodlibeta,* fols. 81vb ff and article 5 in *In quatuor libros sententiarum commentaria* (Paris: D. Moreau, 1647; rep. Farnborough: Gregg, 1966), p. 300b, B.

16 *Scriptum super tertium sententiarum* (Paris, 1517), fol. 50vb.

17 *Ed. cit.,* p. 132a-b.

18 999a1 and 1016b32; Junctas, vol. VIII, fol. 49rb and 114va.

19 Following previous procedure, Suárez explains the opinion first and the authoritative and rational support usually given for it (§ 7) and then goes on to argue against it (§ 8).

20 *Pars prima...,* vol. V, p. 425a-b, but the text says nothing about this matter.

21 Art. 3. *Ed. cit.,* vol. III, pp. 327b ff. See also the *Nona conclusio* in a.1, pp. 257b-258b.

22 Bk. V, q. 18; ed. cit., p. 760b.

23 *De veritate,* vol. XIV, p. 364a.

24 In § 9 the opinion is explained and supported; in § 10 it is criticized.

25 *In duodecim libros metaphysicae,* ed. M. A. Zimara (Venice: Hieronymus Scotus, 1553; rep. Frankfurt/Main: Minerva, 1966), fols. 76va-77ra.

26 By "heatings" *(calefactiones)* is meant the various acts of heating produced by various fires in, for example, the same wood. I have consistently used the gerund to translate terms that could be rendered by the circumlocution "acts of x."

27 Last opinion discussed. § 11 presents the different authors who adhere to this view and the reasons they give. In §§ 12-14 Suárez dismisses the view and the arguments proposed in its favor.

28 Sect. 2. *Ed. cit.,* cols. 599F-600F.

29 *Ed. cit.,* vol. II, fol. 229ra.

30 *Epitome...,* fol. Evb.

31 *Quaestiones in librum tertium sententiarum,* ed. Wadding, in *Opera omnia,* vol. XIV (Paris: Vivès, 1894), p. 365a.

32 Q.7 instead. *Ed. cit.,* fol. 39va ff.

33 This subtitle as well as the ones given at the beginning of § 14 and § 16 are most likely editorial additions.

34 In fact, Suárez begins with the former, namely that "these things are partially false." The latter, namely, that "these things are partially unsatisfactory" is discussed in § 14.

35 More on this in Disp. IV. Ed.'s note.

36 See n. 31 above.

37 That is, the relation involved in being a creature, i.e. being related to the Creator as one of his products.

38 Bk. V, Ch. 10, q.1. *Ed. cit.,* cols. 604 ff.

39 *Ibid.,* cols. 611F-612A.

40 See n. 10 above.

41 The Solution extends from § 15 to the end of the Section. It is divided into two parts. The first extends from § 15-§ 19. In it Suárez points out three things of which he is certain concerning this matter under dispute. The first is stated in the first paragraph of § 15 and defended in the second. The second certainty is stated and defended with traditional, but not completely satisfactory, in Suárez's view, arguments in the first paragraph of § 16. Suárez's own support is provided in the second paragraph. The third certainty is stated in the first paragraph of § 17. Three arguments are given in its support, the first in the second paragraph of § 17, the second in § 18, and the third in the first paragraph of § 19. The second paragraph of § 19 reaches the conclusion of the first part of the *Solutio,* namely, that "the view that distinguishes between absolute and relative accidents is closer to the truth." The second part of the *Solutio* (§§ 20-24) presents Suárez's view and the rejection of a rival view. Suárez states his position in § 20 and the first paragraph of § 21. The second paragraph of § 21 introduces the rival view which is then refuted in §§ 22-24.

42 Actually three: The first (§ 15) that the "universal negative proposition, 'No plurality of accidents of the same species can be [present] in the same subject,' cannot be verified absolutely and without qualification;" the second (§ 16), that "it cannot happen naturally in any species of accident that many accidents differing only numerically be simultaneously [present] in the same subject;" and the third (§ 17), that "accidents of the former sort [i.e. those that 'differ in such a way that outside the distinction of entities they have certain similarity and agreement in everything else, such as in function...'] cannot be multiplied numerically in the same subject, although those of the latter sort [i.e. those that 'although they may agree in specific nature and differ under it only in number, nevertheless do not have so much similarity among themselves, but differ either in function or in relation...'] can be multiplied." The third, although specifically called "third" by Suárez, may be considered a modification or a corollary of the second. This is perhaps the reason why Suárez mentions only two certainties at this point.

43 The term of the relation of "creature" is only one because creatures are said to be related to God, but God is not related to creatures. This was a standard doctrine among scholastics, although a difficult and complicated one. For Suárez's statement of it see the Glossary.

44 'Knowledge' is not exactly equivalent to '*scientia.*' *Scientia* is always universal and demonstrative, while there are also other kinds of knowledge which are not so, such as knowledge of the particular. For the latter Suárez uses the term 'cognition' three lines below and elsewhere in this Disputation.

45 Henceforth translated thus.

[46] *In primum librum sententiarum,* ed. A. Montifalconio (Venice, 1521; rep. Frankfurt: Minerva, 1968). I have not found anything in d.17. *In secundum librum sententiarum,* same ed., I have found no text to support this reference in either one of d.1's two parts.

[47] This 'however' (*tamen*), like that which introduces § 22, refers to the second paragraph of § 21, where the rival view is presented. It is intended to introduce the second part of Suárez's rejection.

[48] Q̆.4 instead. *Super primum et secundum sententiarum* (Venice, 1522; rep. St. Bonaventure/Louvain/Paderborn, 1955), fol. 111rb.

[49] *Super quattuor...,* I, *ed. cit.,* vol. III, sect. R.

[50] *Ed. cit.,* p. 201a.

SECTION IX

WHETHER IT IS INCOMPATIBLE WITH THE INDIVIDUATION OF
ACCIDENTS THAT MANY [ACCIDENTS] DIFFERING ONLY IN
NUMBER BE SUCCESSIVELY [PRESENT] IN THE SAME SUBJECT[1]

1. Many accidents are said to be successively [present] in the same subject when the subject first had an accident and then lost it and afterwards acquires an accident of the same species. And then the question is whether the latter accident necessarily is or can be numerically distinct from the former.

Some defend the individuation of accidents by the subject so stubbornly that they think impossible that even in this way there [can] be many accidents different only in number [present] in the same subject.[2] Whence it is inferred that in the same subject the numerically same accident which had been destroyed before is always reproduced, namely, the same heat, the same light, and consequently the same place *(ubi),*[3] the same local motion, particularly if it is in the same space; for the reason is the same for all of these. And Scotus in part defended this opinion, at least when the agent is the same and the subject is the same. He does not base [it] on individuation, however, but on the fact that the same agent is by nature determined to produce the same [effect] in the same subject, [and that no] sufficient reason can be given why it should produce it distinct in number.

Indeed, Aristotle points out in *Metaphysics* VIII, text 11,[4] that if the agent and the matter are numerically one, the effect too is numerically one. This is explained in this way: For if I continue with open eyes to look at this wall for an hour, I do and preserve the numerically same act. Therefore, if I close my eyes a little and I open [them] again, I do again the numerically same act; for the interruption does not hinder in any way that that power, during all that hour and in any part of it taken by itself, could cause and receive the numerically same act. If you object that it follows [from this] that also the numerically same substantial form is reproduced in the same part of matter whenever [something] similar in species is induced, and consequently, that the same individual that had existed before is naturally reproduced, which is to say that the resurrection can be produced naturally, there is no lack of those who accept it. For example, this can be seen in Paul of Venice, Bk. II, [*Commentary on*] *On Generation,* toward the end.[5] Others, however, deny the nature *(rationem)* to be the same, because the substantial form requires predisposed *(dispositam)* matter and it never concurs with the same dispositions.

2. There is, however, another view which is at the opposite extreme [to this one], namely, that not only can many accidents differing only in number be successively [present] in the same subject, but that it is necessarily so whenever an accident similar in species is reproduced in the same subject. This was held by Durandus, Marsilius and others to be necessary even in terms of God's absolute power. I discussed these and Scotus' opinion in detail in [my *Commentary on Thomas' Summa theologiae*], vol. II, Part III, Disp. XLIV, Sect. IX.[6] The basis of Durandus' [view] is that whenever that production takes place, an action distinct from the one that existed before is renewed, for actions cannot be reproduced, just as successive beings cannot [be reproduced]; therefore, the end-term of the action must be distinct as well. Whence it is confirmed, because if such permanent accidents, produced successively in the same subject, were not distinct, successive accidents also would be able not to be distinct, and so the numerically same time could be reproduced. [And] this everyone thinks impossible.

Solution to the Question

3. But a middle way must be held [in this matter]. It must be said, [first],[7] that it can happen for many accidents differing only in number to be successively [present] in the same subject. Indeed, if understood in terms of God's power, this is evident, because it involves no inconsistency, and it follows *a fortiori* from what has been said that they can even be [present in the same subject] simultaneously, [and]

therefore, all the more [can they do so] successively. This is enough to show that accidents of the same species do not derive intrinsic numerical and entitative distinction from the subject or from a relation to numerically this subject. Otherwise, they could be distinguished in no way, even if the production or reproduction took place at diverse times; because, as I shall show immediately, temporal diversity alone is not sufficient by itself for this distinction, if there were no sufficient foundation of individual distinction and difference in other respects in the very forms produced. If, moreover, the assertion is understood in terms of the power and order of natural agents, then it is also true, as will become clear *a fortiori* from what will be said.

4. Second, I say that it is not only possible, but also true in fact in the natural order, for accidents distinct only in number to be successively produced in the same subject. This is the more common view among philosophers (*Physics* V, Ch. 4 and *On Generation* II, last chapter)[8] and theologians (*On IV, [of the Sentences]*, dists., 43 and 44). About this I have said something in [my commentary to Thomas' *Summa theologiae*] vol. II, Part III, Disp. XLIV, Sect. VII,[9] where I showed that the numerically same accident that had been corrupted is not reproduced in the same subject in the natural order; for it is inferred from this principle that it should be distinct, which is what we intend here.

It is not easy, however, to point out the first cause and root of this natural necessity.[10] For Durandus, above, [i.e. in *Commentary on the Sentences*], derives it from the diversity of action or change.[11] And Henry agrees with this in *Quodlibet* VII, q.16,[12] although he differs from Durandus because he does not posit this necessity in relation to God's power, as Durandus [does]. He [i.e. Durandus] erred more seriously on this, as I showed in the aforementioned place,[13] because God in his activity does not depend on time or any other circumstances on which natural agents can depend, because they act by motion and transformation. For this reason, Aristotle said in *Physics* V, Ch. 4, that unity of time is required for unity of motion,[14] an argument which Toletus accepts in Bk. II, [*Commentary on*] *On Generation*, q.13.[15]

5. But this argument is difficult and does not seem satisfactory: First, because the numerical unity of change is to be taken from the numerical unity of the term or produced form rather than vice versa, as Aristotle taught in the same place of *Physics* V.[16] Therefore, when produced accidents are said to be numerically diverse because the actions are diverse, one falls into a vicious circle. Second, because even if we granted that the actions are diverse, it does not follow that the forms are diverse, because many [more things] are required for the unity of action than the unity of produced form, according to

Aristotle himself, in the cited place. And besides, form does not have unity and distinction from action, but from something else. Whence it happens that the numerically same light produced by one lamp would be preserved by another, [something] which is necessarily the result of a diverse action. Third, because concerning the actions themselves there remains the question of why it is necessary that in terms of the natural order they be numerically distinct. Indeed, what is said concerning the diversity of times is not satisfactory. For, either [a] one is speaking of extrinsic time — which is [the one] considered in the motion of the heavens — , and this seems to have no relation to the intrinsic individuation or numerical distinction of actions, because from this time is taken only a certain extrinsic denomination of those [things] which are said to be in such a time, and numerical unity or distinction does not consist in extrinsic denomination. Again, because the numerically same action, even an indivisible [one], can permanently endure and coexist with a prior or posterior extrinsic time, as is clear from the actions of illuminating, seeing, and similar [ones]. Or [b], one is speaking of time or duration intrinsic to the same action and change whereby it is produced; and so, since such duration in reality is nothing other than the existence of the action itself, to say that these actions are distinct because they are produced at diverse times is to say they are distinct because they have diverse durations and existences, which is either the same or equally obscure. This is what we ask: Why is it necessary that the durations, existences or entities of those actions be distinct, and not rather the same repeated again and again? For, when God reproduces the numerically same form, it is certainly possible [for him] to reproduce it by the numerically same action whereby he had produced it in the first place; for this involves no inconsistency, as was pointed out in detail in the aforementioned place. Therefore, in order for the action to be distinct or in order that it may have a distinct intrinsic duration, it is not enough that it be produced twice, that is, with extrinsic prior and posterior time. Therefore, in order to show with respect to the general agent that these actions are necessarily distinct one must look for a reason elsewhere.

6. Nor is the reason given by those authors convincing, namely, that if the numerically same action could be reproduced, successive [actions] could be reproduced as well; which seems plainly contradictory. For if this reason were valid, it would apply even in terms of God's absolute power. Whence it seems necessary to say that in successive things it is possible to consider that which is real and positive, and that which is included in the succession as a negation or privation. For succession intrinsically means that something has been and now is not, and that something will be in the future but is not [now].

With respect to this negation or privation, therefore, a successive being cannot be reestablished, because in this respect there is no potency with respect to the past. With respect to what is positive, however, there seems to be no incompatibility [in the fact] that, just as
the same heat is reproduced by God, the same heating may also be
reproduced; and just as the sitting [is] the same and the place *(ubi)*
[is] the same, so consequently [is] local motion the same. For all
these express real positive modes, which have their individuation of
themselves and do not depend more on extrinsic time than other
things [do], but [rather they depend] on intrinsic duration; therefore, the same reason applies in this case as in the others. Therefore,
no sufficient reason why this should be incompatible with natural
agents can be given from the part of the action.

7. Others say,[17] therefore, that the cause and reason for this depends on another question, namely, whence the second cause is determined to cause numerically this effect here and now rather than
another. For the same [thing] which is the cause of this determination should also be the cause whereby, provided the second cause
acts again, it is determined to cause a new and distinct effect from all
the preceding ones. For, from the power of the efficient cause alone
or from the capacity of the subject alone, no sufficient reason *(causa)*
can be given for this thing, since the power of the agent as well as the
capacity of the subject itself is always the same and remains whole,
and is of itself equally indifferent to act upon or to receive any individual. Therefore, some say about the aforementioned question that
the whole cause and root of this determination must be reduced to
divine will and predefinition. For, once God sees that this agent here
and now is disposed to change *(immutandum)* this subject to a particular specific form, and that it is of itself indifferent to this or that
form in the individual and that it cannot from itself choose or determine its action to this rather than that, he decrees by his will to co-
operate *(dare concursum)* in the production of such an individual in
particular at this instant and in this subject. And because a secondary cause cannot act without God's cooperation *(concursum)*, consequently it is determined to actualize such an individual here and
now and not another.

I discussed this manner of speaking in passing in the mentioned
place, and I pointed out that it did not please me, because the argument does not seem philosophical enough, and because it presents
some difficulties in relation to free acts. Now, however, having considered the matter more carefully, I judge it to be very probable, not
only because I see that Gregory, *On I* [*of the Sentences*], dist. 17, q.4.
a.2, *ad* 7, and dist. 35, q.1, a.1,[18] and other nominalists are attracted
to it,[19] but also because so are many, very learned, modern writers.

For Toletus, [*Commentary on*] *Physics* VIII, q.3, concl. 2, arg. 3,[20] derives from this the freedom of the First Cause, which only by its will determines secondary causes to individual effects. Fonseca also, [*Questions on*] *Metaphysics* I, Ch. 2, q.3, sect. 8, says that in certain effects it is necessary to have recourse to divine determination and predefinition,[21] [something] which he repeats in Bk. V, Ch. 2, q.9, sect. 2, arg. 9, where he proves the essential dependence of secondary causes on the First [Cause] with respect to action.[22] And the Coimbra Group teach the same, Bk. II, [*Commentary on the*] *Physics,* Ch. 7, q.15, a.2.[23] Then also because it is not voluntary or beyond physical and natural reason that the First Cause help secondary causes and make up for their lacks in those things in which they seem to be defective. And, in the present [case], it seems they lack a mode whereby they could be determined to certain singular effects rather than others. This matter will be raised again below, in the Disputation on causes.[24] Now, therefore, according to that view, it must be said, consequently, that God has determined his cooperation *(concursum)* with secondary causes in order to produce always new and distinct effects, and not in order to produce again the effect which had existed before and does not exist anymore.

8. But it will be rightly asked of the authors of this view, whence it is established that the First Cause has determined in this way its cooperation *(concursum).* For either this was in some way due to the secondary causes themselves, that is, founded on their natural way of acting, or it is due only to God's will, just as [the case of] the production which is determined to this individual rather than another. If the second is said, the matter will remain quite uncertain, since we do not have a revelation of God's will [and] it could not be either demonstrated by reason or deduced from any natural principles. If, however, the first is said, then the primary and as it were last reason of this determination does not come from the divine will, but from the nature of proximate causes. And [then] this is what we ask: How could the nature of proximate causes be the foundation of this, particularly if the determination for the production of numerically this effect rather than another is not founded on it?

9. Because of this someone could say that secondary and finite causes contain any singular effect in their power only once, — if I may put it so — , and thus, that after such a cause has produced some effect once, no power to produce that effect again remains in it, nor to renew the action whereby it produced it. For its power was, as it were, exhausted by the first production insofar as it can be terminated in numerically such an effect.

But this is said gratuitously and without proof, and it is not even intelligible. For the active power by itself and insofar as it is such does not operate by some diminution or change *(immutationem)* of itself, but by the change *(immutationem)* or production of another. Whence its efficacy remains as whole and perfect as if it had produced nothing. Therefore, from having produced an effect once, the [active] power of production does not remain powerless to renew the same effect over and over again, provided there otherwise be no incompatibility from the part of the effect itself. For this reason, any active power, however finite, can act successively to infinity if it is preserved whole in its being, because it remains whole as well in its efficacy, and the succession or multiplication to infinity is not incompatible with the effect. Therefore, the same will be [the case] with respect to the reproduction of the same effect, provided there be no incompatibility on its part. I say this, because, after a thing has been produced once and remains in being, it cannot be produced by the agent again, even if its active power remained whole, because it is incompatible with the effect, *ex natura rei.* However, that what is not may [still] be produced cannot be incompatible with itself, even if [what is not] had existed before. For, what can stop it from being produced again if it does not exist anymore, since already it is as distant from being as if it had never existed? Therefore, if, on the other hand, the active power were to remain whole, the reason for this necessity cannot be taken from its inefficacy.

10. Therefore, it can be added finally that natural agents, although from themselves they may have power, as it were, general and indifferent to many individuals of the same species, nevertheless from themselves they require a certain norm *(modum)* and order in the use and exercise of such a power; so that the nature may be determined to actualize a particular individual in a particular subject, here and now, and after that another and after this another, and so on with the rest. For the very nature seems to require this determination and order, so as not to involve a certain indetermination and confusion. Therefore, from this comes [the fact] that the same effect is never repeated in acting, but a new one is always produced. I chose this manner of speaking in the aforementioned place, because in [such] an obscure and difficult matter nothing completely satisfactory occurred [to me], nor does it come to me now.[25] Indeed, this very [thing] which is attributed to the nature of such agents does not seem to be satisfactorily substantiated *(fundari)* or explained. For, since the natural power of acting is of itself simple and completely the same, there does not seem to be a way in which this natural determination could be founded on it or whence it could be established. Nor can extrinsic circumstances as such help in this regard, as it was shown above concerning time. And the same reason applies completely to place, insofar as it expresses an extrinsic surface or a relation to extrinsic bodies.

Therefore, it must be granted that either this depends on divine will alone or, if it has a natural cause, it is hidden from us. And at most it can be said that, since these natural powers are ordered to the multiplication of individuals and they naturally tend to it, it is more agreeable to their nature that they always receive the cooperation *(concursum)* for new effects. For this reason, [the fact] that in the generations of men new souls are always produced and that the ones that are already created once and exist separately are not united again to the bodies is based not only in God's will, but also in the very natures of things.

NOTES

¹ This Section roughly follows, like most of the others, the structure of a medieval question. After briefly clarifying the problem at stake in the first paragraph of § 1, Suárez proceeds to present the first opinion in the two remaining paragraphs. In § 2 a second view, at the opposite extreme to the first one, is presented. This is followed by Suárez's *Solutio* or answer to the problem (§ 3 and first paragraph of § 4). It has two parts, as can be gathered from the text. The second paragraph of § 4 raises a new issue for which Suárez lists two different opinions. The first is stated in the second paragraph of § 4 and rejected in §§ 5 and 6. The second opinion, favored by Suárez, is stated in § 7. In §§ 8 and 9 Suárez raises some difficulties which are finally settled in § 10.

² This is the first view of the two Suárez is going to reject. The second is presented in § 2. The two views are presented as extremes between which Suárez finds his own middle position.

³ Literally "where;" see Glossary.

⁴ Ch. 4, 1044a15; Junctas, vol. VIII, fol. 218vb.

⁵ *Expositio super libros de generatione et corruptione Aristotelis* (Venice, 1498), fol. 101rb.

⁶ *Ed. cit.,* XIX, p. 763a.

⁷ A 'first' is missing here, since there is a 'second' in the next paragraph and no preceding 'first.'

⁸ This reference is not so much to Aristotle as to those philosophers, like Averroes and others, who commented on the referred texts. All the same, see 227a3 ff and 337a34 ff.

⁹ *Ed. cit.,* XIX, p. 764b ff.

¹⁰ This is a new issue, which will concern Suárez for the rest of the Section. Two views are proposed: the first is given in this paragraph and rejected in §§ 5 and 6; the second is given in § 7.

¹¹ In Bk. III, d.8, q.3, *ed. cit.,* fol. 228vb.

¹² *Ed. cit.,* vol. I, fol. CCLXXr.

¹³ The reference is to Durandus' argument. Suárez cited some authoritative texts against Durandus after he stated his views; he now proceeds to argue against him on the basis of reason.

¹⁴ 227b25; Junctas, vol IV, fol. 232va.

¹⁵ *Commentaria una cum quaestionibus in librum de generatione et corruptione Aristotelis* (Lyon: Veyrat, 1598), p. 307.

16 Ch. 4; 227b22 ff.

17 This is the second view and the one favored by Suárez.

18 *Ed. cit.,* fol. 110rb G and fol. 114va L.

19 From this statement and others found in this Disputation it can be gathered that Suárez had a high regard for the opinion of nominalists. Indeed, his view concerning the individual as expressed in this Disputation is very close to that of Ockham. In view of this, it is not entirely accurate to say, as Ross does, that "there is no evidence whatever for calling Suárez a nominalist" (see *op. cit.,* p. 26). Perhaps not if one only takes into consideration Disp. VI, (on universals), but if one examines Disp. V, it becomes clear that Suárez's view of the individual was closer to that of Ockham than to that of, for example, Thomas Aquinas, and that, to this extent, he is closer to nominalism than one might at first think.

20 *Commentaria una cum quaestionibus in octo libros Aristotelis de physica auscultatione* (Lyon: Veyrat, 1598), p. 704.

21 *Ed. cit.,* col. 205A.

22 Arg. 6 instead. *Ed. cit.,* cols. 141 E ff.

23 *Copulata Conimbricensia.* The reference is to the group of scholars from Coimbra, then one of the major European universities, under the tutelage of Peter Fonseca. They put together the *Cursus Conimbricensium.* For the text, see *In octo libros physicorum, prima pars,* q.15 (Cologne, 1609), cols. 361 ff.

24 Disp. XII. Actually these issues are not raised there, but in Disp. XXII, where Suárez discusses the relation between the First and secondary cause.

25 This sort of statement is occasionally found in Suárez's writings. It shows how far he was from the narrow and doctrinaire dogmatism which is usually but mistakenly associated with late scholasticism.

GLOSSARY

This Glossary is composed primarily of the technical metaphysical terms used by Suárez in Disputation V. Since metaphysics and epistemology, however, were not considered to be separate disciplines by scholastics and since theological issues entered often in their metaphysical discussions, both epistemological and theological terms of importance have also been recorded. In a few instances, ethical and historical terms have been listed for the benefit of the reader unfamiliar with the period.

The bulk of the text in each entry is taken up by Suárez's own discussion, when available and located, of the term in question. This is usually preceded either by texts or by a discussion of views of other important scholastics who influenced Suárez in a especial way—Thomas Aquinas, Duns Scotus and William of Ockham. This gives not only an idea of the common usage of the term among scholastics, but also puts Suárez's understanding of it in historical context, making possible in many instances a provisional appreciation of his doctrinal perspective. In cases where Suárez's understanding of the term involves substantial doctrinal differences with that of other major scholastics, the differences have been explicitly stated. Moreover, in order to clarify Suárez's position within the Aristotelian tradition and the relation of his text to Aristotle's *Metaphysics,* selected passages from the latter have also been added when appropriate.

The entries have been made in Latin for two reasons. First, that there is not at present a clear consensus on how to translate most technical scholastic terms. To have given only this translator's rendition of these terms would have greatly limited the usefulness of the Glossary. Second, that in most cases there is simply no English term that gathers within it all the meanings of the Latin. To balance this lapse into erudition, an English-Latin Index has been added, to which the reader who has difficulty with the Latin may refer.

Abstracta, abstract, separate, abstractions; from *abstraho,* to draw away from, withdraw, divert, abstract. Scholastics opposed the abstract to the concrete (see *concretum*). The first literally means "taken away from" and the latter "grown together." For example, a white (in a white thing) is concrete, but whiteness is abstract. That something was "abstract" was taken to mean (1) that it was separate from that from which it was abstracted or taken away and/or (2) that it was not material. Suárez distinguished between metaphysical and physical *abstracta* in Disp. VI, Sect. X, § 1: "I call those [things] 'metaphysical abstractions' which are abstracted through metaphysical concepts, like 'animality,' 'rationality,' and the like; and I call them 'metaphysical abstractions' in order to distinguish them from physical (abstractions) like 'white,' 'color,' etc." See *praecisio.*

Abstractio, abstraction, separation; see *praecisio.*

Accidens, accident, accidental characteristic, an accident or chance, occurrance; from *accido,* to fall upon, to happen, to belong. If substance is, for Aristotle, that which is neither predicable of a subject nor present in a subject, an accident is precisely that which is either predicable of a subject or present in a subject (*Categories* I, Ch. 2, 1a204). In this sense, anything which is not a substance is an accident. In *Topics I*, Ch. 5, 102b5, Aristotle points out another sense of accident: "an accident is something which may possibly either belong or not belong to any one and the self-same thing, as the 'sitting posture' may belong or not belong to some self-same thing" (see also *Metaphysics* V, Ch. 30, 1025a13). That is, an accident is a feature or characteristic of a thing which is not essential to it. In this sense 'accident' was one of the predicables (see *praedicabilia*) and contrasted with other predicables such as properties (see *propria*) and specific differences (see *differentia*). Scholastics followed Aristotle, regarding as fundamental these two features of accidents, (Thomas, *Summa theologiae* III, 77, 1, *ad* 2). Because an accident is essentially related to a subject, its definition must include the subject, being in itself "incomplete" (Thomas, *On Being and Essence,* Ch. 6, § 1) or, as Suárez puts it, "imperfect" (Detailed Index to Aristotle's *Metaphysics,* Bk. VII, Ch. 4, q.2). A common definition of accident among scholastics is the following: "An accident is what can be present or fail to be present in a subject without the corruption of the subject" (Ockham, *Summa logicae* I, Ch. 25). This definition stresses the fact that the subject remains substantially the same with or without the accident. Suárez discusses the nature of accidents in Disp. XXXVII.

Accidens completum, complete accident. The distinction between complete and incomplete accidents, or accidents in complete and in incomplete acts, is carefully discussed by Suárez in Disp. XXXIX,

Sect. I, §§ 13-15. In § 13 he makes the distinction: "That accident is called complete which is a whole and total form in the nature *(ratione)* of accidental form; that accident is called incomplete, on the other hand, which has a partial nature *(rationem)* of the whole...Moreover, that accident is called physically complete which is neither related of itself to nor composed essentially *(per se)* of another accident, because then it truly has the nature *(rationem)* of whole or complete accident...That accident will be physically incomplete, therefore, which physically composes or is part of some accident one by itself, such as, for example, the parts of continuous quantity, which, while in the continuum, are only incomplete accidents; also the degree of intensity of the same heat can be called a physically incomplete accident." The result is that an accident can be considered complete or incomplete depending on the perspective taken. For example, the line, if considered as having a length of its own, is complete, but, considered as a term of another form, for example the rectangle, is incomplete. Suárez also distinguishes accidents metaphysically complete and metaphysically imcomplete, in § 14: "Metaphysically an accident is called complete when it has the complete essence of some accident." The examples given are quantity, heat and habits. On the other hand, "properly speaking, metaphysically incomplete accidents are differences of accidents, and genera are such, if taken with precision as parts, not, however, taken absolutely."

Accidens incompletum, incomplete accident; see *accidens completum.*

Accidentia absoluta, absolute accidents. This term was used by scholastics to refer to accidents falling into eight of the Aristotelian nine accidental categories. The category excluded was that of relation. The term was opposed to *accidentia respectiva* or relative accidents, which fall within the category of relation. In another way, however, all accidents were called relative to emphasize their dependence and difference from substance. Suárez discusses this distinction briefly in Disp. XXXIX. Sect. 1, § 18, where he gives it little importance: "The same must be said concerning the division [of accidents] into absolute and relative. For this division also pertains more to the common nature *(rationem)* of being than to the proper [nature] of accident. Furthermore, if relative...includes the relative transcendental accidents...then there is no accident that may not be relative; whence the division does not hold. If, however, relative is taken properly for the category of relation, then there is no use in such division, not only because, since only one genus is said to be relative, all the rest are called absolute, but also because this term 'absolute' hardly expresses anything common to the other eight genera except the negation of relation itself." In spite of what he says in this text, however, Suárez occasionally used this terminology.

Accidentia communia, common accidents; see *accidentia propria.*

Accidentia propria, proper accidents. Proper accidents were distinguished both from properties *(propria)* and from just accidents. An accident was usually defined by scholastics as that which may be present or absent in a substance without the corruption of the substance. "White" and "tall" are accidents of man, for example. A property on the other hand is a characteristic "which occurs in the entire species, in it only and always," such as the capacity to laugh in man (see *proprium*). Some claimed that it follows from the definition of the species as a logical consequent. A proper accident, then, is one which occurs in a species alone, although a particular individual of the species may not have it. A good example is the very act of laughter. Since only man is capable of laughter, only human beings laugh, but although they are always capable of laughter (property) they may or may not be laughing at a particular moment (proper accident). Proper accidents are opposed to common accidents *(accidentia communia)* or accidents shared by other species. In the case of man, for example, "weight" or "height". Suárez discusses briefly this distinction in Disp. XXXIX, Sect. II, § 20, where he points out that it does not refer to the nature of accident as such, but to the way accidents follow *(dimanatio)* from the subject.

Accidentia relativa or **respectiva,** relative accidents; see *accidentia absoluta.*

Actio, action; see *actus* and *passio.*

Actualitas, actuality; from *actus,* act (see *actus*). Actuality is opposed to potentiality, just as act is opposed to potency (see *potentia*). Real actuality *(actualitas realis)* is opposed to conceptual actuality *(actualitas conceptualis)*. A man is actually real when he exists as a separate and concrete individual; the concept "man" is actually conceptual when someone has it in the mind. A man is potentially real when he does not yet exist as a man but may do so — say, when he is still a child; "man" is potentially conceptual when it is not yet in anybody's mind, but may be so.

Actualitas conceptualis, conceptual actuality; see *actualitas.*

Actualitas realis, real actuality; see *actualitas.*

Actus, the moving or driving of a thing, motion, act, performance, part of a play; from *ago,* to act, drive, govern, do, perform, etc. For scholastics it referred either to an operation, such as the act of understanding, or to anything that determines or perfects a thing, such as a form; in both cases it is a modality of being. It should not be confused with *actio,* action, one of the Aristotelian categories and, according to Thomas, the origin of motion, *Summa theologiae* I, 41, 1, *ad* 2: "*Actio,* according to the first imposition of the name, means 'the origin of motion'. For just as motion, insofar as it is in the mobile from some [mover], is called a *'passio,'* so the origin of that motion, as it begins from something else and is terminated in that which is moved, is called *'actio.'* Therefore, if the motion is taken away, *actio* means nothing else than 'the order of origin,' according to which it proceeds from some cause or principle into that which is from that principle." Actio is opposed to *passio, actus* to potency (see *potentia).* Suárez discusses the various meanings of *'actus'* in Disp. XIII, Sect. V, § 8: "...the name *actus* can be taken in many ways. Sometimes it is taken absolutely, while other times relatively. For sometimes [something] is said to be an act because it acts on [i.e. actualizes] something; in this way the form is the act of matter. I call this a relative act, because it is the act of something else. Sometimes, however, [something] is called an act because it is something actual in itself, and not potential, although it may not act on [i.e. actualize] anything else; in this way God is called an act. I call this an absolute act. In turn each of these acts can be subdivided, for the act which acts [i.e. actualizes] is [1] physical and formal, such as the physical form or [2] metaphysical, which is multiple, or [3] essential, as it is the difference, or [4] existential, as it is existence; and to this can even be added [5] the act or mode of subsistence. On the other hand, the absolute act is either so without qualification or in a certain respect. The first is the act which in the genus of being as such, that is, of substance, is so complete that it is neither constituted by a physical act distinct from itself, nor is it acted upon [i.e. actualized] by it or needs of it for its existence. This can also be explained in another way: That being is called an act without qualification which in virtue of its actuality alone includes the formal perfection which composite beings usually have from the substantial informing act. Whence, although in this sense the absolute act may not be an informing or actualizing act, nevertheless it can be called a formal act in an eminent way, that is, that it has by itself the complement of perfection which is usually conferred to entities completed through composition by the informing act. Moreover, that being is called an act in a certain respect which has actuality insofar as it is actually outside nothingness *(nihil).* But the actuality it has is incomplete and imperfect, because it is not sufficient that it may not need another act, whether in order to be completed in the nature *(ratione)* of being as such, or in order to exist." Suárez adds in § 15 that act is the principle of operation and distinguishes it from potency in Disp. XLIII, Sect. V, § 10.

Actus primus, first act; opposed to *actus secundus,* second act. This distinction was generally used among scholastics to distinguish an agent from its actions or, to put it another way, the perfections or powers of an agent as agent in contrast to the exercise of those perfections or powers. The first act of an agent is that it exists with its faculties and powers. For example, a man is in first act insofar as he exists and is capable of reason. The second act is the actualization of the powers and faculties of the agent through their exercise. In the example given, a man is in second act when he sees, thinks, etc. This distinction was widely accepted and used among scholastics, who found it among other places in Avicenna, *Al Shifa, Meta.* IX, Ch. 6. Thomas discusses the distinction in *Summa theologiae* I, 48, 5, where he states that "first act is the form and integrity of the thing, while second act is the operation." Cajetan, commenting on *On Being and Essence,* q.17, § 139, points out repeatedly that the first act is to exist *(esse).*

Actus secundus, second act; see *actus primus.*

Ad aliquid, to something, relative to something, relation; see *relatio.*

Addo, to add, bring, join, annex, augment. In the Middle Ages and particularly in theological and philosophical contexts, the term was used to explicate the relation between the individual and the common nature. It is without a doubt a remnant from early medieval neo-Platonic discussions of this issue. As used by Medieval neo-Platonists an addition implied some sort of real distinction between what is added and that to which it is added and therefore a realist doctrine of universals: The individual was said to add something to the common nature because the latter was real in some sense and distinct from the individual. Aristotelians in general, and particularly nominalists, encountered difficulties when using the term and either discarded it altogether in the contexts of ontological discussions or made clear that they did not accept its realistic connotations. Ockham, for example, rejected the real distinction between individual and common nature and accepted only a relation of conceptual addition between them. Suárez, as it is evident in Sect. II of this Disp., follows Ockham in the rejection of a real distinction while maintaining a real addition. What this means is that for him a real addition does not presuppose a real distinction and therefore is not at all an addition in the strict sense. According to him, a real addition implies only that the individual as individual is real, and therefore cannot be considered not to add something real. At the same time, however, the individual cannot be distinguished really from the nature, since the nature is nothing apart from the individual; the reality of the nature is the reality of the individual, since its unity and being are individual unity and being (for further details see my article, "What the Individual Adds to the Common Nature according to Suárez," *The New Scholasticism* 53 (1979), and the Introduction). Suárez also discussed various kinds of additions: negative and positive, (this Disp., Sect. I, § 7); intrinsic and extrinsic (this Disp., Sect. VI, § 2), and others. It should be clear from what has been said that all these uses of 'to add' are quite different from the contemporary usage in, for example, "John adds a room to his house" or "Peter adds 7 to 5." Here the term is used as in "7 adds 2 to 5," meaning that 7 is 2 more than 5.

Ad rem, in reality; see *in re*.

Aequivocatio, meaning literally "the same calling," is a term commonly used by scholastics to refer to the logical fallacy of equivocation, which happens when a term is used with two different meanings within the same argument. William of Sherwood discusses the term in *Introduction to Logic,* Ch. 6, (in Kretzmann's trans., Univ. of Minn. Press, 1966, p. 135): "Equivocation is diverse signification on the part of one and the same word. This can occur in three ways: Either the word signifies [A] more than one thing on its own *(de se)* or [B] as a result of its connection with something else; and there are two varieties of [A] — viz., it signifies [more than one thing] [A1] properly or [A2] transumptively." For the source of this doctrine see Aristotle, *Categories,* Ch. 1. See also *univoce*.

Aevum, uninterrupted, never-ending time, eternity, age, generation, aeviternity; see *coevum*.

Agens, efficient, effective, powerful, agent. For scholastics the term referred to the Aristotelian efficient cause, the active element in causation, what initiates and stops action and change rather than receives it. The agent is opposed, therefore, to the patient *(passum)*. The exact nature of the distinction between these was a point of dispute among scholastics. The controversy centered around the issue of whether the agent and the patient must be distinct in reality — as Aristotle's text from *Physics* VII seems to indicate — or whether they can be the same. The issue was particularly disputed in the contexts of knowledge and self-locomotion, since in these the efficient cause and what is moved seem to be the same in reality: a man is the efficient cause of his movements, for example. Suárez discusses the problem at length in Disp. XVIII, Sect. VII.

Aliquid, something. Generally a thing is *aliquid* or *hoc aliquid* if it is (1) a numerically different substance or (2) an individual being. Some scholastics classified *aliquid* among the transcendental properties of being. '*Aliquid,*' when coupled with '*hoc*' (this) in the expression '*hoc aliquid,*' meant to translate Aristotle's τόδε τι *(Categories,* Ch. 5, 3b10). This term is opposed to '*quale quid,*' which translates ποιόν τι. According to Suárez, in Disp. III, Sect. II, §§ 5 and 6, '*aliquid*' can be understood in two ways: as something, and then it is opposed to "nothing;" or as some other thing, and then it is opposed to "the same."

He writes: " '*Aliquid*' can have two etymologies or interpretations. One is [to interpret it] as the same as something having some quiddity; for, whether this is the first derivation of the word or not, it seems to be commonly used in this way now; for *aliquid* and *nihil* (nothing) are thought to be contradictory or opposed. Moreover, '*nihil*' signifies the same as non-being or not-having-any-entity; therefore, *aliquid* is the same as what has some entity or quiddity. In this sense, then, it is clear that '*aliquid*' is not an attribute *(passio)* but a synonym of 'being.' For this reason, to say that something is *aliquid* or that it is a being is the same thing in terms of the form or concept....The other etymology...is that '*aliquid*' be taken as 'other something.'...Taken in this sense, this attribute, ['*aliquid*'], either is not different *(diversum)* from 'one' or it is included in it as its consequence. For that is said to be one which is undivided in itself and divided from any other...therefore, the negation which is carried by the word '*aliquid*' or which is reduced to it is included in the notion of 'one'. For this reason this attribute does not increase the number of attributes [of being]."

Alteratio, alteration. Scholastics interpreted alteration as change occurring within the category of quality. A fruit, for example, undergoes alteration when it changes color. This kind of change is opposed to locomotion (change of place), augmentation and remission (quantitative change), and generation and corruption (substantial change). See *mutatio*.

Anima, soul, life, mind; see *anima rationalis*.

Anima rationalis, the rational soul for scholastics. The term, *anima* in Classical Latin referred to the animating principle or life of living beings. This notion was derived from the more fundamental one of breadth. It was contrasted with *animus*, which referred to the soul or mind in rational beings. In the Middle Ages, however, the second term fell into disuse and the first one took on the meaning of both. In most cases the context made clear the meaning, but often the term *rationalis* was added to it in cases where the term was used to refer to the soul of man in order to dispel any possible ambiguity not resolved by context. In addition to the rational soul scholastics spoke of vegetative and animal souls, i.e. the principles of life in plants and animals. Thomas, following Aristotle, identified the rational soul of man with the substantial form, which united to matter, the body, constituted an individual human being *(Summa theologiae* I, 76, 3). Suárez follows Aristotle and Thomas on this, as it is clear from Disp. XV, Sect. I,§ 6: "A man consists of a body as matter and of a rational soul as form. Therefore, this soul is the substantial form, since, as we shall explain later, the name 'substantial form' signifies nothing other than a certain partial substance which can become united to matter in such a way that it may compose with it a whole and essentially one substance which is a man."

Angelus, messenger, angel. Suárez, following Thomas and other scholastics, identified the angels of Christian doctrine with the Aristotelian movers of the celestial spheres. He refers to the traditional philosophical and theological texts in support of this view in the Prologue to his *Treatise on Angels.*

Angeli mali, evil angels or demons. These are the angels that followed Lucifer to hell when he sinned and was banned from heaven. According to Suárez, the distinction between evil and good *(boni)* angels coincides with the distinction between terrestrial and heavenly angels. The latter distinction is based on the place of habitation. See *On the Nature of Angels,* VII, Ch. 1, §§ 8-16.

Annihilo, to bring to nothing, to annihilate, from *nihil,* nothing. It is to be distinguished from *corruptio,* which involves a change in the category of substance. A substance is corrupted when its form ceases to exist and it is substituted by another. The substance is not annihilated because a part of it, the matter, continues to exist under another form. But matter, on the other hand, is not corrupted, although it can cease to exist altogether, that is, be annihilated (see *corruptio*). Suárez discusses this notion in his *Commentary and Disputations on the Third Part of Thomas' "Summa,"* Disp. L, Sect. VII. He points out that annihilation signifies, as it were, a complete and whole change which makes a thing cease to exist completely" (§ 5). And in § 9: "Annihilation is the cessation of the whole being in itself." It is for this reason that annihilation cannot be brought about by a positive action (§ 6), "because a positive action ends necessarily in a positive term, and, if the cessation of some thing's existence follows from it, that thing cannot be completely destroyed, because it is essentially *(per se)* presupposed by that action; and thus such [action] cannot be conceived as annihilation." The contrast between annihilation and corruption is explained in § 8: "For, since corruption is opposed to generation, which is accomplished by the union of form with matter, which is the subject of that action, thus generation can immediately and necessarily follow from corruption. Annihilation, however, is properly opposed to creation, and it signifies the destruction of the being as being or as having being through creation. Creation, moreover, is not concerned with the subject, and thus the being of the thing insofar as it depends from it cannot be destroyed by an action incompatible with it. Furthermore, annihilation cannot follow from a positive action, as corruption does."

Antecedens, antecendent; see *consequentia.*

A parte rei, in reality; see *in re.*

Aptitudo, aptitude; from *apto,* to fit, adapt, prepare, get ready, put in order. Scholastics used the term to refer to a natural inclination or ability. For example, heavy things were said to have an aptitude for falling or man for thinking.

Artifex, artist, artificer, master in liberal arts, author, maker, artisan, skillful; from *ars-facio,* I make art. The artist is one that has art or skill. Aristotle distinguished art from science in *Posterior Analytics* II, Ch. 19, 100a5-9: "So out of sense-perception comes to be what we call memory, and out of frequently repeated memories of the same thing develops experience; for a number of memories constitute a single experience. From experience again—i.e. from the universal now stabilized in its entirety within the soul, the one beside the many which is a single indentity within them all—originate the art of the craftsman and the knowledge of the man of science, art in the sphere of becoming and science in the sphere of being." Art and science are distinguished in terms of their object but also and more importantly in terms of their nature and end: Science is knowledge of cause; art is knowledge of rules. The point is well put by the Pseudo-Grosseteste, *Summa philosophiae* II, Ch. 8 (in McKeon, *Selections from Medieval Philosophers* I, p. 312): "Moreover, there seems to be this difference between science and art, that science contemplates and examines principally certain causes of its truth, but art considers rather the manner of operating according to the truth transmitted and proposed. Consequently, the philosopher and the artist have a common matter but different precepts or principles and end." It should be clear then that 'artist' as used in this context has more in common with 'artisan' than with 'plastic artist.' Suárez discusses the differences between divine and human artists in Disp. XXV, Sect I, §§ 17-25.

A se, from itself; see *per se.*

Augmentatio, augmentation, increase, quantitative change; see *mutatio.*

Capacitas, capacity, ability, power; see *capax.*

Capax, wide, large, capable, good, fit, potential, possible, and the medieval substantive form, *capacitas,* capacity, ability, power, were interpreted by scholastics both in a positive and negative way. Positively, a capacity was thought to be a power or ability of a thing to change or alter itself or others; negatively it was interpreted as a receptivity to be changed or altered in certain ways. In both cases this power or receptivity could arise out of the nature of a thing, and then it was called a natural capacity; or out of some particular divine act, and then it was called supernatural. In the case of man, for example, he was conceived as having the natural capacity to laugh but the supernatural capacity to enjoy God's fellowship owing to Christ's sacrifice for him. What was interpreted as natural and supernatural, of course, varied from thinker to thinker, depending on the views of human nature and divine operation held. Aristotle discussed the Greek equivalent of this term in *Metaphysics* V, Ch. 12, 1019a22ff.

Casus, a falling, error, accident, misfortune, chance, event, case, instance, example. For scholastics the term was used technically to mean "chance." They found a long explanation of this notion in Aristotle's *Physics* II, Chs. 5 and 6. Most scholastic discussions centered around the theological problem of God's creation, providence, and causality: Given God's omnipotence and omniscience, does he cause events in the world necessarily or by chance? If necessarily, then that would seem to imply determinism; if by chance, then that would seem to imply some limitation in God's casual connection to the world. Suárez discusses these issues in Disp. XIX, Sect. XII. He explains the notion of chance in §§ 2 and 3: "The name 'chance' properly signifies effect rather than cause, and it is said of any unexpected effect...however, usage has extended it to signify cause as well, since the effect cannot lack a cause....Therefore, that is called a casual effect which, accidentally, unexpectedly and without intention, is united by itself to an effect of a cause, such as, for example, when a treasure is found while digging earth. This is clear from the common meaning of the word, for a casual effect is the same as one which happens rarely and unintentionally. And so there are two [aspects] to that notion: One is that it happens rarely...and this must be understood in a composite sense (if I may put it thus), that is, presupposing a particular cause. For it happens often that the effect is rare because the cause is rare, although once it [i.e. the cause is present, the effect follows regularly; but then the cause] is not casual, since it can be essential (*per se*), unless its presence or the concurrence of many causes is also casual. In another way, therefore, the effect follows rarely from the cause present, and in this way the effect is said to happen rarely. However, since a particular effect always results from the concurrence of many causes, it is necessary that the concurrence do not have a certain and definite cause in the universe, from which it also results that it happens rarely. Therefore, and eclipse is not a casual effect, nor is any other effect which is regularly united together with an essential (*per se*) effect. Secondly, it belongs to the notion of such an effect that it be outside the intention of the causal agent. For example, when Peter passes and a stone falls, that is called a casual event, because such an event was outside the intention of the man passing by, of the falling stone, and of the cause that moved the stone. If such event (*concursum*) were intended for Peter by someone, the effect would not be called casual in that respect, but essential (*per se*) in its genus..." For these reasons, chance is always accidental (§ 5). It must be distinguished as well from fortune, which is chance in human affairs (§ 9).

Causa, cause, reason, motive, occasion, judicial process. Scholastics found to their surprise that Aristotle, in spite of his extensive use of the notion cause, did not give any single and clear definition of it. They proceeded to disagree in their understanding of this notion. Some emphasized the text from *Physics* II, Ch. 7, 198a15-17, where Aristotle says that "the number of causes is the same as that of the things comprehended under the question 'why.' " Others, following Aristotle's definition of principle in *Metaphysics* V, Ch. 1, 1013a18-20, interpreted cause as "that from which something follows" (see *principium*). Still others defined a cause as "that from which something depends essentially." Suárez, in Disp. XII, Sect. II, § 4, rejects the first two views and modifies the third to read: "A cause is a principle which essentially instills *(influens)* being in another." He changes 'that' to 'principle' because principle is the genus of cause, and 'depends essentially' to 'essentially instills being' in order to exclude privation and accidental cause. All scholastics accepted the Aristotelian division of cause into four: formal, material, efficient, and final (*Physics* II, Ch. 3, 195a15-28).

Causa efficiens, efficient cause, one of the Aristotelian four causes. It is what initiates and terminates the process of change. Aristotle defines it in *Metaphysics* V, Ch. 2, 1013a30-32, as "that from which the change or the resting from change first begins; e.g. the adviser is a cause of the action, and the father a cause of the child, and in general the maker a cause of the thing made and the change-producing of the changing." Some scholastics regarded this cause as the cause *per se,* since it was not only the most obvious to us but, unlike the end, the form, and the matter, it seemed to have a clearly real influence on the effect and to be mediated by nothing. For Suárez, however, no cause is more essentially a cause than any other. Each of the four causes is equally a cause and equally necessary for the production of the effect (see Disp. XII, Sect. III, § 6). He dedicates Disp. XVII entirely to the discussion of efficient causality. In Sect. I, he discusses the Aristotelian definition, which he finds in need of modification. He gives his own in § 2: "Efficient cause is an essentially extrinsic principle in virtue of which change occurs in the first place." He then proceeds to explain the various kinds of efficient cause: essential and accidental (§§ 2-5), physical and moral (§ 6), principal and instrumental (§§ 7-19), first and second (§ 20), univocal and equivocal (§ 21), etc.

Causa extrinseca, extrinsic cause. For Suárez, even before the division into formal, material, efficient, and final, causes were divided
into intrinsic, those that "give being to their effects, conferring on
them their numerical entity and composing them internally," and
extrinsic, those that "do not intrinsically compose the effect." The
formal and material were causes of the first type; the efficient and
final of the second. See Disp. XII, Sect. III, § 19. Other scholastics,
such as Thomas, speak of "external" and internal" formal causes
(Com. on Sentences I, d.8, q.1, a.2 *ad* 2). But this way of speaking
should not be confused with Suárez's. For Thomas the extrinsic formal cause is either the exemplar or the object of knowledge. Suárez
explicitly rejects the formal causality of the object of knowledge in
Disp. XII, Sect. III, § 17. He grants only efficient causality to it.
And he concludes the same with respect to exemplary causes — their
causation is primarily efficient (see Disp. XXV, Sect. II, §§ 12-14).

Causa finalis, final cause, one of the Aristotelian four causes. It is
the end or purpose of change, as when a man takes medicine for the
sake of health. Aristotle defines it in *Metaphysics* V, Ch. 2, 1013a32-35
as "the end, i.e. that for the sake of which a thing is; e.g. health is the
cause of walking. For 'Why does one walk?' we say; 'that one may be
healthy'; and in speaking thus we think we have given the cause."
Within the teleological framework of Aristotelian philosophy this is
without a doubt the most important cause. Indeed, it is the way the
Unmoved Mover moves the world *(Metaphysics* XII, Ch. 7,
1072b1-5). This was generally recognized by scholastics. According
to Suárez, in Disp. XXIII, dedicated entirely to this notion, it was
not only the most important but also the first cause. It is placed last
in discussions of causality because "it is more obscure than the others
and it was for this reason that it was almost unknown to the
ancients." He explains further the "primacy" of the end and the
nature of its causality in Disp. XII, Sect. III, § 3: "Concerning the
end, however, there can be reason for doubt, because no real being
is presupposed in it whereby it can cause...however, although the
end is last in execution, it is nevertheless first in intention and under
that aspect *(ratione)* it has the true nature *(rationem)* of principle. For it
is the first [thing] that exercises or moves the agent to act. Moreover,
it is not a fictional principle, but true and real, because it truly exercises and moves. Hence, since it has as much being to actualize [lite-
rally, to exercise] such a nature as a principle, it also has the nature
(rationem) of cause. Moreover, that being, even in the mind, is not
outside the realm of real being, and hence it can be sufficient for
such a nature *(rationem)* of cause. Moreover, this kind of principle is
not accidental, but essential *(per se)*; indeed, the agent has from it the
causality through which it regularly and essentially *(per se)* tends

toward the effect; and for this reason it essentially (*per se*) gives it being. Therefore, the definition of cause truly and properly pertains to the end as well."

Causa formalis, formal cause; see *forma.*

Causa intrinseca, intrinsic cause; see *causa extrinseca.*

Causa materialis, material cause. For Aristotle, the substratum or material out of which a thing is generated — the marble or bronze in a statue, for example. He defines it in *Metaphysics* V, Ch. 2, 1013a25, as "that from which, as immanent material, a thing comes into being, e.g. the bronze is the cause of the statue and the silver of the saucer, and so are the classes which include these." The scholastics gave various interpretations of Aristotle's view. Suárez deals with these in detail in Disp. XIII: "The Material Cause of Substance." In Disp. XII, Sect. III, § 3, he explains Aristotle's definition thus: "Matter is defined by Aristotle as 'that from which, as something intrinsic *(insito),* something is made.' In this definition matter is distinguished from other causes by the term 'from' appropriately taken. And by the term 'something intrinsic' matter is distinguished from privation and the proper influx whereby matter, and in general the subject, is explained, so that from it the being of the whole may come...for matter is, as it were, a certain beginning or foundation of the being itself..."

Causa prima, first cause. Efficient causes were classified by scholastics into first *(prima)* and second *(secunda)* causes. The first cause was identified with God; all other causes were regarded as secondary because they depended from the first, while the first did not depend from them. This distinction constituted the basis of the so called "arguments for the existence of God." Suárez discusses it in Disp. XVII, Sect. II, § 20: There is a cause "that is completely independent in [its] operation, and this is called 'first.' There is another, however, which is dependent, even though it may operate by a principal [note: efficient causes were also divided into principal and instrumental — first and second causes were species of principal causality] and proportionate operation, and this is called 'second cause.' That both of these kinds of causes exist in the order of things is very evident. For either there is in reality a principal cause which depends on another for [its] operation, and from this term [i.e. the second] the other [i.e. the first cause] is necessarily inferred, because one cannot proceed to infinity in [a series of] dependent causes, and therefore one must stop in some independent [cause]...[Or], having granted an independent cause, it is then necessary to infer the other term [i.e. the second cause], because not all causes can be independent. Indeed, such a cause cannot be but unique..."

Causa proxima, proximate cause. A proximate cause is the immediate cause of any change. It is opposed to *causa remota,* or remote cause, the mediate cause of any change. Effects, then, are properly caused by proximate or direct rather than remote or indirect causes. Thomas gives a good example of this principle in *Summa theologiae* I, 14, 13, *ad* 1: "…even if the supreme cause is necessary, nevertheless the effect can be contingent owing to a contingent proximate cause; for example, the growth of a plant is contingent owing to a proximate contingent cause, even though the first cause, the motion of the sun, is necessary. Similarly, the things God knows are contingent owing to proximate causes, although God's knowledge which is the first cause, is necessary." This distinction applied to all four causes, although it was derived primarily from the final cause or end. The end which is immediately desired for itself is the proximate end or final cause; the one that is desired for the sake of another is a remote cause. A medicine, for example, is taken for the sake of health and is therefore a remote cause; health, however, is the proximate cause. Suárez discusses this distinction in Disp. XXIII, Sect. II, § 14. In the case of the efficient cause, the distinction functions in a slightly different way. The proximate cause is the one that directly causes the effect, such as the medicine, which causes health; the remote cause is the one that indirectly causes the effect, such as God's will, which maintains the natural order in operation.

Causa remota, remote cause; see *causa proxima.*

Causa secunda, secondary cause; according to the scholastics, all causes other than God, who was the *causa prima,* or first cause. God was called first cause not in a temporal sense but in a metaphysical one; all other causes ultimately depended on him for their existence and efficacy. Suárez discusses these issues in Disp. XXII; see *causa prima.*

Coaptatio, an accurate joining together, union, fitting coadaptation, adaptation to each other; from *coapto,* to adjust together, fit, join, adapt. This term comes from the same root that has given us 'apt,' 'aptitude,' 'adapted,' etc. In general it means a proper or suitable union.

Coevum, cotemporal, coeval; from *aevum,* time, eternity, never ending, aeviternity. Scholastics used the term loosely to mean just "of the same age." Properly, however, *aevum* referred to an intermediate measure between time — the measure of motion according to prior and posterior (Aristotle, *Physics* 219b) — and eternity — the measure of a thing unchanging both in terms of substance and duration. Time was the measure of physical things, eternity the measure of God, and *aevum* the measure of the heavenly bodies and the angels of the medievals. The text of Thomas from *Summa theologiae* I, 10, 5 is well known: "Since eternity is the measure of permanent being, in the respect in which anything recedes from permanence of being, in that respect it recedes from eternity. Some [things] recede from permanence of being in such a way that their being is the subject of change and consists in change, and [things] of this sort are measured by time, as all motion and also the being of all corruptible [things]. Some [things], on the other hand, recede less from permanence of being, because their being neither consists in change nor is it the subject of change, yet they have change joined to them, either in actuality or in potentiality. This is clear in [the case of] celestial bodies, the substantial being of which is unchangeable; nevertheless they have unchangeable being [together] with changeability with respect to place. This is also clear in [the case of] angels, because they have unchangeable being [together] with changeability with respect to decision, in so far as that pertains to their nature, and [together] with changeability of intelligences and affections and places in their [own] fashion. Therefore, [things] of this kind are measured by *aevum*, which is a medium between eternity and time. On the other hand, the being which eternity measures is neither changeable nor joined to changeability. Thus, time has prior and posterior; *aevum* does not have in itself prior and posterior, but it can be joined to them; and eternity does not have prior and posterior, nor is it compatible with them." See also P. Redpath's doctoral dissertation, *The Ontological Status of Time in Thomas' "Com. on the Sentences," "Com. on the Physics," and "Summa theologiae"* (Buffalo, 1974). Suárez discusses the various kinds of durations in Disp. L: "On the Category of When, and in General on the Durations of Things." In Sect. V, § 2, he explains the various usages of the term *aevum:* The term 'aevum' "is sometimes taken for eternity, because in Greek the term for eternity is not different, and sometimes it is taken for prolonged duration. Properly speaking, however, according to the usage of theologians, *aevum* is taken for the duration of incorruptible beings." And in § 8 he adds that *aevum* is "permanent duration." *Aevum,* therefore, is the measure of beings incapable of substantial change, that is, of generation and corruption.

Communicabilis, communicable, and the corresponding substantive *communicabilitas,* communicability, are Medieval Latin derivatives of *communico,* to communicate, impart, share, divide something with one, unite, have intercourse with an inferior. Scholastics used the term in widely different ways. For example, Thomas Aquinas speaks of the "communicability of names" in *Summa theologiae* I, 13, 9. The most frequent senses of the term were explained by Cajetan in his *Commentary on Thomas' On Being and Essence,* q. 10 (trans. Kendzierski and Wade, Marquette Univ. Press, 1964, p. 199), as follows: "Communicability is threefold: First, there is communicability together with division of essence, as the universal is communicable with particulars. Second, there is communicability by identity without any division of essence and existence *(esse)*, as the divine essence is common to three supposits. Third, there is communicability by being able to be assumed into a hypostatic union, as human nature is communicable to all divine supposits." The first sense of communicability is the most often encountered in philosophical works and one that is frequent in the present Disputation. It is the communicability of universals to particulars, sometimes also referred to as the communicability of superior to inferior, particularly in the context of the Porphyrian tree. The genus is communicated to the species (animal to man and dog, for example), and the species to individuals (man to Peter and Paul, for example). As such it expresses a kind of relational characteristic. Its reverse is called *participatio*. While man is "communicated" to Paul and Peter, these two "participate" in man. This terminology is very Platonic and used frequently by medieval neo-Platonists (see, for example, John Eriugena's *Periphyseon* III, 3-10). It gave a lot of trouble to Aristotelians, particularly late scholastics with lean ontologies in which universals were seen only as mental realities, and natures as individuals. The second meaning given by Cajetan is the one present in Suárez's text in the first objection of Sect. I (§1), as it becomes clear in the answer to the objection in §6. The third meaning is a purely theological one, seldom found in philosophical works. Suárez's own view on communicability and communication is found in Disp. XXXIV, Sect. V, §§54-57: First, he tells us, "there is an intentional extrinsic communication, that is, [a communication] in the genus of final cause; this is the way in which the end or good is said to be communicated to itself, promoting its being loved....There is another kind of extrinsic communication as well that is real and effective; this is the way in which the efficient cause is said to be communicated to its effects....Besides these there is an intrinsic and formal communication. And I call formal not only that which is in the genus of formal cause, but everything in which a thing *(res)* communicates or gives its own entity or formality to something. In this way also matter is said to be intrinsically and formally communicated to the composite. This communication, however, can be divided further, for one is only conceptual, that is, a conceptual communication, in the way the species, genera, and other higher predicates are said to be communicated to the lower ones [this corresponds to Cajetan's first]. Another is the real communication of the same singular thing to many really distinct supposits or beings. This in turn can be understood in two ways, namely, either by identity or only by union." Both of these last two senses of communicability apply only to the divine nature, according to Suárez, for, "even though the divine nature is singular and essentially subsistent, it is also common to the three really distinct persons, in terms of its whole perfection and its very absolute subsistence...and can be communicated with a hypostatic union to many natures, at least supernaturally, since naturally this is not possible." In § 57 Suárez adds another sense of communication: "the communication of one thing *(res)* to another by a formal union or a kind of conjunction, in the way form is communicated to matter." Communicability, i.e. the ability to be or to be made common, should not be confused with commonality (or community, as the medievals would say), the characteristic of being common. Many things are communicable and not common, that is, do not have commonality, although every thing which is common must be communicable.

Communicabilitas, communicability, ability to be or to be made common; see *communicabilis.*

Communis, common to several or to all, general, universal, public. For the various senses in which something may be common, see *communicabilis.*

Complementum, that which fills up, completes, a complement; from *compleo,* to fill up, complete, cover, perfect, fulfill. A complement is, therefore, what completes or fulfills something.

Compositio conceptualis, conceptual composition; see *compositio metaphysica.*

Compositio metaphysica, metaphysical composition. Scholastics differed widely in their understanding of the notion of metaphysical composition and its distinction from physical and conceptual compositions. For Suárez, physical composition is real and therefore consists in the union of two beings in act, such as it is the case in the union of this matter and this form when they compose this individual. Metaphysical composition, however, such as the one resulting from the union of specific nature and individual difference, is not real, but conceptual, because it is not a union of two beings in act. In the example used by Suárez, the union of individual difference and specific nature is conceptual because the specific nature is not a being in act, but only a nature. The point is explained in Disp. XXXI, Sect. XIII, § 12: "Therefore, for real composition it is essentially *(per se)* necessary that the terms be real beings in act; but not so for conceptual composition. Whence, three types of conceptual composition can be distinguished: one, the composition of terms which in reality are beings in act, but not distinct in act; another, [the composition] of terms real in capacity or real objective formality, but abstracting from the actuality of existence; and finally another, [a composition], as it were, in the middle, in which one of its terms is only a real nature *(ratio)* or essence conceived with precision and the other an actual existence." Both the physical composition of matter and form and the metaphysical composition of genus and difference were "essential," according to Suárez in the *Commentary on the Third Part of Thomas' "Summa,"* Disp. VIII, Sect. II, §§ 4-7. As such they are distinguished from (a) the composition of material parts, (b) the composition of essence and existence proposed by Thomists, and (c) the composition of the nature and the supposit discussed in the *Metaphysical Disputations.* In the latter work Suárez considers the composition of nature and supposit as a metaphysical one and thus as conceptual.

Compositio physica, physical composition; see *compositio metaphysica.*

Conceptus, concept; see *conceptus objectivus.*

Conceptus formalis, formal concept; see *conceptus objectivus.*

Conceptus objectivus, the objective concept is the thing as it is conceived in the mind; as such an objective concept is quite different from a thing's *ratio,* or intelligible structure, strictly speaking. A concept resides in the knower, the *ratio* in the known. The latter is related to the former as a principle or cause, for it is because things are intelligible that we intellect, i.e. conceive, them. *Ratio intellecta,* on the other hand, refers to the *ratio* as understood, and therefore residing in the mind. Often, however, Suárez uses the terms indistinctly. *The conceptus objectivus* is also to be contrasted with the *conceptus formalis* or formal concept. The latter is the act of understanding itself and can never be "confused" or "true," while the objective concept may be either. Suárez explains the distinction between the two in Disp. II, Sect. I, § 1: "The act itself, or, what is the same, the word *(verbum)* whereby the intellect conceives a thing or a common nature *(rationem)* is called the objective concept. It is called a concept because it is, as it were, a product of the mind. It is called 'formal' either [1] because it is the last form of the mind or [2] because it formally represents the known thing in the mind, or [3] because in reality it is the intrinsic and formal end of mental conception, in which it differs, if I may say so, from the objective concept. The thing or nature *(ratio)* which is properly and immediately known or represented by the formal concept is called objective concept. For example, when we conceive a man, the act which we produce in the mind to conceive him is called a 'formal concept.' However, the man known and represented in the act is called 'the objective concept;' it is called a concept by extrinsic denomination from the formal concept, through which its object is said to be conceived, and hence correctly called 'objective,' because it is not a concept as a form intrinsically ending [i.e. determining] the conception, but as the object and matter about which the formal conception is, and to which the whole power of the mind directly tends....Whence it is gathered the difference between the formal and objective concept, because the formal [concept] is always a true and positive thing and, in creatures, a quality inhering in the mind; the objective [concept], on the other hand, is not always a true positive thing. For sometimes we conceive privations and other [things] which are called beings of reason, because they only have objective being in the intellect. Again, the formal concept is always a singular and individual thing, because it is a thing produced by the intellect, and inhering in it. But the objective concept sometimes can be a singular and individual thing insofar as it can be objectified and conceived by a formal act, but often it is a universal or confused, and common, thing, such as man, substance, and similar ones...the objective concept of being as such, in all its abstraction, is the object of metaphysics...." Suárez does not clarify exactly where in the mind these concepts reside. Such clarification can be found in Cajetan's *Commentary on Thomas' "On Being and Essense"*, q.2, § 14 *(trans. cit.,* pp. 67 ff)*: "A formal concept is some likeness which the possible intellect forms in itself and is objectively representative of the thing. Philosophers call it an intention or a concept and theologians call it a word. An objective concept, however, is that which, represented by the formal concept, terminates the act of knowing. For example, the formal concept of lion is that representation which the possible intellect forms of a leonine quiddity, when we want to know it; the objective concept of the same thing is the leonine nature itself, represented and known." This distinction between formal and objective concepts developed in late medieval philosophy tended to emphasize the representational nature of knowledge and therefore to introduce a dichotomy between mental content and reality. The point becomes critical in Suárez because metaphysics is interpreted by him as dealing with the objective concept of being rather than being itself, opening the doors to the modern rejection of the uncritical realism common among earlier scholastics.

Concretum, grown together, concrete, compound, hard, solid, united, material; from *concresco,* to grow together, harden, increase, and opposed to *abstractum,* abstract. This is not a very common term among early medieval authors; it becomes more popular with time, however. Most often it means simply a material individual or substance. At other times it refers to the way accidents or properties are signified. If they are signified together with the subject or as they are in the subject, they are said to be signified in the concrete. Example: white or black in a man. If, on the other hand, what is signified is the property or accident considered in itself, without reference to the subject in which it is, it is said to be signified in the abstract (see *abstracta*). Cajetan discusses this issue at length in his *Commentary on Thomas' "On Being and Essence,"* q. 18, §§153 ff. A third usage of this term refers to composites of subject and attribute or form. There are three kinds of these composites or *concreta:* Logical, as "a perceived house," the composite of house, a physical reality, and the perception, a mental one; physical, as "a shaped body," a composite of the body and its shape, both physical realities; and metaphysical, as "merciful God," a composite of God and his mercy, which is not really distinct from him, but neither a result of logical consideration alone.

Concursus, a meeting together, union, cooperation, event. Scholastics used this term generally to refer to God's willingness to act in accord with those natural causes that would bring about a particular effect. Suárez dedicates Disp. XXII in the present work to the issue of God's cooperation *(cooperatio, concursus)* with secondary causes. He discusses it also in other works, but particularly in *Grace's Help* III, Chs. 25 ff. The issue became very important in the Middle Ages from the time of Augustine and Pelagius onwards, because it involved the whole problem of free will vs. determinism. In Disp. XXII Suárez declares himself in favor of the view which holds that "God works essentially and immediately in every action of the creature and that this influence of his is absolutely necessary in order for the creature to cause anything." (§ 6). He also adds, first, in § 15, that "the divine cooperation insofar as it is something *ad extra,* is by itself something essentially similar to an action or at least to a kind of production immediately emanating from God;" and second, in § 19, that "the divine cooperation does not necessarily include something ...as a principle of its action or as a necessary condition of it."

Conditio necessaria, necessary condition; see *conditio requisita.*

Conditio per se, essential condition; see *conditio requisita.*

Conditio requisita, required condition, also called *conditio necessaria* or *sine qua non,* necessary condition or condition without which no [effect follows], contrasted with *conditio per se,* essential condition. Although scholastics were aware of the difficulties involved in determining what were necessary and *per se* conditions in particular cases, they had no difficulty distinguishing the two notions. This was possible because they held the view that beings had essences: any condition related to the essence, such as the formal cause or the efficient cause, were regarded as *per se;* all others, whose presence was a requisite for the effect to happen but which, like contiguity, were not related to the essence, were classified as necessary. Naturally, philosophers who reject the distinction between essence and accident find it very difficult to make any sense out of this distinction and its close relative, the distinction between necessary and sufficient conditions. Indeed, even Suárez, who accepts the distinction between essence and accident, finds difficulties with the distinction between necessary and *per se* conditions, difficulties arising no doubt from some of his anti-realist commitments. In Disp. XVII, Sect. II, § 5, he voices them: "...among the accidental causes there are some conditions necessary for action, which do not essentially *(per se)* influence the effect or action, such as the proximity of the agent and patient, the suppression of some obstacles, and any similar ones. These are usually called conditions *sine qua non.* Nevertheless, although it [i.e. this type of condition] is accidental with respect to proper and direct causality, with respect to physical necessity and insofar as it can be the object of science, it is in some way essential *(per se)*....I only point out that, since the *conditio sine qua non* is similar *(convenit)* to the essential *(per se)* principle of action in that it is necessarily required, it is not easy to discern in which of the two ways a disposition or property of a thing is related to an action, namely, whether as essential *(per se)* principle, or only as condition *sine qua non.* Therefore, sometimes this can be known from the general nature *(ratione)* or mode of the particular property, as we easily understood in the case of proximity, since proximity is only either a relation or mode of presence.... Sometimes, however, it [i.e. the matter] is more obscure and determined through some special feature *(ratio)* of the thing in question, as it is the case in the popular question concerning whether the knowledge of an object is only a necessary condition for the appetite's motion, or if it is also an essential *(per se)* co-efficient principle....At any rate, two general points must be made: One is that whenever we are certain by experience that a property is necessary for an action and no other sufficient reason of that necessity can be given, except proper and essential *(per se)* causality, then we do not have to appeal to the condition *sine qua non,* but that is a sufficient sign of essential *(per se)* causation. The best example of this is the necessity of the impressed species for seeing....However, when a sufficient reason for the necessity of such a condition can be given without essential *(per se)* causality, it will be easily understood that that is only a condition *sine qua non,* particularly if there is in the cause another power sufficiently proportioned in order to be understood as sufficient to influence the action...."

Conditio sine qua non, condition without which; see *conditio requisita.*

Consequens, consequent; see *consequentia.*

Consequentia, consequence, to be distinguished from *consequens,* consequent. According to Peter of Spain (*Treatise on Consequences,* tran. J.

P. Mullally, Marquette Univ. Press, 1964, p. 141) "the term *conse-quence*' in one way is taken in an extremely general way, namely, in-sofar as it is extended to both a valid consequence and to an invalid one. Then, it is defined as follows: A consequence is a statement *(oratio)* which contains more than one proposition and denotes that one of these is a sequel of the other....In a second way, *'consequence'* is taken properly and is defined as follows: A consequence is a state-ment having an antecedent and its consequent as its principal parts and also a sign of an inference understood inferentially." In contrast, then, the consequent "taken properly is a proposition which is in-ferred from the antecedent through the mediation of an inferential sign." And the antecedent "is that through which the mediation of the inferential sign implies a consequent or that which antecedes another proposition in a valid consequence."

Constituo, to cause to stand, lay down, set, fix, arrange, order, con-struct, constitute, build, create, make, establish, confirm, dispose, define, determine, agree. Scholastics used the term at least in three important ways: First, things are said to be constituted when they are made or come to be. This applies both to natural and artificial things. An embryo, just like a statue, is said to be constituted when it is first conceived and begins to exist as a distinct reality. Second, things are said to constitute other things when they make them up as their parts or as their components. Man is said to be constituted by matter and form and, vice versa, matter and form are said to constitute man. Third, things are said to constitute other things when they are the causes or principles of their existence. Thus an artist may be said to constitute a statue because he sculps it. In turn each of these senses can be understood as referring to reality and real things or to the mind and concepts. Things may be constituted or constitute other things in reality, that is, they may come to be, or they may be parts or principles of other things. But they may also constitute other things in the mind or be the causes or principles of their understanding.

Contineo, to hold together, keep together, be comprised, be enclos-ed, preserve, keep, retain, comprise, contain, comprehend; from *con*-, with, and *teneo,* to have, keep, hold, conceive. Medieval and scholastic authors used this term to express various logical, metaphy-sical and physical relations. In logic the species is said to contain the individual or alternatively the individual is said to be contained in the species. Similarly, the species is said to be contained in the genus and so on up Porphyry's logical tree. Metaphysically this term was used to refer to various relations among beings: Inferior beings are said to be contained in superior ones, and consequently the highest being, God, is said to contain the perfections of all other beings.

Suárez discusses the problem of "eminent containment" in Disp. XXX, Sect. I, §§ 10-12. He defines eminent containment as "having a perfection of superior nature such that it virtually contains everything present in the inferior perfection. This cannot be better explained than in terms of causality or effect." Those medievals who held the theory of man as a microcosm generally used this term to describe their view: Man is said to contain the created universe. See my article, "Ontological Characterization of the Relation between Man and Created Nature in Eriugena," *Journal of the History of Philosophy* 16 (1978) 155-166. This terminology was derived from Maximus the Confessor and Gregory of Nissa and transmitted to the Latin West by Eriugena and other neo-Platonists. It created many problems for later scholastics in their attempt to put it together with Aristotelian terminology. Thomas, for example, complains about the strange language of the neo-Platonists in the Introduction to his commentary on Pseudo Dionysius' *On the Divine Names.*

Contingens, touching on all sides, contiguous, contingent; from the Classical *contingo,* to touch, partake, be related; opposed to *necessarium* or *essentiale.* Medievals used this term to refer to beings, propositions, and arguments, or to the way their components are related. Thomas discusses three kinds of contingent things in his commentary on Aristotle's *On Interpretation* (18b5), Lect. XIII, § 9: "Some, the ones that happen by chance or fortune, happen infrequently; others are indeterminate to either of two alternatives because they do not tend more to one than to another, and these proceed from choice; still others occur usually, for instance, men turning gray in old age, which is caused by nature." The discussion of necessity continues in Lect. XIV, §§ 8 ff., where Thomas contrasts necessity to possibility. Cajetan in his *Commentary on Thomas' "On Being and Essence,"* q. 11 (*trans. cit.,* pp. 214, 215), gives short, standard definitions of these: "By possible in itself is meant that which has in itself the possibility of non-existence;" "a being, necessary in itself, is one which lacks a potency to existence (*esse*) or non-existence (*non-esse*)...a necessary being is that which cannot be in any other way." Most other medieval thinkers, and logicians in particular, discussed these terms extensively. See, for example, William of Sherwood's *Syncategoremata,* Ch. 15. Suárez discusses contingency in Disp. XIX, Sect. X: An effect is contingent "in one way because it is produced accidentally, without the agent's intention;...in another sense 'contingent' is taken to mean something in between the necessary and the impossible, in the way dialecticians say the contingent includes what can and cannot exist." Suárez discusses necessity in relation to God's will, Disp. XXX, Sect. XVI, §§ 25 ff. In this Disputation "contingent" is frequently contrasted with "essential" — a predicate (or attribute) is said to be contingent if it does not follow necessarily from the nature of a thing. The ability to laugh, although not included in the definition of man—it is neither the genus nor difference and therefore not part of his essence—, is nonetheless a necessary consequence of it. A broken leg, however, is neither included in the essence of man, nor a necessary consequence of it—if it were, all men would have broken legs—, but rather something that a man may have owing to particular circumstances surrounding him. See *necessarius.*

Continuitas, continuity; from *continuus,* continuous, joining, successive, uninterrupted. The notion of continuity is a difficult one and was discussed extensively by scholastics. Following Aristotle, they associated continuity with change and particularly motion. Indeed, Suárez points out, in Disp. XL, Sect. VIII, § 7, that continuity pertains to the essence of motion. Continuity, however, must not be confused with succession. According to Suárez, they are "neither the same nor convertible. For a change can be continuous even if it is not successive, as it is as clear in the continuity of extensions as of intensifications; for if a surface is heated in a moment, just as the heating is continuous in the surface, so also its parts are continuous, even if it is not successive....Succession requires a prior and posterior in duration, while continuity only requires the union of parts having a common term, even if they are produced simultaneously. On the other hand, succession, properly speaking, intrinsically includes some continuity." The discussion is a long one; see §§ 5 ff.

Contraho, to draw together, assemble, collect, cause, produce, conclude a bargain, shorten, diminish, restrain, contract. For scholastics this term was used to refer to the way in which the genus is narrowed down or restricted to species and the way in which the species is narrowed down or restricted to individuals. Man, for example, contracts the genus "animal" and Paul, the species "man." More broadly, the term was used to refer to any determination whereby a being can be viewed as falling within a particular kind or group. In this sense any characteristic acquired by a being "contracts" it in some way. Thomas refers to this meaning of the term in *Summa theologiae* I, 5, 3, *ad* 1: "Substance, quantity and quality, and those things contained in them, contract being, determining *(applicando)* it to certain quiddity or nature."

Convenio, to come together, assemble, meet, unite, combine, agree, conform, be suitable, be proper, belong, pertain. This is an all purpose word in scholastic Latin and can be translated only according to context. There is at least one text from Suárez, however, where he tries to fix the meaning of it. *Commentary on Thomas' "Summa theologiae"* III, 1, 1: "Something can be said to be *conveniens* with something else either because it is appropriate to it or because it is suited to its power or natural inclination, although no suitable thing may come from it."

Coordinatio metaphysica, metaphysical coordination. This is not a term commonly used by scholastics. It refers to the joint arrangement of the various metaphysical elements that compose a being.

Corpus, body. Scholastics distinguished three meanings of this term: (1) Three-dimensional substances, such as an animal or a plant; (2) that which united to form constitutes a three-dimensional substance, such as the body of a man; and (3) three-dimensionality itself, i.e. a species of quantity (see Thomas, *Summa theologiae* I, 18, 2). Suárez used the term often in the second sense, i.e. as a physical part of a physical being (Disp. XV, Sect. X, § 14). As such it unites with substantial form to make up a complete being.

Corruptio, corruption, spoiling; from *corrumpo,* to destroy, ruin, naught, corrupt, spoil, falsify, mislead. For scholastics *corruptio* was opposed to *generatio* (generation) and referred to substantial change. In substantial change a form previously connected with matter ceases to be and another takes its place. The original composite is said to be corrupted in this process and the ensuing one, to be generated. Thomas (*Contra gentiles* I, Ch. 26) puts it thus: "Generation is the way to being, and corruption the way to non-being." And Ockham in *Summa physicae* III, Ch. 8: "Generation takes place when a substantial form is induced anew into matter. Corruption takes place when a substantial form ceases to be in matter." Suárez, following Thomas *(Summa theologiae* I, 27, 2), points out two meanings of the term 'generation' in *On the Trinity,* IX, Ch. 1, § 4: "In the first way it means the production of a substance from preceding matter. In another way it is especially taken to mean the birth or conception of the living." Likewise, we may gather from this, corruption may mean either (1) the cessation of an existing substance or (2) the death of a living being. Corruption and generation, i.e. substantial change, apply only to sublunary being. Celestial bodies and spiritual beings such as angels do not undergo substantial change. There are further discussions of these terms in Disp. XVIII, Sect. II, §§ 17 and 18, and Sect. XI, §§ 8 and 9.

Creatio, creation; see *annihilo.*

Definitio, boundary, limit, explanation, definition, what is decided; from *difinio,* to limit, end, determine, define, explain, finish. Scholastics generally accepted Aristotle's explanation of the meaning of the Greek equivalent of the term 'definition' given in *Topics* I, Ch. 5, 101b38: "A definition is a phrase signifying a thing's essence." Aristotle included definition among the predicables (see *praedicabilia*), but medieval logicians, following Porphyry, substituted species and difference for it. They introduced as well various distinctions between essential, nominal, natural, metaphysical and logical definitions, although not all of these distinctions were generally accepted. Ockham, for example, argues against a purely logical definition in *Summa logicae* I, Ch. 26: "Definition has two senses. In one [sense of the word we speak of] a definition as expressing the what of a thing and, in another [sense, we speak of] a definition as expressing the what of a name. The definition expressing the what of a thing has two senses, namely, in the broad sense it covers not only strict but descriptive definition. In another [sense], the name 'definition' is taken strictly, and in this way it is a complex expression *(sermo)* expressing the whole nature of a thing without indicating anything extrinsic to the thing defined. This can happen in two ways. For sometimes in such a [complex] expression *(sermone)* will be included [expressions in one or more of the] oblique cases expressing essential parts of the thing...this can be called a natural definition. If no expression is in the oblique case...then it [i.e. the definition] is called metaphysical....Besides these two [kinds of] definitions no other is possible." Suárez follows Aristotle and medieval logicians in his view of definition. In the Index to Aristotles's *Metaphysics* VII, Ch. 4, he writes: "It must be said that what a thing is, taken logically, is nothing other than the essential or quidditative definition of the thing, which as it is formally in the mind or in word belongs to dialectics; however, as the essence of the thing presented *(obiecta)* to the mind or explained by the definition is a metaphysical essence..." A proper definition by contrast is one which always accompanies that which it defines (see *proprium*). It is proper, then, because it belongs to the defined, following, like all properties, from the essence. Suárez rejects the view that only substances (man, dog, etc.) can be defined; accidents (white, long, etc.) insofar as they are real are also definable, although their definition is imperfect, because it must include reference to substance. The individual is not definable.

Demonstratio, indication, a showing, designation, description, demonstration. Scholastics used this term to refer to valid deductive arguments (syllogisms) whose premisses are (1) true and (2) either (i) first principles (or principles deducible from them) or (ii) conclusions of syllogisms who premisses are first principles (or principles deducible from them). Such syllogisms were taken to show cause and therefore to produce knowledge of cause ($\xi\pi\iota\sigma\tau\acute{\eta}\mu\eta$ for Aristotle) or science for scholastics (see *scientia*). Many sorts of demonstrations were accepted by scholastics. The most important ones, derived from Aristotle, *Posterior Analytics* I, Ch. 13, are the following: *propter quid* (from cause to effect — called also *a priori* by Ockham, *Summa* *logicae* III, 2, ch. 17, and *a priori* or ostensive by Suárez) and *quia* (from effect to cause — called also *a posteriori* by Ockham and Suárez). These correspond to Aristotles's δtότι or "demonstration of the reasoned fact" and ότι or "demonstration of fact." Suárez discusses both of these in Disp. III, Sect. III, § 6: "The first [i.e. *demonstratio ostensiva*] is essentially *(per se)* and directly a requisite of science. It proceeds from cause to effect and from the essence of a thing to the demonstration of its attributes *(passiones)* — for we are speaking of an *a priori* and *propter quid* knowledge *(scientia)*... The second kind of demonstration is not essentially *(per se)* required; it is used often owing to human imperfection, ignorance or pride. It is useful not only to reach conclusions but also to establish and prove the first principles, [something] which cannot be done in the first way [i.e. through ostensive demonstration]." See also Thomas' well known discussion of this in *Summa theologiae* I, 2, 2.

Denominatio, denomination, substitution of the name of an object for that of another to which it is related in some way, as the name of the cause for that of the effect, of the property for that of the substance, etc.; also a derivation, determination, designation; from *denomino,* to name, denominate, specify. The term *'denominatio'* and its derivatives, *'denominative,' 'denominationes,'* etc., were of common use in philosophy and logic until relatively recent times. J.S. Mill, for example, uses the term in his *System of Logic,* 1862, 5th ed. The source of the term is a text in *Categories,* Ch. 1, 1a13-14, where Aristotle says that "things are said to be named 'derivatively,' which derive their name from some other name, but differ from it in termination." The Greek term used in this text, παρώνυμα (whence the term 'paronym' in modern English), was translated into Latin by the term *'denominative,'* which was in turn substantivized into *denominatio.* The examples Aristotle gave were 'grammarian,' which is a derivative from 'grammar' and 'courageous,' which is a derivative from 'courage.' Originally, this doctrine was interpreted grammatically, but subsequent writers used the notion of paronymy freely. Priscian, for example, extended the term to cover any sort of derivation from a name (noun or adjective). As usual it was Boethius who became the most important channel through which this notion entered the medieval West. In his *Commentary on Aristotle's "Categories"* (PL 64, 167D) he points out three requisites of paronymy: a) participation of the thing paronymously named into something else, b) participation of the paronymous name into another name, and c) non-identity of paronym and original name. Measured by these criteria, the English term 'grammarian' is a paronym of grammar (the grammarian participates in grammar, and the term 'grammarian' is derived from the term 'grammar,' but the terms are not identical) and 'musician' of 'music,' but, in Latin, *'musica'* (woman musician) is not a paronym of *musica* (the art of music) since these terms are identical. In the early part of the Middle Ages the grammatical and philosophical dimensions of paronymy were discussed at length, as it is clear from Anselm's dialogue *De grammatico* (see D.P. Henry's annotated translation of this work in *The "De grammatico" of St. Anselm: The Theory of Paronymy,* Univ. of Notre Dame Press, 1964, and his *Commentary on "De grammatico,"* Reidel, 1974). Later, in the thirteenth and following centuries, the notion of denomination or paronymy was expanded to include the use of a term to refer to something (x) because the term is primarily applied to something else (y) which is related in some way to the first thing (x). Thus 'healthy' is said denominatively of medicine because medicine causes health. Thomas frequently used the term in this way and so did many other scholastics, including Suárez. The latter refers, for example, to *denominatio per attributionem* (Disp. XXVIII, Sect. III, § 14). Used in this way the term becomes a synonym of 'analogy.' In the thirteenth century and later, various kinds of denominations were distinguished. Thomas, for example, distinguishes between intrinsic and extrinsic denomination, *Contra gentiles* II, Ch. 13: "There are two ways in which something is predicated denominatively: For it may be denominated by that which is outside itself, as when something is said to be 'somewhere' owing to a place and 'at some time' owing to a time; and something may be denominated by that which is in it, as a white is from whiteness. However, a thing is not denominated by something existing, as it were, outside it when it is denominated owing to a relation, but rather by something inhering in it; for someone is not denominated 'father' except from the paternity which is present in him." And in *On Truth,* q.21, a.4: "A thing is denominated in relation to something else in two ways: [a] when the very relation itself is the meaning of the denomination. Hence, urine is called healthy in relation to the health of the animal, for the meaning of 'healthy' as predicated of urine is to serve as a sign of the health of the animal. In such cases, what is relatively denominated does not receive its name from a form inherent in it, but from something extrinsic to which it is related. And [b] a thing is denominated in relation to something else when the relation is not the meaning of the denomination but the cause. For example, air is said to be bright from the sun, not because the very fact that the earth is related to the sun is the brightness of the air, but because the placing of the air directly before the sun is the cause of its brightness." Later, Ockham offered a different kind of distinction in *Summa logicae* I, Ch. 13: "A denominative term can for the present be taken in two senses, namely, strictly, and so it is a term which begins as the abstract [term] but does not have a similar ending, and signifies accident, for example, 'brave' from 'bravery,' 'just' from 'justice.' In another way, taken broadly, it is a term having a similar beginning as the abstract [term] but not having a similar ending, whether signifying accident or not. For example, 'living' from 'life.' " Suárez mentions many kinds of denominations: artificial and natural, real and conceptual, intrinsic and extrinsic, simple and composite, etc. See Disp. XXX-IX, Sect. II. He also uses the term broadly to mean "similarity" or "analogy." In some instances in the translation I have rendered this term and its derivatives by terms such as 'derivatively,' 'derivation,' 'determination,' etc. In such cases the Latin has been recorded within parentheses.

Determinatio, boundary, conclusion, end, determination; from *determino,* to bound, limit, prescribe, determine, fix, settle. Scholastics used this term in these and other non-technical senses, as when a *quaestio* or a dispute was "to be determined." Technically, however, this term referred primarily to two things: First, God's movement of his or someone else's will and activity (as when men are said to be determined to salvation, or an earthquake is said to be determined to happen), and, second, when a less specific thing becomes more specified through some action or influence. In this sense, for example, the genus is said to be determined by the specific difference and the species by the individual unity. Conversely, the genus and the species are said to be determinable. For the first, see Suárez's discussion in Disp. XXX, Sect. XVI, §§ 45 ff.

Dialectica, dialectics, logic. This term has a long history. For Aristotle it referred to reasoning which started from probable rather than self-evident principles; as such was contrasted to demonstration (see *demonstratio*). This is the way Thomas and other scholastics interpreted it strictly speaking *(Commentary on Posterior Analytics* I, Lect. 1). Very often, however, the term 'dialectic' was used simply as a synonym for logic, and dialecticians were simply logicians. Suárez discusses his views on logic in *On the Soul* IV, Ch. 9, § 14 (logic is both practical and speculative) and in the Index to Aristotle's *Metaphysics* II, Ch. 3, § 2 (logic is both an art and a science).

Differentia, difference, diversity, species, distinctive feature. Scholastics used the term technically to refer to the specific difference or feature which distinguishes a species within the genus. For example, rationality is the difference which distinguishes man (the species) from other animals (genus). Difference is one of the predicables. Porphyry and subsequently the medievals divided difference into three: the *differentia communis* accidentally distinguishes one thing from another, such as this man from another because this man is relaxed, the other tense; the *differentia propria* accidentally distinguishes one thing from another, but by a feature which is not separable from the thing, such as this black man from that white man; the *differentia maxime propria* essentially distinguishes one thing from another, such as "rational," which separates a man from a horse. *(Isagoge,* Ch. on Difference). In *De Trinitate* I, Boethius gave another classification of differences — generic (between plant and animal), specific (between man and horse), and numerical (between a man and another man). Strictly speaking, difference is to be contrasted with diversity *(diversum)* — things may be diverse and yet not different, such as the ten categories, diverse from each other but not properly different. Things which are different must differ or be distinguished from each other in something, but things which are diverse may be distinguished by themselves. 'Diverse' is usually contrasted to *idem* (the same) and 'different' to *similis* (like). Suárez discusses the relation between genus and difference in Disp. VI, Sect. XI.

Dimanatio, dimanation; medieval substantive, derived from the rare Classical verb *dimano,* to flow different ways, to spread abroad. The term has a neo-Platonic flavor reminiscent of the doctrine of emanation. This term was used by scholastics, particularly late ones, to refer to the way properties and accidents "flow" or result from or are produced from substances or even other accidents. In this way, one might say the capacity to laugh comes, results, flows or is produced from man's nature, for example. Often this term was interchanged with *resultantia.* Suárez discusses two ways in which accidents are produced in Disp. XVIII, Sect. III, § 2: "In one way, [accidents are produced] by a proper action, as when light is produced by illumination or the 'where' *(ubi)* by a proper local motion. Second, by natural result, as relation results from the foundation, once having posited the term, — if it is a mode distinct from the foundation —, or as figure results from division..." The distinction between these is further clarified in § 9: "When the dimanation is such that it can never be accomplished by itself and separately, but only as connected to a prior action and to its term, then it is not judged a proper and essential *(per se)* action, and much less a change, but only as it were an accidental complement of the prior action....When such result is accomplished by itself and separately, however, as in the reduction of water, then it is judged an essential *(per se)* action and a proper change, essentially *(per se)* tending to such accidental term. This difference is not so much in reality as in a denomination taken from the separation or from the concomitance of actions."

Dimensiones interminatae, indeterminate dimensions, contrasted with *dimensiones terminatae* or *determinatae,* determinate dimensions. This term was used by scholastics primarily in two ways: (1) to refer indiscriminately to any dimension rather than to a specific one, for example "three feet wide;" and (2) to refer specifically to one dimension rather than to a particular instance of that dimension — "three feet tall" rather than "this three feet tall." Suárez understands the term in the first sense in Disp. V, Sect. III, § 11: "For dimensions can be said to be indeterminate only because they do not signify a certain limit of length or width." A most important text on this distinction is found in Thomas' *Commentary on Boethius' "On the Trinity,"* q. 4, a. 2: "Dimensions, however, can be considered in two ways: In one way according to their determination, and I say that they are determined according to limited measure and figure; and so, as complete beings, dimensions are classed in the genus of quantity....In another way, dimensions may be considered without this certain determination, merely in the nature of dimensions, although they never could exist without some kind of determination; just as the nature of color cannot exist without determination to white or black; and according to this aspect dimensions are classed in the genus of quantity as imperfect..."

Dimensiones terminatae, determinate dimensions; see *dimensiones interminatae.*

Dispositio, arrangement, ordering, direction, disposition; from *dispono,* to distribute, dispose, arrange. For scholastics this term meant also nature, determination, tendency, or even just characteristic. It was used in metaphysics as well as logic. For its logical use see William of Sherwood, *Syncategoremata,* in *Mediaeval Studies* 3 (1941), 46-93. Its metaphysical use was taken from Aristotle's *Metaphysics* V, Ch. 19, 1022b1 ff., where he states: " 'Disposition' means the arrangement of that which has parts, in respect either of place or of potency or of kind; for there must be a certain position, as even the word 'disposition' shows." This text gave rise to various different views in the Middle Ages. See, for example, Thomas Aquinas, *Summa theologiae* I-II, 49, 1. Suárez discusses the issue in Disp. XLII, Sect. III, §§ 5-8: Disposition "...is the constitution or as it were the form of the whole thing that emerges in the whole when the parts take their place." This is further divided with respect to place, power, and form. See also Disp. XIV, Sect, III, §§ 26 ff. and *habitus.*

Distinctio essentialis, essential distinction, a distinction between essence and essence, such as that between "alligator" and "ladybug" or "oak" and "crow."

Distinctio ex natura rei is an important technical term for Suárez. According to him, this distinction is intermediate between the real and the conceptual distinctions. The real distinction is "a distinction between thing and thing" and it points to "the fact that one thing is not another, and vice versa." It holds between things that are separate,

such as two supposits or two accidents of distinct supposits, and between things that are united, such as matter and form, quantity and
substance. The conceptual distinction holds "between things not as
they exist in themselves, but only as they exist in our ideas, from
which they receive some denomination." Such is the case of two of
the divine attributes and of identity when, for example, Paul is said
to be the same as himself. Note that, according to Suárez, conceptual distinction does not imply distinction between concepts, since,
as it is clear in the examples provided, Paul and the divine attributes
are not concepts, but real beings. The distinction *ex natura rei* holds
somewhere between these two. It is found "in nature prior to any
activity of the mind, but it is not so great as the distinction between
two altogether separate things or entities." For this reason it may be
called "real," although in order to differentiate it from the real distinction properly speaking, Suárez prefers the term *ex natura rei* or
"modal distinction." This points to the fact that this distinction holds
only between a thing and its mode, such as between quantity and its
inherence in the supposit. (For a discussion of modes see Disp. XX-
XII, Sect. I, and *modus*). In order to avoid confusing this distinction
with the real distinction I have kept the term *ex natura rei* untranslated. For further information on this distinction and its relation to
the others, see Disp. VII, Sect. I, where Suárez discusses it at
length.

Distinctus, separate, apart, distinct, divided; from *distinguo,* to distinguish, separate, part, divide, decorate. Scholastics used the term
technically to refer to individual or singular things. A thing is said to
be distinct from another if it is not numerically one with it. The
abstract substantive '*distinctio,*' however, was used in a variety of
ways to refer to any diversity or division between things, whether
real (between Peter and Paul), conceptual (between man and rational animal), or in between (modal, formal, etc.). As such the term
was contrasted with 'one' or 'common.' It is for this reason that
Suárez discusses this notion and its various sorts in Disp. VII, after
having discussed individual and formal unities in Disps. V and VI
respectively.

Diversum and *diversitas,* diversity, difference; see *differentia*.

Divisio, division, separation, distribution, distinction, difference;
and the corresponding verb, *divido,* to separate, divide, distribute,
distinguish. For scholastics this term referred primarily to the separation of the genus into species by the specific difference. This was
called formal or essential division. However, since in the Porphyrian
tree there are various genera, the essential or formal division was
subdivided to accommodate these. Cajetan explains these divisions

in the *Commentary on Thomas' "On Being and Essence,"* q.6, § 58 (*trans. cit.,* p. 144): "Between Socrates and this lion, granted that lion and man are in the same proximate genus, there is formal division by means of proper essential principles, namely, by means of ultimate differences. Between Socrates and this plant there is a greater formal division by means of principles, namely, the principles common to Socrates and many other species, that is, the division between sensible and non-sensible. Between Socrates and this stone there is still greater formal division by means of common principles, namely, the division between animate and inanimate. And thus, always ascending, formal division becomes wider and wider, until finally we come to the point where we have the greatest formal division between Socrates and this whiteness. It is a division by means of proper and most common essential principles, namely, between the substantive and the dispositive, constitutive of the modes of predicamental being." The term *'divisio'* was also used to refer to the division of the species into individuals. In this case the division was called "material" or "numerical." For other uses of the term, see W. of Ockham's *Summa logicae* I, Ch. 34 and Boethius' *Commentary on Porphyry's "Isagoge,"* where he distinguishes between substantial and accidental division and its various kinds. Suárez discusses this term in Disp. XXXIV, Sect. V, §§ 2 and 3 and in Disp. IV, Sect. VII, where he raises the issue of the order of priority between division and indivision, a point of controversy at the time.

Doctor, teacher, instructor. For scholastics this term refers to the holder of a title officially conferred by the Roman Catholic Church on those authors whose teaching is approved and thus worthy of study and consideration. Although most doctors are saints, these two titles are independent from each other — authoritative and orthodox teaching is independent, at least in principle, from personal holiness. Moreover, not all teaching from a doctor is necessarily to be taken as true or correct. Doctors may on occasion, and sometimes often, err. Indeed, even some of the teachings of the most famous ones, such as Thomas Aquinas, were condemned by segments of the Roman Church at one time or another. For this reason, consensus among doctors is a higher form of authority than any particular view from an individual doctor. This principle is adopted by Suárez in matters of faith (*lex*) in *On the Laws* VI, Ch. 1, § 6.

Duratio, duration; from Classical *duro,* to harden, last, remain, endure. For scholastics this term meant "temporal continuity" or what some contemporary philosophers call "identity" or "sameness through time." See my article, "Numerical Continuity through Time: The Principle of Identity in Thomistic Metaphysics," *The*

Southwestern Journal of Philosophy 10 (1979), 73-92. For Suárez to exist and to endure are the same thing in reality, and since to exist is always to exist as an individual, endurance always implies individual continuity. Therefore, he rejects the Thomistic view that individual being is really distinct from its duration, favoring the nominalistic position, derived from Ockham and Gabriel Biel, that held that the distinction in question is only conceptual. What the concept of duration adds to individual being is explained in Disp. L, Sect. II, § 10:"...duration, properly taken, formally means a positive permanence in existence, which differs from existence only in concept *(ratione)* or in a certain intrinsic connotation. To clarify this, I assume nothing properly endures in the first instant of our time in which it begins to exist. For this is quite in line with the proper and rigorous meaning of the word and the common way of thinking, two things which are very important for this matter, since this whole distinction is primarily based on our way of thinking. The verb 'to endure,' if we pay attention to the force of the Latin, signifies a certain permanence in the thing or an already started action; therefore, since a thing has no permanence in being in the single instant, it cannot be properly said to endure in that instant."

Eductio, a moving out, removal, formation, from *educo,* to draw out, lead forth, educate, rear, produce, support. I have transliterated *eductio* into 'eduction' to preserve its distinction from 'production.' 'Production' is a broader term than 'eduction.' For example, creation *ex nihilo* is a kind of production, but not an eduction. 'Eduction' is generally used in contexts where it is clear that there is a production from already existing entities. In most cases it refers to the production of something out of an existing potency. Eduction is to be distinguished as well from induction, which in this metaphysical context refers to the introduction of something into something else, such as the introduction of form into matter. Strictly speaking, scholastics used the term 'eduction' in connection with the production of forms out of matter. Suárez discusses at least two different explanations of the way forms are educed from matter in Disp. XV, Sect. II, §§ 14 and 15, before he gives his own: The first view states that "since those forms [i.e. the ones educed] are contained in the potency of matter and being produced as it were out of that potency by the agent's action, not because they exist outside matter and do not act on [i.e. actualize] its potency and do not adhere to it, but because, being previously contained in it only in potency and cause, they exist afterwards in act and outside the cause, so they are educed to act from the potential being of matter in which they were contained by the power of the agent which accompanies the matter." The second view is that "for the form to be educed from the potency of matter is to be made in matter and dependent from it in being and production." According to Suárez, however, for form to be educed from the potency of matter is "to be produced by the same action whereby the composite of a prior matter, not produced in the action, is produced." Eduction, therefore, is "an action or change dependent essentially and by itself from matter."

Effectus, effect. For scholastics this term referred primarily to what follows from an efficient cause. They divided effects into essential — those which a cause is ordered from nature to produce, as a house from a builder — and accidental — those which a cause is not ordered from nature to produce, but which follow from chance or fortune, as health when caused by a builder and not a physician. There was disagreement, however, as to how to define these terms exactly. Suárez defines them in Disp. IV, Sect. III, § 2 as follows: An essential effect is one "that is produced from the power and intention of the agent; an accidental effect, on the other hand, is what happens due to chance and fortune, outside the intention of the agent." Aristotle discussed these notions in *Metaphysics* VI, Ch. 2, 1026b1 ff. See *casus.*

Efficacia, Classical *efficacitas,* efficacy, efficiency, power; from *effica,* efficacious, powerful, efficient. For scholastics it signified the power of an efficient cause to produce an effect, as for example in "the efficacy of grace," the power of grace to move the will.

Ens, being, a being, an existing thing; participle of the verb *sum,* to be, or, when used in second position as in "I am," to exist. Although scholastics recognized that being cannot be defined since it is a most general and simple notion, they often argued about the meaning of the term '*ens.*' Some, following Avicenna, emphasized the existential import of the term and relegated its non-existential import to logic, i.e. to the mind. Thomas Aquinas, for example, points out in *On Being and Essence,* Ch. 1, (*trans. cit.,* p. 29), that "the term '*ens*' in itself has two meanings. Taken one way it is divided by the ten categories; taken in the other way it signifies the truth of propositions. The difference between the two is that in the second sense anything can be called *ens* if an affirmative proposition can be formed about it, even though it is nothing positive in reality. In this way privations and negations are called beings, for we say that affirmation *is* opposed to negation, and that blindness *is* in the eye. But in the first way nothing can be called *ens* unless it is something positive in reality. In the first sense, then, blindness and the like are not beings." Suárez, however, takes a different view, which has made him a target of the Thomists' criticism. According to him, *ens* can signify even those things that are not something positive in reality as long as they are possible beings, i.e. beings that although not existing at a particular time, may exist at another. Indeed, it is this type of being, along with actually existing beings, that constitutes the subject of metaphysical investigation. As such, then, metaphysics is not restricted to or even primarily concerned with existing reality. As he puts it in Disp. II, Sect. IV, § 3: " '*Ens*'...is taken sometimes as a participle of the verb to be *(sum)*, and as such it signifies the act of being *(actus essendi)* as exercised and it is the same as the act of existence *(existens actu)*. Sometimes, however, it is taken as a name formally signifying the essence of a thing which has or can have being *(esse)*, [and it can be said to signify the very being *(esse)*] not as an exercised act, but as a potency or aptitude; just as 'living' *(vivens)*, as a participle, signifies the actual use of life, but as a name signifies only that which has a nature which can be the principle of living operations...'*Ens*,' therefore, even taken for real being...is not attributed to existing things alone, but also to real natures considered in themselves, whether they exist or not. This is the way in which metaphysics considers *ens*, and in this way *ens* is divided into the ten categories."

Ens per accidens, accidental being; see *ens per se*.

Ens per se, being as such, essential being; opposed to *ens per accidens*, accidental being. Scholastics used these expressions in at least three different contexts: (1) if the expressions referred to the mode of existence of a thing, then substances were said to be *entia per se* and accidents were said to be *entia per accidens;* (2) if the expression was used in the context of causation, then *entia per se* were effects that followed naturally or intentionally from their causes, while *entia per accidens* were beings that were produced by chance; and (3) if the expression was used to refer to the kind of unity a being has, then *entia per se* were those beings that were one *per se* and *entia per accidens* those that were one *per accidens*. This latter usage was derived from Aristotle's difficult text in *Metaphysics* V, Ch. 7, 1017a7 ff. There were at least two interpretations of it — Suárez discusses them in Disp. IV, Sect. III, §§ 4 and 5: One regards as unity *per se* the type of unity characteristic of one and the same being; unity *per accidens* that characteristic of several entities which although united are different beings. Another view held that an *ens per accidens* consisted of several beings in act while an *ens per se* consisted of a being in potency and its act. Suárez finds fault with both views and settles for the following, § 6: "The nature *(ratio)* of being *per se* consists in this, that it has precisely what is *per se* and intrinsically required for its essence, the wholeness or completeness of such a being in its genus....Consequently...that being will be called strictly and properly *ens per se* which has one essence or entity....Any other being will be called *ens per accidens*." See *ens* and *per se*.

Entia actualia, actual beings, or beings in act. The notion of act, actuality, or being in act is central to Aristotelian metaphysics. It is contrasted to the notion of potency or potentiality. In spite of its importance, actuality cannot be defined, according to Aristotle; like being, it is too general to be determined in a definition; it can only be "illustrated" with examples. In *Metaphysics* IX, Ch. 6, 1048a30, Aristotle explains it thus: "Actuality, then, is the existence of a thing not in the way which we express by 'potentially;' we say that potentially, for instance, a statue of Hermes is in the block of wood and the half-line is in the whole, because it might be separated out, and we call even the man who is not studying a man of science, if he is capable of studying; the thing that stands in contrast to each of these exists actually." For Suárez's view see *actus*.

Entitas, entity; from *ens,* a being. This term has two general meanings in scholastic thought: (1) the character or property of being, and (2) a being. Suárez describes it as "the real essence of a thing as it exists outside its causes" (see Disp. VII, Sect. I, §§ 12 and 19). 'Entity' has a much wider extension than the term 'substance.' It includes not only substances, i.e. concrete individual beings that exist by themselves, such as a horse or a man, but also accidents and even the principles of substance like matter and form. For Suárez this term acquires great importance in this Disputation, since he identifies the principle of individuation with a thing's entity (see Sect. VI).

Esse, to be, exist, be present, live, be found; also a being. All these senses are present in Medieval Latin. For Aquinas, however, *'esse'* was a technical term that referred to the act whereby existing beings exist (see *existentia*).

Esse rationis or *ens rationis,* a being of reason, opposed to a real being, *esse* or *ens reale*. Suárez distinguished the different scholastic uses of the term *ens rationis* in Disp. LIV, Sect, I, §§ 5 and 6: "Since *ens rationis,* as the very name suggests, expresses a relation to reason, there are usually appropriately distinguished as many kinds of *entia rationis* as different relations [to reason]. For there is a being which is effectively produced by reason, by a true and real efficacy, and in this sense all artificial [things] can be called *entia rationis* since they are the product of reason....Another is related to reason as to a subject of inherence, and this is a more proper use of the term...and so all the perfections inhering in the intellect...can be called beings of reason." These two uses of the term, according to Suárez, do not point strictly speaking to beings of reason — the first is not even common and the second points to real beings, i.e. qualities, etc., falling within the ten categories. There is, however, another way in which something is said "to be in reason," i.e. "after the fashion of an object, for, owing to the fact that knowledge is produced by a certain assimilation and, as it were, attraction of the known thing to the knower, a known thing is said to be in the knower, not only inherently through its image, but also objectively through itself." If this objective being has in itself real being, then this objective being is not strictly speaking an *ens rationis*. On the other hand, if "it has no other real and positive being beyond being the object of the intellect or reason that knows it, then this is most properly called an *ens rationis*.... Therefore, an *ens rationis* is usually and correctly defined as that which has objective being only in the intellect or as that which is thought by reason as a being, although it has no being in itself." This definition is expanded usually to exclude beings which although not existing are capable of existence, such as my non-existing son. Strictly speaking, then, a being of reason is a being whose only reality is mental, i.e. this sort of being is the product of human reason alone. For Suárez, as for most scholastics, there are three kinds of *entia rationis:* negations (ex. a man's inability to fly), privations (ex. a man's blindness), and relations of reason (ex. identity). There was considerable divergence of opinion among scholastics about the status, causes, definition, classes, etc. of beings of reason. Some, like Francis of Maironis, in *Quodlibet,* q.7, went so far as to deny their existence. For other texts see Thomas, *Summa theologiae* I, 16, 3 and *Commentary on the Metaphysics* IV, 1.4. See also Joannes J. Urraburu, *Ontologia* (Paris-Rome, 1891, 2nd ed.), pp. 98 ff.

Essentiale, essential, following from the essence; see *contingens, accidens.*

Existentia, existence; medieval substantive derived from *existo,* to spring, emerge, appear, exist, be. Used primarily by later scholastics to refer to a thing's existence as opposed to its essence. The term '*existentia*' was not always used in this connection. Thomas Aquinas, for example, preferred the term '*esse*' to refer to a being's existence in order to stress the dynamic nature of the latter. The position which holds that existence strictly speaking is the principle of individuation in created substances is intelligible only in light of the medieval tradition which regarded existence as something really distinct from essence. If existence is seen only as "presence" or, as some existentialists put it, as "being there," then to ask whether existence is the principle of individuation would be pointless. If the principle of individuation is interpreted as the metaphysical foundation of the individual's individuality, it is clear that "mere presence" cannot be such a foundation. The tradition that regarded existence as somehow distinct from essence goes back to Avicenna (*Al-Shifa', Meta.* IX, Ch. 6) among the Moslems and William of Auvergne (*De Trinitate* 2) among the Latin Christians. It was, however, Thomas Aquinas who formulated it with greater precision and gave it impetus. According to him, existence is an act and perfection in the individual really distinct from its essence. In every being, except in God, there is a real composition of essence, i.e. what the being is, and existence, its act of being. This act is a distinct reality, just as the act of running *(currere)* is a distinct reality from the runner. This doctrine was adopted, discussed and modified by many medieval thinkers after Thomas Aquinas, and it is perhaps for this reason that it became connected with the problem of individuation. Duns Scotus already discusses it in this connection in *Opus oxoniense* I, d.3. For a discussion of Thomas' doctrine see A. Maurer's Introduction to *On Being and Essence* (Toronto: PIMS, 1968). E. Gilson has given a succinct account of the history of the language of being and existence in "Notes sur le Vocabulaire de l'Etre," *Mediaeval Studies* 8 (1946), pp. 150-158. Suárez's own view on the distinction between essence and existence is contained in Disp. XXXI, Sect. I: "Whether the existence *(esse)* and the essence *(essentia)* of created beings are distinguished in reality." He concludes the Section thus (§ 13): "This third opinion is to be interpreted as comparing actual existence *(actualem existentiam),* which they call 'being *(esse)* in exercised act,' and the actual existing essence. And thus this view affirms that existence *(existentiam)* and essence are not distinguished in reality, although essence, conceived abstractly and with precision, [insofar] as it is in potency, may be distinguished from actual existence, as non-being and a being. And I think this view interpreted thus is completely true." J. Owens thinks that the terms of the distinction, as Suárez saw it, were different from those used by Thomas and thus that "this controversy does not touch the doctrine of St. Thomas" although, according to him, Suárez showed conclusively that there was no real distinction between the terms discussed by Suárez. According to Owens, in Thomas "the entitative distinction falls between the essence and any being whatsoever the essence may possess. If the expression *esse essentiae* is to be used, the distinction of St. Thomas will fall between the *esse* and the *essentia*—all *esse* that belongs to the essence is entitatively distinct from it. The only being of essence is existence." *An Elementary Christian Metaphysics,* Ch. 9 (Milwaukee: Bruce, 1963), p. 134, n. 8. See also his article "The Number of Terms in the Suarezian Discussion on Essence and Being," *The Modern Schoolman* 34 (1957), 148-191; and J. Gómez Caffarena, "Sentido de la composición de ser y esencia en Suárez," *Pensamiento* 15 (1959), 135-154. Owens' interpretation is supported by the fact that Suárez's notion of *esse* is not like Thomas'; for him *esse* is more entitative than actual—at least that is the usual interpretation given by Gilson and his followers (*Being and Some Philosophers,* Ch. 3). See, for example, Disp. XXXI, Sect. VII, §§ 1-6, and also Sect.

VIII, §§ 6 ff. On the other hand, that Suárez uses the terms *esse essen-tiae* and *esse existentiae* at times rather than just *esse* and *essentia* is no reason to believe that he is discussing a different problem from the one that concerned Thomas. For the term '*esse essentiae,*' just as its English counterpart, 'the being of essence,' can be interpreted in two ways as meaning "the being (or existence) belonging to essence" or "essential being (or existence)." And, on the other hand, existence may not be interpreted strictly, but just as subsistence or entity.

Extensio, extension, a stretching out; from *extendo,* to extend, spread out, increase, continue. Scholastics generally used this term to refer to continuous quantity or magnitude. Their various inter-pretations were based on Aristotle's text in *Physics* V, Ch. 13, 1020a9 (see *quantitas*). Suárez, who claims to follow Aristotle closely in this matter, discusses continuous quantity at great length in Disp. XL. He dedicates much space to it because "the essential nature of quan-tity is given by continuous quantity," that is, extension. Not all kinds of extensions are to be included here, however. Suárez distinguishes three kinds in Sect. IV, § 15: "One is entitative and does not pertain to...quantity...but can be found among the parts of substance and quality without quantity. Another can be called locational *(localis)* or situational *(situalis)* extension in act, and this is posterior to quantity. Finally, another is a quantitative extension, which can be called situational in aptitude, and it is this one that we posit as the formal nature *(rationem)* of quantity. This is clear between two matters or two bodies, for [the fact is] that the matter of this body, substantially and really distinct from the matter of that one, is not the result of quantity...but of its own entity. However, that those two matters are affected in such a way that they must be necessarily extended or separated in place comes formally from quantity."

Extrinsice, extrinsically; see *intrinsice.*

Falsum, false, deceptive, spurious, a liar; and *falsitas,* falsehood, falsity. Corresponding to the various theories of truth (see *veritas*), scholastics had various theories of falsity. One was ontological: Often they spoke of things as being false if (a) owing to likeness be-tween two or more things, one of them caused us to conclude some-thing false about another thing (see Aristotle's *Metaphysics* V, Ch. 29, 1024b18 ff); (b) one speaks of impossible things, such as the square circle; and (c) something does not adhere to its exemplar or arche-typal idea, such as a man who behaves irrationally. The other important theory was logical: only propositions were to be called false. Suárez adheres to the latter in Disp. IX, Sect. I, § 17, where he points out that "falsity is properly found in the composition and divi-sion of the intellect," i.e. in judgment. In § 19 he adds: "Speaking properly of it, falsity is the non-correspondence *(disconvenientiam)* or inadequation which exists between the judgment of the intellect which composes and divides, and reality [or a thing] as it is in itself." All other uses of the term 'false' for Suárez are metaphorical or derivative.

Fides, trust, faith, confidence, belief, promise, assurance; from *fido,* to trust, confide. Although scholastics discussed as many as a dozen different meanings of this term, generally the term was used in two basic senses: First and foremost, it was used to indicate a certain gift which God confers on the soul whereby the soul believes in him and his revelation; and second, it was used to indicate simply the body of Christian doctrine. For an extensive discussion of this term, see Suárez's *Treatise on Faith.*

Figura, form, shape, figure, sketch, quality, species; from *fingo,* to touch, form, make, feign. Although this term was used in all these senses by scholastics, technically it referred to the form of quantity, which was found only in corporeal beings. See Thomas Aquinas, *Summa theologiae* I, 7, 3 *ad* 2 and 3; also III, 63, 2, *ad* 1. Suárez discusses this term in Disp. XLII, Sect. III, § 15: "Finally, the name 'figure' has a more determined signification. For omitting other improper and metaphorical [significations], whereby one may speak of the 'figure of the syllogism' and of a 'rhetorical figure,' ['figure'] properly signifies a certain mode resulting in a body from the determination of magnitude." As such Suárez classifies figure within the category of quality, because, as he puts it, "it agrees with other qualities in affecting and perfecting the subject." He distinguishes it from shape in the same paragraph: "The name 'form,' [i.e. shape]..., as found within these species [i.e. qualities], signifies nothing other than figure itself, because [figure] is, as it were, the exterior form of bodies. Whence, it seems these two words signify the same, except that with the name 'figure' it is signified in a mathematical way, abstracting from matter...and with the name 'form' it is signified in a physical way." The point is that figure abstracts from other qualities while, according to Suárez, form or shape does not. The latter includes such qualities as color, for example; hence its more "physical" character. Indeed, one often finds texts, particularly in the early Middle Ages, in which 'form' means simply accident. See, for example, Abelard, *Logic for Beginners.*

Forma, form, figure, shape, appearance, nature, kind, essence. For scholastics form is one of the two constitutive principles of things (the other being matter). Together with matter and privation it is one of the principles of natural change. Following Aristotle (*Physics* II, Ch. 3, 194b27), they identified the form with the formal cause of things.

For Suárez the form was primarily a physical principle which, united to matter, makes up the individual; it actualizes matter. He defines it in Disp. XV, Sect. V, § 1, as "a simple and incomplete substance, which as the act of matter, constitutes with it the essence of the composite substance." This physical form was called the form of the part or partial form *(forma partis)*, because it was only a part of the individual and as such did not express the whole essence. It was contrasted to the form of the whole or total form *(forma totius)*, which is simply the essence and therefore includes matter in it. Thomas discusses this distinction at length in *On Being and Essence*, Ch. 2. Suárez regarded the *forma totius* as metaphysical and therefore not strictly speaking a form or structuring principle (Disp. XV, Sect. XI, § 1). It is this metaphysical form that is often called a nature or essence (§ 4). In addition to the physical or substantial form and the metaphysical or abstract form, Suárez and other scholastics spoke of accidental forms, but these were considered imperfect, since they did not inform matter directly but rather through the individual substance. None of these forms should be confused with the exemplars or divine archetypes, also called divine ideas (Disp. XXV, Intro.).

Formaliter, formally, essentially; see *materialiter.*

Forma partis, form of the part, partial form; see *forma.*

Forma substantialis, substantial form; see *forma.*

Forma totius, form of the whole, total form; see *forma.*

Fortuna, fortune, chance; see *casus.*

Fundamentum, a foundation, basis, bottom, ground-work; from *fundo,* to pour, cast, found, utter, lay the bottom, establish. Scholastics used the term primarily in two senses: In one sense they spoke of arguments, proofs and reasons as the foundations of particular views; in another sense they spoke of principles and causes (see *principium* for the distinction between principle and cause) as the foundations of real things or as their components. In order to distinguish these two meanings I have translated the first as "basis" or "bases" and the second as "foundation" or "foundations."

Generatio, generation; see *corruptio.*

Genus, birth, origin, race, offspring, kind, sort, class, character, genus, gender; from *gigno* or *geno,* to beget, produce, be born, cause. For medievals the genus (for example, "animal") was considered one of the predicables (see *praedicabilia*) and defined as "what is predicated essentially *(in quid)* of many things differing in species" (see Ockham, *Summa logicae* I, Ch. 20, and William of Sherwood, *Introduction to Logic,* Ch. 2, § 2). This is Aristotle's definition as given in *Topics* I, Ch. 5, 102a32. However, since the *Topics* did not become available to the Latins until later in the Middle Ages, the definition was taken from Boethius' translation and commentary on Porphyry's *Isagoge*. Some authors altered this definition in various ways. Thomas Aquinas, for example, defines the genus in his *Commentary to Aristotle's Metaphysics* V, lect. 22, 1119-1123, as "that which is stated first in definition and is predicated of primary substance; and the differences are qualities of it, as in the definition of man 'animal' is stated first, and next 'biped' or 'rational,' which are certain substantial qualities of man." Among the many problems surrounding the notion of genus two worried scholastics considerably: The first concerned the type of distinction between genera, species and *differentiae* (real, formal, conceptual, or others); the second issue concerned the origin of the genus in the thing (matter, form, or other). The first problem is discussed in detail by Suárez in Disp. VI, Sect. IX and the second in Sect. XI.

Genus proximus, proximate genus. The genus to which the species immediately belongs, as animal for man and dog; opposed to remote genera such as living, sensible, substance, for man. This terminology is derived from the Porphyrian tree. The proximate genus is predicable only of the species subordinated to it ('animal' is predicable of man or dog); the remote genus of those species and of the genera and species to which those species belong ('living' is predicable not only of man and dog but also of animal).

Genus remotis, remote genus; see *genus proximus.*

Habitudo praedicamentalis, categorical or predicamental relation; see *habitudo transcendentalis.*

Habitudo transcendentalis or, as it is used elsewhere, *transcendentalis relatio* or *respectus,* transcendental relation; opposed to *praedicamentalis habitudo, relatio,* or *respectus,* predicamental, that is, categorical relation. These terms were commonly used by scholastics, but are seldom explained. Suárez finds great difficulty in determining "their differences." He dedicates a whole Section (IV) of Disp. XLVII to this issue. He rejects two ways of distinguishing between categorical and transcendental relations (§§ 2 and 3). The first is "that the transcendental relation does not require the same conditions posited by the categorical relation. These are primarily three...: first, that the categorical relation requires some real, absolute foundation, as likeness [requires] whiteness, and fatherhood [requires] the power of generating or generation; second, that it requires a real term, really existing; third, that it requires a real distinction, or at least an *ex natura rei* [one], between the foundation and the term." The second way rejected is that "the categorical relation is a certain accidental form coming to the foundation fully constituted in its essential and absolute being,

to which it is compared as a complete form in its accidental genus, affecting and referring it to another. The transcendental relation is, however, not compared as an accident or as a complete form to the thing on which it acts immediately and of which it is a relation, but it is compared as an essential difference and consequently as an incomplete being in the genus to which the thing on which it acts belongs...."
After rejecting these two views, Suárez presents his own in five parts. The first he borrows from Cajetan's *Commentary on Thomas' "On Being and Essence,"* q.16, § 136; he explains it thus (§ 9): "...the categorical relation looks to the term purely under the notion *(rationi)* of term; while the transcendental looks to another, not as a pure term, but as a term under some other determined notion, or subject, or object, or of efficient [cause], or of end." A second difference (§ 12) is that "the categorical relation is such that from nature it cannot be intended essentially *(per se),* and hence it is never essentially produced by an agent's action, but, having posited the foundation and term, it follows....The transcendental relation, however, is often greatly intended essentially by nature, and hence form essentially including such relation is often formally, essentially *(per se)* and primarily, produced by a proper action. For example, heat as inhering is produced by heating, and in it [i.e. heat] is intimately included a transcendental relation...." A third difference (§ 13) is to be found in the fact that "the categorical relation has not been established in the order of things to carry out a particular function, but it is said to accompany other things in order that some things be related to each other in virtue of some real nature *(rationis)* or foundation which is posited in them, and hence such relation is nothing other than the relation resulting from the foundation and the term, but never produced essentially *(per se).* The transcendental relation, however, comes to some form or entity or mode of being, insofar as it is by nature essentially *(per se)* instituted and ordered to some particular function which can be essentially *(per se)* intended by an action." From this follows the fourth difference, that (§ 14) "the pure and categorical relation is never a principle of action...while the form signifying a transcendental relation...is often essentially *(per se)* a principle of action, as it is clear concerning science, power and similar things." Finally, (§ 15) "the categorical relation is to be conceived as a minimal and accidental form which does not confer to the subject any being, except its relation to another, nor does it serve for anything else in nature. The transcendental relation, however is not to be conceived as a complete form, whose function is only to refer, but it is an essential mode or difference of a form or entity, insofar as it has been primarily and essentially *(per se)* instituted to cause or operate in some way on other things, or conversely, insofar as it depends essen-

tially from them." The distinction between categorical and transcendental relations has come under fire from contemporary Thomists, who blame John of St. Thomas (1589-1644) for its dissemination within Thomism. See Owens, *An Elementary...* p. 189.

Habitus, the condition or state of a thing, appearance, habit, dress, quality, character, disposition; from *habeo,* to have, keep, contain, be able, hold, make, render, consider, take, accept, know, intend, etc. According to Thomas Aquinas there were at least four ways of considering *habitus:* (1) as a postcategory (categories which are consequences of the ten fundamental categories — opposition, priority, posteriority, simultaneity, motion, condition), (2) as a category, (3) as the first species of quality, and (4) as the habit of religion (see *Summa theologiae* I-II, 49, 1; II-II, 186, 7, *ad* 2, and 188, 1, *ad* 2). As a category, 'habit' signifies a relation like that of dress to the dressed; as a postcategory it is that according to which man, or any other being for that matter, is said "to have" or possess something (see *Summa theologiae* I-II, 49, 10, *ad* 2); as a quality *habitus* signifies a disposition of potency to act or to nature. The distinction between *habitus* as a category and as a quality is further clarified in Thomas' *Commentary on Aristotle's "Metaphysics,"* lect 20: "The first of these [havings] is something in between that which has and that which is had. For habit, although it is not an action, signifies nevertheless something like an action. Therefore, habit is understood as a medium between the having and the had, and, as it were, a kind of action, just as heating is understood as a medium between the heated and the heating, whether the medium be taken as an act, as when the heating is taken actively, or as a motion, as when the heating is taken passively. For, when one thing makes, and another is made, the medium is the making....In the second way, habit means a disposition according to which something is disposed well or ill, as by health one is disposed well, by sickness ill." Suárez discusses these and other senses of *habitus* in various parts of the Disputations. In Disp. XLII, Sect. III, §§ 2-4, he points out the following: "Generally speaking, the name *'habitus'* can be taken as a participle or as a name. As a participle, it is derived from the verb 'to have,' and can be used in as many different ways as that verb....In this way, it is clear that it does not signify any category in particular....*'Habitus'* can be taken in another way, as a name, and then it also has various meanings. In terms of the present discussion, however, three meanings seem pertinent: One is that this word signifies any disposition of a thing or mode of having *(se habendi),* and in this way it is said of any form, and particularly of any quality, and in this way it is usually attributed to the parts of the body and to inanimate things; thus is said 'the habit of place,' '[the habit] of the mouth,' etc....Second, *'habitus'* signifies a dress or bodily garment. Third and final, *'habitus'* is taken as signifying the form which confers the ease and promptitude of operation and, because operation follows being, hence this meaning is usually extended to the qualities which favourably or unfavourably dispose things in their being, in the manner health is called a habit and physicians call a good or a bad habit of the body a natural disposition of the body, from which it comes that all its organs and parts carry out, well or badly, their functions. In this third meaning, *habitus* is always some quality or a proper mixture of qualities...[*habitus*] is always a quality and because of this I think *habitus,* properly taken constitutes the first species of quality...." Although from this text it seems that, for Suárez, dispositions are a kind of habit, strictly speaking this is not so. Scholastics debated the point widely, using as their point of departure the Aristotelian text in *Categories,* Ch. 8, 8b27: "Habit differs from disposition in being more lasting and more firmly established." Such things as knowledge and virtue are habits and such things as disease and health are dispositions for Aristotle. Suárez discusses this in Disp. XLII, Sect. VII, §§ 12-18. His solution is eclectic and circumstantial — the difference between habits and dispositions depends on the particular habits and dispositions in question. For example, in terms of the first act of the understanding or the will there is no distinction; in other cases, such as the ones cited by Aristotle, there is.

Haecceitas, thisness; from *haec,* this. Term used by Scotists. It is not clear whether Scotus favored the term himself or whether it became common only with his followers and critics — we will know when all of Scotus' works are critically edited. It refers to that principle whereby a thing is "a this," i.e. an individual thing, Petrinity in Peter, for example. This principle is formally distinct from the nature. Scotus explains the point in *Opus oxoniense* II, dist. III, q.6: "Hence, this being [i.e. *haecceitas*] is not matter, nor form, nor the composite, insofar as any of these is a nature; but it is the ultimate reality of the being which is matter, or which is form, or the composite, so that anything common and yet determinable can still be distinguished, however much it is one thing, into several formally distinct realities, of which this is not formally that. But this is formally the being of a singular, and that is formally the being of a nature. And these two realities cannot be as thing and thing, as can the realities from which genus and difference are taken...but in the same thing, whether part or whole, they are always formally distinct realities of the same thing." In many ways the notion of *haecceitas* is similar to the contemporary notion of "bare particular," since (1) its only function is to individuate, (2) it cannot be analyzed into further principles, and (3) it is posited on the bases of dialectical or theoretical considerations alone.

There are, however, important differences as well. The most important of these is that *haecceitas* is a substantial principle, not an accidental one. Scotus, unlike most contemporary philosophers who use the notion of bare particular, adheres to the substance-accident distinction. Unless otherwise noted, the term *haecceitas* is rendered by 'thisness' throughout this translation.

Hoc aliquid, this something; see *aliquid.*

Ideas universalium, ideas of universals. The terms 'idea' and 'universal' were seldom used as synonyms by scholastics, and least of all by Suárez. Universals are the various genera and species, such as man, animal, dog, etc., considered as they are related to the particulars that instantiate them. Consequently, the problem of universals in the Middle Ages consisted in the determination of the ontological status of genera and species and their relation to particulars — their instances. Ideas, however, a term medievals borrowed from Augustine and the neo-Platonic tradition, are the various genera and species as they are related to God and his nature. Consequently, the problem of divine ideas consisted in the determination of the ontological status of genera and species in relation to the divine nature and being. The problem of divine ideas was inherited from Plotinus, via Augustine, who placed Plato's ideas in the *Nous,* later identified by Augustine as the *Logos* or Christ, the second person of the Trinity. Thus, although Plato and Aristotle were addressing the same problem when they spoke about ideas and universals, the medievals were not. Whence it was possible for Suárez to write concerning "the ideas of universals." He makes the point clear in Disp. XXXV, Sect. VI, § 9, where he distinguishes ideas from specific natures and in Disp. XXV, introd., where he identifies them with exemplars. In his view, the most important difference between ideas and universals is that the former can exist separate from things (in God), while universals cannot. Indeed, universals exist only in things or in someone's mind; ideas exist in God's mind. We use universals in the process of knowing; God uses ideas in the process of creating. Sometimes, however, the term 'idea' was also used to refer to the forms of things as they are in the mind of the knower, and therefore as principles of cognition. In *Summa theologiae* I, 15, 1, Thomas explains the point thus: " *'Idea'* in Greek is translated by *'forma'* in Latin; whence by ideas are understood the forms of things existing outside the things themselves. But the form of anything existing outside the thing itself, can be in two ways, either as the exemplar of that of which it is said to be the form, or as the principle of cognition of it, according to which the forms of knowable [things] are said to be in the knower."

Idem, the same; see *identitas.*

Immediate, directly, immediately, without intermediary; from *medium*, the middle. For the medievals something was said to exist *immediate* if its existence was not mediated, i.e. dependent, on something else. In this sense individuals were said to exist *immediate*, but natures were not. Some authors speak as well of substances existing 'immediately" while accidents exist only mediately, through substances. In logic, expressions such as "immediately contradictory predicates" mean that the predicates in question are both exclusive and exhaustive.

Identitas, sameness, identity; from Classical *idem*, the same, identical. The deficiencies in Aristotle's discussion of sameness found in *Metaphsics* V, Ch. 10, prompted a long-lasting controversy on the issue in the Middle Ages, beginning with Boethius' text in *On the Trinity* I (Loeb trans., p. 7): "Sameness (*idem*) is predicated in three ways: By genus, e.g., a man and a horse, because of their common genus, animal. By species, e.g., Cato and Cicero, because of their common species, man. By number, e.g., Tully and Cicero, because they are numerically one." For Suárez sameness can be taken in two ways: relatively (also called formally), and in this sense it is a mental relation; and negatively (also called fundamentally), and in this sense it is the same as individual unity, whereby and individual thing is not diverse or divided from itself. In the second sense, Suárez calls it a passion or attribute of being. He explains the point with an example in Disp. VII, Sect. III, § 2: "This [i.e. the distinction] is clear in the sameness whereby somebody is said to be the same as himself. For, if this [statement] is taken relatively and formally, it expresses only a mental relation....For there can be no real relation of the same to itself, since there must be a true opposition between a relation and its term, which cannot be between the same and itself. Nevertheless, in this sense, that is, formally, no one will be said [to be] the same as himself, that is, to be referred to himself with such a relation, except when he is thus conceived or compared in the mind. But without some kind of comparison or intellectual fiction somebody is said [to be] the same as himself fundamentally or negatively, since he is not diverse or divided from himself."

Indifferens, indifferent, careless, indistinct, neither good nor evil, indeterminate. This term has a long history in the Middle Ages. It was used by William of Champeaux to explain the ontological status of universals, and savagely criticized by Abelard in his *Logic for Beginners* (in *Beiträge zur Geschichte der Philosophie des Mittelalters*, XXI, 1, pp. 29 ff.). It was also frequently used by later scholastics in an ethical context to refer to the freedom of the will (indifferent to good and evil and therefore capable of doing either). See Suárez, Disp. XIX, Sect. V, § 22.

Inferior, inferior; see *superior.*

Induco, to induce; see *educo.*

Infinitas, infinity; medieval term derived from *infinitum,* the infinite, endless, countless, indefinite. For the Greeks this notion involved a lack of determination and form and was, therefore, regarded as an imperfection; the infinite could never be in act (see Aristotle, *Physics* III, Chs. 5-8, 204a10 ff.). For scholastics, on the other hand, infinity was a perfection predicable of God, although they differed in their understanding of it. Some understood it positively while others understood it negatively or, in some cases, as a privation. Suárez explains how this notion is applied to God in Disp. XXVIII, Sect. I, §§ 18 and 19: "A body is quantitatively finite insofar as it attains a determinate limit and is not extended beyond [it]; and among finite quantities we understand one to be greater than another because it attains a limit beyond [that of the others] and in order to explain the magnitude of a certain thing we use some definite measure, through the multiplication of which we know a thing to be of a particular, greater or lesser, quantity. Using a similar analogy we explain the entitative perfection and active power of things. In things we apprehend a certain, as it were, hierarchy in the perfection of being, in which there are degrees and, as it were, parts of perfection, and in the case of each being we understand it to be finite and limited by a certain appropriate degree of perfection, which is so limited in its perfection that it prescinds from them [i.e. the degrees of perfection] and does not include them in itself in any way, neither formally nor virtually; it is in this sense that we call created beings limited and finite. And among them we conceive one to be greater than another, because we understand it to participate in a greater number of these perfections or because it participates in, as it were, a greater portion of perfection from the whole hierarchy of being. Since, however, all these beings participate in the perfection of a superior being, we understood it to be necessary that a being in which all possible perfection in the hierarchy of being be contained in some way, either formally or eminently, exist. This being we call infinite without qualification, not in quantity of mass, but in excellence of perfection. Hence, this infinity does not consist in some unlimited extension, but in such perfection of being that, although one and indivisible in itself, does not prescind from other beings in such a way that it may not contain in itself in some way the perfections of all...properly [speaking], this infinitude is not understood privatively, but negatively, with respect to the being to which it is attributed. By this is meant an unlimited perfection without any capacity for limitation...." For various medieval doctrines of infinity as related to the divine being see, Leo Sweeney, "Bonaventure and Aquinas on the Divine Being as Infinite," in *Bonaventure and Aquinas,* ed. R. W. Shahan and F. J. Kovach, Univ. of Oklahoma Press, 1976, pp. 133-153. He provides bibliographical data on the issue.

Infinitas extensiva, extensive infinity. For scholastics the notion of extensive infinity referred either to the number of perfections a being may have or to the number of instances there may be of a particular perfection. In the first sense something was said to be extensively infinite if it lacked no perfections; extensively finite if it did. In this way only God was extensively infinite — all creatures were extensively finite. In the second sense something was said to be extensively infinite if the number of its instances was potentially infinite. For example, animality as a perfection may be considered extensively infinite because the number of animals is potentially infinite. Intensive infinity, on the other hand, referred to the degree or intensity of any of the perfections a being possesses. Thus, something was said to be intensively infinite with respect to a particular perfection, e.g., goodness, if it possessed it to the highest degree, intensively finite if it did not. Again, God was thought to be the only intensively infinite being, for he has all perfections to the highest degree. All other beings are intensively finite. See also *intensio.*

Infinitas intensiva, intensive infinity; see *infinitas extensiva.*

Informo, to give form, shape, sketch, instruct, educate, give information. Scholastics used the term technically to refer to the property of forms whereby they shape and become united to matter. Forms may also, in a secondary sense, inform the intellect, i.e. become united to it in the act of understanding. Suárez holds in Disp. XX-VI, Sect. II, § 10, that "to inform is a real predicate, since it is nothing other than to give proper being while acting...composite being is the result of the information of form." This doctrine creates some difficulties for Suárez, since it seems to imply the natural priority and, consequently, entitative priority of form to the composite. The answer, according to Suárez, (§ 13), is that the form does not exist with natural priority in itself, before its union to matter, but that it exists only with precision with natural priority to its existence in such and such a fashion, while it informs matter.

Infundo, to pour upon, administer, cast, communicate, impart, infuse. The term was used generally in the context of the theological doctrine which explains God's role in the creation of an individual soul and its placement in a body.

In re, in reality, in the/a thing. Expressions such as *in re ipsa, in re, reipsa, secundum rem, a parte rei, ad rem* and other similar ones carry the same meaning and are rendered in this translation by 'in reality' or its adverbial and adjectival derivatives. The exceptions are *in rerum natura*, translated as "in the order of things" and *ex natura rei*, which has been left untranslated because it is a technical term of great importance in Suarecian metaphysics without an exact equivalent in English. It is important to keep in mind that for most scholastics not only actually existing substances and accidents, such as a man or the color of his hair, are real, but also metaphysical principles, such as matter and form.

Intellectus, a perceiving, discernment, understanding, meaning of a word or sentence, idea, knowledge, faculty of understanding or intellect; from *intellego,* to perceive, understand. Although all of these meanings and more are present in scholastic writing, creating sometimes some confusion among contemporary commentators, the most widespread use of this term was as a faculty of the understanding. In this way scholastic writers discussed primarily the divine, angelic and human intellects, distinguishing within these various faculties or functions, such as the passive and active intellects, the formal and material, the possible and actual, etc. The distinction between active and passive intellects is easily traced to Aristotle, *On the Soul* III, Chs. 4 and 5; the others are to be found primarily in Aristotle's Muslim commentators (see my article, "The Agent and Possible Intellects in Gonsalvus Hispanus' Question XIII," *Franciscan Studies,* 29 (1969), 5-36). The divergence of opinion among scholastics concerning these various distinctions produced a number of treatises on this problem, such as Thomas' *On the Unity of the Intellect against Averroists.* There was also divergence of opinion as to whether these distinctions applied to the human intellect alone or were to be extended to the angelic intellect as well. Suárez discusses the latter in detail in *On the Nature of Angels* II, Ch. 1.

Intensibilis, intensifiable, subject to or capable of intensification or increase. See *intensio.*

Intensio, effort, increase, intensity; from *intendo,* to extend, stretch, turn, use, state as a proposition of a syllogism. For the scholastics this term referred to a property of certain qualities: Both to the capacity to be intensified or increased and to the degree of intensity of the quality. Consequently, its translation must necessarily vary according to context. In Disp. XLII, Sect. VII, § 4, Suárez writes: "The second property of qualities (the first is contrariety) is the capacity to be subject to intensification or remission." He dedicates Disp. XLVI to the study of this notion. In the introductory remarks he distinguishes two senses of '*intensio:*' "In the first and most used sense, [*intensio*] is taken for the change by which the same quality is perfected more and more in the same part o.· entity of the same subject....In another sense *intensio* can be taken for the extension or mode of the entity of a form subject to intensification and remission, by reason of which it is capable of that change which is called *intensio.*"

Intentio, in Classical Latin it meant a stretching, tension, increase, directing of the mind toward something, effort, major premise in a syllogism. The medievals primarily used the term to translate the Arabic word for concept (*ma'na,* a notion, meaning), although the term was also used in moral contexts with a meaning similar to that of the English word of the same root. In *Summa logicae* I, Ch. 12, Ockham defines an intention "as something in the soul [capable] by nature *(natum)* of signifying something else," and later adds "that [thing] existing in the soul which is the sign of a thing [and] out of which a mental proposition is composed...sometimes is called an intention of the soul; sometimes a concept of the soul; sometimes an impression *(passio)* of the soul; sometimes the similitude of the thing...." The main problem that concerned the medievals was not the definition of intentions but rather their causes and ontological status: Was an intention a product of the mind or not? Was it a quality of the soul separate from the act of understanding, or was it simply the act of understanding itself? Suárez adopted the view that it was separate from the act of understanding (see *species intentionales*), while Ockham finally settled for the opposite view. Intentions were generally divided into first — concepts which are signs of things which are not concepts, for example, "dog" — and second — concepts which are signs of concepts, for example, "species." For the Thomistic doctrine of first and second intentions see, R. Schmidt, *The Domain of Logic according to St. Thomas Aquinas* (The Hague, 1966).

Intrinsice, intrinsically, from the inside, inwardly. For scholastics to say that something followed from something else intrinsically or that something was intrinsic to something else meant that it did not come from the outside, but was a result of the thing's nature. For this reason 'essentially,' 'naturally,' and 'intrinsically' are often used interchangeably. Strictly speaking, however, the term 'intrinsic' denotes only the notion of "from within," while the term 'nature' denotes the notion of "from birth," and 'essence,' "from being" or "from kind." Certain accidents, for example, white, black, three feet tall, etc. were regarded as intrinsic because they affected the being which had them. Others, such as near, sitting and the like, were called extrinsic because they did not affect or modify the thing itself.

Locus, place, position, spot, location, subject matter, argument, ground of proof. There was wide discussion and disagreement among scholastics as to the exact meaning of this term and its relation to *ubi* (where) and *situs* (position) — fifth and seventh respectively of Aristotle's categories. Suárez thought that most of the disagreement surrounding the meaning of these terms was purely linguistic. Following Toletus (*Physics* IV, q.8), he makes a distinction between intrinsic and extrinsic place in Disp. LI, Sect. II, § 4: "There are two certain things in this matter: The first is that there is an intrinsic mode in corporeal bodies existing in a place, by reason of which they can be the end of local motion. The second is that, beyond this intrinsic mode, generally there is in bodies an extrinsic circumscription of one body by another which is close and next to it." The first of these modes is what Suárez called intrinsic place or *ubi;* it is a true accident intrinsically affecting and determining *(denominans)* a body. The second, on the other hand, is called extrinsic place or just place *(locus)* because "although it is in itself an accident with respect to the subject in which it is (since it is its boundary), nevertheless, with respect to the body that it circumscribes it is not a true accident, because neither does it truly affect nor does it modify such a body, but is only next to and determines *(denominat)* it extrinsically; for this reason it participates in the nature *(rationem)* and name *(praedicationem)* of accident only by a certain analogy and proportionality." (§ 9) *Ubi* and *locus,* then, do not belong to the same category. *Ubi* belongs to or rather constitutes a category of its own, while *locus* falls in different categories or in none at all depending on how it is interpreted. If it is considered as an extrinsic term or end, then it does not belong to any category, since it does not carry out any formal modification. If it is considered in terms of its relations to what is in place, then it is a relation. If it is considered as what protects and preserves what is in place, then it is a cause. And if it is considered as an extrinsic form, then it seems to have the same nature as the one a habit (garment) has to a dressed man. (§ 10) One word of caution: The distinction between intrinsic and extrinsic place does not imply that intrinsic place should be understood as an absolute such as Plato's receptacle, Newton's space or Kant's *apriori.* The latter's view makes space something prior to substance. This contradicts the basic Aristotelian doctrine that substance is the fundamental constituent of the universe. For Suárez, and scholastics in general, place, even intrinsic place, is an accident and therefore dependent on substance; indeed, it is thanks to substance that place exists at all. This brings out another important point: In spite of this emphasis on the non-absolute nature of place, place should not be taken to be something unreal, an extrinsic and purely mental way of perceiving things. Place, at least intrinsic place *(ubi),* is not the product of the mind, but a real accident of things.

Lumina, literally "illuminations," that is, the diffusion of light *(lux)* through a medium. I have translated it as "light" because the English noun seems to include the notion of illumination and the Latin *lumen* seems to include the notion of light. Both are ambiguous. The sense becomes clear in context. Suárez explains this terminology in *On the Soul* III, Ch. 14, § 2: "*Lumen* is an accidental act belonging to the category of quality...it is neither a substantial form, nor some body; therefore it is an accidental form...*Lux* and *lumen* are distinguished [as follows]: *Lux* is said to be an illuminating quality, as it is in an illuminating source or body, such as the *lux* inhering in the sun. *Lumen,* however, is the quality received in the medium; and it is called a ray *(radius)* insofar as it tends to the eye in a direct or reflected line, and it is called brightness *(splendor)* when it shines on a smooth and polished body." The theological issues connected with the creation of light are discussed by Suárez in his work *On the Six Days* II, Chs. 1 ff. The main sources of medieval discussions of light were Aristotle's *On the Soul* III, Ch. 7, and Augustine's *Literal Commentary on Genesis.* Out of these and other sources grew an impressive body of literature. A good example of this available in English is Robert Grosseteste's *On Light,* trans. C. G. Wallis, St. John's Bookstore, Annapolis, 1939.

Materia, matter. The scholastics, reflecting various combinations of the Aristotelian and Platonic doctrines of matter, proposed various views. Some, like Thomas, relied primarily on Aristotle (see *Physics* I, Ch. 9; *On the Heavens* III, Ch. 8, etc.), while others, particularly the Franciscans, adopted a more Platonic attitude. The latter was based primarily on Chalcidius' translation and commentary of part of Plato's *Timaeus* and on a number of medieval neo-Platonic writings by such authors as Augustine, Eriugena, members of the School of Chartres, and others. For Aristotelians matter was primarily the subject of change; it was identified with the material cause of substance. For this reason it was called *materia prima* or prime matter. This is the position adopted by Thomas, who concluded further that prime matter in itself is not actually something; it is pure potentiality, receiving all its actuality from form. See his commentary on *Metaphysics* VII, lect. 2, § 1285 and VIII, lect. 1, § 1687, and *Summa theologiae* I, 4, 1. Cajetan expands on the Thomistic doctrine in his commentary on *On Being and Essence,* Ch. 3, § 50, *(trans. cit.* p. 125), where he explains the unity of prime matter: "When you hear that the unity of prime matter is a numerical unity, understand this negatively, not positively. For something is said to be one in number in two ways, that is, positively and negatively. Something is one in number positively which is one by the presence of a property or a numerical difference, for instance, Socrates. And in this way, prime

matter in itself is not one in number, because it includes no individual property. Something is one in number negatively which,
because it is not universal, is not many in number; and this is what
includes within itself nothing distinctive, whence it could have plurality and number. Taken in this way prime matter in itself is one in
number, and this sort of numerical unity is based upon a determinate entity, namely, upon that entity which is matter, which includes within itself nothing distinctive, since it is stripped of all act,
whose function it is to distinguish." Suárez disagreed with this view
of matter as lacking all act. He discusses his view in Disp. XIII,
"The Material Cause of Substance." In Sect. I, § 3, he defines prime
matter as "that matter which does not presuppose any previous subject." In Sect. IV, § 13, he points out that "prime matter has in itself
and by itself the entity or actuality of existence distinct from the existence of form, although," he qualifies, "it may be dependent from
form." This dependence is the result of the fact that (§ 14) the existence of matter "is so imperfect that matter cannot exist naturally
without form." Moreover (§ 15), "matter does not have actual entity
or existence from itself without an efficient cause, but rather it is
necessary for it to receive it from another being, namely, God." He
adds elsewhere (§ 2) that prime matter has "a real and substantial
entity, really distinct from the entity of form." Prime matter is to be
contrasted with "second mater" *(materia secunda)*. The distinctive feature of the latter is that it presupposes the first and adds to it some
form or disposition. Because of this various things are called second
matter, according to Suárez (§ 3): the substantial composite with
respect to accidents, the composite of matter and form of corporeity
with respect to other substantial forms (for those who accept the
multiplicity of substantial forms — Suárez does not), and the matter
disposed or modified by accidents with respect to other accidents.
For a discussion of this notion in Suárez, see John F. McCormick's
"Suárez on Matter and Form," *Proceedings. Annual Convention, Jesuit
Educational Association* (Chicago: Loyola Univ. Press, 1931), pp.
172-183, and Russell Hatton, *"The Role of Materia in Suárez's Metaphysics,"* Doctoral dissertation, State Univ. of New York at Buffalo,
1979. *Materia signata,* designated matter, is a kind of second matter; it
is prime matter designated or determined by quantity. Thomas used
this notion to explain the individuation of material substances.
Suárez discusses his view in great detail in this Disp., Sect. III.

Materialiter, materially, substantially, circumstantially; opposed to
formaliter, formally, essentially. Strictly speaking, for scholastics
something is said or predicated materially when it is said or predicated by reason of the matter or of the subject; formally, when it is
said or predicated by reason of the form or the essence. Loosely

speaking, however, what the material or formal aspects are depends on the particular situation. What is formal at one time can be considered material at another and vice versa. A man, for example, is materially large and formally animal, but he is also materially animal and formally rational or materially rational and formally "a this." In these cases, the last determination is always formal, the basic one, material.

Materia prima, prime matter; see *materia.*

Materia secunda, second matter; see *materia.*

Materia signata, designated matter; see *materia.*

Mediate, mediately; see *immediate.*

Metaphysica, metaphysics. This term originates from the title of Aristotle's text. As it is well known, Aristotle himself did not use the term 'metaphysics;' it was the editor of his works that used it to gather all the treatises that go under that title today. In the *Metaphysics* Aristotle does not give a single and clear definition of the science under discussion. What he often calls "first philosophy," "wisdom," "theology," or just "philosophy" is defined in four different ways — as the study of causes (*Metaphysics* III, Ch. 2), of being *qua* being (IV, Ch. 1), of substance (VII, Ch. 1), and of the divine (VI, Ch. 1). The relation of these different definitions and their import for an understanding of Aristotle and of metaphysics in general is something still debated today. The medievals differed widely on this subject. Suárez's own view is given in Disp. I, "On the Nature of First Philosophy or Metaphysics." In it he concludes, among other things, that metaphysics is a speculative (Sect. IV, § 2), perfect, and *a priori* science (Sect. III, § 1). Its object is being insofar as it is real (Sect. I, § 26).

Modus: measure, bound, limit, end, manner, way, method, mode. In philosophy the term does not seem to acquire any definitive technical meaning in metaphysics (for its logical use see William of Sherwood, *Introduction to Logic,* Ch. 1, §§ 21 ff.) until the latter part of the thirteenth and early part of the fourteenth centuries. Thomas, for example, had little to say about modes. Durandus, however, discussed modes in *On I Sent.,* dist. 30, q.2, and Giles of Rome mentions them in *On the Composition of Angels,* q.5. It is, nevertheless, in late scholasticism and the Renaissance that modes are given more attention (Astudillo, *On generation* I, q.5; Fonseca, *On Metap.* V, Ch. 6, Sect. II), in particular by Suárez, who provided the first systematic treatment of them, and from whom, no doubt, modern doctrines spring. His most clear explanation of what a mode is appears in Disp. VII, Sect. I, § 17. "I assume that in created things, in addition to their entities, [which are,] as it were, substantial or (if I may put it so) radical, there are found certain real modes that are something positive and of themselves modify the very entities by conferring on them something that is outside [their] complete essence as individual and as existing in reality. This is clear from induction. For in quantity, for example, which inheres in a substance, two [things] may be considered: one is the entity of quantity itself, the other is the union or actual inherence of the quantity in the substance. The first we call simply the reality of quantity, comprising whatever pertains to the essence of the individual quantity as it is found in reality, and remains and is preserved even if quantity is separated from [its] subject. It is impossible to preserve this thing which is this numerical quantity without including the essence of quantity [together] with its intrinsic individuation and actual existence....The second, that is, the inherence, we call a mode of quantity, but not in the general sense in which every quality is usually called a mode of substance... nor is it [i.e. the term 'mode'] used in the general sense in which every contracting or determining [principle] is usually called the mode of [the thing thus] contracted....[Lastly,] this word is not taken in the general [sense] in which every determination or limitation affixed to a finite thing according to its measure is usually called a mode...the inherence of quantity is called its mode because it is something affecting it [i.e. quantity] and, as it were, ultimately determining its state and manner *(rationem)* of existing, without adding to it a proper new entity, but merely modifying a preexisting [one]...[in § 18] their nature *(ratio)* seems to consist in this, that they do not of themselves suffice to constitute a being or an entity in reality but are intrinsically directed to the actual modification of some entity without which they are incapable of existing." As such, therefore, strictly speaking, modes cannot exist as entities by themselves, since they depend on other entities and their only function is to modify them. Suárez divides them into substantial and accidental. Both of these are "real modes." Conceptual modes are the result of human understanding. For further details see, Peter Nolan, "The Suarezian Modes," *Proceedings. Annual Convention. Jesuit Education Association* (Chicago: Loyola Univ. Press, 1931), pp. 184-200. Nolan collects and translates most of Suárez's important texts on this topic.

Motus, motion, change, alteration; see *mutatio.*

Multiplico, multiply, increase. For scholastics to multiply means to make many out of one, either [1] through division of a whole into parts or [2] of a species into individuals or [3] through actual reproduction of many things similar to an original one. Suárez generally uses the term 'multiplication' to refer to numerical multiplication, that is, the production of plurality within the species. See, for example, Detailed Index to Aristotle's *Metaphysics* III, Ch. 1, q.11.

Mutabilis, changeable, mutable; from *mutatio,* change, alteration, modification, mutation, exchange; in turn from *muto,* to move, change, alter, modify, abandon. For scholastics to be mutable was to be subject to *mutatio.*

Mutatio, change, alteration, mutation, modification, exchange; from *muto,* to move, change, alter, modify, abandon. For scholastics *mutatio* referred to the most general kind of change. It included substantial change, which is instantaneous, as when a man dies, and accidental change, which takes place in time. Accidental change was divided in turn into qualitative change, usually called alteration, quantitative change, called augmentation and decrease, and local motion. Only the last one was properly called motion *(motus),* in order to distinguish it from the other two kinds of accidental change, although those were also often called motions. Suárez discusses change briefly in Disp. XXX, Sect. VIII, §§ 2 and 3.

Natura, birth, nature, character, inclination, order, course, substance, essence, the universe, the world; from *nascor,* to be born, to be begotten, to rise, grow, to be produced. This term has a wide range of meaning both in Latin and in Greek *(physis).* Aristotle catalogued and explained some of these meanings in *Physics* II, Ch. I and in *Metaphysics* V, Ch. 4. In general, however, the Greeks emphasized the relation of nature to movement and change in the physical world and therefore the more material aspect of nature. As Aristotle puts it in *Physics* 192b22: "Nature is a source or cause of being moved and of being at rest in that to which it belongs primarily." And even in *Metaphysics* 1015a12-20, where he identifies nature with the essence of things, the things in question are always "movable" ones: "...it is plain that nature in the primary and strict sense is the essence of things which have in themselves, as such, a source of movement; for the matter is called the nature because it is qualified to receive this, and processes of becoming and growing are called nature because they are movements proceeding from this. And nature in this sense is the source of the movement of natural objects, being present in them somehow, either potentially or in complete reality." This emphasis on the "movable" and "material" created a problem for scholastics, who wanted to speak as well of spiritual and even of divine natures. Often, when commenting on the text of the *Physics,* they follow Aristotle and interpret nature as "the principle of motion and rest" (see Thomas, *Com. on Physics* I, lect. 1). At other times they content themselves with pointing out various usages of the term, some derived from Aristotle, some not. Thomas, for example, writes in *Com. on Sentences* II, d.37, q.1, a.1: "The name of nature is used in many ways. For, in the first way, nature is used as that which is related commonly to all things that are, as nature is defined as all that which can be in any way understood by the intellect. In a second way, it is proper only to substances; and thus nature is said to be that which can act or suffer. In a third way, nature is that which is the principle of motion or rest in those things in which it is essentially and not accidentally. In a fourth way, each thing informed with a specific difference is called a nature." On the other hand, when on their own, scholastics usually modified the Aristotelian definition to suit their own views. In *On Being and Essence*, Ch. 1, § 4, for example, Thomas makes this move when he states that "the term 'nature' seems to mean the essence of a thing as directed to its specific operation, for no reality lacks its specific operation." This view is still restrictive since it includes the modifier 'specific,' and God, for example, is a member of no species. Suárez goes farther than this, dropping the restrictive modifier and identifying the nature with the essence as such, although adding to it the notion of "being related to operation." In Disp. XV, Sect. XI, § 6, he writes: "...in terms of the reality signified and speaking metaphysically rather than physically ...this word [i.e. 'nature'] absolutely and primarily signifies the essence, without qualification and wholly, of each thing, as it is signified by the whole form. And in immaterial things it is simple; while in material things it is composed of matter and form, because neither the matter [alone] nor the form [alone] is the whole nature of the thing, but only a part of it...." It is for this reason that each thing owes to the nature its being what it is and its essential distinction from other things (§ 4). However, although metaphysically the same, conceptually the nature adds a relational aspect to essence (§ 4): "The nature, as it is commonly accepted, expresses a relation to operation, [being this] the only [aspect] in which it differs from essence, because the name 'essence' is taken from the relation to being, while the name 'nature' is taken from the relation to operation; it is for this reason that it is called 'nature,' because, as it were, it makes something to be born." There is no problem then in speaking about a "divine" nature, for God's nature is simply his essence in its operational dimension. All substances, therefore, have natures, whether divine, spiritual or material. And even accidents have natures, although their nature is not whole or complete, but, as Suárez puts it (§ 6), partial and imperfect.

Natura communis et specifica, common and specific nature. See *natura.* The common and specific nature is the opposite of the individual nature—man as opposed to this man. For Suárez, the first, considered as common and specific, had ontological status only in someone's mind, after the operation of the intellect (Disp. V, Sect. III). He makes the point clear as well in this Disp., Sect. I.

Necessarius, unavoidable, indispensable, requisite, necessary. Scholastics frequently debated the exact meaning of this term and its derivatives. Their discussions were prompted by Boethius' *Commentary on Aristotle's "On Interpretation"* III, and Aristotle's own text in *Metaphysics* I, Ch. 5, 1015a20 ff. Part of the latter's text reads: "We say that that which cannot be otherwise is necessarily as it is. And from this sense of 'necessary' all the others are somehow derived; for a thing is said to do or suffer what is necessary in the sense of compulsory, only when it cannot act according to its impulse because of the compelling force — which implies that necessity is that because of which a thing cannot be otherwise; and similarly as regards the conditions of life and of good; for when in the one case good, in the other life and being, are not possible without certain conditions, these are necessary, and this kind of cause is a sort of necessity. Again, demonstration is a necessary thing because the conclusion cannot be otherwise, if there has been demonstration in the unqualified sense; and the causes of this necessity are the first premises, i.e., the fact that the propositions from which the syllogism proceeds cannot be otherwise." The ambiguities of this text caused medievals to formulate all sorts of necessities and necessary things: Beings were called necessary (as opposed to possible/impossible) if they could not notexist or if they could not be otherwise than they were (see Cajetan's *Commentary on Thomas' On Being and Essence,* q.9, § 94). God is a necessary being in this sense. Propositions were called necessary (as opposed to contingent) if they were based on nature or followed necessarily from nature. 'God exists' is such a proposition. And arguments or proofs were called necessary, the so called "necessary reasons" (as opposed to probable), if they were valid arguments based on necessary propositions. In all these cases, however, the fundamental point was the nature — what follows from nature either in reality or in its apprehension was said to be "necessary." What is necessary was often opposed as well to what is suffient *(satis, sufficiens).* In the order of causation in particular, a cause was necessary if the effect did not take place without its presence, but the cause did not of itself bring about the effect. The cause was sufficient if its presence insured the occurrence of the effect. For Suárez's discussion of Aristotle's view of necessity, see the Detailed Index to Aristotle's *Metaphysics* V, Ch. 5. He discusses necessity in connection with God and his activity in Disp. XXX, Sect. XVI, §§ 25 ff. For other, earlier, and less clear medieval views of necessity see my article, "The Structural Elements of Necessary Reasons in Anselm and Llull," *Diálogos* 9 (1973), 105-129 and Desmond Paul Henry, *Commentary on "De grammatico,"* n.3, 232 a, *et passim.* See also Thomas, *Summa theologiae* I, 83, 1.

Negatio, negation; see *privative.*

Nihil, nothing; see *aliquid.*

Nomen, name, word, noun, depending on context. Aristotle defines the Greek equivalent of this term thus: "By a noun we mean a sound significant by convention, which has no reference to time, and of which no part is significant apart from the rest." (*On Interpretation,* Ch. 2, 19a19). William of Sherwood modified the definition to read: "A name is an utterance *(vox)* significant by convention, apart from time, finite and direct, no part of which, taken by itself, signifies anything." (*Introduction to Logic,* Ch. 1.) This was the standard definition of the term, used by almost everybody. Defined as such, a name included such things as adjectives, which are not included today in what we call nouns. For this reason it is better to translate '*nomen*' by 'name' rather than 'noun.'

Nominales, nominalists. The nominalists received their name from the fact that they said universals were names *(nomina).* The term seems to have been introduced in the twelfth century when medievals were trying to distinguish realists (those who held universals to be *res*) from those who held universals to be words (*sermones, nomina, voces*). However, no one really held universals to be mere words in the Middle Ages, except perhaps for Abelard's teacher, Roscelin, who called a universal a *flatus vocis* or mere emission of sound. The nominalists, therefore, were those who, like Ockham, rejected the view that universals (or natures in the thirteenth and fourteenth centuries) had more than a conceptual reality, i.e. unity and being apart from the unity and being they have in the mind. It should also be clear that to be a realist did not imply a doctrine in which the individual is somehow composed of (or qualified by, as some contemporary philosophers prefer to say) universals. Everyone in the Middle Ages, with the exception of early figures, such as John Eriugena, held that there is nothing universal (or common) in the individual. What realists held was rather that the nature considered in itself is neither common nor individual (Thomas' so called "moderate realism") or that it has some unity and being of its own (Scotus' realism). The view that an individual is a bundle of universals, common before 1150 A.D. (Eriugena, John of Salisbury, Boethius, etc.), was not defended again after Abelard's incisive criticism in his *Logic for Beginners.*

Objectum adaequatum, adequate object. Strictly speaking, a proper or adequate object is the object toward which a power, or a science is naturally directed. By association scholastics also spoke of objects toward which natures were directed as "adequate objects." The primary sense, however, is epistemic. The point comes through clearly in Thomas' discussion in *Summa theologiae* I, 1, 7: "Properly speaking, the object of a power or habit is that aspect *(ratione)* under which all things are referred to the power or habit. For example, man and stone are referred to sight insofar as they are colored; hence, the colored is the proper object of sight." Suárez discusses three ways of understanding the unity of the adequate object of the species in *On the Nature of Angels* II, Ch. 14, § 7: "First, [the adequate object may be understood as having] a real unity in the existing order of things. Second, it [may be understood] to be one by the formal conformity of all the [things] represented by such a species in a difference, or predicate, or common degree in the genus of being, as is [the case with] one genus or one species. Third, only by conformity in some condition, under which all [things which are represented by one species] are represented or known by the same act." Of these he accepts the third only, rejecting the first, which he identifies as Scotus' view, and the second, which he sees as the position of Cajetan and Ferrara.

Objectum proximum, proximate object; opposed to remote object *(objectum remotum).* An object for scholastics is that toward which any power or science is directed. The proximate object is that toward which the power is immediately directed; a remote one, that toward which the power is mediately directed. For example, the universal is the proximate object of the intellect, while the particular is a remote object. See also *objectum adaequatum.*

Objectum remotum, remote object; see *objectum proximum.*

Omnis, all, every. In order to preserve the number of the Latin text, *omnis* has been translated as "all" when it is used together with a plural noun, as in *omnes res;* but it has been rendered as "every" when it is used together with a singular noun, as in *omnis entitas.* In no case should this be construed as implying that medieval authors rigidly distinguished between the singular and plural forms of *omnis* as some modern logicians do concerning the English terms 'all' and 'every' when they say that these terms have collective and distributed reference respectively. Medieval logicians believed the reference of *omnis,* whether in plural or singular, varied depending on the case. See Ockham, *Summa logicae* I, Ch. 4, and William of Sherwood, *Syncategoremata,* Ch. 1. See also *totum.*

Ordo, order, norm, rule, nature. There is order between two or more things if one is said to be prior or posterior to the other (see *prior).* There are many orders: of perfection, nature, cause, time, place, height, etc. But scholastics divided them into two basic kinds: essential and accidental. In the first the order stems from the nature or essence of the things involved; in the second, from some accidental feature.

Pars, a part, piece, portion, share, role or character on the stage, function. Scholastics followed Aristotle's fundamental distinctions in his explanation of the Greek equivalent of this term in *Metaphysics* V, Ch. 25, 1023b26 ff.: " 'Part' means (1) (a) that into which a quantum can in any way be divided...e.g. two is called in a sense a part of three; (b) of the parts in the first sense, only those which measure the whole — this is why two is not called a part of three in another sense...; (2) the elements into which a kind might be divided apart from the quantity...the species are parts of the genus; (3) the elements into which a whole is divided, or of which it consists — the 'whole' meaning either the form or that which has the form, e.g. of the bronze sphere or of the bronze cube both the bronze...; (4) the elements in the definition which explains a thing...the genus is a part of the species...." Scholastics made many other distinctions concerning this notion (see Suárez, Disp. XV, Sect. X). Most important of these was the distinction between essential part (when the whole could not continue to exist apart from the part in question, e.g. form in the matter-form composite of a dog) and accidental part (when the whole could continue to exist apart from the parts, ex. an arm in a man).

Participo, to share, partake, participate, impart, take part of. This is the term used by Platonists to indicate the relation of particulars to the forms. It carries with it the notion of something divided into parts which are shared by the participants. Whiteness, for example, is shared by many subjects, i.e. all white things. It seems to have been used by some pre-Socratic philosophers (see Parmenides, in Diels' *Die Fragmente der Vorsokratiker,* ed. W. Kranz, Berlin: Weidmann, 1934-37, 28B, 9.4), but it was Plato who made most of it, although he saw some of the difficulties it involved (see *Parmenides,* 131). Scholastics found the term in the writings of medieval neo-Platonic authors, such as Boethius and Eriugena, who used the term in the Platonic sense. Aristotelians, however, frequently used the term in a less metaphysical vein to mean simply that a notion is related to another with some sort of logical dependence. Most often the term was used as expressing formal causality as understood by Aristotle. In this sense, man is said to be participated by men because it is their formal cause, i.e. that which determines them to be what they are. The correlative term of *participo* is *communico,* to communicate, which describes the relation of the form to the particulars that participate in it (see *communicabilis*).

Passio, passion, a suffering, property, attribute. Scholastics distinguished two important meanings of *passio.* In one way this term was used synonymously with *proprium* and as such it indicated a characteristic always accompanying the species (see *proprium;* also Ockham, *Summa logicae,* Chs. 24, 37). In another way, however, *passio* refers to the tenth category, the category of suffering or affection (Aristotle, *Categories* IV, 1b25). As such it signifies the act of the patient or subject being acted upon by the agent. Thomas points out (*On Sent.* III, d.15, q.2, a.1) that "it is required by the nature of passion that the quality introduced be extraneous and the quality forced out be connatural, and this is so because passion involves a kind of victory of the agent over the patient; but all that which is conquered is, as it were, drawn beyond its proper bounds to extraneous bounds; and therefore, alterations which occur beyond the nature of the thing altered are most properly called passions, as are sicknesses more properly than states of health." Ockham (*Summa logicae* I, Ch. 58) points out the various senses of *passio* thus: " 'To suffer' is taken in many senses, namely, to receive something from something [else]. In this sense a subject suffers as does the matter receiving a form. In another more general sense [the term] is used to cover the first case as well as the case where something is moved without receiving anything as a subject, as when something is moved locally. In the third sense [the term] is used for what is common to the first two cases as well as the case where something is caused or produced. In this sense it refers to a category." Suárez dedicates Disp. XLIX to the study of this notion. He outlines the different meanings of the term *passio* in the introduction: "The name 'passion' as used by philosophers and theologians is equivocal as it is clear in Aristotle, Bk. V, *Metaphysics,* Ch. 21, and in St. Thomas, [*Summa theologiae*] I-II, 22, 1 and in other places, and in other authors. For not only the affections of the soul are usually called passions, but also certain qualities of the third species [i.e. category] are called passions, as it is clear from the Ch. on quality, and from *Physics* III, Ch. 3. Moreover, something is said to suffer *(pati)* primarily when it receives *(patitur)* something outside its nature, or when it loses something. Broadly speaking, however, the reception of any form, whatever it may be, is called a passion. And this is the sense in which [the term] is taken at present. In this sense [passion] is opposed to action, although not to every [action], but to the one produced from a presupposed subject. However, since action and passion, taken thus, have with each other the greatest kind of connection and agree in many [things], thus, many [things] which are said about action, maintaining the appropriate proportion, can also be applied to passion." In another sense, the transcendental attributes of being are called *passiones* (see *transcendens*).

Passum, patient; see *agens.*

Per accidens, by accident, accidentally; see *per se.*

Per aliud, by another, accidentally; see *per se.*

Perfectio, a finishing, completing, perfection; from *perficio,* to achieve, execute, finish, conclude, perfect. A perfection for scholastics is that in virtue of which something is called perfect. The perfect was defined as "that which lacks nothing" (see Suárez, Disp. X, Sect. I, § 15). This definition was a modification of the second of three definitions Aristotle gives of "the complete" in *Metaphysics* V, Ch. 16, 1021b10 ff: (1) "that outside which it is not possible to find any, even one, of its parts, e.g. the complete time of each thing is that outside which it is not possible to find any time which is a part proper to it; (2) that which in respect of excellence and goodness cannot be excelled in its kind, e.g. we have a complete doctor or a complete flute player, when they lack nothing in respect of the form of their proper excellence...; (3) the things which have attained their end, this being good, are called complete...." Suárez distinguishes further between perfect and good. 'Perfect' can be understood to mean two things: (1) absolutely good, in which case there is only one perfect being, namely God, and perfect and good are not equivalent; and (2) good in relation to some essence, in which case beings other than God can be perfect if they measure up to that essence. In this latter sense good and perfect are coextensive, for in reality whatever is perfect, insofar as it is perfect, is good and whatever is good, insofar as it is good, is perfect. Their notions, however, are not the same: perfect involves the notion of "not lacking" while good involves the notion of "being desirable" (§ 18). From this it follows as well that to be perfect and to be in act are coextensive, since to possess a perfection is to be in act with respect to some form. Indeed, for some scholastics these two notions are not only coextensive but equivalent, a point supported by the fact that the distinction between first and second perfection present in Islamic sources (Avicenna, *Al-Shifa, Meta.* I, Ch. 6) was translated into Latin by the terms first and second acts. For the notions of privative and negative perfections see Suárez, Disp. XXX, Sect. I, § 1.

Perplexitas, perplexity; from Classical *perplexus,* entangled, involved, intricate, confused, unintelligible, ambiguous.

Per se, by itself, through itself, essentially, substantially; opposed to *per accidens,* accidentally, or *per aliud,* by another. *Per se,* therefore, refers to anything which has to do with the nature of a thing, whether rooted in it or following from it. All essential predicates and properties, such as the capacity to laugh and rationality in man, are *per se.* On the other hand, *per accidens* refers to what is not necessarily connected to a thing's essence, and which a thing may or may not have, such as fat in a man. Thomas Aquinas points out that "whatever is present *per se* in a thing either is [derived] from its essence or follows from essential principles, from which principles is [derived] the first root of the distinction of things. Everything which is present *per accidens,* since it is external to its nature, must come to it owing to some external cause." (*On the Power,* q.10, a.4, concl.). The cause of *per se* characteristics is the thing's essence; that of accidental ones, something other than the thing's essence. *Per se* should not be confused with *a se,* from itself. Something is *a se* if it is uncaused or caused by itself. Consequently, there is only one being whose perfections are *a se,* God. This particular feature of God is sometimes called *aseitas,* (aseity). The appearance of the term in Latin texts can be directly traced to translations of Arabic sources. Suárez discusses *per se* and *per accidens* in the Detailed Index to Aristotle's *Metaphysics* VIII, Ch. 6. *Per se* is generally translated here as "by itself," otherwise the Latin is included in parentheses.

Per se nota, self-evident, known through itself; usually applying to propositions or principles; also, non-technically: evident, clear, obvious. Scotus defines self-evident principles as principles whose terms "are so identical that one necessarily includes the other. Consequently, the intellect uniting these terms in a proposition, from the very fact that it grasps these terms, has present to itself the necessary cause, and what is more, the evident cause of the conformity of this proposition with the terms that compose it. This conformity, then, the evident cause of which the intellect perceives in the terms, cannot help but be evident to the intellect. That is why the intellect could not apprehend these terms and unite them in a proposition without having this relationship of conformity arise between the proposition and the terms, anymore than two white objects could exist without a relationship of similarity arising between them. Now, it is precisely this conformity of the proposition to the terms that constitutes the truth of a judgment. Such terms then cannot be combined in a judgment without being true, and so it is that one cannot perceive this proposition and its terms without also perceiving the conformity of the proposition to the terms, and therefore, perceiving the truth. For what is first perceived evidently includes the perception of the truth of the proposition." (*Opus oxoniense* I, dist. III, q.4; in A. Wolter, *Duns Scotus: Philosophical Writings,* N.Y.: Nelson, 1963, pp. 106-107). Thomas' well known definition of a *per se nota propositio* appears in *Summa theologiae* I, 2, 1: "Something is self-evident in two ways: in one way in itself, but not to us; in another way in itself, and to us. From this it follows that a proposition is self-evident when the predicate is included in the notion of the subject, for ex., 'Man is an animal,' for 'animal' is contained in the notion of man." See also Thomas' commentary on Aristotle's *Posterior Analytics* I, lect. 4, where he points out that an "immediate proposition" (another term for *per se* *nota propositio*) cannot be denied by anyone who understands it. Suárez's use of the term is sometimes considerably weaker than the ones outlined, meaning simply "quite clear" or "following quite clearly." He uses the term in stronger senses often as well.

Perspectivi, perspectivists; practitioners of the science of optics and related disciplines.

Phantasia, idea, notion, fancy, phantom, phantasy. For scholastics it referred to various things: 1) the internal sense which perceives objects absent but previously perceived; 2) the faculty of imagination; and 3) the very impressions of the internal sense in contrast to the images of the external sense. All these meanings were extracted from Aristotle's discussion in *On the Soul* III, Ch. 3, 427b28-429a9. Suárez discusses this term in various places, but he pays particular attention to it in *Treatise on the Soul* III, Ch. 30. In § 4 he gives the standard scholastic definition derived from Aristotle and refers to the Greek etymology of the word: "*Phantasia* is the interior sense that can know sensible things in their absence; this operation is common to us and animals and hence it is to be attributed to some sense." The scholastic debate concerning *phantasia* centered on whether it was really distinct from the interior sense, memory and other powers of the soul. Suárez rejects all views that draw a real distinction between these powers and decides in favor of just one interior power or sense. These various terms signify only different perfections of a single power.

Philosophi, philosophers. In the Middle Ages this term was reserved for Plato, Aristotle, Averroes, Avicenna and other thinkers of Antiquity or the Islamic world who discussed philosophical problems. Medieval Christian writers were called saints or fathers if they lived in the early Christian centuries, doctors if their writings had been specifically approved by the Church, or masters if they were currently teaching at the university; all were regarded as theologians (excluding masters of arts) even though some of them, such as Thomas and Ockham, also wrote purely philosophical treatises and commentaries. By the time of Suárez, however, the term 'philosopher' was more liberally applied to include as well theologians who engaged in some philosophical speculation. When the term was used in the singular it was usually reserved for Aristotle, who for scholastics was the most authoritative of the philosophers.

Possibile, possible. Suárez, following Aristotle, defines it as "that from whose existence nothing impossible follows" (Index to Aristotle's *Metaphysics* IX, Ch. 3, q.2). In *Treatise on Law* I, Ch. 9, § 17, he points out that "the term 'possible' can be taken in two ways: First, without qualification, as opposed to impossible; in another way, as opposed to difficult, serious, and burdensome." The term was also used in a less precise manner to mean "potential" and, therefore, it was opposed to "actual."

Positivum, positive. This is a term of common use among scholastics, but its meaning is seldom discussed. Even Suárez does not give it separate treatment. The reason for this may be that it never acquired a definite technical meaning (except in grammar). Most often it is used in conjunction with other terms such as 'real,' 'actual,' to refer to beings or perfections such as humanity, sight, etc. and in opposition to others, such as 'negative,' 'unreal,' 'privative,' which referred to imperfections and lacks, such as inhumanity and blindness. For the relevant Aristotelian texts see *Categories,* Ch. 10, 11b20 ff. and *Metaphysics* V, Ch. 10, 1018a20.

Potentia, might, force, power, capacity, faculty, potency, potentiality; from *potens,* to be able, have power. Scholastics found two texts in Aristotle's *Metaphysics* (V, Ch. 11, 1019a15-32; IX, Ch. 1, 1046a5-35) and one in *On the Soul* (II, Ch. 5, 417a21-35) that discussed various meanings of the Greek counterpart of this term. These seem to fall into two groups: In one sense a potency is an originative source or principle of change; in another it refers to a capacity a thing has. This scheme was expanded and refined by scholastics. For Suárez potency can be understood in two ways, transcendentally, i.e. as common to all categories, or predicamentally (categorically), i.e. as particular to any one of the categories. As he points out in the Introduction to Disp. XLIII: "in the first sense every being is divided by potency and act or, as others say, this is one of the disjunctive properties of being." Transcendental potency is divided into possibility and physical potency. In the former are included two things, according to Suárez (Disp. XLII, Sect. III, §9): "one is, as it were, negative,...the non-contradiction in being, and this is usually called logical possibility, and to it corresponds a logical potency, which is so called because it is not a simple and real capacity (*facultas*), but only a non-contradiction of the terms (*extremorum*), and so it concerns more the order of mental composition and division which pertains to the logician....The other, found in a possible reality as such, is a positive determination (*denominatio*) (for which reason it is called possible), which is taken from a real potency, whether active or passive; for that is called possible in this way which is contained in the potency of something; and that is called impossible, which is above the potency of a thing or is not contained in it." Real, i.e. physical, potency for Suárez can be taken broadly to include such different principles as prime matter, habits, qualities, etc. Strictly speaking (§10) potency is taken as a proximate principle, connatural to the created agent, for the purpose of some action. In this way it is always an accident, for the substantial form is not a proximate principle, but the principal one. And in this sense potency refers only to a quality. Its definition as such is given in Disp. XLIII, Sect. III, § 2: "Potency is the proximate principle of an operation for which it has been instituted and ordained by nature."

Potentia absoluta, absolute power. This expression refers to God's power since only his power can be absolute. God's absolute power was contrasted with his relative power. The first was God's power as it is in itself, without any limitation except for the principle of non-contradiction. The second was God's power in relation to his will and knowledge, that is, as limited and governed by these. In late medieval thought references to God's absolute power were used to show that something was not impossible. Since God was supposed to be able to do anything except what involved a contradiction, this was a common way of showing or illustrating—not proving, it was seldom used as a proof—that a particular view did not involve a contradiction, and thus that it was possible. This is not unlike some of the science fiction examples so common to contemporary philosophical literature. For the distinction between absolute and relative power, see Thomas Aquinas, *Summa theologiae* I, 25, 5. Suárez discusses God's power, which he identifies with his omnipotence, in Disp. XXX, Sect. XVII. Following Thomas, he sets contradiction as the only limit to it (§§ 10-14 and 25). Otherwise, God can do anything (§ 15); his power is infinite (§ 3).

Potentia receptiva, receptive potency. This is a capacity to receive something, such as the capacity of a substance to receive an accident. Many scholastics, including Cajetan, accepted the view that substances had a capacity to receive accidents which was distinct from the substance itself. But Suárez rejects this view. In Disp. XIV, Sect. II, § 7, he explains his reasons: In inanimate corporeal substances there is no receptive potency except for quantity, and quantity is not essentially and primarily a receptive potency, but a form which confers mass and extension to corporeal substance. And animate objects do not have any purely passive potency, at least insofar as they are living beings.

Potentia relativa, relative power; see *potentia absoluta.*

Praecisio, a cutting off, a cut, piece, cutting; from *praecido,* to cut off, separate. Used as an adjective *(praecisus, -a, -um),* in an adverbial form *(praecise),* or in the expression 'with precision' *(cum praecisione),* this term was used by scholastics to signify a mode of abstraction *(abstractio)* by which something is cut off or excluded from something else. In the context of individuation what was cut off or excluded, according to early scholastics like Thomas, was the individuality of the thing being considered with precision. In this sense precision is to be contrasted with abstraction properly speaking, for in the latter a thing is considered without the inclusion or exclusion in its notion of the characteristics that accompany it in reality. It is for this reason, for example, that an essence as "abstract" is predicable of the individual—"man" is predicable of a man; but an essence as "precise" is not—"humanity" is not predicable of a man. Nevertheless, early scholastics held that "precise" notions reflect the nature of reality (see, for example, J. Owens, *An Elementary Christian Metaphysics,* p. 66n). Suárez, on the other hand, did not think that to consider something with precision involved necessarily the consideration of a thing as it was in reality. For him precision could be of two sorts, mental or real. The latter was the actual separation of two things in reality; the former, the separation which results from intellectual consideration, and therefore not necessarily a reflection of the way in which the thing exists. He explains the matter in Disp. II, Sect. II, § 16: "Therefore, it must be noted that the abstraction or precision of the intellect does not require a distinction of things or the precision [i.e. separation] of some notion *(rationis)* or mode, which precedes *ex natura rei* in reality the intellectual precision itself, but in the most simple thing this kind of precision can be made in various ways, namely, either [1] by way of form [prescinding] from subject or [2] contrarily, by way of subject [prescinding] from form, or [3] by way of form [prescinding] from form, as God as such is prescinded in God from his act of will, and the act of will from God, and the act of will from the act of the intellect....Therefore, the intellect so abstracts and prescinds something from something [else] as the common from the particular, not owing to the distinction or precision which precedes in reality, but, owing to its imperfect, confused, or inadequate mode of conceiving. For this reason, it does not comprehend, in the object it considers, all that is in it as it exists in reality, but it comprehends it only in terms of some conformity or similarity which several things have in common, which [things], considered under such notion, [are considered] as one. Wherefore, in order for an objective concept to be conceptually precise from other things or concepts, the precision of things in themselves is not necessary, but a certain denomination from the formal concept representing the objective [concept] is sufficient, because, certainly, by it is not represented the object in all it is in reality, but only in a particular notion of conformity. This is clear in the objective concept of man as such, which is conceptually said to be precise [i.e. separate] from Peter, Paul, and other singulars from which it does not differ in reality...." In the present translation I have used transliterations of this term and

its derivatives whenever possible, but in some cases I have been forced to render it by terms such as 'absolute,' 'abstract' and 'separate'
and their derivatives, depending on context. This does not do vio-
lence to the text, since, as the text of Suárez just cited shows, he
often interchanged this term with others.

Praedefinitio, predefinition, sometimes translated also as predetermination, although strictly speaking these are different notions.
Suárez defines predefinition in the opuscle *On the Cooperation and
Efficacious Help of God* I, Ch. 14, § 2: "Therefore, a certain eternal
decree of the divine will whereby he absolutely decrees that something take place in time is called predefinition; for example, that
Peter's will elicit an act of contrition at a particular time and
place.... Therefore, predefinition properly signifies a decree prior to
a future act, whereby God, before seeing Peter's act of contrition,
absolutely decreed that he should have it, and hence ordained the
means whereby it would be accomplished." The difference between
predefinition and predetermination is that the first (§ 6) "denotes only an internal act of the soul, just as providence or predestination,
while the latter can refer rather to the external act and effect." Both
predefinition and predetermination are to be distinguished from predestination. Predestination, Suárez points out in the treatise *On
Divine Predestination* I, Ch. 4, § 4, "properly signifies an efficacious
ordination of someone to an ultimate supernatural end." For this
reason, predestination applies only to created persons. "It consists of
the acts of foreknowledge and free will of God" (*ibid.,* Bk. II, Ch. 22,
§ 1). For the derivation of the term see the same work, Bk. I, Ch. 1, §
3. The issues surrounding predetermination, predefinition and predestination were primarily theological and based to a great extent on
the issues raised by Augustine in *On Free Will* and other works.

Praedestinatio, predestination; see *praedefinitio.*

Praedeterminatio, predetermination; see *praedefinitio.*

Praedicabilia or *praedicabile,* predicables or predicable; see *species.*

Praedicamenta is the Latin term used to translate the Greek term
kategoriai or categories. Strictly speaking, the term *praedicamentum* in
Latin and its Greek counterpart meant "that which is predicable."
However, the first and most important of the categories, according
to Aristotle, i.e. substance, was not predicable (*Categories,* Ch. 5,
2a10). It was generally accepted that there were ten categories,
although Aristotle never settled for a definite number and allowed
for predicates to fall into more than one of these groups: substance,
quantity, quality, relation, place, time, position, state, action, and
passion. Although in the early part of the Middle Ages the metaphysical and logical roles of the categories were often confused, scholas-

tics generally distinguished between them. The categories, metaphysically understood, were the ten most general classes of things, the ten most general ways of being. Logically, they were thought to be the ten most general ways in which one can think about things. The logical understanding of the categories included both a strictly logical dimension concerned with the classification of terms as they are predicated of other terms, and also epistemic considerations concerned with the way we think about things. The fact that these two functions were not generally distinguished with clarity by scholastics is a further proof of the scholastic disregard for epistemology as a separate philosophical science. Even Suárez, as late as the close of the XVIth century, was still repeating the distinction between the logical and the metaphysical and including the epistemic within the former. See Disp. XXXIX, Sect. I, §§ 1 and 2. On the other hand, many neo-scholastics today consider epistemology a branch of metaphysics (for example, Peter Doffey, *Epistemology,* London, 1917; see also G. Van Riet's *L' Epistemologie Thomiste,* Louvain, 1946, for a history of this issue).

Praedicatum, predicate; see *praedico.*

Praedicatum accidentale, accidental predicate; see *praedicatum essentiale.*

Praedicatum essentiale, essential predicate; opposed to accidental predicate. Essential, also called substantial, predicates are not separable from, i.e. cannot not be predicated of, that of which they are essential, while accidental predicates are. The first are properties or features of things such as the genus, the species and the specific difference, which are part of or follow from their essence and are thus coextensive with them. 'Rational,' 'animal' and 'the capacity to laugh' are such essential predicates in man. Examples of accidental predicates in the same case are "tall," "white," "fat." Suárez discusses essential predicates in Disp. VI, Sect. IX, §§ 9 ff.

Praedicatum metaphysicum, metaphysical predicate. Metaphysical predicates such as 'individual' and 'nature' are to be contrasted with (1) physical, such as 'material,' and (2) logical, such as 'specific.'

Praedico, to make known, proclaim, declare, claim, say, praise, preach, predict, admonish, foretell, predicate. In philosophical or theological contexts it usually means to predicate. In *On Being and Essence,* Ch. 3, § 8, (*trans. cit.,* p. 49), Thomas defines predication as "something achieved by the intellect through its act of combining and dividing, having for its foundation in reality the unity of those things, one of which is attributed to the other." Scholastics usually made two types of distinctions within predication: formal vs. material (or fundamental), and *in quid* vs. *in quale.* Formal predication refers to the mental relation between concepts expressed in a judgment; material predication refers to the real conjunction of the thing predicated and the subject in which the predicate inheres — the white present in a piece of paper and the paper, when it is true that the paper is white. The term *'in quid'* is derived from *quidditas* (whatness); the term *in quale* from *qualitas* (quality). To predicate *in quale* means to predicate a term as qualifying a subject, as 'white' in the proposition 'The paper is white.' 'White' expresses a quality of the paper which qualifies it. In *in quid* predication, however, the predicated term signifies the subject or its essence, as 'substance' in 'John is a substance.' Terms such as 'whiteness,' 'rationality,' and 'substance' are always predicated *in quid*. Terms such as 'white,' 'rational' and 'substantial' are always predicated *in quale*. For other kinds of predication (primary, secondary, analogical), see Cajetan's *Commentary on On Being and Essence* q.3, §§ 18 ff. Suárez discusses some issues surrounding predication in Disp. VI, Sect. X.

Principium, principle, beginning, origin, source, foundation, element; from *princeps,* first in time or order, chief, most eminent. Aristotle explains this notion in Bk. V of the *Metaphysics* (1013a18-20): "It is common to all principles *(arché)* to be the first point from which a thing either is, or comes to be, or is known; but of these some are immanent in the thing while others are outside." Following the implications of this statement, scholastics distinguished three kinds of principles: logical, physical, and metaphysical. Logical principles, such as the principle of non-contradiction, the rules of inference, and even just premises of particular demonstrations, are the starting points of knowledge. Physical principles, such as a father of a child, are causes and, therefore, external to the things of which they are principles. Metaphysical principles fall in between these two. Like logical principles, they are not separable from the things of which they are principles, but unlike them and like physical principles they are really distinct from that of which they are principles. As such they are neither physical things nor mental concepts but real constituents of things. The most universally accepted of these among scholastics were form-matter, essence-existence, and substance-accident. See Ernan McMullin, "Matter as a Principle," in *The Concept of Matter in Greek and Medieval Philosophy* (Notre Dame, Ind.: University Press, 1965), pp. 173-212. Suárez discusses the various uses of the term 'principle,' the definition of principle, and the relation between principle and cause in Disp. XII, Sect. I. His detailed discussion is prompted by two factors: First, Aristotle's ambiguous use of 'principle' both as a term standing for something distinct and for something identical with cause, and second, what Suárez calls Thomas' "confusing" definition of principle, in *Summa theologiae* I, 33, 1, as "that from which something proceeds in any way." Suárez points out two common characteristics of principles (§§ 8 and 11): First, "to be in some way prior to what is begun" *(principiato)* and second, "that there be some connection or consequence *(consecutio)* between those things, one of which is called principle of the other." Principles are more general than causes (§ 25). Their difference lies in the fact that 'principle' is predicated of things which do not properly have an influence on other things, while 'cause' is not so predicated. For this reason 'principle' is not predicated only of real things, but also of beings of reason and even of privation, while that is not the case with 'cause.' A good example of this, according to Suárez, is the dawn, which, although called the *"principium"* (beginning) of day, does not cause it (§ 2). If *principium* is understood as having a positive influence, then it is, according to Suárez (§ 5), not very different from cause. But *principium* may also refer to something prior and intrinsically related to another thing, although not positively influencing it (§ 6). From all this it is clear that contemporary attempts to identify principles, as understood in the Middle Ages, with sufficient conditions or, alternatively, necessary conditions, are bound to be unsatisfactory, since the connection between a principle and that of which it is a principle was thought to vary from case to case. It should also be clear that the way particular scholastics classified the principle of individuation — logically, physically, metaphysically — depended largely on their view of individuation. For those, like William of Ockham, who thought the individual was individual *per se,* that is, essentially, the principle of individuation was a logical abstraction, since there was nothing to be individuated in the first place. For those, like Scotus, who held that the nature in itself was not individual and therefore required some real or formal addition to be made individual, the principle of individuation was metaphysical. Finally, for Suárez, who, as can be seen in Sect. IV, identified the principle of individuation with the individual itself, i.e. its entity, the principle of individuation was physical. Finally, it should be clear that, given Suárez's identification of the principle of individuation with a physical being, the question, "What makes an individual individual?" becomes for him the question, "What is the cause of individuation in an individual?"

Prior, prius, former, previous, prior, first, and its medieval substantivized form, *prioritas,* priority. Aristotle discussed the Greek equivalent of this term and its opposite, *posterior,* in *Metaphysics* V, Ch. 11, 1018b9-1019a12: "The words 'prior' and 'posterior' are applied (1) to some things because they are nearer some beginning determined either absolutely and by nature, or by reference to something or in some place or by certain people: some things are prior in place... other things are prior in movement...others are prior in power...

others are prior in arrangement....In another sense (2) that which is prior for knowledge is treated as also absolutely prior [prior in definition, perception, etc.]....(3) The attributes of prior things are called prior....(4) Other things are called prior in respect of nature and substance...." Disagreement among scholastics centered on two issues: (1) the essence of priority (and, of course, posteriority) and (2) its ontological status, that is, whether priority was to be considered a relation, and if it was so considered, whether it was real or merely the product of human understanding. Suárez discusses these issues in the Index to Aristotle's *Metaphysics* V, Ch. 11, q.1: "In general priority consists in a kind of reference *(habitudine)* or relation between those [things] called prior and posterior. Sometimes, however, this relation is measured by a third and is as it were founded on another relation or proximity to and distance from it. On the other hand, sometimes [it is founded] on the condition of the terms which are compared as prior and posterior, because one has existence already, while the other has none as yet, or because one is the cause, the other the effect, or because one is more excellent than the other. Indeed, priority, considered by itself and intrinsically, consists in this relation between the terms themselves; [it consists] in the relation to a third only remotely and fundamentally, or, if I may put it thus, as it were after the fashion of a measure. Moreover, this relation, being a certain order, as its very name indicates *(priori prae se fert)* can take place in the order of place, time, motion, that is generation, causality, cognition, nature, or subsistence....From which it can be concluded that the relation of prior, strictly *(per se)* speaking, is not real, because it is often attributed to those [things] which are not distinct in reality, as for example, when man is said to be prior to Peter in the order of subsistence. Sometimes it is attributed to a non-existing thing, as for example, when I am said [to be] temporally prior to the Antichrist. Sometimes, moreover, the notion of prior is applied to a negation, for something is said temporally prior to another because it has or had existence while the other does not as yet exist. Sometimes, moreover, it consists in a kind of comparison of relations, as when that is said to be prior which is closer to the first. Finally, sometimes this priority has a foundation in nature, sometimes in human consideration and judgment....Therefore, by itself priority does not involve a real relation, although sometimes, insofar as a particular relation concides with another [relation] which is real, it can be real as well. For example, when a cause is said to be prior to an effect, the true relation of prior is none other in reality than the relation of cause, which, owing to some similarity *(convenientiam)* or proportionality, is called priority. In that case the relation of prior will also be real, although perhaps it may not be found to be real in any other way. From all this it is easy to understand that this enumeration of priors is not an univocal division, but an analogical and imperfect one, by proportionality. For there is no attribution to a first signified one, but there is only a kind of proportion [involved]. And it seems indeed that this notion of prior and posterior was first said with reference to motion or time and from these, owing to a kind of proportional similarity, it was applied to the others."

Prius natura, first or prior in nature, or *prioritas naturae,* priority of nature. For scholastics natural priority was contrasted with temporal, logical and other types of priority. Natural priority was considered the most basic or fundamental of these, something which Aristotle had already pointed out in *Metaphysics* V, Ch. 11, 1019a1-1019a12: Other things are said to be prior and posterior "in respect of nature and substance, i.e. those which can be without other things, while the others cannot be without *them* — a distinction which Plato used.... In a sense...all things that are called prior and posterior are so called with reference to this...sense; for some things can exist without others in respect of generation, e.g. the whole without the parts, and others in respect of dissolution, e.g. the part without the whole. And the same is true in all cases." Suárez accepts three types of natural priority: causal (the cause is prior to the effect), perfectional (the more perfect is prior to the less perfect with respect to the perfection in question), and substantial (substance is prior to accident). See Disp. XXVI, Sect. II, §§ 4-10.

Privatio, privation; see *privative.*

Privative, privatively; from *privo,* to deprive, lack. For the scholastics the adverbial and adjectival forms of this term were derived from *privatio* or privation, a lack or absence in a subject of what naturally belongs to it, such as blindness in man. It is to be contrasted with *negatio* or negation, which is a pure lack or absence of what is not natural to the subject, such as the capacity to laugh in a stone. Aristotle discussed the matter in *Metaphysics* VIII, Chs. 1 and 4, 1046a32 ff., and 1055b1 ff. and in Bk. V, Ch. 22, 1022b22-1023a5. Versions of the Aristotelian definition and classification were common among scholastics; see, for example, Thomas Aquinas, *Summa theologiae* I, 33, 4, *ad* 2. Suárez discusses privation and its distinction from negation at length in Disp. LIV. In Sect. V, § 7, he points out that "they differ, first, because privation expresses a lack of form in a subject with a natural aptitude for it; negation, however, expresses precisely the lack without the subject's aptitude; for it is necessary to add this in order to distinguish it from privation or from the general notion of a lack, which can be as common to privation as to negation. But this diversity is not [to be found] in the proper and formal notion which

privation and negation express, but in what is connoted. For privation as such does not intrinsically include the subject or its aptitude,
otherwise privation would not be distinguished from the deprived
subject, which is as it were composed from subject and privation,
and [privation] would not be a pure non-real being, but would consist of the reality of potency and the negation of act or form, and this
goes against the nature *(rationem)* of privation. Therefore, formally
privation expresses only negation, limiting it to the subject capable
of the opposite form, and in this sense it is said to differ from negation obliquely and insofar as it connotes the subject with aptitude for
the opposite form." When privation is called "real" or "true," then,
this does not mean that it is a being such as a substance or an accident, not even a potency, but only, according to Suárez, that as conceived by the mind it corresponds to a real lack in a thing (§ 2). It is
in this sense that Suárez understands how privation can be a principle of generation in things along with form and matter, for "since
generation is essentially the transition from non-being to being,
hence, it essentially *(per se)* presupposes privation...privation is not a
principle of the constitution of things, but of their generation" (Disp.
XII, Sect. I, § 6). The different varieties of privation are discussed in
Disp. LIV, Sect. V, § 8.

Probabilitas, probability, credibility defensibility; from *probabilis*
and ultimately from *probus,* good, proper, serviceable. Hence a view
had probability or was probable if it was good and defensible. With
more precision, scholastics held that a view was probable if, not being demonstrable, still it was more likely to be true than its opposite.
This term became popular after the thirteenth century, when it
became clear that there were many philosophical and theological
matters which had no clear and demonstrable solution. In such cases
scholastics talked about "more or less probable opinions."

Proportio, comparative relation, proportion, analogy, similarity. In
the Middle Ages, the term was used with all these meanings; it was
used also to mean mathematical ratio. This last meaning, which the
medievals found in Boethius' *On Arithmetic,* was regarded by them as
original. Thomas Aquinas points out in *Summa theologiae* I, 12, 1, *ad* 2
and *ad* 4, that "the term *proportio* can be taken in two senses: in one
way [it means] the relation of one quantity to another. In this sense
double, triple and equal are examples of proportion. In another
way, the relation between any two things is called a proportion, such
as the proportion of the creature to God...of effect to cause... potency to act...." This term is usually contrasted, both in its mathematical and non-mathematical uses, with the term proportionality, i.e. a
proportion of proportions. See Thomas Bradwardine's *Treatise on*

Proportions and also my article "Problems of Interpretation in Brad-wardine's *Tractatus de proportionibus,"Divus Thomas* 73 (1970), 175-195.

Propositio, a setting forth, purpose, resolution, statement, proposi-tion. As early as Cicero (*De inventione rhetorica* I, 37, 67) the term was used in logic to refer to the major premise of a syllogism. Early medieval writers seem to have followed this tradition, contrasting *propositio* and *assumptio;* the latter was used to refer to the minor pre-mise (see, Anselm, *De grammatico,* Ch. 6, ed. F. S. Schmitt, in *Opera omnia,* B.A.C. reprint, vol. I., p. 450). More generally, however, the term was used to refer to any premise of a syllogism and, there-fore, it was contrasted with the conclusion. This usage in fact can be traced to the etymology of the word *propositio,* which literally means "placed for" or "positing for," where the 'for' points to the conclusion. See my article "Propositions and Premises of Syllogisms in Medie-val Logic," *Notre Dame Journal of Formal Logic* 16 (1975), 545-547. With time, however, the term came to refer to the meaning of any affirma-tive or negative sentence. For a general study of medieval proposi-tional theory see N. Kretzmann, "Medieval Logicians on the Mean-ing of the Proposition," *Journal of Philosophy* 67 (1970), 767-787. See also D. P. Henry, *Commentary on "De grammatico,"* Reidel, 1974, pp. 93-99 and 123.

Proprietas, property; see *proprium.*

Proprium, proper, not common with others, one's own. Together with accident, difference, genus and definition it is one of the four universal attributes or predicables listed in Aristotle's *Topics,* Ch. 5, 101b37 (see *praedicabilia*). Also called *passiones, propria* are characteris-tics necessarily present in the subject although not included in its definition. Some scholastics claimed they follow logically from the definition. As such *propria* result from the essence but are not part of it, as the capacity to laugh follows from humanity but is not part of the essence of man expressed by the definition. Unlike differences, *propria* do not distinguish the species from the genus. Scholastics differed in detail as to the correct understanding of this notion, but most of them followed in general (see, for ex., Ockham, *Summa logi-cae* I, Ch. 24) Porphyry's definition and classification in the *Isagoge* (trans. E. Warren, Toronto: PIMS, p. 48): "Our predecessors dis-tinguish four meanings of property: (1) what occurs in one species only, although not in every member of the species, as healing and measuring occur in man; (2) what occurs in the entire species, and not in it only, as being twofooted occurs in man; (3) what occurs in the whole species, in it only, and at some time, as becoming gray in old age occurs in every man; and (4) what occurs in the whole spe-cies, in it only, and always, as the capacity to laugh in man....[The latter are said to be] properties in the strict sense...." Suárez distinguishes two meanings of the term in *The Holy Mystery of the Trinity* VII, Ch. 2, § 1, where he points out that in logic *proprium* "means that which intrinsically and always accompanies something, although not alone." He also says that, in another sense, *proprium* "is to be contrasted with common," that is, that *proprium* means particular.

Quaestio, a seeking, inquiry, question, subject of debate, disputed point. This term was used by scholastics to refer to a literary *genre* in which a discussion of a problem, philosophical or otherwise, was framed. The term was used because the problem was posed as a question capable of antithetical answers. Although the structure of the *genre* was never completely standardized, the most frequent structure had four parts: the question or statement of the problem, the *status quaestionis* or state of the question, the *solutio* or *responsio*, and the answer to the objections. The *status quaestionis* was a survey of the various authoritative opinions on the matter. These opinions were gathered in two groups — the ones favoring a positive answer to the question were called the *pro;* the ones favoring a negative answer, the *contra.* In the *solutio* or *responsio*, the writer gave his own opinion. This was done generally by drawing a distinction which opened the door to the possible harmonization of the apparently divergent opinions given in the *status quaestionis.* Finally, in the answer to the objections, the author discussed and interpreted the opinions of the *status quaestionis* contrary to his own. The medieval *quaestio* developed out of the public disputations held at Christmas and Easter at medieval universities. They were divided into two types: quodlibetal and disputed. In the first, the master to conduct the disputation allowed questions on any subject; in the second, only on a previously determined topic. Although the *quaestio* as a literary *genre* clearly originated in the Middle Ages, it is well to remember that the Greeks had already discussed *aporiai,* i.e. difficulties created by the existence of conflicting arguments and views (Aristotle, *Topics* 145b1) and their solution (*euporia* or *lysis*). In the early Middle Ages one can easily find loosely structured *quaestiones,* particularly among those acquainted with Aristotle (Boethius, Abelard, etc.). Suárez uses the basic *quaestio* structure throughout the *Metaphysical Disputations.*

Quale quid, a kind of something, a kind of quiddity; see *aliquid.*

Qualitas, quality, property, nature, state, condition; from *qualis,* how constituted, of what sort. Aristotle had given a rather unsatisfactory explanation of the Greek counterpart of this term in *Categories,* Ch. 8, 8b25, as "that in virtue of which people are said to be such and such." And then he proceeded in *Metaphysics* V, Ch. 14, 1020a33-

1020b10, to list four other uses of the term: (1) "the differentia of the essence, e.g. man is an animal of a certain quality because he is two-footed...(2) that which exists in the essence of numbers besides quantity; for the essence of each is what it is once, e.g. that of 6 is not what it is twice or thrice, but what it is once; for 6 is once 6...(3) all the modifications of substances that move, e.g. heat and cold...(4) quality in respect of virtue and vice and, in general, of evil and good." Given these statements, it is not surprising that scholastics use this term to mean such widely different things as the essential or specific difference, the substantial form, and any accidental modification of things. Indeed, anything that made a thing to be of a certain kind was called a quality. Humanity, therefore, was regarded as a quality, although substantial, and whiteness was also regarded as a quality, but accidental. Accidental qualities are determinations of already specifically determined natures — white of man, for example. Strictly speaking, however, only accidental determinations of a certain sort were classified as qualities and therefore as falling within the third of the Aristotelian categories. Even here there was disagreement as to the nature of quality. After rejecting what he takes to be the Thomistic view (quality is a mode of substance which determines its potency to a particular way of being), Suárez gives his own view in Disp. XLII, Sect. I, § 5: "Within this genus [i.e. accident] quality has this peculiarity, that it is essentially *(per se)* and primarily established intrinsically to qualify and perfect substance so that it be approximately affected in its being or in its active power. Quantity, on the other hand, has been given to corporeal substance for this particular effect, that it have corporeal mass and extension and impenetrability of parts. Relations, moreover (if they are something), are not intended by themselves, but are results since they consist only in a relationship. Action and passion as well, are only ways toward the end....The remaining four categories, moreover, are accidents in an improper way...." Scholastics, Suárez included, generally followed Aristotle (*Cat.,* text cited) in the division of quality into habit and disposition, natural capacity or incapacity, affection and affective quality, and figure and form. A change of quality was called alteration.

Quantitas (or *quantum*), quantity (the quantitative); in Classical Latin it also meant greatness, extent. In scholastic metaphysics the term is used to refer either to the Aristotelian category of quantity or to those accidents and predicates such as "three-feet-long," "two," etc. that fall within it. In either case quantity is real, i.e. a category of reality. Moreover, it is the category closest to substance, for all other categories presuppose it — for something to be white, for example, it must first of all have certain dimensions. Aristotle explains this notion in *Metaphysics* V, Ch. 13, 1020a8-13: " 'Quantum' means that which is divisible into two or more constituent parts of which each is by nature a 'one' and a 'this.' A quantum is a plurality if it is numerable, a magnitude if it is measurable. 'Plurality' means that which is divisible potentially into noncontinuous parts, 'magnitude' that which is divisible into continuous parts; of magnitude, that which is continuous in one dimension is length, in two breadth, in three depth. Of these, limited plurality is number, limited length is a line, breadth a surface, depth a solid." (See also *Categories,* Ch. 6.) Suárez adopts the Aristotelian definition. He discusses continuous quantity, i.e. magnitude or extension, in Disp. XL and discrete quantity, i.e. plurality or number, in Disp. XLI. In addition to "real" or "categorical" quantity scholastics also spoke of mathematical and logical quantities. Mathematical quantity was simply quantity in abstraction, e.g. the number two, the line, etc. In logic "quantity" was used to refer to the extension of propositions. Logicians, such as William of Sherwood, for example (*Introduction to Logic,* Ch. 1, § 14), divide the quantity of propositions into universal, particular, indefinite and singular. Examples of propositions with the first, second, and fourth types of quantities respectively are: 'Every man is running,' 'Some man is running,' 'Socrates is running.' William does not give an example of indefinite propositions, but defines them as propositions in which the subject is a common term not determined by any sign. In Latin, *'Equus est animal'* is indefinite in quantity because it may mean either that every horse is an animal or just that one horse is an animal.

Quid, the what, what; see *quo.*

Quidditas, quiddity, whatness; from *quid,* what, something. The term became commonplace in the thirteenth century. In reality a thing's essence and its quiddity are the same, but in thought one may distinguish between that whereby a thing exists (the essence) and that whereby a thing is a what (the quiddity). Thomas puts it thus in *On Being and Essence,* Ch. 1 (*trans. cit.,* p. 31): "Because the definition telling what a thing is signifies that by which a thing is located in its genus or species, philosophers have substituted the term 'quiddity' for the term 'essence.'....The term 'quiddity' is derived from what is signified by the definition, while 'essence' is used because through it, and in it, that which is has being." See *natura.*

Quo, in which, by which; used sometimes to distinguish what is accidental from what is essential, *quid,* the what.

Raritas et densitas, rarity and density were classified by most scholastics as species of qualities. Suárez discusses the point and agrees with this view in Disp. XLII, Sect. V, § 17.

Ratio, reason, cause, argument, nature, relation, principle, foundation, definition, meaning, order, notion, norm, aspect, kind, idea.
Scholastics used this word in many senses. Thomas distinguished
two primary senses of *ratio* in *Com. on the Sentences* I, d.33, q.1, a.1, *ad*
3: "*Ratio* is taken in two senses, for sometimes that is called reason
which is in the reasoner, namely, the act itself of reason, or the
power or faculty which is reason; but sometimes reason is the name
of an intention, whether that according to which it signifies the definition of a thing, as reason is a definition, or as reason is called argumentation." *Ratio,* therefore, is sometimes synonymous with the
faculty of reason but at other times with *intentio* (a concept) or *argumentum* (argument). Strictly speaking it is the nature or essence of the
thing considered as intelligible and, therefore, as capable of being
grasped or understood by the mind. Sometimes, however, it refers to
the definition as actually present in the mind, although in such cases
it becomes the *ratio intellecta* or *intentio* (concept). In Suárez's text all
these meanings are intertwined. I have translated this term by 'notion,' 'meaning,' 'nature,' 'kind,' 'argument,' 'reason,' and others. Except in cases where it is translated by the English terms 'reason' and
'notion' or used in place of *'argumentum,'* I add the Latin in parentheses next to the term. For further information on this notion see
Thomas, *Com. on Posterior Analytics,* lect. 1, and *Com. on the Sentences* I,
d.2, q.1, a.3. See also J. Pegliaire, *Intellectus et Ratio selon S. Thomas
d'Aquin* (Paris, 1936). *Ratio* is used in conjunction with many other
terms to refer to very specific doctrines, such as *ratio seminalis* (semi-
nal reason, an expression used first by Augustine and widely used by
the Franciscans in the thirteenth century), *ratio aeterna* (eternal reason, again used by Augustine and referring to God's eternal truths or
ideas), *ratio intelligendi* (reason for knowing, used by Scotus, *Opus oxo-
nienxe* I, dist. 2, q.1, a.2, *via secunda,* to mean perhaps "intelligible
species"), etc.

Reductive, reductively; from *reduco,* to lead back, bring back, conduct, withdraw, replace, introduce again, produce, reduce.

Reipsa, in reality; see *in re.*

Relatio, relation; in Classical Latin this term meant a carrying back,
bringing back, a throwing back, retorting, returning. After Augustine the term came to be used for a report, narration or relation of
events. For scholastics, however, this was a technical term which
referred to Aristotle's fourth category, also called *ad aliquid.* Aristotle
explains the notion of relation in *Categories,* Ch. 7, 6a36: "Those
things are called relative, which, being either said to be *of* something
else or *related to* something, are explained by reference to that other
thing. For instance, the word 'superior' is explained by reference to

something else, for it is superiority *over something else* that is meant."
He lists as examples of relations the following: habit, disposition,
perception, knowledge, attitude, and others. Scholastics largely accepted Aristotle's view of relation as expressed in the text cited and in
Metaphysics V, Ch. 15, 1020b25 ff. Their debates centered rather on
the ontological status of relations. Were they real? Did they have the
same sort of being and unity other accidents had? Or were they to be
considered beings of reason (see *ens rationis*)? Suárez dedicates Disp.
XLVII, one of the longest, to the discussion of real relation. Among
the various problems he discusses is the question of the reality of
relations (Sect. I). He rejects Aureol's view that there are no real
relations (§ 8), Soto's view that there are real relations but that they
do not constitute a separate category of being, and adopts the view of
Thomas and others who accepted the reality of relations and their
distinct nature. In Sect. II he raises a related issue, whether real
relations are really or modally distinguished from substance and
absolute accidents. He rejects the view of Cajetan, Ferrara and
Thomas, who held that relations are really distinguished from substances and absolute accidents (§ 2) and the view of Scotus, who
regarded them as having a peculiar reality (§ 7). His own view is
similar to that of the nominalists, Ockham and Gregory, for whom
relations are distinguished only in concept (§§ 12, 22). He puts the
point thus: "It must be clear that a relation expresses certainly a real
form and that it denominates its own relative [term], which it constitutes. It is not, however, a reality or mode distinct *ex natura rei* from
all absolute forms, but it is in reality an absolute form, although not
taken absolutely, but rather as referring to another, which it includes or connotes with a relative denomination. In this way similarity, for example, is a real form existing in the thing called similar;
but it is not distinct from whiteness in the thing, with respect to what
it puts in the thing which is said similar, but only with respect to the
term it connotes. And so, in reality similarity is not other than the
very white as relating to another whiteness of the same or a similar
nature *(rationis)*. And this distinction of reason is enough...."

Relatio creaturae, the relation of creature. The term is applied to the
relation which creatures have to God. Properly speaking, scholastics
explained, this relation is found in the creature, since God's nature is
simple and unchanging. Strictly speaking, God is not related to creatures; he is only the term of the relation. Suárez puts it thus in *On the
Mystery of the Holy Trinity* VII, Ch. 4, § 9: "....the relation of creature
to Creator posits a real distinction from the Creator...because he is
opposed to them in reality, not as a correlative, since there is no corresponding real relation opposed in the Creator, but as a term which
is absolute in itself." This doctrine goes back to the Fathers. See, for

example, Boethius' *De Trinitate* IV; in Loeb's ed., pp. 16 and 17.

Remissibilis, remissible, subject or capable of remission, decrease; from *remissio,* a sending back, releasing, returning, diminishing, remission.

Repugnantia, repugnance, inconsistency, incompatibility, contradiction; the last three meanings are documented in Classical Latin. From *repugno,* to oppose, resist, disagree. Scholastics speak of both a logical *repugnantia,* rendered here by the terms 'inconsistency' or 'contradiction' and a factual *repugnantia,* translated here by 'incompatibility.' Propositions, statements or sentences are contradictory; substances, accidents, natures and other realities are incompatible; views are inconsistent.

Res, a thing, object, being, fact, circumstance, and also reality. Scholastics used the term to refer to the referents of categorical terms, whether substances or accidents and as such it was interpreted by some as an attribute of being, i.e. one of the transcendentals, along with unity, goodness, and truth. Suárez, however, explicitly rejects its inclusion among the transcendental attributes, although he is willing to maintain its transcendentality, that is, its coextension with being. According to him, in Disp. III, Sect. II, § 4, "*res* and *ens* are generally used as synonyms; and sometimes they are predicated of actual existing being, while at other times they abstract from actual existence, for which reason they are not attributes of each other." He refers in the same Section to Thomas' view that *res* is predicated primarily from essence or quiddity while *ens* is predicated primarily from *esse* and therefore that it applies only to existing beings. It is presumably for this reason that some neo-scholastics (e.g. J. Owens, *An Elementary Christian Metaphysics,* Ch. 8, p. 124) refer to *res* as "a potency to being" rather than one of its attributes. Scholastics also talked about principles and concepts as *res.* Thomas, in his *Commentary on I Sent.,* dist. 25, q.1, a.4, explains the meaning of *res* as follows: "There are two points to be considered in a thing; namely, the quiddity and reason of it and also the being of it, and the name 'thing' is taken from the quiddity. And since the quiddity can have being both in the singular which is external to the mind and as it is apprehended in the mind by the intellect, therefore, the name 'thing' applies to both, to that which is in the mind, as 'thing' *(res)* is derived from 'knowing' *(reor),* and to that which is outside the mind, as thing is spoken of as something known *(ratum)* and firm in nature." In dist. 37, q.1, a.1, he adds: "The name 'thing' is taken in two senses. For that is called a thing absolutely which has a known and firm being in nature; 'thing' is used in this way, taking the name 'thing' to indicate it as it has a certain quiddity or essence; but it is called 'a being,' as it has being. But because a thing is knowable through its essence, the name of 'thing' is extended to all that which can fall in knowledge or understanding, in the sense that 'thing' is derived from 'knowing' *(reor)*, and in this manner things of reason are spoken of, which do not have a known being in nature, and in this way negations and privations can be called things too, just as they are called beings of reason."

Resisto, to stand back, stop, stay, continue, oppose, resist, rise again. This term became important among scholastics because some of them used its substantive form, *resistentia,* to describe a third kind of potency in addition to active and passive potencies. Suárez rejects this view, holding that resistance is in reality nothing different from active or passive potency. He explains the meaning of the term *resisto* in Disp. XLIII, Sect. I, §§ 8-9: "There are two ways in which a thing resists another: First, formally, through immediate incompatibility; second, radically and as it were by the diminution of the power of the other thing. In this latter way the heat of fire resists cold water, stopping its action as far as it can and diminishing its power. Similarly, between men one is said to resist another if, foreseeing an attack, he cuts his hand or in some other way diminishes his power. Therefore, this resistance is nothing in fact but a kind of action, and differs only in name and relation. For it is called action insofar as it is an acting principle and it is called resistance insofar as it diminishes the powers of another so that it may not act....Concerning this [i.e. the first] mode of resistance it must be said that it does not consist in a positive act coming from the power which is called power of resistance, but it consists rather in a privation of act. Hence, such resistance is a lack of potency *(impotentia)* and a kind of incapacity rather than a potency proper...."

Satis, also *sufficiens,* sufficient, enough; see *necessarius.*

Scientia, knowledge, science, skill; from *sciens,* to know. Among scholastics this term is used often to mean knowledge of what is true. Strictly speaking, however, they restricted its meaning to that of Aristotle's knowledge (ἐπιστήμη) through demonstration, that is, they thought of it as the conclusion of a demonstrative syllogism expressing a causal relation. Suárez makes the point clear in Disp. I, Sect. IV, § 6: "The word *'scientia'* or *'scire,'* used by Aristotle in many ways, can be taken in general to mean any knowledge or understanding of truth, but especially to mean that understanding which is perfect and which has the proper nature of science, that is,...knowledge of a thing through cause, with evidence and certainty." See also Disp. XXX, Sect. XV, § 2. *Scientia,* therefore, is a kind of relation between the thing known and the knower. Sometimes terms such as *'scientia,' 'disciplina,' 'doctrina'* and others were used interchangeably. The pseudo-Grosseteste, however, makes clear that these are not to be confused: "Knowledge is either the name of the condition by which the understanding speculates easily what is true, and what is false, and understands actually — and thus it is properly called *scientia* — for condition is midway between potentiality and actuality; or else it is that act of speculating or understanding — and thus it is properly called consideration; or it is the disposition of the act of knowing or the condition in learning, whether the learner begins to know by his own exercise, and that is called investigation, or instructed by someone else, which is properly called in the person teaching, doctrine, in the person learning, discipline." (From McKeon, *Selections from Medieval Philosophers* II, p. 492.)

Secundum quid, in a certain respect, relatively; see *simpliciter.*

Secundum rem, in reality; see *in re.*

Sentio, to sense, perceive, feel, suffer the effects, observe, think, judge, imagine, declare. The primary meaning of this term has to do with sensation and feeling; it is only secondarily that it is used to mean judging or thinking. Since the same ambiguity is present in English in the term 'to feel' I have used the latter to render *'sentio'* in most instances in this translation.

Separatio, separation, division, a severing; from *separo,* to sever, disjoin, divide, separate. This term is usually reserved by scholastics to describe the state of the soul apart from the body after death — see Suárez's Commentary to the third part of Thomas' *Summa theologiae,* Disp. LI, Sect. 2, § 12 — or of angels and other spiritual beings who exist apart from matter. Sometimes, however, it is used as well to describe the relation of forms to particulars in Plato's theory of forms.

Signum, sign, indication, token, signal, image, picture, seal. For scholastics it meant something which, besides its usual function, was used to cause an understanding of something else. This is how Suárez uses the term: "As dialecticians say, a sign is that which besides the species it produces in the senses, makes us come to the knowledge of something else." (Disp. XXX, Sect. XIII, § 8.) Ockham gives a more precise definition in *Summa logicae* I, Ch. 1: "It should be noted that 'sign' is taken in two ways: In one way [it can be taken] to mean anything which, when apprehended, brings something else to the mind, although it may not bring that to the mind for the first time, but, as has been shown elsewhere, [makes] it actual after it has been [known] habitually. In this way, a word is a natural sign, the effect is a sign of its cause, and a barrel-hoop is a sign of the wine....In another way, 'sign' is taken to mean anything which brings something to the mind and [1] naturally supposits for it, or [2] is added to [a sign of] this sort in a proposition...or [3] is naturally composed of things that are signs of this sort."

Similis, similar, like; see *similitudo.*

Similitudo, likeness, resemblance, similitude, similarity; from *similis,* similar, like. The term was commonly used for two things: (a) the relation of similarity between two or more things, such as the similarity existing between two white things, and (b) the image or likeness of something, such as man, who is the likeness of God. In scholastic metaphysics *similitudo* was used primarily to refer to the relation of two qualities of the same species and intensity. As such *similitudo* is a kind of unity, less than numerical, which requires unity of essence and degree, e.g. two whites are similar if they are the same kind of white and the intensity of the quality is the same in each case. Thomas puts it thus in *Com. on the Sentences* I, d.2, q.1: "*Similitudo* signifies a relation caused by a unity of quality, requiring distinct subjects, for the *similitudo* of different things is the same [kind of] quality. For this reason the nature of what causes *similitudo* reveals a unity of essence, which is the same goodness and wisdom or whatever else is signified by the mode of quality." Suárez discusses this notion briefly in Disp. XLII, Sect. VII, § 5 and Disp. XLVII, Sect. XI, § 14.

Simpliciter, simply, absolutely, strictly, plainly, naturally, directly, openly, frankly; from *simplex,* simple, plain, uncompound. For scholastics the term was opposed to *secundum quid* (in a certain respect) and, therefore, meant, depending on context, either "absolutely" or "without qualification." Thomas' explanation of the term in *Summa theologiae* III, 50, 5, is well known. "*Simpliciter* can be taken in two ways: In one way '*simpliciter*' is the same as 'absolutely,' in this way 'that is spoken of simply which is spoken of without the addition of something else'...and in another way, '*simpliciter*' is the same as 'completely' or 'totally.'" The source of this term is Aristotle, *Topics* II, Ch. 11, 115b34. In this translation '*simpliciter*' has been rendered by the term 'without qualification.' In the few instances where another term has been used, the Latin has been added in parentheses.

Singulare, singular, single, separate, unique and therefore not predicable of many, as Aristotle points out in *On Interpretation,* Ch. 6, 17a37. In reality what is singular is also individual and particular. All these terms refer to the same thing although in different ways. 'Singular' is opposed to 'plural' or 'multiple,' while 'individual' is opposed to 'collective' and 'particular' to 'universal.' Individuality has to do with indivisibility. An individual *qua* individual is what cannot be divided into other individuals of the same specific kind as itself, as Suárez points out in Sect. I, § 3 *et passim.* As such it is different from

the species and the genus. The individual is said to be particular
because it is considered as part of or as partaking of a universal
essence. Thus a man is particular while man is not. The individual
(or singular, or particular) exists undivided in itself and divided, i.e.
separate, from other things; it represents the last stage of divisibility
in beings as expressed by the Porphyrian tree. Various authors viewed these terms in various ways. See, for example, William of Ockham, *Summa logicae* I, 19. In this Disputation, Suárez uses the terms
interchangeably with each other and with 'numerically one' except
when specified, and he opposes individual or singular to common or
universal.

Situalis, situational; adjectival form of *situs,* situation, local position, site, disposition, and, for Suárez, also place.; see *situs.*

Situs, situation, position, disposition; from *sino,* set down, allow,
suffer, give up, place, situate. The scholastics, following Aristotle,
identified *situs* with the seventh category. Suárez dedicates Disp. LII
to its investigation. He finds that *situs* and *ubi* (where — fifth of the
ten categories) are very closely related and therefore that his discussion of *situs* need not be long since *situs* only adds "a certain categorical denomination to *ubi*" (*ubi* is discussed in Disp. LI). Indeed,
Suárez finds difficult to explain the classification of *situs* as separate
from *ubi.* There are, according to him, three ways of understanding
the term *situs* (Sect. I, § 1): "First, as signifying generally the intrinsic
place *(locum)* in which a thing is situated, which [place] is neither a
form nor an accident of the thing, but, as it were, its support *(substen-
taculum),* as if you say that the portion of earth in which a tree is
planted is its place *(situm),* and so it seems evident that *situs* is not a
category in this case. Second, it can signify a certain relation of
order, as being above or below, or in a prior or posterior place *(loco),*
that is, in a more dignified or less dignified [place], which relation,
when real, corresponds to the category of relation *(ad aliquid).* In a
third way it signifies the position of parts with respect to place
(locum); and it is in this sense that [*situs*] is judged to constitute this
category." Suárez, however, rejects these three views and understands *situs* or *positio* (§ 7) as "an intrinsic mode of the situated body,
from which the body is said to be sitting, or lying or something similar." The difference between *situs* and *ubi* is not great (§ 9): "*situs* or
position is the same as *ubi* conceived under a different aspect *(ratio),*
so that, just as a conceptual distinction is sufficient for the distinction
of action and passion, so likewise in this case it is sufficient to distinguish *situs* and *ubi.* The conceptual distinction consists in this, that
ubi as such expresses the mode only insofar as it constitutes the thing
as present in some place, and thus we always explain the *ubi* by relations of distance, or proximity, or inner presence, because we con-

ceive it only as their foundation. *Situs* as such, however, signifies the mode as denominating a thing disposed in itself in this way, by a disposition resulting from the local coordination of parts; in which denomination neither the notion of presence nor properly the order with respect to space, are taken into consideration, but [only] the order of parts among themselves. Moreover, we understand order not as expressing a categorical relation, but just as being its foundation."

Species, a seeing, look, outward appearance, shape or form, beauty, aspect, vision, image, kind, species; from *specio,* to look, behold. Although used sometimes in these senses, in the Middle Ages the term was used mostly as a technical term to refer to one of the predicables, that is, to the various ways in which predicates are predicated of subjects. Originally, according to Aristotle, there were only four of these: definition (as when 'rational animal' is predicated of man), property (capable of laughter), genus (animal) and accident (white); see *Topics* I, Ch. 4, 101b35. Porphyry, in his *Isagoge,* changed this list, adding species and difference and dropping definition. The elimination of definition is not very significant since the definition can be obtained by adding the difference to the genus. But the inclusion of species among the predicables is a serious departure from Aristotelian orthodoxy, for, according to Aristotle, species is not to count as a predicable but as a subject. The reason for this is that the species is numerically divisible into individuals (see E. A. Moody, *The Logic of William of Ockham,* N.Y.: Russell and Russell, 1935, p. 67, and a more sympathetic interpretation of Porphyry's addition by E. W. Warren, in *Porphyry the Phoenician. Isagoge.* Toronto: PIMS, 1975, p. 11, n.). The Porphyrian list was passed on to the Middle Ages by Boethius. In the *Isagoge,* Porphyry listed the various meanings of species as "the shapeliness of an individual...that under the defined genus... what is ordered under the genus and what the genus is predicated of essentially...that predicated essentially of many things which differ in number." The latter is the one that is repeated throughout the Middle Ages. See, for example, William of Sherwood's *Introduction to Logic,* Ch. 2, § 3, and William of Ockham, *Summa logicae* I, Ch. 21. Species differs from genus because the genus is predicated of the species and not vice versa. For example, 'animal' is predicated of man, but 'man' cannot be predicated of animal. See *genus.*

Species intentionales, intentional species. For scholastics an intentional species is a certain likeness of a thing in the mind through which the thing is known. In *Summa theologiae* I, 13, 9, Thomas distinguishes two kinds of species: One is the nature immediately communicable to many individuals, such as man, and the other is the intention in the mind. The nature, definition and ontological status of these intentional species was extensively debated by scholastics. In Disp. XLII, Sect. V, § 16, Suárez classifies these species as habits, and since habits are qualities, he argues, they must also be qualities. Later, in Disp. XLIV, Sect. I, he points out that habits can be considered in two ways. In one way they are "qualities added to our faculties to help them in their operations, serving to unify the object to the faculty." And a bit later, in the same paragraph, he writes that "they are certain qualities which are, as it were, seeds or instruments of objects, by means of which the objects unite their power to the knowing faculties in order to determine and constitute them in the first act to achieve knowledge." Suárez's most thorough discussion of intentional species is found in *Treatise on the Soul* III, Ch. 2, where he gives the same definition given in the *Metaphysical Disputations,* adding a very detailed discussion of their ontological status. He draws four basic conclusions: "All [intentional] species are accidents" (§ 2); "the notion of [intentional] species and their objects are not the same" (§ 9); "intentional species are spiritual and indivisible only in the intellect; in other knowing faculties they are material and divisible" (§ 16); and "intentional species do not represent objects formally, but only effectively" (§ 20). Suárez's views contradict a number of doctrines common at the time. In particular, compare assertion four with Thomas' view as expressed in *Contra gentiles* II, Ch. 98 and III, Ch. 49.

Subicio (or *subjicio* in scholastic Latin), to bring under, subject, place under, subordinate. This is the term that gives us 'subject.' In the passive, as used often, it means that something is subordinated or placed under something else. Sometimes this term is used interchangeably with '*subordino,*' to subordinate, although the latter and its substantive form, '*subordinatio,*' apply more often to causes (see Suárez, Disp. XXII, Sect. V, § 19) or to beings arranged in a certain metaphysical hierarchical order of superior to inferior, as the etymology of the term suggests. In the case of *subicio* the order of arrangement may just be logical, as when the individual is said to be "under" or to be subordinated to the species because the latter is predicable of it or because the former belongs to it along with other individuals of the same kind.

Subiectum, subject, foundation; from *subicio,* to bring under, subject, subordinate, comprehend. 'Subject' was a term used in logic, metaphysics and physics. Ockham clarifies some of its standard usages in *Summa logicae* I, Ch. 30: "...something is called a subject because it really underlies another thing that inheres in it and is really present in it. In this way subject is taken in two ways: Strictly, [something] is called a subject in relation to the accidents which really inhere in it [and] without which it can continue to subsist. Broadly, [something] is called a subject because it underlies something else, whether the thing which it underlies is an accident really inhering [in it] or a substantial form which informs the thing to which it [i.e. the form] adheres. In this way matter is said to be a subject with respect to substantial forms. In another sense [something] is called a subject, because it is that part of a proposition which precedes the copula and of which something [else] is predicated." Suárez refers briefly to the distinction between subject of inherence and subject of predication in this Disp., Sect. III, § 7. For the distinction between subject and substance, see *substantia*.

Subiectum primum, first or primary subject, literally the first that lays under. Metaphysically a subject, for scholastics, was that which lays under properties and accidents; logically that of which predicates are predicated; and epistemically that which constitutes the basis of knowledge. The term 'primary subject' was generally used in a metaphysical context to refer either to the individual or to prime matter. The first is a primary subject insofar as it is the foundation for accidents and accidental change; the second is so because it is the foundation of all form and of all substantial change.

Subordinatio, subordination; see *subicio*.

Subsistentia, subsistence; recorded in Cassiodorus and Boethius to refer to the "substance" or "reality" of something; from *subsisto*, to take a stand, to stop, sustain, support; and technically, "to exist as a substance." Scholastics used it variously to mean existence, essence, nature, entity, non-material being, etc. Suárez rejects the view that identifies existence and subsistence. He explains the distinction between the two in Disp. XXXIV, Sect. IV, § 23: " 'To exist' *(existere)* of itself expresses only to have entity outside causes in the order of nature; hence, [to exist] is of itself indifferent to the mode of existing, relying on another as sustaining, and [relying] on itself for the mode of existing with independence from anything sustaining. However, 'to subsist' *(subsistere)* expresses a determinate mode of existing by itself and without dependence from [something] sustaining; whence it is opposed to 'exist in' or to 'be in,' and it expresses a determinate mode of existing in another. Therefore, while existence is not determined by the mode of existence in itself and by itself, it is still incomplete and in a, as it were, potential state, and hence as such it cannot have the nature *(rationem)* of subsistence. Moreover, if it is affected by the mode of existing in some thing whereby it is sustained and from which it depends, it also is in an incomplete state, because it is in another from which it depends and it is ordered to enter in the composition of some complete being." He defines created subsistence in Sect. V, § 1: "Created subsistence is a substantial mode which ultimately determines the substantial nature and renders a thing subsistent by itself and incommunicable." Divine subsistence differs from created subsistence because it is communicable. Notice that this text clearly points to subsistence as principle of incommunicability. This does not conflict, of course, with Suárez's view in the present Disputation. For, as he pointed out in Sect. I, incommunicability is a result of individual unity rather than individual unity itself. The principle of individual unity is entity. For comparison see Thomas Aquinas, *On Sentences* I, d.23, q.1, a.1.

Substantia, that of which a thing consists, the essence, being, contents, material, substance, property; from *substo,* to stand or be under or among, to stand firm. Scholastics used the term in various non-technical senses. Its technical meanings were derived primarily from Aristotelian texts, particularly *Categories,* Ch. 5, 2a10, and *Metaphysics* V, Ch. 8, 1017b22. The first reads: "Substance, in the truest and primary and most definite sense of the word, is that which is neither predicable of a subject nor present in a subject; for instance, the individual man or horse." The second: "...'substance' has two senses, (a) the ultimate substratum, which is no longer predicated of anything else, and (b) that which, being a 'this' is also separable — and of this nature is the shape or form of each thing." In these texts and others Aristotle seems to present substance both as a substratum or subject of accidents and as an independently existing thing. Scholastics were aware of both of these senses of the term and generally saw the second as primary. Suárez makes the point in Disp. XXXIII, Sect. I, § 1: "The etymology of the word 'substance' is twofold: either from subsisting *(subsistendo)* or from standing under *(substando)*....'To be under' is the same as to be under others as their support and foundation or subject....According to this interpretation, there are two notions or properties indicated by the verb 'standing under' and the name 'substance': One is absolute, namely, to exist in itself and by itself, something which, owing to its simplicity, we explain as the negation of existing in a subject; the other is relative, it has to do with supporting the accidents." In § 3 Suárez points out that the etymology based on the verb 'to subsist,' like that based on the verb 'to stand under,' has a twofold sense — to exist or be a real essence and to be under other things as their foundation. As such, then, it is irrelevant which etymology is pursued. In both cases the outcome is the same: To be a substance is primarily "to exist in itself *(in se)* and by itself *(per se)*" and only as a result of this "to be the subject of accidents." This view of substance was common among scholastics. In *Summa theologiae* I, 3, 5, *ad* 1, for example, Thomas writes:

"The name 'substance' does not signify only what is by itself existing, because what exists as such cannot be a genus...but it signifies an essence to which it belongs to exist in a certain way, that is, by itself, although existence does not belong to its essence." This scholastic view of substance is quite different from the purely substratum view of Locke which relegated substance to a decharacterized subject — a something I know not what *(An Essay Concerning Human Understanding* II, 23, 1). Substance for the scholastics was not primarily a subject but primarily a being. As such it was always characterized. Indeed, its very nature included properties without which the substance would not exist. It is in the nature of a dog, for example, to have a body, although its shape, color, etc. might be subject to variation and change. In this sense the scholastic view of substance is different as well from the contemporary notion of bare particular (for this notion see E. B. Allaire, "Bare Particulars," *Philosophical Studies* 16 (1963)), where the subject of characteristics is nothing more than the subject of characteristics. The scholastic view is closer to the recently proposed notion of a characterized particular, that is, a characterized whole, which as a whole is the subject of other characteristics (for this notion see D. C. Long, "Particulars and Their Qualities," *Philosophical Quarterly* 18 (1968)). On the other hand, the scholastic view should not be confused either with the Cartesian view of substance as "a thing that so exists as to be in need of no other thing for its existence" (see *Principia Philosophiae* I, 51). Descartes interpreted this definition, which he borrowed from the scholastics, to mean that a substance must be completely independent. He accepted, moreover, the obvious corollary of this view, namely, that there is only one substance in the universe, God. According to the scholastic formula, a substance was a thing that existed in itself *(in se)* and by itself *(per se),* but for them this did not mean complete existential autonomy. It only meant that a substance was, from its own essence, independent, i.e. that it did not receive its being except through its own essence or form. Of course, all substances are in one way or another dependent on other substances for their efficient causation, and, according to scholastics, on God for their creation. But for their formal causation they do not depend on anything else, since there is no reference to other substances or beings in their definition. In this way they differ from accidents, which are always defined in terms of another and, therefore, are dependent on something else. True, the terms *per se* and *in se* can be literally interpreted to mean just what Descartes interpreted them to mean. But scholastics did not interpret them thus. Indeed, some scholastics went so far as to say that God, the only substance according to Descartes, is not a substance at all, since he, unlike all other essences, does not *have* being but *is* being (Thomas,

Contra gentiles I, 25). Finally, it should be pointed out that the definition of substance given by scholastics is only, as Suárez puts it, a
"nominal definition," and not a proper definition, since substance, as
the first of the categories is not definable. Thomas explains the point
clearly in *Contra gentiles* I, 25: " 'Being by itself' does not enter into the
definition of substance. For from what has been said of 'being,' it
could not be a genus, because it has already been proved that 'being'
does not have the nature *(rationem)* of genus. Similarly, from what
has been said of 'by itself' *(per se)*, [it could not be a genus,] because it
seems to mean only a negation, for it is called 'being by itself' *(ens per
se)* because it is not in another, [and] this is a pure negation which
cannot constitute the nature *(ratio)* of a genus, because then the
genus would not express what the thing is, but what it is not. The
nature *(ratio)* of substance, therefore, must be understood in this
way, that substance is a thing to which it is proper not to be in a subject, but the name 'thing' is imposed from quiddity, just as the name
'being' *(ens)* [is imposed] from being *(esse)*. And thus it is understood
in the nature of substance that it has a quiddity to which it is proper
not to be in something else." Substances were classified in many
ways. One of the most important classifications was into material
and immaterial (or spiritual) substances.

Substantia completa, complete substance; see *substantia imcompleta.*

Substantia composita, composite substance. Most often, when
scholastics used the term 'composite' in connection with 'substance,'
they were referring to the composition of matter and form. There
were, however, other kinds of compositions in substances: act and
potency, substance and accident, essence and existence, nature and
supposit, genus and difference, part and part, etc. None of these was
ever assigned of God, who was conceived as absolutely simple. But
there was ample disagreement as to the acceptability of these distinctions and their application to beings other than God, particularly
angels. Some medievals, following Avencebrol (Ibn Gabirol, author
of *The Fountain of Life*) posited a hylomorphic composition in angels;
others, following Thomas (*On Spiritual Creatures,* a.1), rejected their
hylomorphic composition but accepted an essence-existence one.
For Suárez, angels are composed of nature and supposit. He deals
with the question of simplicity in Disp. XXX, Sect. III. See also *On
the Divine Substance* I, Ch. 4.

Substantia creata, created substance. For scholastics all substances
were created except God. Yet many of them believed that it was only
God who was essentially and properly a substance since he "subsisted" by himself, while all the others "subsisted" only because of
him. Suárez explains the distinction between created and uncreated

substance in Disp. XXXII, Sect. I, § 7: "Uncreated substance is by itself substantially and essentially subsistent, and so it has the complete nature *(rationem)* of substance in virtue of its own essence; created substance, on the other hand, if incomplete, for that very reason lacks the proper nature *(ratione)* of substance, and of itself either does not subsist in act except in another [thing], that is in the whole, or it subsists neither perfectly nor completely in an absolute [sense], but in order to compose a whole; ex. prime matter. If, however, created substance is complete, although subsisting in act, it does so not formally and precisely in virtue of its essence, but through a mode or act of its essence, and therefore, substantial created nature...is not an act essentially subsisting, but [an act subsisting] by an adaptation *(aptitudine)*." See also Disp. XVIII, Sect. III, §§ 19-21.

Substantia incompleta, incomplete substance. Scholastics called matter and form, the constitutive principles of a substance, incomplete substances. They were called substances because they have, as it were, a certain priority over substance, i.e., over the substantial composite such as a man or a dog. In this sense they are in contrast with the "parts" of a substance, such as the accidents, e.g., eyes, nose, arms in a man, because (1) they are necessary conditions for the existence of substance, while accidents and other integral parts of substance are not, and (2) they do not, unlike accidents, presuppose the substance, but rather the reverse. Matter and form, however, are not substances in the same way a man is, since they enter into composition to make up a substance, e.g., a man. For this reason they were called "incomplete" substances, while men and dogs were called "complete" substances. The use of the term 'substance' *(ousia)* to refer to matter and form is found in Aristotle, *Metaphysics* VII, Ch. 3, 1028b32ff. Suárez uses this terminology often — see, for ex., Disp. XXXII, Sect. II, § 30, where he speaks of the rational soul and prime matter as incomplete substances.

Substantia increata, uncreated substance; see *substantia creata.*

Substantia simplex, simple substance. This substance has no composition of any kind, and there is only one of its kind, God. See *substantia composita.*

Superior, comparative form of *superus,* what is above, superior, higher. Scholastics used the term in many different ways. Logically, it refers to the relative position of a general predicate within the Porphyrian tree. The higher the place, the more superior a predicate was said to be. Superiority, therefore, meant greater extension. The term was also used to refer to degrees of being, particularly by neo-Platonists. In this sense beings were considered as hierarchically

ordered in a pyramidal structure with God at the top and matter at
the bottom. At each level, except for the first and last, a being was
said to be superior to those below it and inferior to those above it.
Man was believed to occupy the middle position in this hierarchy
and thus to participate through his body of what was inferior to him
and through his soul of what was superior to him. For this reason he
was called a microcosm. See my article, "Ontological Characterization of the Relation between Man and Created Nature in Eriugena,"
Journal of the History of Philosophy 16 (1978), 155-166.

Suppositum, that which is placed under, subject, supposit; from *sup-*
pono, to put or place under, to substitute, falsify, forge, subject, sub-
mit. For scholastics, generally speaking, the supposit is in reality the
same as primary or individual substance, but conceptually it is the
individual substance considered as subsisting and/or as the metaphysical foundation of properties and accidents. Thomas defines it
thus: "it is an individual subsisting in the nature" (*Summa theologiae*
III, 2, 2). It should not be confused with the logical notion of subject
of predicates, although again, in reality the subject of predicates is
the same as the *suppositum* or substance. Sometimes the term *supposi-*
tum is used also to refer to matter as the ultimate substratum of
change and other times to persons. For these and other uses of the
term see: Thomas Aquinas, *On the Power* IX, 2, *ad* 13; Cajetan, *Com-*
mentary on Thomas' "On Being and Essence," q.9, § 85; and William of
Ockham, *Summa logicae* I, Ch. 19. Suárez discusses extensively the
notions of supposit, substance, subsistence, nature, hyposthasis, and
person in Disp. XXXIV. Following what was by this time standard
procedure among scholastics (see Cajetan, *op. cit.*), he distinguishes
between the notion of *suppositum* as applied to God, to intellectual or
rational creatures, and to non-rational creatures. In the case of God,
the supposit and the substance, i.e. the subsisting thing, although
the same in reality, are not the same conceptually, for, according to
Suárez, in God the nature subsists by itself and is communicable to
several supposits (the three divine persons), while "it is in the nature
of a supposit to be incommunicable to another supposit" (§ 1). On
the other hand, in the case of creatures the supposit and the substance are the same both in reality and in thought (§§ 9 and 12). The
conceptual identity, however, is restricted to the concept of the thing
itself; considering the mode of conception, the supposit and the substance can be distinguished conceptually (§ 12). Third, the only
difference between rational and non-rational creatures in this respect
is that in rational creatures the supposit is called "a person," while in
non-rational creatures it is not (§ 13). In § 14 Suárez adds that the
term "hyposthasis" means the same thing as *suppositum,* the only
difference being its Greek origin. It is clear then, that, for Suárez,

the differentiating characteristic of the supposit is incommunicability, while that of substance is subsistence.

Syncategorematice, syncategorematically. This term was primarily used in logic in connection with other terms such as 'every,' 'whole,' 'both,' etc., which had no independent signification. William of Sherwood explains its etymology thus (*Treatise on Syncategorematic Terms,* trans. Kretzmann, Univ. of Minnesota Press, 1968, Intro., p. 16): "The name *'syncategorema'* comes from 'sin-' — i.e., 'con-' — and *'categoreuma'* — i.e., 'significative' or 'predicative' — as if to say 'conpredicative,' for a syncategorematic word is always joined with something else [a categorematic word] in discourse." See also Ockham, *Summa logicae* I, Ch. 4. In metaphysical contexts, however, the term was used to mean "potentially": species and perfections are said to be syncategorematically infinite, for example, because they are "potentially" infinite.

Terminus, boundary, limit, end, term; from *termino,* to limit, define, determine, end, finish, terminate, close. Besides the obvious logical and grammatical uses of *terminus,* scholastics used this word to refer to a number of things, such as: the terms of a relation (the father and the son in a father-son relation), the result of a motion or change (the generation of a new substance in the act of procreation), the passive receiver of an action (the receiver of a blow in a fight), the last determining factor of a sequence (the individual difference in an individual), and others. I have translated *terminus* as end-term, end, determination, or just term, depending on context.

Theologus, theologian, one who treats of the deity. For scholastics this term referred both to practitioners of revealed theology, the science about God based on God's supernatural revelations to man, and natural theology, the science about God based on God's natural revelations to man. The supernatural revelations consisted primarily in the sacred Scriptures *(sacra pagina);* the natural, in God's imprint in his creatures.

Totum, the whole, all. As in the case of part, scholastics followed Aristotle in their understanding of the notion of whole. The key text appears in *Metaphysics* V, Ch. 26, 1023b27-1024a10: " 'A whole' means (1) that from which is absent none of the parts of which it is said to be naturally a whole, and (2) that which so contains the things it contains that they form a unity; and this in two senses — either as being each severally one single thing, or as making up the unity between them....And (3) of quanta that have a beginning and a middle and an end, those to which the position does not make a difference are called totals, and those to which it does, wholes." The last point introduces a discussion of distribution. For Suárez, who discusses this passage in the Detailed Index to Aristotle's *Metaphysics* V, Ch. 26, the distributive use of *omne* and its distinction from *totum* constitute a purely verbal matter which depends on usage (see *omnis*).

Transcendens, transcending, literally "climbing-beyond" or "climbing-across." This notion was applied by scholastics to being and to those of its attributes which either (1) were common to the ten categories, or (2) were outside the ten categories. Being and these attributes were called *"transcendentalia"* (transcendentals). The first meaning is the most commonly found and the one adopted by Suárez in Disp. III, where he discusses the various attributes of being. The second can be illustrated with reference to Scotus, who, in his *Subtle Questions on Aristotle's "Metaphysics,"* Prol., argues that community to all beings is not essential to transcendence. What is essential is that the attribute or predicate in question be "not contained under any genus." Indeed, to be a transcendental is simply "not to have any predicate above itself except 'being.' " For this reason "a transcendental may be predicated of God alone, or of God and some creature. It is not required that a transcendental as transcendental be predicated of every being, unless it be convertible [i.e. coextensive] with the first transcendental, namely, 'being.' " A point often disputed by scholastics had to do with the number of transcendentals. Scotus included among them such disjunctive predicates as 'possible-or-necessary,' 'act-or-potency,' etc. The standard list of the times, however, included only being *(ens)*, thing *(res)*, something *(aliquid)*, one *(unum)*, true *(verum)*, and good *(bonum)* — beautiful *(pulchrum)* was usually placed under good. All of these predicates are coextensive with each other and therefore common to the ten categories — whatever is a being is also a thing and something, as well as true insofar as it is the basis of a true judgment, good, insofar as it is capable of being desired, and one insofar as it is an individual. The notion of "transcendental" should not be confused with the notion of "attribute of being" according to Suárez. "Being," of course, is not an attribute of itself, while "thing" and "something" are just verbal variants for the same thing. Among the transcendentals there are only three attributes: one, true, and good (Sect. II, § 3). For the history of this problem see my article, "The Convertibility of *unum* and *ens* according to Guido Terrena," *Franciscan Studies* 33 (1973), 143-170, and also: D. H. Pouillon, "Le premier Traité des Propriétés transcendentales. La *Summa de bono* du Chancelier Philippe," *Revue Néoscolastique de Philosophie* 42 (1939), 40-77; G. Schulemann, *Die Lehre von den Transcendentalien in der scholastischen Philosophie,* Leipzig, 1929; A. B. Wolter, *The Transcendentals and Their Function in the Metaphysics of Duns Scotus,* Washington, 1946. It should be added that the term 'transcendental' or 'transcending' also had a more common use in expressions such as "transcending time" or "transcending matter." In such cases it meant no more than "outside" or "not subject to."

Transcendentalia, transcendentals; see *transcendens*.

Transmutatio, transformation, change. Scholastics used this term and *mutatio,* change, interchangeably. *Transmutatio* carried with it a stronger sense of changing into something else. For this reason it referred primarily to the change of something — whether substance or accident — into something else, rather than the accidental change of a subject. A man would be "transformed" into ashes or the color of his hair (black) into the color of his ashes (grey), but a man was not "transformed" when the color of his hair changed from black in youth to gray in old age — only the color was "transformed." Like change *(mutatio),* transformation was usually divided into accidental and substantial, depending on the subject of the change. Suárez discussed the notion of transformation briefly and incidentally in Disp. XIII, Sect. I, §§ 6-12.

Unitas arithmetica, arithmetic or mathematical unity; see *unitas individualis*.

Unitas essentialis, essential unity; also called formal unity and sometimes unity *per se.* In one way, as opposed to accidental or *per accidens* unity, essential or formal unity is the same as substantial unity (see Suárez's extensive discussion of this in Disp. IV, Sect. III, §§ 6 ff.). In another way, however, essential unity is contrasted with material, numerical or individual unity and then it is the unity of the essence considered as separate from individual differences — as such it is taken with precision (see *praecisio*). The discussion of this notion and the problems surrounding it, known as the problem of universals, takes up Disp. VI. In Sect. I, §§ 8-11, Suárez remarks: "It must be said, first, that there is in things a formal unity belonging by itself to each essence or nature....Again, because, since 'unity' expresses 'lack of division,' there are as many kinds of unity as there are kinds of divisions. But in things there is a material and a formal, or an entitative and an essential, division; therefore, there will be similarly a formal unity in addition to the material unity. As a result, any individual, for example, Peter, is not only one in number, but also one essentially; and [the individual] has both unities in reality and not as a result of the operations of the mind....Secondly, it must be said that this formal unity is distinguished at least by reason from individual unity....Whence, I say, thirdly: these unities are not distinguished in reality or *ex natura rei* [see distinctio *ex natura rei*]...and fourthly, it must be concluded, that this formal unity, insofar as it exists in things prior to any operation of the intellect, is not common to many individuals, but that formal unities are multiplied as many times as there are individuals." There is, moreover, another use of the term 'essential unity' recorded among scholastics, where it refers to the unity of the species, i.e. the unity of the concept whereby an individual thing is understood to be of a certain kind.

Unitas individualis, individual unity. According to Aristotle, the negation of division of a thing and its "division," i.e. separation, from everything else. Aristotle listed several kinds of unities in *Metaphysics* V, Ch. 6, 1016b30 and 1015b15 ff. In one group he placed numerical, specific, generic and analogical; in another, continuous, formal, generic, absolute, and the unity of definition (according to Suárez, he also added specific unity and unity of difference to this group.) This gave rise to considerable controversy among scholastics, who inquired not only about the nature and distinction between these different unities but also about their number and extension. Suárez expounded his doctrine of unity in Disps. IV, V, VI, VII (Sect. III), XXXIX (Sect. II), XL, and XLI. The most important of these is the first, where he discusses transcendental unity, which is, according to him, the basis of all unity. Transcendental unity, so called because it is not restricted to any of the categories, but is common to all of them, since it is convertible (i.e., coextensive) with being, is real unity; on the other hand, mathematical or arithmetical unity is the result of mental consideration alone. The first is a real attribute of being; the second a principle whereby things are counted. (This distinction is traditional among scholastics. See, for example, Thomas Aquinas, *Summa theologiae* I, 11, 1 and 2, and I, 30, 3. Its immediate source for the Latin Middle Ages is to be found in Boethius, *On the Trinity* III). In Suárez's view, transcendental unity adds a negation of division to being and, as a result, a division from others. Therefore, in a sense, it is a privation. This separates Suárez from Scotus, who thought unity added something really distinct to being, and from Bonaventure and Alexander of Hales, who held that it added a positive concept to being. It allied him with Thomas Aquinas, who also thought that "unity, insofar as the negation it adds to being, is opposed to multiplicity by privation" (see *Summa theologiae* I, 11, 2, *ad* 2, for example). But Suárez goes farther by pointing out that even to interpret unity as a negative addition to being is excessive, for this negation is not in fact added to entity, since it is something in the very nature of entity. Transcendental unity and individual unity are in actuality the same, although conceptually they may be distinguished. Consequently, Suárez extends the notion of individual unity not only to material being but also to spiritual beings and even to God. It is this individual unity, common to all the categories, that is the basis of all other unities. For further details see the Introduction above.

Unitas numerica. Numerical unity is also called individual unity, although, strictly speaking, individual unity refers particularly to the unity of the individual considered as indivisible, while numerical unity refers to the unity of each individual considered as *one* among many real or possible beings. A thing, then, is said to have numerical unity, or conversely that it differs numerically from others, when apart from any differences it may have from others it is considered as separate from them. Boethius divided unity into generic (a man and a horse are both animal), specific (Cato and Cicero are both men), and numerical (Tully and Cicero are both the same man). He contrasted the latter with abstract or arithmetical unity: "There are in fact two kinds of number. There is the number with which we count and the number inherent in things counted. 'One' is a thing—the thing counted. Unity is that by which oneness is signified. Again 'two' belongs to the class of things as men or stones; but not so duality; duality is merely that whereby two men or two stones are signified; and so on. Therefore, a repetition of unities produces plurality when it is a question of abstract, but not when it is a question of concrete things, as, for example, if I say of one and the same thing, 'one sword, one brand, one blade.' It is easy to see that each of these names signifies a sword; I am not numbering unities but simply repeating one thing, and in saying 'sword, brand, blade,' I reiterate the one thing and do not enumerate several different things any more than I produce three suns instead of merely mentioning one thing thrice when I say 'Sun, Sun, Sun.' " (*On the Trinity* III, in Loeb, p. 13; see also I). Most medievals followed Boethius' terminology and distinction closely, although some introduced significant changes. See for ex., Ockham, *Summa logicae* I, Ch. 39, and Thomas, *Summa theologiae* III, 3, 6 *ad* 1 and 7, *ad* 2; I, 11, 1 *ad* 2. Suárez is aware of the basic distinction between generic, specific and numerical unities and the distinctions between numerical and arithmetical and between numerical and individual unities, but in practice he does not distinguish between numerical and individual unities, using these terms interchangeably to refer to the unity by which a thing is indivisible in itself and separate from other things. (See this Disp., Sect. I and Sect. III, § 17, and the Introduction above).

Unitas transcendentalis, transcendental unity; see *unitas individualis.*

Universale, universal, belonging to all; from *universus,* the whole. Aristotle defined "universal" as "that which is of such nature as to be predicated of many subjects" and contrasted it to "individual," that which is not thus predicated. "Man" is a universal, "Callias" an individual (*On Interpretation,* Ch. 6, 17a37). In the Middle Ages there were many views of the universal and its ontological status. For Thomas Aquinas, for example, the universal was always in the mind, since universality is a characteristic of species and genera. (*On Being and Essence,* Ch. 3, §§ 1 and 5; see also *Summa theologiae* I, 85, 3, *ad* 1 and *On VII Metaphysics,* lect. 13, 1570 ff). Suárez agrees with Thomas to the extent that in his view universality is a kind of unity resulting from the operation of the intellect, although the basis or occasion of universality is taken from singular things themselves (Disp. VI, Sect. V, § 1). This separates Suárez both from Scotus — for whom there is a common unity of nature in the individual — and Ockham — for whom the unity of the universal is explained in terms of similarity resulting from mental consideration alone — and allies him with Thomas, Durandus, Avicenna and Averroes. He explains his view in Disp. VI, Sect. II, § 9: "I assume something Aristotle often taught, that the nature of universality as such consists in two things, namely, in unity and in communicability. For these two are included in the definition according to which the universal is said to be 'one in many and of many' or 'beyond many.'....For, if the nature were not in some way one, then it would not be universal at all, but would be a multitude or aggregate of things. If, however, it were not capable of being in many, it would not be universal, but singular. And it is indeed necessary that it be in many things in a manner opposed to singularity or individuality, that is, that it be in many inferiors which can be multiplied and enumerated under this common notion. Therefore, these two, namely, unity and community, are to be explained in such a way that it will be clear that the aspect *(rationem)* properly constitutive of the universal is not to be found in things apart from the intellect."

Univoce (or *univoca, univocalis* and *univocatio*) univocally; from the Classical *univocus,* literally one naming or calling, univocal, that has but one meaning. A term is univocal or used or predicated univocally if its definition does not change. Univocity is opposed to equivocity *(aequivocatio),* the property of a term used in two different senses. Scholastics inherited these notions from Aristotle, *Categories* Ch. 1, 1a6: "Things are said to be named 'univocally' which have both the name and the definition answering to the name in common. A man and an ox are both 'animal,' and these are univocally so named, inasmuch as not only the name, but also the definition, is the same in both cases." And in 1a1: "Things are said to be named 'equivocally' when, though they have a common name, the definition corresponding with the name differs for each. Thus, a real man and a figure in a picture can both lay claim to the name 'animal;' yet these are equivocally so named, for, though they have a common name, the definition corresponding with the name differs for each." Thomas Aquinas and other medievals held that these two possibilities were not exhaustive. They introduced analogy as a third alternative (see Thomas, *Summa theologiae* I, 13, 5). According to Thomas a term is used analogically if, although not used univocally or equivocally, it still conveys some meaning, such as it is the case, for example, with 'healthy' when predicated of urine, medicine, and a man. The urine is said to be healthy because it is a sign of health, the medicine is called healthy because it causes health, and a man is judged healthy because he has the quality of health. In each case the meaning of 'healthy' is not entirely different or entirely the same; it is therefore similar or analogous (see *Summa theologiae* I, 13, 5). There were many other definitions and views of univocity and equivocity in the Middle Ages. William of Sherwood, for example, defined equivocation in *Introduction to Logic*, Ch. 6, 3.1.1, (*trans. cit.*, p. 135), as "diverse signification on the part of one and the same word." And he adds that this can happen in three ways: "Either the word signifies [A] more than one thing on its own (*de se*) or [B] as a result of its connection with something else; and there are two varieties of [A] — viz., it signifies [more than one thing] [A1] properly or [A2] transumptively." Duns Scotus defined "univocal concepts" in *Opus oxoniense* I, dist. III, q.1, thus: "I call that concept univocal whose unity is such that it is sufficient to fall into contradiction by denying and affirming it of the same thing." Suárez contrasts analogous and equivocal "names" in Disp. XXVIII, Sect. III, § 3: Analogous names "agree with equivocal ones in [the fact] that they are not posited to signify many [things] by means of only one imposition, but by many. The difference between the two [i.e. analogous and equivocal] lies in [the fact] that it is only a casual happening that an equivocal name be used to signify other things, while in the case of the analogous name, the imposition to signify one thing is made first, and then it is extended by similarity or proportion to another." See also Cajetan's classic discussion of analogy, univocity and equivocity in his *Commentary on Thomas' "On Being and Essence,"* q.3.

Verbum divinum, divine word. This refers to Christ, second person of the Trinity. The term 'word' is a standard way of referring to Christ in Christian circles. This usage of the term was based on the Vulgate Latin translation of the Bible, Gospel of John, where the translator rendered the Greek term '*logos*' by the Latin '*verbum.*'

Veritas, truth, verity, reality, nature, integrity; from *verus*, true, real, actual. This is one of the most complicated notions discussed by scholastics and one in which there was wide range of disagreement. The most widely accepted definition among late scholastics is the one attributed to Isaac Israeli, a ninth century author who defined truth as the *adaequatio rei et intellectus*, the correspondence of reality and understanding (see G. B. Phelan, "*Verum sequitur esse rerum,*" *Mediaeval Studies* 1 (1939), 12-14), Suárez dedicates Disp. VIII to the investigation of this notion. He gives two definitions of truth depending on whether it is considered as a matter of reality or as a matter of reason. For the first he uses Isaac's definition; the second he defines as the correspondence of the significative proposition and the thing signified. There are, according to him, three kinds of truth: "of signification, of knowledge, and of being. The first is properly found in spoken or written words or also in concepts not called ultimate. The second is in the intellect that knows things, or in the knowledge and conception of those things. The third is in things themselves, which because of it are called true. Therefore, the consideration of the first kind of truth concerns the logician; the second concerns the physicist insofar as it considers the mind *(anima)* and its functions; and the third is proper to this science [metaphysics]...." (Introd.) The first is what is today called "logical" truth; the second "epistemological" and, the third "metaphysical" or "ontological." For Suárez all truth was ultimately based on metaphysical truth, i.e. the transcendental property of being whereby being can become the subject of apprehension and judgment. Metaphysically, then, transcendental truth is prior to all other truths and the others are in a sense "derived" from it. The complete answer to this issue, however, is much more complex. For further details see Sect. VIII, "Whether Truth is Primarily Predicated of Logical *(cognitionis)* or Ontological *(rei)* Truth and How."

Virtualiter, virtually; medieval derivative of *virtus,* manliness, vigor, courage, excellence, virtue, power, perfection. Usually coupled with *contineo* (to contain). Scholastics spoke of one thing being contained in another "virtually" if the second had the power to produce the first. In this sense every effect is virtually contained in its cause. To be "virtually contained," however, implied (1) that the effect had yet to be produced and therefore was not actually anywhere, and (2) that it was not part of the form of the thing in which it was contained. Whence the reason why "virtually" is opposed to "formally" sometimes. This term was also used in logic to express a loose relation of implication between two propositions.

Vulgaris, usual, common, ordinary, belonging to the multitude, vulgar; from *vulgus,* the multitude, people. In the expression *vulgaris modus loquendi* it refers to the ordinary manner of speaking as opposed to the strict or precise *(praecise, simpliciter, per se)* manner of speaking.

A Select Bibliography of Recent Discussion on Suarez's Metaphysics

This bibliography concentrates on the years 1947 to the present. A few important items from 1940-1947 are included, although those years produced little secondary material of interest and depth owing to the second World War. For items published before 1940, see C. C. Riedl, *Jesuit Thinkers of the Renaissance* (Milwaukee, Wis.: Marquette Univ. Press, 1939). Bibliographical material pertinent to the subject matter of Disputation V published before 1940 is to be found in the footnotes at the appropriate places.

Adúriz, Joaquin. "Para el estudio de la criteriología suareziana," *Ciencia y Fe* 4 (1948).

Alcorta, J. I. *La teoría de los modos en Suárez.* Madrid, 1949.

Alejandro, José María. "Gnoseología de lo singular según Suárez," *Pensamiento* 3 (1947), 403-425 and 4 (1948), 131-152.

Aleu Benítez, José. "Juicio y objetivación en Suárez," *Pensamiento* 26 (1970), 397-417.

Allers, Rudolf. "The Intellectual Cognition of Particulars," *Thomist* 3 (1941), 95-163.

Baciero, Carlos, "Contexto filosófico del axioma 'actiones sunt suppositorum' en Suárez, Vásquez y Lugo," *Miscelánea Comillas* 50 (1968), 21-36.

Baena, J. G. *Fundamentos metafísicos de la potencia obediencial en Suárez.* Medellín, 1957.

Barale, Paolo. "Critica del Rosmini alla definizione suareziana del concetto," in *Atti del XII Congresso internazionale di filosofia. Venezia, 1958,* Vol. XII. Firenze: Sansoni, 1960, pp. 9-16.

Bartolomei, Tommaso M. "La conoscenza intelletuale del singolare corporeo e la funzione della cognitiva," *Divus Thomas* 61 (1958).

Basabe, Fernando. "Teoría tomista de la causa instrumental y la crítica suareciana," *Pensamiento* 16 (1960), 5-40.

Basabe, Fernando. "Exposición suareciana de la causa instrumental," *Pensamiento* 16 (1960), 189-223.

Berube, Camille. "La Connaissance intellectuelle du singular material au XIIIe siècle," *Franciscan Studies* 11 (1951), 157-201.

Boeder, H. "Leibniz und das Prinzip der Neueren Philosophie," *Philosophisches Jahrbuch* 81 (1974), 1-29.

Burns, J. Patout. "Action in Suárez," *New Scholasticism* 37 (1964), 453-472.

Cabada Castro, M. "Die Suarezische Verbegrifflchung des Thomasischen Seins," *Theologie und Philosphie* 49 (1974), 324-342.

Castellote Cuvells, Salvador. "La posición de Suárez en la historia," *Anales del Seminario de Valencia* 2 (1962), 5-120.

Connell, D. "Malebranche et la scolastique," *Etudes Philosophiques* 4 (1974) 449-463.

Copleston, Frederick. *A History of Philosophy,* Vol. III. New York: Doubleday, 1963.

Cronin, Timothy J. "Eternal Truths in the Thought of Suárez and Descartes," *Modern Schoolman* 38 (1960-1), 269-288.

Cronin, Timothy J. "Objective Being in Descartes and in Suárez," *Analecta Gregoriana,* Roma: Gregorian U.P., 1966.

Cronin, Timothy J. "Objective Reality of Ideas in Human Thought: Descartes and Suárez," *Wisdom in Depth: Essays in Honor of Henri Renard, S.J.* Milwaukee, Wis.: Bruce, 1966.

Dalledonne, Andrea. "A proposito di 'Postille'," *Divus Thomas* 76 (1973), 393-395.

de Vos, A. F. "L'aristotélisme de Suárez et sa théorie de l'individuation," *Actas. Congreso internacional de filosofía, Barcelona, 1948,* Vol. III. Madrid: Instituto Luis Vives de Filosofía, 1949, pp. 505-514.

de Vries, Josef. "Die Erkenntnislehre des Franz Suárez und der Nominalismus," *Scholastik* 3 (1949), pp. 321-349.

Doyle, John Patrick. "The Metaphysical Nature of the Proof for God's Existence according to Francis Suárez," Doctoral Dissertation, Toronto, 1966.

Doyle, John P. "Suárez on the Reality of the Possibles," *Modern Schoolman* 45 (1967-8), 29-48.

Doyle, John P. "Suárez on the Analogy of Being," *Modern Schoolman* 46 (1968-9), 219-249.

Doyle, John P. "Suárez on the Analogy of Being II," *Modern Schoolman* 46 (1968-9), pp. 323-341.

Doyle, John P. "Heidegger and Scholastic Metaphysics," *Modern Schoolman* 49 (1972), 98-103, 201-220.

Elorduy, Eleuterio. "El concepto objetivo en Suárez," *Pensamiento* 4 (1948), pp. 335-424.

Elorduy, Eleuterio. "La acción de resultancia en Suárez," *Anales de la cátedra Francisco Suárez* 3 (1963), pp. 45-71.

Elorduy, Eleuterio. "Duns Scoti Influxus in Francisci Suárez Doctrinam," in *Acta. Congressus Scotistici Internationalis Oxonii et Edimburgi.* Roma, 1968, pp. 307-337.

Elorduy, Eleuterio. "San Agustín y Suárez," *Augustinus* 13 (1968), 167-212.

Elorduy, Eleuterio. "Filosofía cristiana de San Agustín y Suárez," *Augustinus* 14 (1969), 3-42.

Elorduy, Eleuterio. "San Agustín y Suárez. Conclusiones y nuevas perspectivas," *Augustinus* 16 (1971), 113-122.

Fernández, C. "Metafísica del conocimiento en Suárez," *Estudios Onienses* 3 (1954).

Ferrater Mora, José. "Suárez and Modern Philosophy," *Journal of the History of Ideas* 14 (1953), 528-547.

Fleckenstein, Otto. "Der aristotelismus von Suárez und der Funktionalismus in der wissenschaft del Leibnizens," in *Actas. Congreso Internacional de Filosofía, Barcelona, 1948.* Vol. II. Madrid: Instituto Luis Vives, 1949, pp. 317-326.

Gallego Salvadores, J. "La aparición de las primeras metafísicas sistemáticas en la España del XVI: Diego Más (1587), Francisco Suárez y Diego de Zúñiga (1597)," *Escritos del Vedat* 3 (1973), 91-162.

García López, Jesús. "La concepción suarista del ente y sus implicaciones metafísicas," *Anuario Filosófico* 2 (1969), 137-167.

García y Martínez, F. "El sentido de la realidad en la metafísica suareciana," *Miscelánea Comillas* 9 (1948), 309-322.

Gemmeke, Elisabeth. "Die Metaphysik des sittlich Guten bei Franz Suárez," in *Freiburger Theologische Studien* 84 (1965).

Gnemmi, Angelo. "Fondamento metafisico e mediazione transcendentale nelle *Disputationes Metaphysicae* di F. Suárez," *Rivista di Filosofia Neoscolastica* 58 (1966), 1-24, 175-188.

Gnemmi, Angelo. *Il fondamento metafisico. Analisi di struttura sulle "Disputationes Metaphysicae" di F. Suárez.* Milano: Vita e Pensiero, 1969.

Gnemmi, Angelo. "Postille. A proposito di fondamento metafisico e di F. Suárez," *Rivista di Filosofia Neoscolastica* 65 (1973), 410-417.

Gnemmi, Angelo. "Nuova postilla a proposito di fondamento metafisico e di F. Suárez," *Rivista di Filosofia Neoscolastica* 67 (1975), 622-624.

Gómez Arboleya, E. *Francisco Suárez. Situación espiritual, vida y obras, metafísica.* Granada: Publicaciones de la cátedra F. Suárez 2, 1946.

Gómez Caffarena, J. "El sentido de la composición de ser y esencia en Suárez," *Pensamiento* 15 (1959), 34-154.

González Torres, J. *El concepto de potencia y sus diversas acepciones en Suárez.* Quito, 1957.

Gracia, Jorge J. E. "Suárez's Criticism of the Thomistic Principle of Individuation," *Atti. Congresso Internazionale di Filosofia, 1974.* Roma, 1978.

Gracia, Jorge J. E. "What the Individual Adds to the Common Nature according to Suárez," *New Scholasticism* 53 (1979) 221-233.

Hellín, José. *La analogía del ser y el conocimiento de Dios en Suárez.* Madrid, 1947.

Hellín, José. "Abstracción de tercer grado y objeto de la metafísica," *Pensamiento* 4 (1948), 433-450.

Hellín, José. "Sobre el ser esencial y existencial en el ser creado," in *Actas. Congreso Internacional de Filosofía, Barcelona, 1948.* Vol. II. Madrid: Instituto Luis Vives, 1949, pp. 517-562.

Hellín, José. "Esencia de la relación predicamental según Suárez," *Las Ciencias* 23 (1958), 648-697.

Hellín, José. "El ente real y los posibles en Suárez," *Espíritu* 10 (1961), 146-163.

Hellín, José. "El concepto formal según Suárez," *Pensamiento* 18 (1962), 407-432.

Hellín, José. "Las verdades esenciales se fundan en Dios, según Suárez," *Revista de Filosofía* 22 (1963), 19-42.

Hellín, José. "Relaciones divinas y principio de identidad comparada," *Espíritu* 24 (1975), 135-142.

Hoeres, Walter, "Bewusstein und Erkenntnisbild bei Suárez," *Scholastik* 36 (1961), 192-216.

Hoeres, Walter. "Wesenheit und Individuum bei Suárez," *Scholastik* 37 (1962), 181-210.

Hoeres, Walter. "Francis Suárez and the Teaching of John Duns Scotus on *univocatio entis,*" *Studies in Philosophy and the History of Philosophy* 3 (1965), 263-290.

Iriarte, Joaquin. "La proyección sobre Europa de una gran metafísica," in *Pensadores e historiadores,* vol. I. Madrid, 1960, pp. 482-520.

Iturrioz, I. "Estudios sobre la metafísica de Francisco Suárez," *Estudios Onienses* 2 (1949).

Juncosa Carbonell, Arturo. "Los conceptos de espacio y tiempo de la teoría de la relatividad contrastados con la filosofía de Francisco Suárez," *Convivium* 11-12 (1961), 3-43.

Kainz, H. P. "The Suarezian Position on Being and the Real Distinction: An Analytic and Comparative Study," *Thomist* 34 (1970), 289-305.

Knight, David M. "Suárez's Approach to Substantial Form," *Modern Schoolman* 39 (1961-2), 219-239.

Maurer, Armand. "St. Thomas and Eternal Truths," *Mediaeval Studies* 32 (1970), 91-107.

Murray, Michael V. *The Theory of Distinctions in the Metaphysics of Francis Suárez.* Doctoral dissertation, Fordham University, 1944.

Neidl, Walter M. "Der Realitästsbegriff des Franz Suárez nach den *Disputationes Metaphysicae,*" *Münchener Theologische Studien* 2, Bd. 33, (1966).

Owens, Joseph. "The Number of Terms in the Suarezian Discussion on Essence and Being," *Modern Schoolman* 34 (1956-7), 147-191.

Peccorini, Francisco L. "Suárez's Struggle with the Problem of the One and the Many," *Thomist* 36 (1972), 433-471.

Peccorini, Francisco L. "Knowledge of the Singular: Aquinas, Suárez and Recent Interpreters," *Thomist* 38 (1974), 606-655.

Rábade Romeo, Sergio. "La metafísica suareciana y la acusación de esencialismo," *Anales de la Cátedra Francisco Suárez* 3 (1963), 73-86.

Roig Gironella, Juan. "Carácter absoluto del conocimiento en Suárez," *Pensamiento* 15 (1959), 401-438.

Roig Gironella, Juan. "Para la historia del nominalismo y de la reacción antinominalista de Suárez," *Pensamiento* 17 (1961), 279-310.

Roig Gironella, Juan. "La oposición individuo-universal en los siglos XIV-XV, punto de partida de Suárez," in *Die Metaphysik im Mittelalter. Internationalen Kongresses für Mittelalterliche Philosophie,* vol. II, Berlin: Water de Gruyter, 1963, pp. 667-678. Also in *Espíritu* 10 (1961), 189-200.

Rosanas, Juan. "El principio de individuación, según Suárez," *Ciencia y Fe* 6 (1950), 69-86.

Rosenberg, Jean R. *A Comparative Study of St. Thomas, Scotus, and Suárez.* Washington, D. C.: The Catholic Univ. of America Press, 1950.

Ross, J. F. "Suárez on 'Universals'," *Journal of Philosophy* 59 (1962), 736-748.

Ross, J. F. "Introduction," in *Francis Suárez. On Formal and Universal Unity.* Milwaukee, Wis.: Marquette Univ. Press, 1964, pp. 1-27.

Sagües Inturralde, José F. "Escoto y la eficacia del concurso divino ante Suárez," *Acta. Congressus Scotistici Internationalis Oxonii et Edimburgi 1966,* Vol. IV. Roma, 1968. Also in *Estudios Eclesiásticos* 41 (1966), 483-514.

Schneider, Marius. "Der angebliche philosophische Essentialismus des Suárez," *Wissenschaft und Weisheit* 24 (1961), 40-68.

Seigfried, Hans. "Wahrheit und Metaphysik bei Suárez," *Abh andlungen zur Philosophie, Psychologie und Pädagogik* 32 (1967), 185-194.

Seigfried, H. "Metaphysik und Seinsvergessenheit," *Kant-Studien* 61 (1970), 209-216.

Sepich, Juan R. "Naturaleza de la filosofía primera, o metafísica, en Francisco Suárez," in *Actas. Congreso Internacional de Filosofía,* Barcelona, 1948. Vol. III. Madrid: Instituto Luis Vives, 1949, 491-504.

Siewerth, Gustav. *Das Schicksal der Metaphysik von Thomas zu Heidegger.* Einsiedeln, 1959, pp. 119-195.

Specht, Reiner. "Zur Bezeichnung unzureichender Zweitursachen bei Francisco Suárez," *Philosophisches Jahrbuch* 68 (1959), 382-392.

Specht, Reiner. *Francisco Suárez. Über die Individualität und das Individuationsprinzip.* Hamburg: Meiner, 1976, 2 vols.

Stengren, George L. *The Doctrine of Being in the Metaphysics of Suárez.* Master's dissertation, St. John's University, 1956.

Stengren, George L. *Human Intellectual Knowledge of the Material Singular according to Francis Suárez*. Doctoral dissertation, Fordham University, 1965.

Ssekasozi, Engelbert. *A Comparative and Critical Analysis of the Metaphysical Theories of William of Ockham and Francis Suárez as regards the Principle of Individuation.* Doctoral dissertation, Kansas, 1976.

Treloar, John Lawrence. *Francis Suárez: A Metaphysics for Body and Soul.* Doctoral dissertation, Michigan State Univ., 1976.

Tusquets, Juan. "Francis Suárez: sa métaphysique et sa critériologie," in *Apports hispaniques à la philosophie chrétienne de l'Occident*. Louvain: Publications Universitaires, 1962, pp. 73-116.

Ulrich, F. *Inwiefern ist die Konstruktion der Substanzkonstitution massgebend für die Konstruktion des Materiebegriffes bei Thomas von Aquin, Duns Scotus und F. Suárez?* Dissertation, Munich, 1955.

Vollert, Cyril. "Introduction," in *Francis Suárez. On the Various Kinds of Distinctions.* Milwaukee, Wis.: Marquette Univ. Press, 1947; second printing 1976.

Wells, Norman J. "Suárez, Historian and Critic of the Modal Distinction between Essential Being and Existential Being." *New Scholasticism* 36 (1962), 419-444.

Wells, Norman J. "Objective Being, Descartes and His Sources," *Modern Schoolman* 45 (1967), 49-61.

Yela Utrilla, Juan Francisco. "Espacio y tiempo en Suárez," in *Actas. Congreso Internacional de Filosofía, Barcelona, 1948.* Vol. II. Madrid: Instituto Luis Vives, 1949, 145-182.

English–Latin Index

This Index is not intended as a dictionary-aid or even as an English-Latin exhaustive list of the terms contained in the translation; for many terms, including very obvious ones, have been omitted. It is primarily a guide to the Glossary intended for those who do not have sufficient familiarity with technical terms in scholastic metaphysics. For this reason, only those terms recorded in the Glossary are listed. Moreover, only the main occurrences of the terms in the Glossary have been rᵉ corded. Since most of them appear frequently throughout the text and in some cases almost on every page, to mention all of these references would have been useless.

Index of Ancient
and Scholastic Authors
Cited by Suarez

Names are listed in alphabetical order according to the form and spelling used in the text. Terms within square brackets or placed after a comma are additions of the translator. Dates have been placed within parentheses. Page numbers within parentheses refer to Suárez's text.

MEDIAEVAL PHILOSOPHICAL TEXTS IN TRANSLATION

Translation #1: "Grosseteste: On Light"
by Clare Riedl-Trans.
This treatise is significant as an introduction to an influential thinker and man of science of the Middle Ages.

Translation #2: "St. Augustine: Against the Academicians"
by Sister Mary Patricia, R.S.M.-Trans.
Augustine aims to prove that man need not be content with mere probability in the realm of knowledge.

Translation #3: "Pico Della Mirandola: Of Being and Unity"
by Victor M. Hamm-Trans.
In this work Pico tried to discover the genuine thought of Plato and Aristotle on being and unity.

Translation #4: "Francis Suarez: On the Various Kinds of Distinction"
by Cyril Vollert, S.J.-Trans.
Suarez propounds his theory on distinctions, a point of capital importance for a grasp of Suarezian metaphysics.

Translation #5: "St. Thomas Aquinas: On Spiritual Creatures,"
by Mary C. Fitzpatrick-Trans.
This book falls into two general divisions: an introduction and the translation from the Latin.

Translation #6: "Meditations of Guigo,"
by John J. Jolin, S.J.-Trans.
A series of reflections by Guigo, 12th century Prior of the hermitage Charterhouse.

Translation #7: "Giles of Rome: Theorems on Existence and Essence,"
by Michael V. Murray, S.J.-Trans.
An essay dealing with the *a priori* deductions of being and its conditions.

Translation #8: "John of St. Thomas: Outlines of Formal Logic"
by Francis C. Wade, S.J.-Trans.
A standard English translation of the Logic of John of St. Thomas.

Translation #9: "Hugh of St. Victor: Soliloquy in the Earnest Money of the Soul,"
Kevin Herbert-Trans.
The purpose of the work is to direct the soul toward a true love of self, an attitude which is identical with a love of God.

Translation #10: "St. Thomas Aquinas: On Charity,"
by Lottie Kendzierski-Trans.
This treatise is significant as an expression of St. Thomas' discussion on the virtue of charity in itself, its object, subject, order, precepts, and principal act.

Translation #11: "Aristotle: On Interpretation-Commentary by St. Thomas and Cajetan,"
Jean T. Oesterle-Trans.
This translation will be of particular value to teachers and students of logic.

Translation #12: "Desiderius Erasmus of Rotterdam: On Copia of Words and Ideas,"
by Donald B. King and H. David Rix-Trans.
One of the most popular and influential books of the 16th century is made available here for the first time in English.

Translation #13: "Peter of Spain: Tractatus Syncategorematum and Selected Anonymous Treatises,"
by Joseph P. Mullally and Roland Houde-Trans.
The first English translation of these tracts now makes it possible for scholars of logic to better appreciate the continuity of Formal Logic.

Translation #14: "Cajetan: Commentary on St. Thomas Aquinas' On Being and Essence,"
by Lottie Kendzierski and Francis C. Wade, S.J.-Trans.
A basic understanding of the relation between Cajetan and St. Thomas.

Translation #15: "Suarez: Disputation VI, On Formal and Universal Unity,"
by James F. Ross-Trans.
The study of late mediaeval philosophy and the decline of scholasticism.

Translation #16: "St. Thomas, Sieger de Brabant, St. Bonaventure: On the Eternity of the World,"
by Cyril Vollert, S.J., Lottie Kendzierski, Paul Byrne-Trans.
A combined work bringing together the writings of three great scholars on the philosophical problem of the eternity of the world.

Translation #17: "Geoffrey of Vinsauf: Instruction in the Method and Art of Speaking and Versifying,"
by Roger P. Parr-Trans.
This text, of one of the most important mediaeval literary theorists, is here for the first time translated into English.

Translation #18: "Liber De Pomo: The Apple, or Aristotle's Death,"
by Mary F. Rousseau-Trans.
A significant item in the history of mediaeval thought, never previously translated into English from the Latin.

Translation #19: "St. Thomas Aquinas: On the Unity of the Intellect Against the Averroists,"
by Beatrice H. Zedler-Trans.
This is a polemical treatise that St. Thomas wrote to answer a difficult problem confronting his times.

Translation #20: "The Universal Treatise of Nicholas of Autrecourt,"
by Leonard L. Kennedy C.S.B., Richard E. Arnold, S.J. and Arthur E. Millward, A.M.
This treatise gives an indication of the deep philosophical skepticism at the University of Paris in the mid-fourteenth century.

Translation #21: "Pseudo-Dionysius Aeropagite: The Divine Names in Mystical Theology"
by John D. Jones-Trans.
Among the most important works in the transition from later Greek to Medieval thought.

Translation #22: "Matthew of Vendôme: Ars Versificatoria (The Art of the Versemaker)"
by Roger P. Parr-Trans.
The text of this, the earliest of the major treatises of the *Artes Poetical* is here translated in toto with special emphasis given to maintaining the full nature of the complete original text.

Translation #23: Suarez on Individuation
Translation by Jorge J. E. Garcia